Ariel Dinar
BGU   5/13/92

Y0-DBO-671

Microeconomic Studies

Edited by W. Güth, J. McMillan and H.-W.Sinn

Microeconomic Studies

J.-M. von der Schulenburg (Ed.), Essays in Social Security Economics.
XII, 222 pages. 1986.

B. Gutting, Taxation, Housing Markets, and the Markets for Building Land.
VIII, 138 pages. 1987.

H. Verbon, The Evolution of Public Pension Schemes.
XII, 287 pages. 1988.

M. Funke (Ed.), Factors in Business Investment.
VIII, 263 pages. 1989.

K. F. Zimmermann (Ed.), Economic Theory of Optimal Population.
X, 182 pages. 1989.

Rüdiger Pethig (Ed.)

Conflicts and Cooperation in Managing Environmental Resources

With 46 Figures

Springer-Verlag

Berlin Heidelberg New York
London Paris Tokyo
Hong Kong Barcelona
Budapest

Professor Dr. RÜDIGER PETHIG
Fachbereich Wirtschaftswissenschaften
Universität Gesamthochschule Siegen
Hölderlinstr. 3
D-5900 Siegen, FRG

ISBN 3-540-54968-4 Springer-Verlag Berlin Heidelberg New York Tokyo
ISBN 0-387-54968-4 Springer-Verlag New York Berlin Heidelberg Tokyo

This work is subject to copyright. All rights are reserved, whether the whole or part of the material is concerned, specifically the rights of translation, reprinting, reuse of illustrations, recitation, broadcasting, reproduction on microfilms or in other ways, and storage in data banks. Duplication of this publication or parts thereof is only permitted under the provisions of the German Copyright Law of September 9, 1965, in its version of June 24, 1985, and a copyright fee must always be paid. Violations fall under the prosecution act of the German Copyright Law.

© Springer-Verlag Berlin · Heidelberg 1992
Printing in Germany

The use of registered names, trademarks, etc. in this publication does not imply, even in the absence of a specific statement, that such names are exempt from the relevant protective laws and regulations and therefore free for general use.

2142/7130-543210 - Printed on acid-free paper

Preface

This volume contains the proceedings of a conference at Freudenberg, Germany, that brought together some forty (environmental) economists from seven European countries and the U.S. in November 1990 to analyse "Conflicts and Cooperation in Managing Environmental Resources". I should like to thank the Volkswagen–Stiftung whose financial support made this conference possible. Additional funding by the Forschungsinstitut für Geistes– und Sozialwissenschaften at the Universität – Gesamthochschule Siegen is also gratefully acknowledged.

The papers and formal comments published in this volume emerged from those presented at Freudenberg. Thorough and competent discussions during and after the conference as well as an anonymous reviewing process led to major revisions which improved the quality of all contributions. I am grateful to the authors for their constructive collaboration before and during the conference as well as during the editing process. The authors demonstrated convincingly that they are not only able to scrutinise the inefficiencies of non–cooperation in their research work, but that they also succeeded to learn this lesson by avoiding delays of the editing process at the expense of the remaining players.

My special thank is due to Klaus Fiedler, Rainer Hickmann, Peter Marx, Ute Müller, Michael Rapp, Ekkehard Seiler, Uwe Seja and Monika Siebel for their devoted effort in supporting the organisation of the conference and/or the editing of this proceedings volume. It is my pleasure to forward to them a large share of the participants' unanimous praise of the stimulating and enjoyable research atmosphere of the Freudenberg conference.

Siegen, August 1991   Rüdiger Pethig

CONTENTS

Chapter 3

Critical Loads and International Environmental Cooperation

KARL—GÖRAN MÄLER

Chapter 4

Environmental Conflicts and Strategic Commitment

JASON F. SHOGREN, KYUNG H. BAIK, and THOMAS D. CROCKER

Chapter 5

The Choice of Environmental Policy Instruments and Strategic International Trade

ALISTAIR ULPH

Chapter 6

Economic Models of Optimal Energy Use under Global Environmental Constraints

HANS W. GOTTINGER

Part 1: The CO_2 Problem in Basic Models of Optimal Use of Fossil Fuels

PART 2: MONITORING AND ENFORCEMENT

Chapter 7

Monitoring and Enforcement of Pollution Control Laws in Europe and the United States

CLIFFORD S. RUSSELL

Chapter 8

The Economics of Negotiations on Water Quality – An Application of Principal Agent Theory

WOLFGANG J. STRÖBELE

Chapter 9

Monitoring the Emission of Pollutants by Means of the Inspector Leadership Method

RUDOLF AVENHAUS

Chapter 10

Illegal Pollution and Monitoring of Unknown Quality – A Signaling Game Approach –

WERNER GÜTH and RÜDIGER PETHIG

Editor's Introduction

Environmental resources are used for a variety of consumptive and productive purposes, in particular as a life–supporting system and as a receptor of waste products stemming from the processes of production and consumption. In the absence of exclusive property rights and markets, conflicts over competing uses are unavoidable. In the Pigouvian tradition the remedy called for is a tax–subsidy scheme to "internalise" externalities. From this perspective, there does not seem to be any need for cooperation, and conflicts of interest do not seem to matter even though taxes or subsidies generate winners and losers. Many environmental economists maintain, however, that in case on non–exclusive, attenuated or uncertain property rights the utilisation of environmental resources necessarily involves strategic behavior of self–interested agents, bargaining, cooperation or other efforts to generate or settle conflicts. This is not only true for transfrontier or global environmental conflicts but also when pollution has purely domestic sources and impacts. Consequently, any modelling of environmental resource allocation should explicitly capture the conflicts involved. This is not to deny the necessity of policy design and professional consulting of government. On the contrary, to understand the preconditions of successful policy implementation, descriptive analysis of that type is indispensable.

To model environmental conflicts, game theory is obviously an appropriate approach, since its central focus is on strategic uncertainty. In most papers of the present volume game theoretic methods are applied to environmental conflicts in an effort to make use of recently developed advanced game theoretic concepts. The first six papers focus on international conflicts and cooperation (Part 1) while the other contributions address conflicts and cooperation arising in the context of monitoring and enforcing emission constraints (Part 2).

Part 1 starts with the paper *"International Environmental Agreements as Games"* (**Chapter 1**) by SCOTT BARRETT. He focuses on the question as to why international environmental agreements become less effective the greater the number of countries involved. At the core of this question is the well–known Olson problem of group formation and collective action. Even though the members of such groups have special interests in common like the reduction of global pollution, they are reluctant to voluntarily contribute to the cost of pollution control because they hope for a free ride. BARRETT views international environmental agreements as games and shows that, with increasing number and heterogeneity of countries, agreements will become very difficult to reach, in particular, when they are based on simple rules like uniform abatement levels without side payments. On the other hand empirical observation shows that such simple rules predominate when international treaties are negotiated which explains why international cooperation is not always successful. Nonetheless, a number of important agreements have been reached. With regard to these agreements the important question arises whether they are sustainable in spite of the signatories' strong incentives to cheat. BAR-RETT addresses the issue of monitoring and enforcement of international agreements (thus establishing a link between Part 1 and Part 2 of this volume) by discussing various 'retaliating' strategies such as increasing emissions by the other signatories or trigger strategies. He shows that enforcement of international environmental agreements becomes less effective as the number of countries increases.

While BARRETT analyses the conditions for successful negotiations for emission abatement regulations, tradeable permits and emission taxes, MICHAEL HOEL focuses exclusively and in greater detail on the issue of emission taxation in his contribution *"Emission Taxes in a Dynamic International Game of CO_2 Emissions"* (**Chapter 2**). He presupposes an international agreement on CO_2 taxes with a scheme of reimbursing total tax revenue and then investigates how emissions are determined as the outcome of a non—cooperative game. In a static (one shot) game it is shown that tax rates which are uniform across countries do not necessarily yield a Pareto optimal outcome. Since CO_2 affects the climate through cumulative emissions, HOEL's main interest is to study this problem with the help of dynamic games applying the solution concepts of open loop and Markov perfect equilibrium. First the properties of these equilibria are derived in the absence of taxation. For the same level of cumulative stock of CO_2 emissions in the end state, a comparison of these equilibria reveals that, under plausible conditions, the Markov perfect equilibrium involves higher CO_2 emissions than the open loop equilibrium until the final stock of pollution is reached. HOEL then derives the surprising result that in spite of this difference, there is a time path of increasing CO_2 tax rates (to which the countries have to commit themselves) which establishes the social optimum in both types of equilibria. Such a long—term commitment of governments to predetermined tax rates may not be expected in the arena of international politics, however, as argued by OTTO KECK in his comments.

In HOEL's dynamic game, the public bad affecting all countries was a stock of pollutants, the aggregate cumulative CO_2 emissions, which could not be "depreciated" by nature. In contrast to this hypothesis, KARL—GÖRAN MÄLER points to the relevance of nature's self—cleansing forces which he takes explicitly into account in his analysis by introducing the ecological concept of critical load defined as the maximum deposition of a pollutant that leaves the environmental resource unaffected in the long run. He discusses various ways to specify this concept and suggests to consider the critical load as a stock–independent, country–specific amount of pollutants which is subtracted in each period from the stock of pollutants. Then he investigates the impact of this ecological hypothesis on cooperation in global pollution problems. MÄLER considers first a single country seeking its social optimum and then the dynamic non–cooperative international game with countries either using open loop and closed loop strategies. He shows that in all these cases the time path of the solution approaches a steady state in which emissions are equal to critical loads. The same is true for the cooperative solution with the decisive difference however, that in case of cooperation, the stock of pollutants in each country will be less than in the non–cooperative solution. According to MÄLER, cooperation among countries may be promoted by focusing attention on the determination of these critical loads for each country.

Quite a different international dimension of environmental problems is addressed by ALISTAIR ULPH in his paper "*The Choice of Environmental Policy Instruments and Strategic International Trade*" (**Chapter 3**). He considers two countries forming a world--market duopoly for some commodity. This is produced with the help of an energy input which causes pollution (e.g. CO_2 emissions). But in contrast to the previous contributions the countries do not strategically interact (explicitly) in a transfrontier pollution problem. They are only concerned with domestic environmental policy by imposing a limit on domestic emissions. As possible policy instruments ULPH examines the choice between quantity controls and price controls. First, he recalls the well–known result that both countries are indifferent between using standards or taxes in a one–shot game with Cournot–Nash strategies. Then he assumes Stackelberg behavior and demonstrates that under certain conditions both countries will be better off if the Stackelberg follower uses standards rather than taxes irrespective of what instruments the Stackelberg leader uses. In another model, both countries simultaneously select the level of the non–polluting input and then proceed to choose the amount of output and hence their emission level. It is shown that the choice of standards by both countries is a Nash equilibrium which Pareto dominates the choice of taxes by both countries. Within this framework of strategic international trade ULPH makes an interesting and innovative contribution to the long–debated question as to why standards are so often preferred in actual environmental policy to price controls in spite of the economists' permanent and unanimous recommendation for the latter.

Since environmental pollution stems from waste products released into the environ ment, damage from harmful residuals can be avoided along three lines: (i) Residuals need not be discharged in the first place; instead, they can be abated ("neutralised") within industry. This important route of settling environmental conflicts plays a constitutive role for the contributions in Part 2 of this volume. (ii) Nature's self—cleansing capacity protects eco—systems and human beings from damage — at least up to some critical load. This conflict—reducing property of environmental resources was center stage in MÄLER's contribution and will be also considered by GOTTINGER. (iii) People exposed to pollution may engage in self—protection actions to the effect that the burden of pollution is shifted to others. Since in this way environmental conflicts are transferred rather than resolved, these phenomena have rightly been denoted transferable externalities (Bird).

JASON SHOGREN, KYUNG BAIK and THOMAS CROCKER take up this concept of transferable externalities in their paper on *"Environemental Conflicts and Strategic Commitment"* (**Chapter 4**) in order to study the implied environmental conflicts in a game—theoretic framework. Players in these game models could be individuals involved in neighborhood externalities. But many of the authors' examples indicate the relevance of their approach to interregional, international and even global environmental problems. First SHOGREN, BAIK and CROCKER show that the failure to cooperate leads to inefficient over—protection. Their next set of models assumes that all agents face the same damage but that the probabilities of damage depend on self—protection in an a-gent—specific way. As a result of non—cooperation, some agents (underdogs) are more likely to be damaged than others (favorites) whereas the cooperative solution requires zero—effort of self—protection for all agents. Various leader—follower games with endogenous strategic timing are investigated which according to SHOGREN, BAIK, and CROCKER help to understand e.g. the pattern of play between Canada (underdog) and the United States (favorite) with respect to acid deposition—control policy. The last part of the paper introduces two or more identical agents making simultaneous efforts of self—protection in order to win a prize — such as an improvement in (local) environmental quality. Agents have the option to form a team whose members share the prize in case that this is won by a team member. Various aspects of strategic team formation, e.g. restriction of entry and efficiency, are discussed.

In his paper on *"Economic Models of Optimal Energy Use under Global Environmental Constraints"* (**Chapter 5**) HANS W. GOTTINGER addresses the issue of global warming caused by accumulated carbon dioxide emissions from burning fossil fuels (assumed to be available in unlimited supply). In most sections the analysis is based on a highly aggregated world model ("there is only one world region") so that, unlike in all proceeding contributions, strategic interactions are not considered. The perspective is one of centralised optimal control to contribute to better policy making through improving the theoretical rationale for policy decisions. GOTTINGER assumes that global warming adversely affects production, but otherwise has no direct impacts on consumers. The physical production damage is either modelled as a continuous negative externality or as a catastrophe by which production is smashed to zero once accumulated atmospheric CO_2 exceeds some positive threshold level. (Observe that the physical damage function as depicted in Figure 1 of MÄLER's paper corresponds to this hypothesis). The atmospheric stock of CO_2 is reabsorbed, or "depreciated", at a rate proportional to the stock. It is worth noting that such an ecological hypothesis differs from that applied by MÄLER who takes reabsorption to be stock–independent. The application of competing, incompatible ecological hypotheses clearly reinforces TULKENS's call for the need of more detailed empirical information on that matter. After the optimal trajectories of the basic models have been characterised, GOTTINGER uses these models for analysing the impact of various forms of technical change, the impact of international cooperation (with the world split up into two regions), and that of structural uncertainty on the optimal intertemporal allocation.

It is shown that the optimal steady state stock of pollution may rise or fall with a shift in technological change depending on the type of that change. The discussion of international cooperation uses the catastrophe version of physical damage. In conformity to one's intuition it turns out that cooperation has the effect of extending the time interval before the end of which the critical pollution level is reached.

As for structural uncertainty, GOTTINGER assumes that the decision maker is imperfectly informed about the critical pollution. Suppose, some probability distribution is known for this threshold and the decision maker adopts the "certainty equivalent approach". Then he may arrive at significantly higher than optimal values of CO_2 emissions as compared to the case that he takes proper care of uncertainty in his decision process.

Part 2 of this volume deals with monitoring and enforcement of pollution control rules resulting either from voluntary agreements (contracts) between pollutees and polluters or — more often — from anti–pollution legislation. First, CLIFFORD S. RUSSELL scrutinises the issue of "*Monitoring and Enforcement of Pollution Control Laws in Europe and the United States*" (**Chapter 7**). He starts out by developing a taxonomy of monitoring and enforcement problems and then proceeds to discuss the key dimensions of monitoring and enforcement system design such as probability of monitoring visits, (absence of) prearrangement of those visits, definition of violations and penalties. RUS-SELL's description and comparison of specific approaches to monitor and enforce environmental laws in several European countries and the U.S. is very illuminating. Loosely speaking, he finds that, on the whole and notwithstanding occasional deviations for the better, monitoring and enforcement is not taken too seriously in all country under investigation, and that there is no significant difference in that respect between the U.S. and European approaches — even though a wide range of difference in institutional arrangements is observable. Improvements and a benchmark for other countries may be expected from the new National Rivers Authority in the United Kingdom but it remains to be seen to what extent the paper form of these recently established enforcement rules can be preserved in the process of implementation.

Even though reliable empirical estimates of the degree of non—compliance are not available, there is wide agreement that non—compliance is neither a negligible nor a transitory empirical issue. In the introduction of his paper, RUSSELL observes that the issue of monitoring and enforcement has not yet received due attention in the literature on environmental economics which tends to define the problem away by assuming perfect compliance — or costless monitoring and enforcement, for that matter. In fact, RUS-SELL conjectures that environmental economists refrain from the design and analysis of monitoring and enforcement systems, because this "... is at once unglamorous and technically difficult".

In an effort to improve upon this unsatisfactory state of the arts, the last three papers of this volume contribute to this neglected research area centering around the conflicts arising between a monitoring agency (a pollutee, respectively), and a polluter which has an incentive not to abide to the rules. In his contribution "*The Economics of Negotiations on Water Quality — An Application of Principal Agent Theory*" (**Chapter 8**), WOLFGANG STRÖBELE considers the design of a contract between a principal, say a downstream producer of drinking water, and an agent, say an upstream river—polluting firm, which has both the right to pollute and an incentive to do so.

The principal's objective is to induce the agent to reduce her waste emissions by offering her a (linear) compensatory payment scheme taking into account that water quality is a random variable whose distribution depends on, but is not completely determined by, the abatement effort of the upstream agent. The agent knows, of course, her own abatement effort, but the principal observes the stochastic water quality only. STRÖBELE determines the non—cooperative negotiation game for different assumptions about the players' risk aversion and for two different specifications of the probability distribution of water quality (normal and beta). Even though the building blocks of the model are rather simple parametric functions, the analysis is of great formal complexity. In case of the normal distribution STRÖBELE offers an explicit general solution, whereas for the beta distribution, which is obviously the more realistic concept, he is only able to provide a numerical solution.

STRÖBELE's model places the pollutee in a very unfavorable position: Owing to the prevailing property–rights regime she has to "bribe" the polluter to reduce his emissions (pollutee–pays–principle) without being able to directly monitor the polluter's abatement activity. In many empirical situations the opposite property–rights regime is in place: environmental laws deny polluters any discharge of pollutants into the environment at least any emissions above some legally fixed limit. To enforce these emission standards, a monitoring agency (inspector, controller) is needed whose task it is to check whether polluters abide to the rule. Strategic interactions between inspectors/controllers and polluters are the principal focus of the last two papers.

RUDOLF AVENHAUS's contribution is about *"Monitoring the Emission of Pollutants by Means of the Inspector Leadership Method"* (**Chapter 9**). The polluter must not exceed some upper emission limit per unit of time (without being compensated as in STRÖBELE's setup). The inspector observes the polluter's releases of pollutants as random variables and announces to the polluter the procedure according to which he determines whether the polluter violated the standard. This gives room for strategic behavior on part of the polluter, since with his incentive to violate the emission standards he will use that strategy which minimises the inspector's chance to call a violation.

AVENHAUS starts with a simple simultaneous move model in which the inspector chooses the probability of giving a false alarm of illegal pollution which, in turn, determines for the violator the probability not getting detected. The next game, called the inspector leadership game and considered by the author to be more appropriate than the first for the problem at hand, is a game in which the inspector moves first by choosing an alarm probability. After having learned about this choice the firm's move is to decide whether to abide to the rule or not. The Nash equilibrium always yields full compliance. The paper proceeds by generalising this inspector leadership game in that the players' strategy space are enlarged. In particular, the inspector can now choose among different monitoring procedures in an effort to minimise the violator's probability not to be detected. At the same time the polluter maximises this probability by choosing the best (excess) emissions strategy. As before, the result is that the inspector succeeds in enforcing legal behavior.

Enforcement of predetermined emission standards is also the central topic of the paper *"Illegal Pollution and Monitoring of Unknown Quality — A Signaling Game Approach"* (**Chapter 10**) by WERNER GÜTH and RÜDIGER PETHIG. In their model the polluting firm faces an inspector — called controller, this time — who, with some positive a priori probability may be an expert or not in detecting illegal polluters. The potential polluter has the option of undertaking a small–scale deliberate "exploratory pollution accident" to get a hint about the controller's qualification before deciding on how to dispose of his waste. The controller may or may not respond to that "accident" by a thorough investigation thus, perhaps, revealing her type (expert, non–expert) to the polluter.

It is this sequential decision making process along with the asymmetric distribution of information that constitutes a signaling game during the play of which the type of the controller may but need not be signaled to the (potential) polluter. After having introduced the game model, GÜTH and PETHIG discuss several so–called equilibrium scenarios, i.e. non–degenerate submodels whose equilibria are considered typical and especially interesting for the issue at hand. There are non–signaling scenarios, in which both types of the controller react to an exploratory accident in the same way (pooling behavior) so that the firm must rely on its a priori knowledge when determining the amount of illegal emission — which may range from zero to some maximum positive amount. There are also scenarios the equilibria of which signal the controller's type to the polluter yielding valuable information for his subsequent choice of illegal emission.

Having set up a rather complex game model the price to be paid is, as in many game theoretic analyses in other fields, the multiplicity of equilibria — even within one and the same equilibrium scenario. Such multiplicity clearly weakens the predictive capacity of the model. To overcome this drawback GÜTH and PETHIG address concepts of equilibrium refinement and selection on a fairly technical level. It is shown that the set of equilibria is reduced — not to a singleton, though — by applying the refinement concept of uniformly perfect pure strategy equilibria. Unique solutions are obtained by reference to the equilibrium selection theoretic concepts of cell and truncation consistency, of payoff dominance and of risk dominance.

PART ONE

International Dimensions

Chapter 1

Scott Barrett

International Environmental Agreements as Games

Abstract. It is often asserted that international environmental agreements (IEAs) become less effective the greater the number of countries involved. This paper, which views IEAs as games, shows why. As the number of countries increases, so do the differences between them. Agreement on the basis of simple rules like uniform abatement levels without side payments will then become very difficult to reach; and yet this is often the basis upon which treaties are negotiated. Even if agreement can be reached, it may not be sustainable. As the number of countries increases, the incentive for signatories to punish non–signatories falls, and free riding becomes more irresistible.

1. Introduction

If a fishery is subject to open access, every fisherman will harvest too many fish because each has little to gain from conservation. If the current rate of harvest is reduced, growth in the total stock of fish is likely to be greater, and hence the stock should support a greater rate of harvest in the future. But if one fisherman reduces his harvest, and this fisherman is only one among many, he could hope to recover (at best) only a small portion of the extra future harvest; most (if not all) of it will be grabbed by the other fishermen. Every other fisherman faces exactly the same incentive. Although every fisherman could be better off if use of the resource were reduced by all, each has a private incentive to overexploit the fish population[1]. The outcome need not be disastrous, for private incentives may offer some protection. For example, as a fishery is depleted, harvesting costs may become so great that it will not pay open access fishermen to reduce the stock below its minimum viable population. Or, if demand for the product is very

---

[1] Whether every fisherman would be made better off depends on how the reduced harvest is effected, and in particular whether the rents arising from the reduced harvest are retained by the fisherman or appropriated by the regulator. See Dasgupta (1982, 25–30), for a demonstration of this point.

elastic, price may fall so quickly as the catch is increased that it will not pay the fishermen to harvest at an unsustainable rate. Still, even where extinction is avoided, well–being can be enhanced by effective management of the resource. Where private incentives
make exhaustion individually optimal, better management can save the resource from
extinction.

The fisheries example illustrates a phenomenon that is common to many social and
economic problems. The private incentives of individual agents (fishermen in the above
example) prevent the agents from reaching an outcome which makes each and every
agent better off. It is a particularly serious feature of many environmental problems,
including pollution of the air and water.

Where open access resources fall under the jurisdiction of a single state, use of the
resource can be regulated by the central authority, and the inefficiencies of open access
can be eliminated. But where such resources fall under the jurisdiction of two or more
states, the problem is not resolved so easily. For with no state having full authority over
the resource, we are back to the open access game where the players are the states themselves. The only way of avoiding overexploitation, short of merger or annexation, is
cooperation. International cooperation in the management of environmental resources is
in fact common. It is usually codified in the form of international agreements, of which
there are now well over 140 (see Barrett, 1991b). These establish rules for the management of such resources as international fisheries and river basins, Antarctica, migratory
and endangered wildlife, pollution at sea, and atmospheric pollution.

While the details of each management problem are different, they all have in common two features. The first is that while every country may agree that *something* needs
to be done, they may disagree on exactly *what* should be done by *whom*. The second is
that commitments made by potential signatories can only be sustained if free riding can
be deterred.

This paper views international environmental agreements (IEAs) as the outcome of
a game where these two problems are resolved[2]. The resolution will generally improve
upon the non–cooperative outcome, but may still leave us far from the full cooperative
outcome. Agreement by all parties may prove impossible; some may not sign the agreement because the terms of the agreement are so onerous that they would do better with
no agreement at all; others may not sign because, while they would do better with an

---

[2] Other aspects of IEAs are discussed by Hahn and Richards (1989). For a more general
discussion of the problem of achieving international cooperation in environmental protection, see Barrett (1990).

agreement than without one, they do better still by free riding on those who do sign the treaty.

The paper employs a model of an open access pollution problem where environmental damage is independent of the location of emissions and where the pollutant does not accumulate. Section 2 considers the problem where countries must reach agreement on who does what. It is assumed here that commitments are binding, and so free riding is not a problem. We shall see that if countries are identical, they will have no problem reaching agreement. If countries are different, treaty obligations are uniform and side payments are forbidden, then agreement will be more difficult to reach and full agreement may prove impossible. The success of negotiations will depend in part on the nature and extent of the differences, and on the *instrument* that is used to effect emission reductions. The instruments considered in this paper are abatement obligations, pollution taxes, and internationally tradeable pollution permits.

Section 3 focuses on the free rider problem. Here I assume that countries are identical, and hence that agreement on who does what is not a problem. However, I now also assume that binding commitments cannot be made, and hence that the success of negotiations depends on whether free riding can be deterred. We shall see that in general only a fraction of countries will sign the agreement, and that this fraction will fall as the number of countries involved increases, all else being equal. The reason is that as the number of countries involved increases, it becomes more difficult for signatories to punish non—signatories without making themselves worse off.

2. Reaching agreement

Different countries will usually have different views on the obligations which they and others should carry. This is because the costs and benefits of any given obligation often vary widely. It can also be because countries have different views about the "just" obligation. Many developing countries have argued that the responsibility for forestalling or averting global climate change lies with the high—income countries because they are largely responsible for the great accumulation of greenhouse gases in the atmosphere. Some industrial countries have responded by arguing that past emissions are irrelevant because the dangers of potential climate change did not become apparent until recently. They also argue that since all countries are responsible for incremental additions to atmospheric concentrations, all should play a part in abatement.

Despite these differences, IEAs usually involve *uniform* obligations, if not for all countries then at least within a broad group of countries, or obligations based on fairly arbitrary rules — like population or GDP. One reason for this is that these obligations serve as good focal points (Schelling, 1960, 67):

> "In bargains that involve numerical magnitudes...there seems to be a strong magne-
> tism in mathematical simplicity... . The frequency with which final agreement is
> precipitated by an offer to 'split the difference' illustrates the...point, and the differ-
> ence that is split is by no means always trivial. More impressive, perhaps, is the
> remarkable frequency with which long negotiations over complicated quantitative
> formulas or *ad hoc* shares in some costs or benefits converge ultimately on some-
> thing as crudely simple as equal shares, shares proportionate to some common mag-
> nitude (gross national product, population, foreign exchange deficit, and so forth),
> or the shares agreed on in some previous but logically irrelevant negotiation."

The phenomenon is seen repeatedly. Thus, the original Montreal Protocol required a 50% reduction in chlorofluorocarbons (CFCs); the draft revisions to the Protocol de-mand a complete phasing out of CFCs; the 1963 Nuclear Test Ban Treaty prohibits atmospheric and under water testing; and Protocols to the 1979 Convention on Long—Range Transboundary Air Pollution impose a 30% cut in sulphur emissions and a stabi-lization of nitrogen oxide emissions. Proposals for a treaty on global warming call for a stabilization in greenhouse gas concentrations, or a stabilization in CO_2 emissions, or a 20% reduction in these emissions, or a tradeable permit scheme where permits to pollute are allocated initially on the basis of population or GNP.

These treaties and proposals are not the outcome of a sophisticated bargaining pro-cess. They are not perfectly efficient[3]. And they would not have been viewed as being the best outcome by all or even any of the signatories. The reason for such outcomes is unsophisticated but compelling (Schelling 1960, 70): "The rationale may not be strong at the arbitrary 'focal point', but at least it can defend itself with the argument 'If not here, where?'"

Below we shall consider the outcomes that might emerge from negotiations on uniform obligations. One reason for undertaking this exercise is to determine the dis-crepancy between the outcome with uniform obligations and the fully efficient outcome.

---

[3] One must be careful in making this assessment. The International Whaling Commission has banned comercial whaling from 1986, and the 1973 Convention on International Trade in Endangered Species prohibits (with a few exeptions) international trade in species threatened with extinction. These obligations may represent focal points, but they may also be efficient. Spence (1984) has shown that moratorium can be the most efficient policy for managing the blue whale population.

Another reason is that such an analysis can help lead policy. As Schelling (1960, 75) argues, "If the analysis provides anything ... it is not a judgment of the probability of successfully reaching tacit agreement but a better understanding of where to look for the terms of agreement." The analysis presented below considers not just uniform abatement but also uniform pollution taxes and uniform allocations of tradeable pollution permits.

Consider the problem where N countries emit a pollutant that is both uniformly mixed and quickly assimilated by the environment. These last assumptions ignore the spatial and temporal dimensions of many environmental problems, but allow us to focus on the other important forces that determine the success or failure of international cooperation.

Assuming that all marginal abatement benefit and cost schedules are linear in abatement, the ith country's benefit and cost functions can be written

$$B_i(Q) = b_i\left[a_i Q - \frac{Q^2}{2N} \right],$$ (1)

$$C_i(q_i) = \frac{c_i q_i^2}{2},$$ (2)

where $Q = \overset{N}{\underset{i=1}{\Sigma}} q_i.$

Notice that i's marginal abatement benefits are zero where $Q = a_i N$.[4] For any given problem, N will be fixed, and if the level of abatement where marginal abatement benefits are zero is the same for all countries, then a_i will be the same for all i. In the analysis that follows it shall be assumed that a_i is the same for all i and equal to 10.[5] It is

---

[4] This specification will prove helpful later for evaluating the free rider problem. In that case our interests will lie partly in comparing problems for which N varies. Consider analyzing a problem where N is given, and then ask what will happen if N increases by one unit. If the additional country increases emissions, then it must be the case that the level of global abatement where marginal abatement benefits are zero increases. It is for this reason that N is included in (1).

[5] This choice of value is entirely abitrary. Later in the paper we shall see that the value of the parameter a (assumed here to equal 10) can be taken to represent emissions in the absence of abatement. For example, if it is assumed that any positive level of emissions results in some damage, then Equation (1') implies that if all countries abate all their emissions, the benefit of further reductions is zero.

also assumed that $N = 2$.[6] Hence (1) can be rewritten

$$B_i(Q) = b_i \left[10 \, Q - \frac{Q^2}{4} \right].$$ (1')

Table 1 and Figures 1–5 present some possible negotiation outcomes for five cases. What distinguishes these cases is the nature of the net benefit functions and the instruments that are used to reach agreement. The instruments considered include a uniform abatement level, a uniform emission tax, and an internationally tradeable permit scheme where permits are allocated initially on a uniform basis.[7] Revenues from the international tax are assumed to be collected and retained by the national governments; there are no international transfers.[8] It is assumed that international trading in emission permits will be perfect in the sense that trading will continue until all gains from trade have been exhausted. Countries negotiate a uniform allocation of tradeable permits recognizing how their net benefits will be affected by trading *ex post*. Under the trading scheme, resources *are* transferred internationally.

A number of solution concepts are considered; for details, see the Appendix. The noncooperative outcome assumes that each country determines its unilateral abatement level by setting *its* marginal benefit of abatement equal to *its* marginal cost of abatement. In other words, each country chooses its best reply to the other's abatement level. This constitutes the Cournot–Nash equilibrium to this game. The noncooperative outcome is taken to be the threat point for negotiations; it determines the payoffs which the two countries receive if negotiations fail.

The negotiated outcomes are of three types. The first assumes that country *1* chooses the uniform obligation (i.e., the uniform abatement level, emission tax or allocation of tradeable permits). The second assumes that country *2* makes this choice. The virtue of these outcomes is that they show whether a uniform abatement obligation falls within the bargaining range. If the uniform abatement obligation which maximizes

---

[6] Consideration of the case where $N > 2$ can complicate matters, for a complete analysis would then have to examine whether countries might prefer to form coalitions consisting of more than one but less than N countries.

[7] The countries are assumed to have the same base level of emissions. Hence, uniform abatement is equivalent to uniform percentage abatement, and uniform allocations of abatement permits are equivalent to uniform allocations of emission permits.

[8] It is further assumed that the tax does not alter the abatement cost function. If revenue from the pollution tax allows the tax authority to reduce distortionary taxes like income taxes (which alter the trade–off between work and leisure), then the pollution tax may enhance economic performance. Such a possibility is not considered here.

	Country 1				Country 2				Total	
	Allocation	Tax	Abatement	Net Benefit	Allocation	Tax	Abatement	Net Benefit	Abatement	Net Benefit
Case 1: $b_1=b_2=1$; $c_1=c_2=1$										
Noncooperative	—	—	5.00	62.50	—	—	5.00	62.50	10.00	125.00
1 chooses $q_1=q_2$	—	—	6.67	66.67	—	—	6.67	66.67	13.34	133.34
2 chooses $q_1=q_2$	—	—	6.67	66.67	—	—	6.67	66.67	13.34	133.34
Nash $(q_1=q_2)$	—	—	6.67	66.67	—	—	6.67	66.67	13.34	133.34
Full Cooperative	—	—	6.67	66.67	—	—	6.67	66.67	13.34	133.34
Case 2: $b_1=b_2=1$; $c_1=1$, $c_2=2$										
Noncooperative	—	—	5.71	51.09	—	—	2.87	59.16	8.58	110.25
1 chooses $q_1=q_2$	—	—	6.67	66.67	—	—	6.67	44.42	13.34	111.09
2 chooses $q_1=q_2$	—	—	5.00	62.50	—	—	5.00	50.00	10.00	112.50
Full Cooperative	—	—	8.00	52.00	—	—	4.00	68.00	12.00	120.00
Case 3: $b_1=b_2=1$; $c_1=1$, $c_2=2$										
Noncooperative	—	5.71	5.71	51.09	—	5.71	2.86	59.16	8.57	110.25
1 chooses $t_1=t_2$	—	7.06	7.06	52.94	—	7.06	3.53	65.40	10.59	118.34
2 chooses $t_1=t_2$	—	9.23	9.23	47.93	—	9.23	4.62	69.23	13.85	117.16
Nash $(t_1=t_2)$	—	7.33	7.33	52.86	—	7.33	3.66	66.30	11.00	119.16
Full Cooperative	—	8.00	8.00	52.00	—	8.00	4.00	68.00	12.00	120.00
Case 4: $b_1=b_2=1$; $c_1=1$, $c_2=2$										
Noncooperative	—		5.71	51.09	—		2.86	59.16	8.57	110.25
1 chooses $\hat{q}_1=\hat{q}_2$	6.92		9.23	69.23	6.92		4.61	47.95	13.84	117.18
2 chooses $\hat{q}_1=\hat{q}_2$	5.29		7.05	65.38	5.29		3.53	52.94	10.58	118.32
Full Cooperative	—		8.00	52.00	—		4.00	68.00	12.00	120.00
Case 5: $b_1=1$, $b_2=2$, $c_1=c_2=1$										
Noncooperative	—	—	4.00	76.00	—	—	8.00	136.00	12.00	212.00
1 chooses $q_1=q_2$	—	—	6.67	66.67	—	—	6.67	155.58	13.34	222.25
2 chooses $q_1=q_2$	—	—	8.00	64.00	—	—	8.00	160.00	16.00	224.00
Full Cooperative	—	—	7.50	65.63	—	—	7.50	159.38	15.00	225.01

Table 1: Negotiation outcomes for five cases.

Scott Barrett

Case 2': $b_1=b_2=1$; $c_1=1$, $c_2=2$

	Country 1			Country 2			Total	
	Percentage Abatement	Abatement	Net Benefit	Percentage Abatement	Abatement	Net Benefit	Abatement	Net Benefit
Noncooperative	–	5.71	51.09	–	2.87	59.16	8.58	110.25
1 chooses $s_1=s_2$	49	7.80	61.00	49	6.34	51.22	14.14	112.22
2 chooses $s_1=s_2$	15	6.33	56.40	15	3.94	60.91	10.27	117.31
Nash $(s_1=s_2)$	21	6.59	57.71	21	4.34	60.62	10.93	118.33
Full Cooperative	53	8.00	52.00	16	4.00	68.00	12.00	120.00

Table 2. Countries choose a uniform percent abatement relative to the disagreement point.

country i's net benefits still leave this country worse off compared with the noncooperative outcome, then no uniform obligation will prove acceptable to i. A threat by i to break off negotiations would then be credible. If a uniform obligation falls within the bargaining range, then the parties will be able to reach agreement (assuming commitments are binding), but the precise nature of the agreement will be indeterminate. One possibility is that countries will negotiate the Nash bargaining solution.[9] This solution is also given where uniform obligations fall within the bargaining range.

The full cooperative outcome assumes that each country's abatement level is chosen so as to equate its marginal abatement cost to the *sum* of the marginal abatement benefits for the two countries, or in other words that abatement is chosen to maximize the total net benefits for the two countries. Our primary interest in this outcome is to see how close the negotiated outcome can get us to the full cooperative outcome.

2.1. Identical countries

Figure 1 illustrates the solution to case 1, where both countries are assumed to have identical net benefit functions. The noncooperative outcome is labelled NC in the figure. All points both north and east of NC are strictly preferred by both countries to the non-cooperative outcome. Hence, if the negotiation instrument can lead the two countries into this territory, agreement between the two parties should not pose a problem. The 45 degree line that passes through the point NC shows the payoffs the two countries receive for various uniform abatement obligations. Hence, points on this line and northeast of the point NC represent uniform abatement obligations that make both countries better off compared to the disagreement point NC. Along the downward sloping line labelled SP in the figure, total net benefits are maximized. The line simply shows how the total net benefits of full cooperation could be allocated between the two countries if side payments were feasible.

If the two countries must negotiate over uniform obligations, country *1* will prefer the outcome that is farthest east, provided that point is also east of NC. Country *2* will prefer the outcome that is farthest north, provided that point is also north of NC. It is obvious from the figure that both countries would like to be at the same point on the figure – the intersection of the uniform abatement locus and the SP line. As Table 1

---

[9] The Nash bargaining solution maximizes the product of the parties' gains from cooperation. There are, of course, other possible bargaining solutions. The Kalai–Smorodinsky solution, for example, gives every party a net benefit which is the same proportion of that party's maximum gain from cooperation.

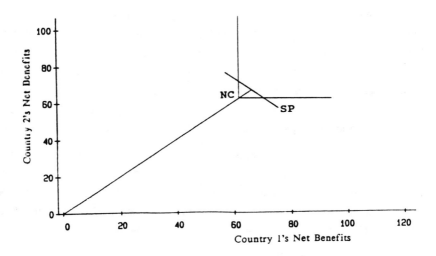

Figure 1: Case 1

shows, each country prefers a uniform abatement level of 6.67 units — the solution which full cooperation would deliver. As Table 1 indicates, this is also the Nash bargaining solution to this cooperative game. Although identical countries do not have difficulty reaching agreement, we shall see in the next section that they may well have difficulty *sustaining* the agreement because of the free rider problem.

Notice that if these two countries were to choose a uniform tax or a uniform allocation of pollution permits, the outcome would be unaffected. Because the two countries are identical, uniform abatement is cost–effective. When a pollutant is uniformly mixed, a uniform tax is also cost–effective. Since both countries are identical, the uniform tax provides an incentive for both countries to choose uniform abatement. Hence, the two countries could do no better than to choose the uniform tax that results in the same uniform abatement level described above (6.67 in Table 1).

The story is similar for internationally tradeable pollution permits. Since the initial allocation must be uniform, and since countries are identical, no trading will take place because any initial uniform allocation will be cost–effective. Since countries have nothing to gain from trading, the uniform allocation that is preferred by each party is the same as the uniform abatement level that is preferred by each party.

2.2. Cost differences

In case 2, country *2*'s marginal abatement cost curve rises more steeply than country *1*'s. As Figure 2 shows, the uniform abatement locus begins to rise from the origin at about 45 degrees (as in the previous case), but as the level of abatement increases the locus quickly reaches a maximum and then turns back as country *2*'s net benefits fall more rapidly than *1*'s. Country *1* will prefer a negotiated outcome in which the abatement obligation is uniform over some range (between about 3.5 and 10 units each), whereas country *2* would refuse to sign an agreement under those terms *even if it is allowed to choose the uniform abatement level;* no point on the uniform abatement locus is north of point *NC*.

Both countries would prefer the full cooperative solution over the noncooperative outcome, but achievement of the full cooperative outcome requires non–uniform abatement. Because the uniform abatement locus never reaches the *SP* line, the full cooperative outcome cannot be achieved as long as abatement must be uniform. It is, however, possible that the two countries might be able to do better than the noncooperative outcome if side payments were allowed. The dashed line labelled *SP'* shows how the maximum total net benefits associated with the uniform abatement could be distributed between the two countries. Because this line passes through the quadrant northeast of *NC*, it is possible that countries could negotiate a uniform abatement obligation, with country *1* agreeing to make a payment to *2* that makes *2* at least as well off as at *NC*.

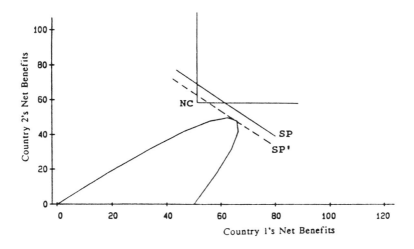

Figure 2: Case 2

Case 3 is the same as case 2 except that countries negotiate a uniform emission tax rather than a uniform abatement level. The solution is shown in Figure 3. The uniform tax locus intersects the y–axis because at very high tax levels country 2 abates much more than 1. The locus passes through the territory northeast of NC, and hence there is scope for negotiation. Country 2 could be made better off with a uniform tax between about 6 and 12 units, while country 1 could be made better off with a tax of between about 6 and 8 units. Hence, the two countries might negotiate a uniform tax over the range 6–8 units. They could in fact negotiate the full cooperative outcome, since the uniform tax locus meets the SP line inside the northeast quadrant. However, the Nash bargaining solution suggests that the negotiated uniform tax may not be the one which achieves the full cooperative outcome (assuming side payments are forbidden).

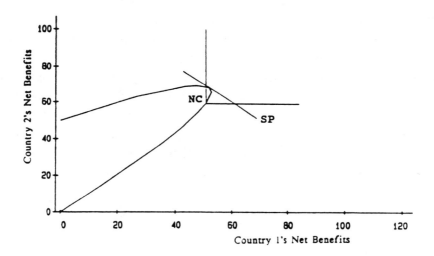

Figure 3: Case 3

Under case 4, countries negotiate a uniform initial allocation of emission permits on the understanding that these could be traded once agreement has been reached. It is assumed that countries believe trading will continue until all gains from trade have been exhausted.[10] In comparing cases 2 and 4, notice that country 1 comes out well in case 4 not only because its costs are low, but also because it will be paid by country 1 to undertake abatement on 1's behalf. Country 2 also does better than in case 2, because country

---

[10] Hoel (1990) considers the case where some countries are large and hence are able to influence the price at which permits are traded.

2 is able to lower its costs by paying 1 to bear a portion of its emission reduction obligation. Because trading lowers the effective cost of a uniform abatement obligation, countries 1 and 2 would both prefer greater obligations when trading is allowed. However,
country 2 still prefers no agreement at all to one involving uniform abatement obligations, even when these obligations can be traded.

Figure 4 shows that the net benefits associated with the full cooperative outcome
can be achieved (by the countries agreeing to each accept an obligation of 6 units). However, this initial allocation will not be acceptable to country 2 unless side payments are
made. Alternatively, the full cooperative outcome could be achieved without side payments if the initial allocation were non–uniform.

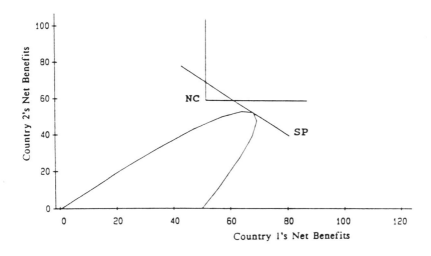

Figure 4: Case 4

In evaluating cases 2–4, notice that the two countries may disagree not only over the
obligations each should carry but also about the appropriate instrument for negotiation.
Country 1 (the low cost country) will prefer a uniform abatement obligation which includes provisions for trading, whereas country 2 (which has higher abatement costs) will
prefer a uniform pollution charge. An IEA specifying uniform abatement would not be
cost–effective in these cases, and would not be acceptable to country 2 (unless, possibly,
accompanied by side payments). A uniform tax would be cost–effective, and might possibly be acceptable to country 1 (1 is better off with the uniform tax set at 8 units than
with no agreement at all, although using different numerical values for the parameters in

the model may change this result). A uniform allocation of tradeable permits would be unacceptable to country 2 unless side payments were made, even though perfect trading would be cost—effective.

2.3. Benefit differences

In case 5, the two countries have identical cost functions but country 2's marginal abate- ment benefit curve is steeper than 1's. In this case, as Figure 5 shows, uniform abate- ment levels are cost—effective, and will be acceptable (over some range) to country 2. However, country 1 can only be made worse off under such an agreement, unless country 2 offers 1 a payment that puts 1 east of the point NC. Hence, country 1 will not accept an agreement on uniform abatement without side payments. The full cooperative solu- tion could be acceptable to the two parties if each country were required to abate 7.5 units and country 1 received a side payment of at least 10.37 from 2.

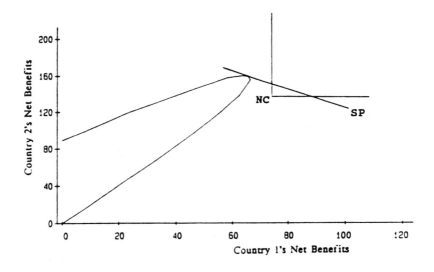

Figure 5: Case 5

Notice that the outcome for case 5 would be unaffected if the countries were to negotiate a uniform tax or a uniform allocation of permits. Because the abatement cost schedules are identical, uniform abatement will be cost—effective. Since a uniform tax is cost—ef- fective, the tax preferred by each party will be the one which results in the same uni form abatement levels shown in Table 1. Likewise, if the allocation of permits is uniform, abatement without trading will be cost–effective and hence no trading will take place. If no trading takes place, then countries could do no better than to choose a uniform allocation of permits that was identical to the uniform abatement level shown in Table 1.

2.4. Choice of a benchmark

The obligations which countries agree to bear are not absolute but relative to a benchmark. Thus, countries could agree to reduce emissions relative to some benchmark level of emissions, or to impose a tax relative to some benchmark price on emissions. The preceding analysis assumed that this benchmark had been agreed, and that it was identical for both countries.[11] However, the benchmark is something that will itself have to be negotiated, and it is unlikely that the benchmark would be identical for all countries when countries differ in important respects.

The benchmark could be some historical emission or price level that was observed before negotiations commenced — perhaps before the environmental problem had even been detected. Alternatively, the benchmark might be taken to be the level that each country would choose if negotiations failed (i.e., the noncooperative outcome). If the latter is chosen, and countries have identical net benefit functions, then our results would not change. The reason is that the benchmark would then be the same for each country (for example, in case 1 each country would abate 5 units if negotiations failed). However, if countries have different net benefit functions, then this will no longer be true; in general, some will prefer to undertake more abatement than others if negotiations failed.

One of the problems with choosing an historical benchmark is that it may convey no information about the disagreement point. If obligations had to be uniform, one would think that negotiations would prove more successful if the point of departure were the disagreement point because small reductions in emissions from this point would have to make both parties better off. If the benchmark is an historical emission level (say, last year's emissions), that need not be so. To see this, suppose country *2* has higher marginal abatement costs than *1*. If both countries would be harmed by the pollution, then both would prefer to abate some of their emissions, even if no agreement is reached. But

---

[11] Provided the benchmark is identical, the precise value of the benchmark is not relevant to negotiation outcomes.

country *1* would want to abate more than *2* if negotiations fail, and *2* knows this. Hence, country *2* may be unwilling to agree to a uniform reduction relative to last year's emissions because *2* knows that country *1* would abate more than *2* if negotiations failed, and hence *2* could receive the benefit of additional abatement by *1* without having to bear the costs of additional abatement itself.

To illustrate this point, Table 2 provides an analysis of case 2 but where countries choose uniform percent abatement relative to the disagreement point.[12] The noncooperative and full cooperative outcomes are unaffected. However, agreement is now easier to reach using uniform obligations.

2.5. Summary

Although these examples are simple, and other cases should be considered, several firm and important conclusions can be made.

(1)   If countries have identical cost and benefit functions, agreement on the full cooperative outcome should not prove difficult.

(2)   If countries have identical benefit functions but different cost functions, uniform abatement will not be cost–effective. Negotiation on the basis of uniform abatement obligations may not be acceptable to high cost countries — at least not without transfers. Hence, if cost differences are great, it seems likely that negotiation will require non–uniform abatement obligations (possibly supplemented by side payments) — unless, that is, a different instrument for negotiation is employed (see below).

(3)   If countries have identical benefit functions but different cost functions, a uniform emission charge will be cost–effective. Negotiation on the basis of a uniform emission charge may prove acceptable, but this is by no means assured; side payments may be required to win acceptance by low cost countries.

---

[12] In case 2', base year emissions are taken to equal *10* for both countries. The benchmark emission level is thus $10 - q_i^n$ for each country i, $i = 1, 2$, where the superscript n refers to the noncooperative abatement level (defined by Equation (A.2) in the Appendix). The actual abatement undertaken by i will be $q_i = 10 - (1 - s)(10 - q_i^n)$, where s denotes uniform percent emission reduction relative to the benchmark emission level. Notice that if $s = 0$, $q_i = q_i^n$, and if $s = 1$, $q_i = 10$. The solutions are found by substituting the above equation for q_i into Equations (A.1), (A.3), (A.5), and (A.16), where the choice variable in these optimization problems now becomes s, the uniform percent emission reduction level (the reduction is relative to the noncooperative level).

(4)   If countries have identical benefit functions but different cost functions, a
       uniform initial abatement obligation with provisions for trading will be
       cost–effective (assuming trading is perfect[13]). But high cost countries may
       threaten (credibly) not to negotiate on these terms. If costs vary significantly,
       agreement on a tradeable permit scheme will probably require non–uniform
       initial abatement obligations and/or side payments.

(5)   If countries have identical cost functions but different benefit functions, any
       agreement on uniform abatement or a uniform emission tax levels or uniform
       initial allocations of tradeable permits will be cost–effective. However, if benefits
       vary significantly, it seems likely that the countries that benefit most from
       abatement will have to offer side payments to the low benefit countries[14].

(6)   When countries have different net benefit functions, agreement will prove more
       effective when uniform obligations are chosen relative to the disagreement point
       than to some arbitrary benchmark such as an historical emission level.

3. Sustaining agreement

Suppose an agreement has been reached and achieves an outcome that is better from the
point of view of all signatories than the non–cooperative outcome. Then each signatory's
marginal benefit of abatement will fall short of its own marginal cost of abatement (see
Barrett, 1991a). There will be an irresistible urge on the part of all countries to cheat.
Yet if all countries cheat, we will end up back where we started — at the
non–cooperative outcome — and all countries will be worse off.

To overcome free–riding incentives, cheating, once detected, must be punished effectively. But punishment for failing to sign or comply with the obligations of a treaty is
particularly difficult to inflict because IEAs cannot be enforced by a central authority. A
polluter that violates a national law can be punished by the regulator or judicial system —

---

[13] Trading is permitted by the Montreal Protocol. However, features of this treaty prevent
trading from being perfect. For a discussion of the cost–effectiveness of this agreement,
see Bohm (1990).

[14] For an application to the acid rain problem, see Mäler (1989).

the polluter can be fined, or forced to shut down, or its managers sent to jail. But there is no world government that can enforce international law. A country that violates a treaty can be taken to the International Court of Justice — but only if the country agrees to go. Even then, the country can refuse to comply with the court's decision. Hence, IEAs must be *self—enforcing*.

There are a number of punishment strategies that might be employed by an IEA. Signatories might agree that if any one signatory fails to meet its agreed obligation, the others will automatically cease all trade with the offending nation, or increase their emissions by twice as much, or perhaps even invade and occupy the country. All these punishment strategies may work if they were implemented. However, such threats may not be credible. The signatories inflicting the punishment may themselves be made much worse off if they actually carried out their threat. Once the one country defected from the agreement, the others would have an incentive not to carry out their threat. The potential defector would know this, and hence would disregard the threat. An effective punishment strategy must be *credible*. Credibility poses a major problem in enforcing IEAs.

One mechanism for punishment is suggested by my (1991a) model of an IEA. In this model, if one country pulls out of the agreement in order to increase its emissions, the remaining countries increase their emissions too. This punishment is credible. In fact, in this model signatories choose their abatement obligations by maximizing the collective net benefits of all signatories.[15] Hence, there is no other choice of emission levels that would make the remaining signatories better off. The model also has a reward mechanism. If a country joins the agreement and undertakes additional abatement, the other signatories abate more. In a sense, the abatement of countries that accede to the agreement is subsidized by the existing signatories. A stable solution exists in the model where signatories do not want to withdraw, and nonsignatories do not want to accede. The stable IEA defined by this model is self—enforcing.

The elements of the model are easily explained. Suppose there are N identical countries, all of which emit the same quantity of a pollutant. Each country has abatement benefit function (1) with b_i a constant equal to b and abatement cost function (2) with

---

[15] Since all countries are identical in this model, signatories have no problem coming to an agreement on obligations.

c_i constant and equal to c.[16] A proportion α of countries form an IEA and agree to maximize net benefits to the group. The justification for this was provided in the previous section. These countries act as leaders insofar as they choose their collective abatement levels while recognizing how the remaining countries will react to their choice. The remaining $(1 - \alpha)N$ countries invoke the usual Cournot conjecture that every country chooses its abatement level on the belief that the abatement levels of all the other countries are given.

Formally, the jth nonsignatory performs the following optimization exercise:

$$\max_{q_j} \; b\left[10(Q_{-j} + q_j) - \frac{(Q_{-j} + q_j)^2}{2N} \right] - \frac{c q_j^2}{2}, \tag{3}$$

where Q_{-j} is the abatement of all countries excluding j. Solving for q_j and summing over all $(1 - \alpha)N$ nonsignatories yields

$$Q_n = \frac{(1 - \alpha)N\left[10 - \frac{Q_s}{N}\right]}{\frac{c}{b} + 1 - \alpha}, \tag{4}$$

where Q_n is total abatement by nonsignatories and Q_s is total abatement by signatories.

Signatories substitute (4) for Q_n in their maximization problem:

$$\max_{Q_s} \; \alpha N b\left[10(Q_n + Q_s) - \frac{(Q_n + Q_s)^2}{2N} \right] - \frac{c Q_s^2}{2 \alpha N}. \tag{5}$$

Maximization of (5) yields Q_s as a function of α. Q_n can then be expressed as a function of α by substituting $Q_s(\alpha)$ into Eq. (4). The solution to the IEA problem, letting q_s

---

[16] For any given problem, N will be fixed, and the marginal benefit of abatement for each country will be zero when $Q = aN$. When N is fixed, a change in a alters the absolute gains from cooperation, but not the qualitative results of the model; see Barrett (1991a). In comparing two cases involving different values for N, the problem can be modelled in two different ways. The first is to assume that countries are identical in the two cases and that an increase in N therefore implies that global abatement must be increased if each country's benefit from abatement is to be unchanged. (i.e., aN is greater when N is greater). The second is to assume that countries are identical for any given N, but not across cases where N varies; the value aN is assumed to be unchanged as N changes. The analysis presented here adopts the first approach by assuming that the parameter a is constant.

denote the abatement by each signatory ($q_s = Q_s/\alpha N$) and q_n the abatement by each nonsignatory ($q_n = Q_n/(1-\alpha)N$), is given by

$$q_s(\alpha) = \frac{10\alpha N\ \theta(\alpha)}{\frac{c}{b} + \alpha^2 N\ \theta(\alpha)}, \tag{6}$$

$$q_n(\alpha) = \frac{\dfrac{10\frac{c}{b}}{\frac{c}{b} + 1 - \alpha}}{\frac{c}{b} + \alpha^2 N\ \theta(\alpha)}, \tag{7}$$

where $\quad \theta(\alpha) = \left[\dfrac{\frac{c}{b}}{\frac{c}{b} + 1 - \alpha}\right]^2$.

The remaining problem is to determine α^*, or the equilibrium number of signatories. Let π_s denote the net benefit of every signatory and π_n the net benefit of every nonsignatory. Then an IEA is defined as being *stable* if

$$\pi_n\left[\alpha - \frac{1}{N}\right] \leq \pi_s(\alpha) \quad and \quad \pi_n(\alpha) \geq \pi_s\left[\alpha + \frac{1}{N}\right] \tag{8}$$

If (8) holds, signatories will not want to withdraw from the agreement; in withdrawing the country would reduce its abatement level and hence its costs, but its withdrawal would weaken the agreement and the resulting loss in benefits would exceed the reduction in costs. Furthermore, nonsignatories will not want to accede to the agreement; although the benefits would increase upon accession, an acceding country's abatement costs would rise even more.

The solution to any particular problem is found by solving an iterative algorithm which is best understood by way of an example. Table 3 shows the net benefits and abatement levels corresponding to each possible α for the case where $N = 10$, $b = 1$, and $c = .25$ (global net benefits are denoted π). To solve for α^*, start at $\alpha = 0$. A nonsignatory gets 476.8 if it joins the agreement and 472.0 if it does not. Hence the country will join. For $\alpha = 0.1$, a nonsignatory gets 474.0 if it joins and 468.1 if it does not. Hence the country will join. Continuing in this way, one finds that it will be optimal for a nonsignatory to join until α equals 0.4. Starting from $\alpha = 1$, one finds that a country gets 487.8 if it remains a signatory and 498.8 if it withdraws. Hence the country will withdraw. Continuing with lower levels of α one finds that it will be optimal for a signatory to withdraw until $\alpha = 0.4$. An IEA consisting of four signatories is the only stable solution to this game. The weakness in this punishment/reward strategy is illustrated by this example. The punishment that is meted out, though credible, may not be severe enough to deter many countries from cheating, and the reward that is given may not be sufficient to lead all countries to sign even though all would be better off by signing. The problem is more acute as the number of countries exploiting the resource increases. Then if any one country accedes to or pulls out of the agreement, the effect will be small — and so too then will be the reward or punishment.

A different punishment/reward mechanism has been proposed by Black, Levi and de Meza (1990). They consider the case where countries must commit themselves to an agreement simultaneously, and where the agreement is binding only if the number of signatories exceeds a designated number. In this case, a country that signs the agreement increases the likelihood of acceptance, and a country that does not sign increases the likelihood of failure.

α	q_s	q_n	π_s	π_n	Q	π
0.0	—	8.0	—	472.0	80.0	4,720.0
0.1	1.9	8.5	476.8	468.1	78.7	4,690.0
0.2	4.2	8.7	474.0	466.6	78.2	4,681.2
0.3	6.7	8.4	472.3	468.9	78.9	4,699.4
0.4*	8.9*	7.6*	472.2*	474.9*	81.1*	4,738.1*
0.5	10.5	6.3	473.7	482.5	84.2	4,781.2
0.6	11.3	4.9	476.4	489.4	87.7	4,816.0
0.7	11.5	3.6	479.5	494.3	91.0	4,839.8
0.8	11.1	2.5	482.7	497.3	93.8	4,855.9
0.9	10.5	1.6	485.4	498.8	95.9	4,867.8
1.0	9.8	—	487.8	—	97.6	4,878.0

Table 3. Stability analysis for hypothetical example

One of the difficulties with the Black, Levi and de Meza proposal, however, is that it prohibits withdrawals and renegotiation. If the actual number of signatories fell short of the minimum, then future cooperation would have to be ruled out. If the actual number of signatories exceeded the minimum, then none could be allowed to renege on its commitment. While it may well be in the interest of countries to commit themselves not to renegotiate or withdraw, such a commitment may not be credible. The fact is that IEAs *are* renegotiated, and all IEAs include provisions for withdrawals.

Yet another punishment mechanism is the trigger strategy. Each country implements its full cooperative abatement level provided all other signatories also implement their full cooperative abatement obligations. If, however, any signatory violates the treaty, each country implements the noncooperative abatement level forever. This strategy provides a strong deterrent to cheating provided detection of cheating is fairly quick and punishment credible. Interestingly, the strategy appears to be built into the North Pacific Fur Seal Treaty. Article 12 of the treaty states that in the event of a violation, and provided signatories cannot agree to "remedial measures," any signatory may give notice of its intention to terminate the agreement, and that the whole of the agreement will then be terminated nine months later. Since signatories must be better off with the agreement than without it, this article provides a strong incentive for full compliance. In this case the trigger strategy is credible, for if one country violated the agreement the others would suffer badly. But only four countries exploit this resource. Were the number of affected countries much greater, the trigger strategy would probably not be credible.

Appendix

Full Cooperative Outcome

The full cooperative outcome is the solution to

$$\max_{q_1, q_2} \ (b_1 + b_2)\left[10(q_1 + q_2) - \frac{(q_1 + q_2)^2}{4}\right] - \frac{c_1 q_1^2}{2} - \frac{c_2 q_2^2}{2}, \tag{A.1}$$

or
$$q_i = \frac{20}{\dfrac{2c_i}{b_i + b_j} + 1 + \dfrac{c_i}{c_j}}, \quad i, j = 1, 2, \quad i \neq j. \tag{A.2}$$

Noncooperative outcome

Each country i takes q_j as given and seeks to

$$\max_{q_i} \; b_i\left[10(q_i + q_j) - \frac{(q_i + q_j)^2}{4}\right] - \frac{c_i q_i^2}{2}.$$
(A.3)

The Cournot–Nash equilibrium is the solution to

$$q_i = \frac{20}{\frac{2c_i}{b_i} + 1 + \frac{c_i b_i}{b_i c_j}}.$$
(A.4)

Preferred uniform abatement obligations

Country i would prefer a uniform abatement obligation $q = q_1 = q_2$ which solves

$$\max_{q} \; b_i\left[20q - \frac{(2q)^2}{4}\right] - \frac{c_i q^2}{2}$$
(A.5)

or $\quad q = \dfrac{20}{\dfrac{c_i}{b_i} + 2}.$
(A.6)

Preferred uniform tax obligations

For any given emission tax, country i will maximize its net benefits by choosing q_i where marginal abatement costs just equal the tax. If the tax rate is t, we therefore have

$$q_i = \frac{t}{c_i}$$
(A.7)

Country i would prefer a uniform tax t which solves

$$\max_{t} \; b_i\left[10\left[\frac{t}{c_i} + \frac{t}{c_j}\right] - \frac{1}{4}\left[\frac{t}{c_i} + \frac{t}{c_j}\right]^2\right] - \frac{c_i}{2}\left[\frac{t}{c_i}\right]^2,$$
(A.8)

or $\quad t = \dfrac{20c_i}{\dfrac{2}{b_i(1/c_i + 1/c_j)} + 1 + \dfrac{c_i}{c_j}}.$
(A.9)

Substituting (A.9) into (A.7) implies an abatement level

$$q_i = \frac{20}{\frac{2}{b_i(1/c_i + 1/c_j)} + 1 + \frac{c_i}{c_j}}. \tag{A.10}$$

Preferred uniform allocation of tradeable permits

If trading is perfect after permits have been allocated, the marginal abatement costs for countries 1 and 2 will be equal:

$$c_1 q_1 = c_2 q_2. \tag{A.11}$$

Let q be the quantity of permits allocated to each country. If country i abates a level of emission q_i, and if permits trade at the market clearing price $c_1 q_1 = c_2 q_2$, then i will earn an amount $c_i q_i (q_i - \hat{q})$ from permit transactions. i's optimization problem then becomes

$$\max_{\hat{q}} \quad b_i(20\hat{q} - \hat{q}^2) - \frac{c_i q_i^2}{2} + c_i q_i(q_i - \hat{q}), \tag{A.12}$$

subject to (A.11) and

$$q_1 + q_2 = 2\hat{q}. \tag{A.13}$$

Substituting (A.11) and (A.13) into (A.12) yields

$$\max_{\hat{q}} \quad b_i(20\hat{q} - \hat{q}^2) - \frac{2c_i \hat{q}_i^2 \left[1 - \frac{1}{1 + c_i/c_j}\right]}{1 + \frac{c_i}{c_j}}, \tag{A.14}$$

the solution to which is

$$\hat{q} = \frac{10b_i(1 + c_i/c_j)}{1 + 2c_i(1 - \frac{1}{1 + c_i/c_j})}. \tag{A.15}$$

Notice that when both countries are identical, the instrument of negotiation is irrelevant; Eqs. (A.10) and (A.15) are the same as (A.6). Hence, it is only when countries are different that choice of a negotiation instrument will be contentious.

Nash bargaining solution

Subject to the constraint that obligations be uniform, the Nash bargaining solution is the value of q which solves

$$\underset{q}{max} \left[b_1(20q - q^2) - \frac{c_1 q^2}{2} - d_1 \right] \left[b_2(20q - q^2) - \frac{c_2 q^2}{2} - d_2 \right], \qquad (A.16)$$

where $d = (d_1, d_2)$ is the disagreement point or threat point. If negotiations fail, country 1 gets a payoff d_1 and 2 gets a payoff d_2. These payoffs are easily calculated by substituting (A.4) into (A.3). The solution to (A.16) is a cubic equation, and evaluation of the three roots yields the Nash bargaining solution.

The Nash bargaining solution to the uniform tax can be obtained following the same procedure but using (A.7) in (A.16).

References

Barrett, S., 1990, "The problem of global environmental protection," *Oxford Review of Economic Policy 6*, 68–79

Barrett, S., 1991a, "The paradox of international environmental agreements," mimeo, London Business School

Barrett, S., 1991b, "Economic analysis of international environmental agreements: Lessons for a global warming treaty," in: OECD, *Climate Change: Selected Economic Topics*, Paris: Organisation for Economic Co–operation and Development

Black, J., Levi, M.D., and de Meza, D., 1990, "Creating a good atmosphere: Minimum participation for tackling the 'greenhouse effect'," mimeo, University of Exeter and University of British Columbia

Bohm, P., 1990, "Efficiency aspects of imperfect treaties on global public bads: Lessons from the Montreal Protocol," paper prepared for the World Institute for Development Economics Research, Helsinki, July

Dasgupta, P., 1982, *"The Control of Resources"*, Cambridge, MA: Harvard University Press

Hahn, R.W. and Richards, K.R., 1989, "The internationalization of environmental regulation," *Harvard International Law Journal 30*, 421–446

Hoel, M., 1990, "CO$_2$ and the greenhouse effect: A game theoretic exploration," prepared for the World Institute for Development Economics Research, Helsinki

Mäler, K.–G., 1989, "The acid rain game, 2," mimeo, Stockholm School of Economics

Schelling, T.C., 1960, *"The Strategy of Conflict"*, Cambridge: Harvard University Press

Spence, A.M., 1984, "Blue whales and applied control theory," in Y. Ahmad, P. Dasgupta and K.–G. Mäler (eds.), *Environmental Decision Making 2*, London: Hodder and Stoughton

Comments by Henk Folmer

The first part of the paper by Scott Barrett presents a game–theoretical approach to the problem of reaching international agreements on environmental problems under identical, respectively different, benefit and cost functions. The success of negotiations under each of these conditions is analyzed for three types of instruments to effect emission reductions, i.e. abatement regulations, pollution taxes and internationally tradeable pollution permits. As most international agreements specify uniform obligations, it is primarily this kind of instruments which is analyzed. Barrett shows that if countries have identical benefit functions but different cost functions, uniform abatement will not be cost–effective. A similar result has been obtained by Hoel (1991) who, moreover, argues that not all countries find it in their interest to participate in such agreements. However, in his analysis of global CO$_2$ emissions reductions, Kverndokk (1991) shows that uniform abatement only moderately deviates from a cost efficient approach.

The second part of the paper deals with the problem of sustaining agreements. In this context Barrett discusses various kinds of strategies, such as increasing emissions by the remaining countries if one country pulls out and the trigger strategy.

Both problems dealt with in this paper are analyzed in isolation from other problems in which the countries concerned may be involved. In practice, countries are typically engaged in several areas of negotiations. The same holds for enforcement of agreements. This applies in particular to institutions like the Single European Market in which the Member States experience a strong increase in domains of cooperation (Folmer and Howe, 1991), but can also be observed in other contexts, such as the growing tendency to relate debt forgiveness to resource saving (Strand, 1990). A basic requirement for the exchange of concessions is the existence of reverse interests which can be linked. For instance, a country which suffers from transfrontier pollution may be an important trade partner of the polluter and could offer trade concessions to induce the latter to cooperate on environmental problems. It might also threaten to withdraw some economic advantage if the polluter defects. Kneese (1988) provides an example of linking of environmental and non–environmental problems. Folmer et al. (1991) analyze the linking of environmental and non–environmental problems as an interconnected game.

Another possible extension of the model developed by Barrett would be to take into account more differences among the countries than those relating to the benefit and cost functions, such as economic and political power. The reasons for such extensions are that reaching and sustaining an agreement is not only affected by the number of countries involved but also by which countries.

References

Folmer, H., and Howe, Ch., 1991, "Environmental Problems and Policy in the Single European Market", *Environmental and Resource Economics 1*, 17–41

Folmer, H., van Mouche, P., and Ragland, S., 1991, "International Environmental Problems and Interconnected Games", paper presented to the second annual meeting of the European Association of environmental and resource economists, Stockholm, June 11–14

Hoel, M., 1991, "International environmental conventions: The case of uniform reductions of emissions", forthcoming in: *Environmental and Resource Economics 4*

Kneese, A., 1988, "Environmental stress and political conflicts: Saling in the Colorado River", paper presented to the conference of the Royal Swedish Academy of Sciences, Stockholm, December 1990

Kverndokk, S., 1991, "Global CO_2 agreements: A cost efficient approach", paper presented to the Second Annual Meeting of the European Association of Environmental and Resource Economists, Stockholm, June 11–14

Strand, J., 1990, "Lending terms, debt concessions, and developing countries' resource extraction", Mimeo, Department of economics , University of Oslo, No. 5

Chapter 2

Michael Hoel

Emission Taxes in a Dynamic International Game of CO_2 Emissions[1]

Abstract. For national environmental problems, appropriately designed emission taxes lead to efficient outcomes. The paper gives an analysis of the properties of a global tax on CO_2 emissions. A uniform CO_2 tax for all countries does not necessarily give a Pareto optimal outcome. The reason for this is that some or all countries may be so large that their own CO_2 emissions contribute non-negligibly to the greenhouse effect, and thus their own welfare.

CO_2 emissions affect the climate through *cumulative* emissions. In a dynamic game of CO_2 emissions, it is shown that the tax giving a Pareto optimal solution is the same for the open loop and the Markov perfect equilibrium, in spite of the fact that these two equilibria differ in the absence of a CO_2 tax.

1. Introduction

One of the most serious environmental problems in the next century will probably be global warming caused by the greenhouse effect. Increased atmospheric concentration of greenhouse gases, of which CO_2 is the most important gas, may increase the average temperature by 1.5-5 degrees celsius within the next century.

The greenhouse problem is a truly global environmental problem: The climate change affects the citizens of all countries, and depends only on the world wide aggregate emissions of CO_2. The *consequences* of climatic changes may be quite different for different countries, but the climatic changes themselves depend only on world wide aggregate emissions.

[1] This paper is part of the research project "Energy and Society" at the Centre for Research in Economics and Business Administration (SF), Oslo. I am grateful to Kjell Arne Brekke, Rolf Golombek, Otto Keck and an anonymous referee for useful comments to earlier versions of the paper.

Global environmental problems are difficult to solve: Each country's own contribution to world wide emissions is small, so there is little a country can do by itself. To solve global environmental problems one therefore needs coordinated actions between countries.

International cooperation typically takes the form of an agreement among the cooperating countries to cut back emissions by some uniform percentage compared with a specific base year. However, it is well known from environmental economics that equal percentage reductions of emissions from different sources gives an inefficient outcome, in the sense that the same environmental goals can be achieved at lower costs through a different distribution of emission reductions.

For national environmental problems, appropriately designed emission taxes lead to efficient outcomes. The purpose of this paper is to study the properties of a global tax on CO_2 emissions. More specifically, it is assumed that the government of each country pays a tax, proportional to its CO_2 emissions, to an international agency. The tax revenue (minus administrative costs) are reimbursed to the governments of participating countries according to fixed distribution parameters. These distribution parameters as well as the tax rates on CO_2 emissions are determined through negotiations between the participating countries. In practice, it may be very difficult to reach an agreement on the size of these variables. It would probably be even more difficult to reach an agreement if one opened up for the possibility of different countries facing different tax rates. Most of the present analysis is therefore restricted to a uniform CO_2 tax, although this may not lead to a first best optimum.

Once the tax rates and the reimbursement parameters are given, the countries' CO_2 emissions are determined as the outcome of a non-cooperative game. Section 2 considers a static game, and shows under which conditions a common CO_2 tax leads to a Pareto optimal outcome. An equal CO_2 tax for all countries does not necessarily give a Pareto optimal outcome, since some or all countries may be so large that their own CO_2 emissions contribute non-negligiably to the greenhouse effect, and thus their own welfare.

CO_2 emissions affect the climate through *cumulative* emissions. This is modeled in Sections 3-7, where CO_2 emissions are given as an outcome of a non-cooperative differential game. Different solution concepts for the game (open-loop and Markov perfect) are discussed in Sections 3-6, where time paths of CO_2 emissions in the absence of a CO_2 tax are derived. In Section 7 it is shown under which conditions a uniform CO_2 tax, which rises over time, gives a Pareto optimal outcome. In particular, it is shown that when a uniform tax rate makes the open loop equilibrium coincide with the social optimum, the same uniform tax rate makes the Markov perfect equilibrium coincide with the social optimum. This is quite surprising, since the two solutions differ in the absence of a CO$_2$ tax. The interpretation of this result is given in the end of Section 7. Finally, in Section 8 it is shown that the result above generally no longer holds if the authorities cannot commit themselves to a time path for the CO$_2$ tax.

2. A static game

Consider N countries, each with a revenue function $R_j(V_j)$, where V_j is the emission of CO$_2$ from country j. Other inputs are held constant, and the revenue function is assumed to be increasing (up to some level $\bar{V}_j$) and strictly concave in V_j. $R_j(V_j)$ measures revenue in excess of the revenue level associated with no emissions, i.e. $R_j(0) = 0$.

Total CO$_2$ emissions S are given by

$$S = \Sigma_i V_i, \tag{1}$$

and each country is assumed to have an increasing and strictly convex damage function $D_j(S)$.

CO$_2$ emission from country j is taxed at a rate t_j by some international environmental agency. The tax revenue is reimbursed to the countries in fixed ratios $\beta_1, \beta_2, ..., \beta_N$, where $\beta_j > 0$ and $\Sigma_i \beta_i = 1$. The determination of the β_j's is beyond the scope of this paper, although it is natural to think of the β vector being determined through international negotiations. A natural requirement for the β vector is that each country's β_j is so large that the country is better off under the arrangement with a CO$_2$ tax than it is in the non-cooperative equilibrium without any tax on CO$_2$ emissions. The reason for such a requirement is the following. As long as there is no international law to force countries to participate in an agreement, each country can choose to be a free rider outside the agreement instead of participating in the agreement. If the country stands outside the agreement it can enjoy (almost) the same benefits of reduced CO$_2$ emissions as if it participates in the agreement, while it doesn't bear any of the costs of reducing emissions. An important motive for a country to participate in an agreement instead of being a free rider is that by being a free rider it increases the risk of the whole agreement breaking down. This motive for participating in the agreement is stronger the more the country has to loose from the agreement breaking down. Obviously, a country which doesn't loose anything from the agreement breaking down has no incentive to participate in the agreement, and it will therefore instead choose to be a free rider.

For all countries to be better off with a CO_2 tax than without, the β vector will to some extent have to reflect the size of the countries. In fact, we shall speak of β_j as a measure of the "size" of country j, although there of course need not be any strict relationship between β_j and GNP or population of country j.

The net benefit of country j is

$$B_j = R_j(V_j) - D_j(S) - [t_j V_j - \beta_j \Sigma_i t_i V_i].\tag{2}$$

The term in square brackets represents taxes minus reimbursements for country j, and may be positive or negative.

The *sum* of net benefits for all countries is

$$B = \Sigma_j [R_j(V_j) - D_j(S)],\tag{3}$$

since the sum of the tax terms is zero. A first-best social optimum follows from maximizing (2.3) with respect to CO_2 emissions, which gives

$$R_j{}'(V_j) = \Sigma_i D_i{}'(S) = D'(S),\qquad\qquad j=1,..,N,\tag{4}$$

where we have defined

$$D'(S) = \Sigma_i D_i(S),\tag{5}$$

In other words, marginal revenues are equal for all countries, and equal to the sum over all countries of the marginal damage of CO_2 emissions. Notice that (4) gives a particular distribution of CO_2 emissions, and thus a particular distribution of net benefits between countries in the absence of side payments. With side payments, however, the conditions (4) do not restrict the possible distributions of net benefits between countries. It is therefore only when side payments of some form are permitted that (4) is the obvious candidate for a cooperative equilibrium.

Consider next the non-cooperative Nash equilibrium of the one-shot game in which all countries choose their CO_2 emissions simultaneously. Each country takes its tax rate t_j and its reimbursement parameter β_j as given. The non-cooperative Nash equilibrium implies that B_j in (2) is maximized with respect to V_j, taking the other choices V_i $(i{\neq}j)$ as given and with (1) inserted into (2). This gives

$$R_j'(V_j) = D_j'(S) + (1 - \beta_j)t_j. \tag{6}$$

From (4) and (6) we immediately see that the noncooperative equilibrium coincides with the social optimum if

$$D_j'(S) + (1 - \beta_j)t_j = D'(S), \tag{7}$$

i.e.

$$t_j = D'(S)\, \dfrac{1 - \dfrac{D_j'(S)}{D'(S)}}{1 - \beta_j}. \tag{8}$$

From (8) it is clear that optimal tax rates are equal for all countries only if

$$\beta_j = D_j'(S)/D'(S) \tag{9}$$

for all countries (at the optimal S). In this case the optimal uniform tax rate t is given by

$$t = D'(S). \tag{10}$$

Whether or not the condition (9) holds depends on the β vector. In principle, the β vector could have been chosen so that (9) holds in equilibrium. However, this could violate the requirement that all countries are at least as well of in this first best optimum as they are in the non-cooperative case without any CO$_2$ tax. In particular, there could be a country which would not be negatively affected by the climatic changes following from increased atmospheric concentration of CO$_2$, i.e. $D_j' \leq 0$ for this country. Clearly, such a country would need to have $\beta_j > 0$ to be willing to participate in an arrangement with a positive tax on CO$_2$ emissions, i.e. $\beta_j > D_j'(S)/D'(S)$.

An interesting special case is the case in which all D_j-functions are identical except for a factor of proportionality. More precisely, $D_j(S) = \alpha_j D(S)$ for all j in this special case, where $D(S)$ is given by (5), and where $\alpha_j \geq 0$ and $\Sigma_i \alpha_i = 1$. One would expect the

α_j-coefficients to be closely related to the size of the countries, i.e. for α_j to be higher the larger country j is. Since the β vector also will be related to the size distribution of the countries, it is not unconceivable that the β vector is chosen so that it is identical to the α vector. If this is the case, condition (9) always holds.

Whether or not (9) holds, (10) inserted into (6) gives

$$R_j{'}(V_j) = D'(S) + [D_j{'}(S) - \beta_j D'(S)] \tag{11}$$

or

$$R_j{'}(V_j) = D'(S)\left[1 + \frac{D_j{'}(S)}{D'(S)} - \beta_j\right]. \tag{11'}$$

It follows from (11') that countries with relatively high marginal damage functions relative to their size (as measured by β_j), will have less CO_2 emissions than what follows from the first-best optimum and conversely for countries with relatively low marginal damage functions.

Notice also that for all countries which are small, the terms $D_j{'}(S)/D(S)$ and β_j will be close to zero. For these countries it is therefore clear from (11') that the tax given by (10) leads to CO_2 emissions which are approximately equal to the CO_2 emissions in the first best optimum. For large countries, such as e.g. USA and USSR (which have 23 and 18 percent of total CO_2 emissions, respectively), $D_j{'}(S)/D'(S)$ and β_j cannot be approximated by zero. Nevertheless, $D_j{'}(S)/D'(S) - \beta_j$ may be close to zero also for these large countries.

Assume that the tax is given by (10), i.e. $t = D'(S)$. Does there, for any given set of D_j-functions, exist a β-vector with $\beta_j \geq 0$ and $\Sigma_i \beta_i = 1$ which makes all countries better off than they are in the non-cooperative equilibrium without any CO_2 tax? The answer is no. To see this, consider the case in which $S = 0$ in the social optimum. In this case, $t = D'(0)$ gives the corner solution $V_j = 0$ for all j, so that there is no tax revenue to redistribute. If there exist countries which are not adversely affected by the climatic change caused by CO_2 emissions, these countries therefore are worse off in the equilibrium with $t = D'(0)$ than they are in the non-ccoperative equilibrium without any CO_2 tax.

Although it may be impossible to find a β-vector making all countries better off with $t = D'(S)$ than with $t = 0$, there always exist a (t, β)-vector with $t > 0$ making all countries better off than with $t = 0$, provided all countries have positive CO$_2$ emissions in the non-cooperative equilibrium. To see this, write the payoff of country j as

$$\Pi_j = \max_{V_j} [R_j(V_j) - D_j(V_j + V_{-j}) - tV_j + \beta_j t(V_j + V_{-j})] \tag{12}$$

where $V_{-j} = \sum_{i \neq j} V_i$. Differentiating with respect to t and evaluating at $t = 0$ gives (by the envelope theorem)

$$[d\Pi_j]_{t=0} = -D_j'(S)dV_{-j} + (\beta_j S - V_j)dt \tag{13}$$

It follows from the first order conditions (6) as well as $R_j'' < 0$ and $D_j'' > 0$ that all V_j decline as t is increased. This implies that $dV_{-j} < 0$, i.e. $-D_j'(S)dV_{-j} \geq 0$. To make all countries better off as t increases from zero, we can set $\beta_j = (V_j/S) + \varepsilon_0$ for countries with $D_j'(S) = 0$ and $\beta_j = (V_j/S) - \varepsilon_1$ for countries with $D_j'(S) > 0$, where ε_0 and ε_1 are positive and sufficiently small, and satisfy $n\varepsilon_0 = (N - n)\varepsilon_1$, where n is the number of countries with $D_j'(S) = 0$.

In the next sections we consider a dynamic extension of the present game. In order to focus on the dynamic features of the game, we shall stick to the special case in which $D_j(S) = \beta_j D(S)$ for all j and S.

3. A dynamic game

The revenue and damage functions R_j and D_j have the same properties as in the static game. However, it is now assumed that S stands for the *cumulative* emissions of CO$_2$. This is clearly more realistic than the assumption made in the static game of Section 2: The climate is not affected by current emissions of CO$_2$, but the atmospheric concentration of CO$_2$, which in term depends on cumulative emissions. Instead of (2.1) we thus assume[2]

---

[2] For the sake of notational simplicity the numbering of equations starts with (1) in each subsequent section. If an equation, say Equation (14), is refered to in the text, it is understood that we mean Equation (14) in the section where the reference is made. If in section y we refer to Equation (14) from section x (x ≠ y), we write Equation (x.14).

$$\dot{S} = \Sigma_i V_i, \tag{1}$$

where the dot represents the time derivative. We shall use τ to denote time, but omit this variable wherever this cannot cause any misunderstanding.

Each country wishes to maximize the present value of current net benefits. Assuming that the interest rate is r in all countries, we thus have the objective functions

$$B_j = \int_0^\infty e^{-\tau\tau}\{R_j(V_j) - D_j(S) - [tV_j - \beta_j t\Sigma_i V_i]\}d\tau. \tag{2}$$

To find the social optimum, we sum over all countries:

$$B = \int_0^\infty e^{-\tau\tau}\{\Sigma_i R_i(V_i) - D(S))\}d\tau. \tag{3}$$

The current value Hamiltonian follows from (1) and (3),

$$H = \Sigma_i R_i(V_i) - D(S) + \lambda\Sigma_i V_i, \tag{4}$$

and necessary conditions for an optimal solution are

$$\dot{\lambda} = r\lambda - \frac{\partial H}{\partial S} = r\lambda + D'(S), \tag{5}$$

$$H_{vj} = R_j'(V_j) + \lambda \leq 0 \quad \text{for all } j, \text{ with equality for } V_i > 0, \tag{6}$$

$$\lim_{\tau\to\infty} e^{-\tau\tau}\lambda(\tau) = 0 \tag{7}$$

In other words, CO_2 emissions should always be at levels equating marginal revenues across countries (for an interior equilibrium) and the common marginal revenue should develop in a particular manner depending on the damage functions (cf. (5)).

We shall assume that $R_i'(0)$ is finite, and define λ^* by

$$\lambda^* = - \max_i R_i{}'(0).\tag{8}$$

From (6) it is clear that $\lambda(\tau) \leq \lambda^*$ implies that $V_j(\tau) = 0$ for all j, i.e. $\dot{S}(\tau) = 0$.

The solution of the optimization problem is illustrated in Figure 1. The optimal trajectory goes from $\lambda(0)$ to λ^*, where λ^* is given by (8). Along this trajectory $-\lambda(\tau)$ is rising, i.e. all positive $V_j(\tau)$ are declining (cf. (6)). Since $\lambda(\tau)$ approaches λ^*, it is clear that the transversality condition (7) holds along this trajectory.

In Figure 1 we have also drawn two non-optimal trajectories (dotted). If $\lambda(0)$ is too large, $\lambda(\tau)$ and $S(\tau)$ will grow for ever. It is clear from (5) that when λ is positive, it will grow at a rate higher than r, so that the transversality condition (5) is violated. If $\lambda(0)$ is too small, CO_2 emissions will stop at some date T while $\lambda(\tau)$ is still declining. After T it follows from (3.5) that $\dot{\lambda} = r\lambda + D'(S(T))$, since $\dot{S} = 0$. This implies that

$$e^{-r\tau}\lambda(\tau) = e^{-rT}[\frac{D(S(T))}{r} - \lambda^*] - e^{-r\tau}\frac{D(S(T))}{r}\tag{9}$$

It is clear from (9) that the transversality condition (7) is satisfied if and only if $\lambda^* = -D'(S(T))/r$. From Figure 1 we see that this only holds if $S(T) = S^*$, i.e. along the

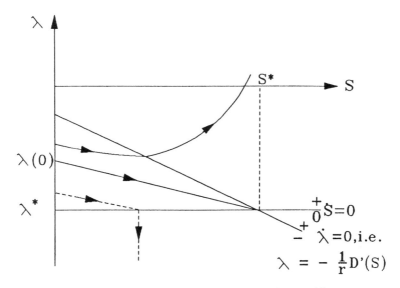

Figure 1: Solution of the social optimization problem

heavily drawn trajectory.

The end point of the optimal trajectory in Figure 1 is characterized by $\lambda^* = - D'(S^*)/r$ Together with (8) this gives

$$\max_i R_i'(0) = \frac{1}{r} D'(S^*). \tag{10}$$

This condition has a straightforward interpretation. It says that CO_2 emissions should stop when the marginal benefit of emissions is equal to the present value of the marginal damage of increased CO_2 in the atmosphere.

We next turn to the non-cooperative game. In a dynamic game of the present type, some choice of equilibrium concept must be made. A natural candidate is the dynamic analog of the Nash equilibrium of Section 2: Each country chooses the time path of CO_2 emissions which is an optimal reply to the other countries' strategies, which are specified as similar time paths. In the literature of dynamic games, this type of equilibrium is often called an open loop equilibrium. The problem with this equilibrium is that it is not a subgame perfect equilibrium (in the sense of Selten (1975)) unless the countries can commit themselves to specific time paths of CO_2 at the beginning of the infinite planning period (Reinganum and Stokey, 1985). An alternative equilibrium concept is to model each country as choosing a decision rule strategy, making its CO_2 emissions at any time depend on the history of the game up to this point of time. With this type of strategies we can derive subgame perfect equilibria.

The present analysis is restricted to simple decision rules in which CO_2 emissions from each player at any date depend only on that date and on the cumulative stock of total CO_2 emissions at that date, i.e.

$$V_k(\tau) = v_k(S(\tau),\tau). \tag{11}$$

It is assumed that v_k is continuous and differentiable in S and τ, except perhaps at $V_k = 0$. The tax rate t may depend both on cumulative CO_2 emissions and on time, i.e.

$$t = t(S, \tau). \tag{12}$$

Finally, we shall use the notation

$$v_{-j}(S, \tau) = \sum_{i \neq j} v_i(S, \tau) \tag{13}$$

and

$$v_{-js} = \frac{\partial v_{-j}(S, \tau)}{\partial S}. \tag{14}$$

The optimization problem of country j is to maximize

$$B_j = \int_0^\infty e^{-r\tau} \{R_j(V_j) - D_j(S) - t(S, \tau)[(1 - \beta_j)V_j - \beta_j v_{-j}(S, \tau)]\} \, d\tau \tag{15}$$

subject to

$$\dot{S} = V_j + v_{-j}(S, \tau). \tag{16}$$

The current value Hamiltonian is

$$H_j = R_j(V_j) - D_j(S) - t(S, \tau)[(1 - \beta_j)V_j - \beta_j v_{-j}(S, \tau)] + \lambda_j(V_j + v_{-j}(S, \tau)), \tag{17}$$

and the necessary conditions for an optimal solution are

$$\dot{\lambda}_j = r\lambda_j - \frac{\partial H_j}{\partial S} = r\lambda_j + D_j{}'(S) - (\beta_j t + \lambda_j)v_{-js} + [V_j - \beta_j \Sigma_i V_i] \, t_s, \tag{18}$$

(where we have inserted the condition $v_{-j} = \sum_{i \neq j} V_i$ in equilibrium),

$$H_{jv} = R_j{}'(V_j) - (1 - \beta_j)t + \lambda_j \leq 0, \tag{19}$$

where $V_j > 0$ implies strict equality and

$$\lim_{\tau \to \infty} e^{-r\tau} \lambda_j(\tau) = 0. \tag{20}$$

We proceed by first characterizing the open loop and Markov perfect equilibria when there are no taxes (Sections 4 - 6). Pigouvian taxes are then discussed for the case in which a commitment can be made about the path of the tax rate (Section 7), and when the future path of the tax rate may be chosen freely at any date (Section 8).

4. The open loop equilibrium without taxes

An open loop strategy is the special case of (3.11) in which $v_{ks} = \partial v_k/\partial S_k \equiv 0$. A Nash equilibrium in open loop strategies implies that the time path $V_k(\cdot)$ is an optimal reply to the other players' strategies when viewed from the initial date (i.e. from $(S(0), 0)$). In our model this equilibrium is also dynamic consistent, in the sense that along the equilibrium path, the continuation of the equilibrium strategies $V_k(\cdot)$ from any $\tau > 0$ onwards remains a Nash equilibrium. However, for an equilibrium to be perfect it is not enough that this consistency property holds along the equilibrium path of $S(\tau)$: Subgame perfection requires that the continuation of the strategies $v_k(S(\tau), \tau)$ constitute a Nash equilibrium when viewed from *any* pair $(S(\tau), \tau)$, i.e. not only from the $(S(\tau), \tau)$ pairs of the original Nash equilibrium path. (See e.g. Fershtman (1989) for a further discussion of the relationship between time consistency and subgame perfection).

In this and the next two sections it is assumed that $t(S, \tau) \equiv 0$. As mentioned above, $v_{ks} = 0$ (for all k) in an open loop equilibrium. From (3.18) - (3.20) we therefore find (for all j)

$$\dot{\lambda}_j = r\lambda_j + D_j'(S), \tag{1}$$

$$R_j'(V_j) + \lambda_j \leq 0, \tag{2}$$

where $V_j > 0$ implies strict equality, and

$$Lim_{\tau \to \infty} e^{-r\tau}\lambda_j(\tau) = 0. \tag{3}$$

Together with equation (3.16) for the development of cumulative CO_2 emissions, the equations above give a specific time path for $V_k(\tau)$ from $\tau = 0$ onwards as an optimal reply to any vector of strategies from the other players (i.e. for any $v_{-j}(S, \tau)$).

The solution to country j's optimization problem is illustrated in Figure 2. Qualitatively, the solution is very similar to the full optimum discussed earlier, cf. also Figure 1. In the present case there is an initial $\lambda_j(0)$ which gives a $\lambda_j(\tau)$- development satisfying the transversality condition. Notice that in the present case we may have $\dot{\lambda}_j < 0$ and $\dot{S}_j > 0$ also after V_j has reached zero, since other countries may continue their CO_2 emissions even if $R_j'(0) + \lambda_j \leq 0$ for country j.

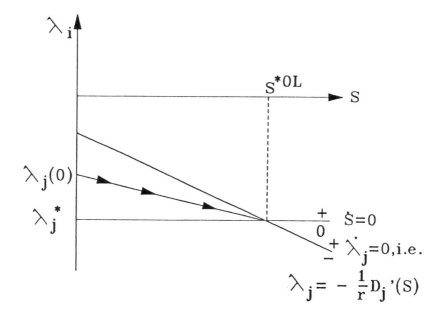

Figure 2: Solution to country j's optimization problem

It follows from the reasoning above that $V_j(\tau)$ gradually declines to zero for *any* strategies $v_k(S, \tau) = 0$ $(k \neq j)$ satisfying $v_{ks} = 0$ and $v_k(S, \tau) = 0$ for $\tau \geq T$. Since this is true for all countries, *all* $V_k(\tau)$ must be declining in τ in the open loop Nash equilibrium.

In order to compare the Nash equilibrium with the full optimum, we use the superscript OL for the *open loop* Nash equilibrium and SO for the *social optimum*. In both cases the auxiliary variables λ and λ_j (for all j) end up with the values given by (3.8), i.e. $\lambda^* = \lambda_j^* = \max_k R_k'(0)$. Since $D_j'(S) < D'(S)$, it follows from Figures 1 and 2 that $S^{*OL} > S^{*SO}$. This is also illustrated in Figure 3, where the optimal trajectories for both equilibria are drawn. These trajectories can never cross each other, since $\dot{\lambda}_j^{OL} < \dot{\lambda}_j^{SO}$ at a hypothetical point at which $S^{OL} = S^{SO}$ and $\lambda_j^{OL} = \lambda_j^{SO} > \lambda^*$. For any given S-value, we therefore must have $\lambda_j^{OL} > \lambda^{SO}$, i.e. $V_j^{OL} > V_j^{SO}$ (from (3.6), (2) and $R_j'' < 0$).

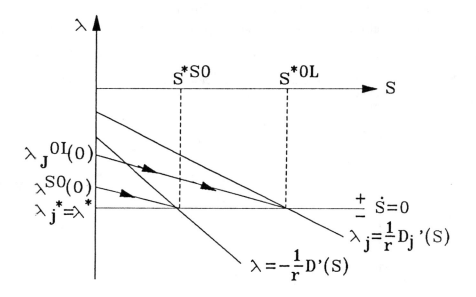

Figure 3: Comparison of open loop with social optimum I

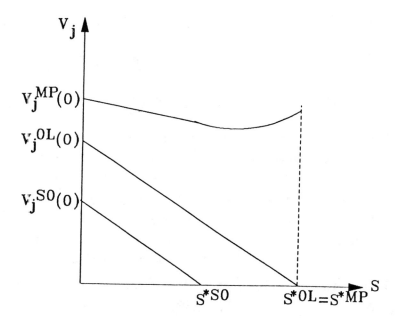

Figure 4: Comparison of open loop with social optimum II

The reasoning above implies that the (V_j, S) - path in the open loop Nash equilibrium must lie above the (V_j, S) — path in the full optimum, as illustrated in Figure 4. In particular, at the initial time point (when $S^{OL}(0) = S^{SO}(0)$), CO_2 emissions are higher in the open loop Nash equilibrium than in the social optimum.

5. The Markov perfect equilibrium without taxes

It is clear that the open loop solution described above is not subgame perfect. Each player is assumed to have a simple time path $V_k(\tau)$ as its strategy. However, it follows from the discussion above that $V_k(0)$ depends on $S(0)$, even if all time paths $V_k(\tau)$ $(k \neq j)$ are given. The conjecture $v_{ks} = 0$ for all k thus is not correct: *If S for some reason moved off its equilibrium path, it would no longer be optimal for the players to stick to their original time paths $V_k(\tau)$.*

We now turn to perfect equilibria. The analysis is restricted to so called Markov perfect equilibria. These are equilibria in which each player's strategy only depends on payoff-relevant variables. (See e.g. Maskin and Tirole (1988) for a further discussion of such equilibria). In the absence of time-dependent taxes, the only payoff-relevant variable for each player at time τ is $S(\tau)$. We must therefore have $v_{k\tau} = 0$ (for all k and τ) for the strategies given by (3.11).

In the open loop equilibrium, there was no CO_2-emission for $S > S^*$, with S^* defined by

$$S^* = \max_j S_j^*, \text{ where } D_j{}'(S_j^*) = rR_j{}'(0) \tag{1}$$

The interpretation of this condition was straightforward, cf. the discussion after (3.10). The same condition is also supported by a Markov perfect equilibrium. To be more precise, we only consider Markov strategies satisfying

$$v_k(S) = 0 \qquad for\ S > S^*. \tag{2}$$

This part of the Markov strategies is obviously subgame perfect: Whatever value of S above S^* is reached, $V_k = 0$ is an optimal reply to $V_i = 0$ from all other countries.

It follows from (2) that the class of Markov perfect equilibria considered here leads to the same total emissions as the open loop equilibrium. Apart from this property, there is little one can say for the general case. We therefore turn to the case in which all countries are equal. Each of the N countries is assumed to have a continuous (for $S \neq S^*$) emission function $V = v(S)$ and an environmental damage function

$$d'(S) = D(S)/N.$$

Cumulative CO_2 emissions develop according to (3.1), which in the present case may be written as

$$\dot{S} = Nv(S) = V + (N-1)v(S), \tag{3}$$

where the time reference is omitted to simplify notation.

The critical value S^* in (2) follows from (1), which in the present case may be written as

$$d'(S^*) = rR'(0). \tag{4}$$

Each country's optimal CO_2 emission is a solution to the problem of maximizing (3.15) (with $t = 0$) subject to (3). Since we shall allow $v(S)$ to be discontinuous at S^*, it is useful to reformulate the optimization problem. Denote T as the time at which $S(\tau)$ reaches S^*. Then the optimization problem can be formulated as choosing the path $V(\tau)$ and the date T to maximize

$$b = \int_0^T e^{-r\tau}[R(V) - d(S)]d\tau + \int_0^\infty e^{-r\tau}(-d(S^*))d\tau \tag{5}$$

subject to (5.3) for $\tau < T$ and the additional constraint $S(T) = S^*$.

The current value Hamiltonian corresponding to this problem is

$$H = R(V) - d(S) + \lambda[V + (N-1)v(S)], \tag{6}$$

and the necessary conditions for an optimal solution are

$$\dot{\lambda} = r\lambda - \frac{\partial H}{\partial S} = [r - (N-1)v'(S)]\lambda + d'(S), \tag{7}$$

$$H_V = R'(V) + \lambda \leq 0 \tag{8}$$

where $V > 0$ implies strict equality,

$$R(V(T)) + \lambda(T)[V(T) + (N-1)v(S^*)] = 0. \tag{9}$$

(7) and (8) are familiar equations, and (9) follows directly from $H(T) - (-d(S^*)) = 0$, which is the condition for optimal T.

In a symmetric equilibrium, we have

$$V(T) = v^* = v(S^*),$$
$$\lambda(T) = \lambda^* = -R'(v^*), \tag{10}$$

where $v^* \geq 0$ is defined as the v-value at T before the jump down to zero (if $v^* > 0$). From (9) we have

$$R(v^*) + \lambda^* N v^* = 0 \qquad \text{or} \qquad \frac{R(v^*)}{Nv^*} = -\lambda^*$$

which together with (10) implies

$$\varepsilon(v^*) \equiv \frac{R(v^*)v^*}{R(v^*)} = \frac{1}{N}. \tag{11}$$

We know that $\varepsilon(0) = 1$ (since $\underset{v \to \infty}{Lim} [R(v)/v] = R'(0)$) and that $\varepsilon(\bar{v}) = 0$, where $\bar{v}$ is the optimal value of v in the absence of environmental considerations, i.e. $R'(\bar{v}) = 0$. It therefore follows from (11) that there exists a $v^* \in (0, \bar{v})$ which satisfies (11).

The special case of $N = 1$ gives the social optimization problem analyzed in Section 3, and for this case (11) confirms $v^* = 0$, i.e. $v(\tau)$ declines continuously towards zero. For $N > 1$ $v(\tau)$ jumps from $v^* > 0$ to $v = 0$ at the date T when $S(T) = S^*$ is reached. If $\varepsilon(v)$ is monotonic, this jump is larger the larger is N. For the limiting case of $N = \infty$ we get $v^* = \bar{v}$.

We now turn to the properties of the function $v(S)$ for $S < S^*$. Since V depends only on S, we must have $\dot{V} = V'(S)\dot{S}$, or, since $v'(S) = V'(S)$,

$$v'(S) = \dot{V}/\dot{S} \tag{12}$$

From (7) and (8) we have

$$-R''(V)\dot{V} = [(N-1)v'(S) - r]R'(V) + d'(S) \tag{13}$$

Together with (3), (12) and $V = v$ this gives

$$v'(S) = \frac{\dot{V}}{\dot{S}} = \frac{[(N-1)v'(S) - r]R'(v) + d'(S)}{-R''(v)\,Nv} \qquad \text{i.e.}$$

$$F(v(S))v'(S) = -rR'(v(S)) + d'(S), \tag{14}$$

where

$$F(v) = N \cdot [-vR''(v) - \frac{N-1}{N}R'(v)]. \tag{15}$$

It is clear from (15) that $F(v) < 0$ for v sufficiently small (at least for $-R''(0)$ finite), and that $F(v) > 0$ for v sufficiently large, since $R'(v) = 0$ for the optimal v in the absence of environmental considerations (i.e. for $v = \bar{v}$). We shall assume that $F(v)$ is monotonic, and define $\hat{v}$ by $F(\hat{v}) = 0$.

Eq. (14) is a differential equation in $v(S)$, with (v^*, S^*) as the fixed end point. If this differential equation can be solved for all $S \in [S_0, S^*]$, then a Markov perfect equilibrium exists. If (14) cannot be solved for $S \in [S_0, S^*]$, then no Markov perfect equilibrium exists[3].

Consider first the case in which $v^* > \hat{v}$, which must hold for N sufficiently large. This case is illustrated in Figure 5. Here it is assumed that $d'(S_0) > 0$, so that the curve for $-rR'(v) + d'(S) = 0$ cuts the vertical axis below $\bar{v}$. As long as $v > \hat{v}$, it follows from (14) that $v'(S) < 0$ to the left of the curve giving $-rR'(v) + d'(S) = 0$ and $v'(S) > 0$ to the right of this curve. Along the equilibrium trajectory, we thus have $v'(S) > 0$ for

---

[3] We are only considering continuous strategies $v(S)$ for $v \neq 0$. There may exist discontinuous Markov perfect strategies even if no continuous function $v(S)$ exists which solves (14) for $S \in [S_0, S^*]$.

S-values close to S^*. If v^* is sufficiently small, we have $v'(S) < 0$ for lower values of S. (It is clear from Figure 5 that $rR'(v^*) > d'(S_0)$ is a sufficient condition for $v'(S) < 0$ for low S-values).

It is clear from Figure 5 that $v''(S) > 0$ where $v(S)$ crosses the curve giving $- rR'(v) + d'(S) = 0$. This is confirmed by differentiating (14):

$$v''(S) = \frac{1}{F}[d''(S) - rR''\cdot v' - F'(v')^2],$$

i.e.

$$v''(S) = \frac{d''(S)}{F(v(S))} \qquad \text{for } v'(S) = 0. \tag{16}$$

Since $d''(S) > 0$, (16) implies that $v''(S)$ is positive or negative (when $v'(S) = 0$) depending on $F(v)$ positive or negative, i.e. on $v > \hat{v}$ or $v < \hat{v}$.

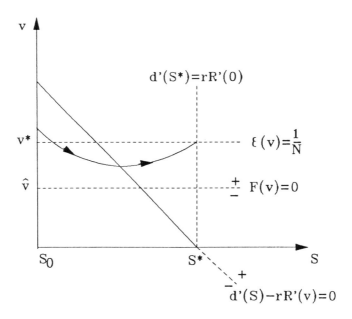

Figure 5: Markov perfect equilibrium for $v^* > \hat{v}$

From the analysis in Section 4, we know that $\dot{v} < 0$ and $rR'(v) > d'(S)$ in the open loop equilibrium whenever emissions are positive. In other words, we are always to the

Michael Hoel

left of the curve $d'(S) - rR'(v) = 0$ in Figure 5. More precisely, in the present symmetric case the open loop equilibrium is characterized by[4]

$$- NvR''(v)v'(S) = - rR'(v(S)) + d'(S) \tag{17}$$

Comparing this equation with (14)–(15), we immediately see that when $F(v) > 0$ and $v'(S) < 0$ in the Markov perfect equilibrium, $-v'(S)$ in the perfect equilibrium is larger than $-v'(S)$ in the open loop equilibrium at the same (S, v)–pair. But since the trajectory in the perfect equilibrium reaches a point above the end point of the open loop trajectory (since $v^* > 0$), this means that $v^{MP}(S) > v^{OL}(S)$ for all $S < S^*$, as illustrated in Figure 4.

The case of $v^* < \hat{v}$ is illustrated in Figure 6. In this case $v'(S) < 0$ for S-values to the right of the curve giving $-rR'(v) + d'(S) = 0$, and $v'(S) > 0$ for S–values to the left of this curve. In this case we thus have $v'(S) > 0$ for small S-values, and $v'(S) < 0$ for

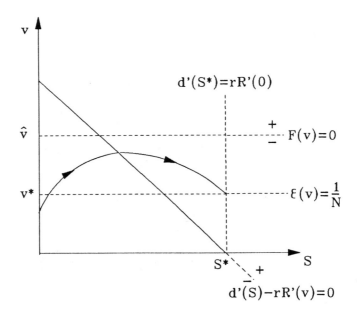

Figure 6: Markov perfect equilibrium for $\hat{v} > v^*$ for "small" S_0

---

[4] This is seen from (13), with 0 instead of $v'(S)$ in the right hand side, and inserting $\dot{V}/\dot{S} = v'(S)$ and $\dot{S} = Nv$.

large S-values. If S_0 is so large that $d'(S_0) > rR'(\hat{v})$, we may have $v'(S) < 0$ for all S, as illustrated in Figure 7. Notice that while the situation in Figure 7 implies $v^{MP}(S) > v^{OL}(S)$, this need not be the case for Figure 6. However, it is clear from the discussion above that one must have $v^{MP}(S) > v^{OL}(S)$ for all $S < S^*$ if S_0 is sufficiently large.

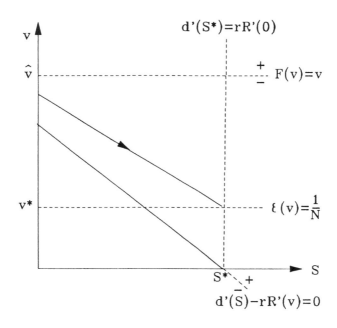

Figure 7: Markov perfect equilibrium for $\hat{v} > v^*$ and "large" S_0

Changing N while the functions $R(V)$ and $d(S)$ are left unchanged implies that the social optimum is also changed. In order to focus on the pure institutional aspects of the number of countries, we shall assume that world revenue is $Q(x)$ and world environmental damage is $D(S)$, and that

$$\dot{S} = x = Nv \qquad (18)$$

and

$$Q(x) = NR(v) = NR\left(\frac{x}{N}\right). \qquad (19)$$

For given functions $Q(x)$ and $D(S)$, a change in N now implies changes of the country functions $R(v)$ and $d(S) = D(S)/N$.

From (18) and (19) we have

$$R'(v) = Q'(Nv) = Q'(x),$$
$$R''(v) = NQ''(x).$$

(20)

To see how the Markov perfect equilibrium depends on N, consider first (11). Inserting (19) and (20) gives

$$\frac{Q'(x^*)\frac{x^*}{N}}{\frac{1}{N}Q(x^*)} = \frac{Q'(x^*)x^*}{Q(x^*)} = \varepsilon(x^*) = \frac{1}{N}.$$

(21)

As above, $\varepsilon(\bar{x}) = 0$ (where $\bar{x}$ is defined by $Q'(\bar{x}) = 0$). If $\varepsilon(x)$ is monotonic, x* is therefore increasing in N, approaching $\bar{x}$ as N goes to infinity.

Since $x = Nv$, we have $x'(S) = Nv'(S)$. From (14) and (15) we therefore have (using (19) and (20))

$$x'(S) = \frac{-rQ'(x) + \frac{1}{N}D'(S)}{-xQ''(x) - \frac{N-1}{N}Q'(x)}.$$

(22)

The critical value $\hat{x}$ making the denominator in (22) zero is given by

$$\frac{-\hat{x}Q''(\hat{x})}{Q'(\hat{x})} = \frac{N-1}{N}.$$

(23)

Assuming that the l.h.s. of (23) is monotonic in x, the denominator of (22) is negative for $x < \hat{x}$ and positive for $x > \hat{x}$. Except for very small values of N, it is clear from (23) that $\hat{x}$ is practically independent of N. Since x^* is rising in N with $\bar{x}$ as its upper limit, and $\hat{x} < \bar{x}$ for all N, it follows that Figure 6 can only be relevant for small values of N. From the discussion above (after (16)) we know that $x^{MP}(S) > x^{OL}(S)$ if Figure 5 is valid, which it is for $x^* > \hat{x}$. It is therefore clear that $x^{MP}(S) > x^{OL}(S)$ for all S if N is sufficiently large.

So far, we have only considered situations in which equilibria exist. However, if $v*$ is sufficiently close to $\hat{v}$ there exists no solution to (22) for all $S \in [S_0, S^*]$. Two such situation are illustrated in Figures 8 and 9: Whenever one starts in the vertical axis, it is not possible to reach the point $(S^*, v*)$. Or looked upon from the end point $(S^*, v*)$: Moving backwards, v reaches $\hat{v}$ before v reaches the curve giving $rR'(v) = D'(S)/N$.

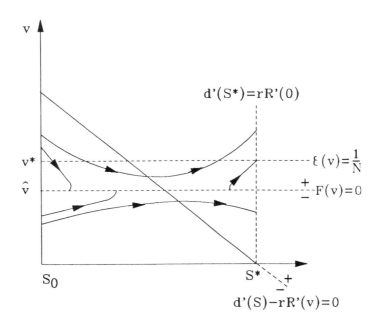

Figure 8: Non–existence of Markov equilibrium with $v > \hat{v}$

Whether or not an equilibrium exists depends on the functions $Q(x)$, $D(S)$ and on N and r. In particular, situations of the type illustrated in Figures 8 and 9 cannot occur if $v* > \hat{v}$ and the curve giving $rR'(v) = D'(S)/N$ lies above $\hat{v}$ except for S-values sufficiently close to S^*. For $v* > \hat{v}$, this will hold if $D'(S)/N < rQ'(\hat{v})$ except for S-values sufficiently close to S^*.

Figure 10 is based on a numerical example in which $D'(S)$ first rises slowly up to about $S = 10$, after which it rises rapidly.[5] In this numerical example, $Q'(x) = 1 - x$, i.e. $x = \bar{x} = 1$ is the optimal choice of x in the absence of environmental considerations, and $x = 0$ gives a marginal revenue equal to 1. CO_2 emissions are zero for $D'(S)/r > 1$ in the social optimum and for $D'(S)/rN > 1$ in the noncooperative equilibria. The interest rate is 5%, and $N = 2$. A larger number of countries gives qualitatively the same picture, but all curves lie closer to $x = 1$ for all values of S.

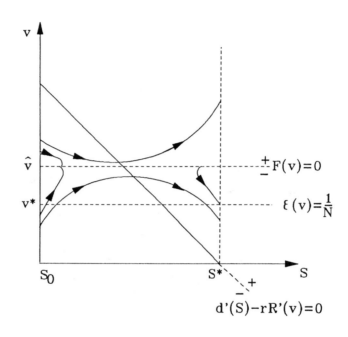

Figure 9: Non–existence of Markov equilibrium with $\hat{v} > v^*$

In this example, optimal CO_2–emissions decline gradually from 0.44 to zero as S rises towards 11, which is the optimal long-run value of S. CO_2–emissions decline gradually towards zero also in the open loop equilibrium. However, initial emissions in this case are 0.60, and emissions are also higher than in the social optimum for any given value of S. In this case emissions are positive until $S = 13$. This S-value is also reached in the Markov perfect equilibrium. In the latter case, emissions decline gradually from

---

[5] The figure is based on calculations of $x(S)$ at discrete intervals for S. For $S = 0, 1, 2,...,$ 15 the values for $D(S)/r$ (for $r = 0.05$) are 0.40, 0.40, 0.41, 0.43, 0.46, 0.50, 0.55, 0.61, 0.67, 0.74, 0.85, 1.00, 1.35, 2.00, 20.00, 100.00.

0.69 until $S = 10.3$ is reached, after which emissions rise from 0.56 towards 0.67. The latter emission level is reached as $S = 13$ is attained, and at this time emissions jump to zero.

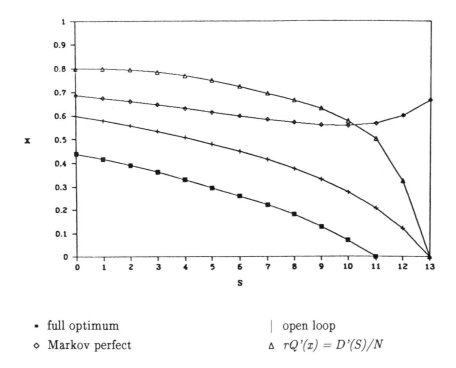

- full optimum | open loop
◇ Markov perfect   ∆ $rQ'(x) = D'(S)/N$

Figure 10: Emission functions for 2 countries

6. Other subgame perfect equilibria

So far, only strategies which are continuous in S (except at S^*) have been considered. If one allows strategies to be discontinuous in S, a continuum of emission paths may be supported by Markov perfect equilibria. To see this, consider again the symmetric case in which each country's emission strategy is given by the same function $f(S)$, defined by

$$f(S) = \begin{cases} g(S) & \text{for } S < S^g, \\ 0 & \text{for } S = S^g, \\ v(S) & \text{for } S > S^g. \end{cases} \tag{1}$$

Here S^g is some emission level below S^*, and $v(S)$ is the continuous strategy (for $S \neq S^*$) discussed in the previous section. The function $g(S)$ is the continuous function which is defined exactly as $v(S)$, except for S^g being the end point instead of S^*.

Assume that S^g is chosen so that all countries are better off with this constant emission level (and no current emissions) than they are under the path $v(S)$ from S^g to S^*. This will obviously be the case if S^g is the maximal level of cumulative emissions under the social optimum, i.e., if $S^g = S^{*SO}$. It will in fact also be the the case for *any* $S^g \in [S^{*SO}, S^*]$ and also for S^g values below, but sufficiently close to S^{*SO}.

If the history of the game has led to a cumulative emission level S^g, the function $f(S)$ defines a Markov perfect equilibrium of the game starting at S^g: For each country, the best strategy is to choose zero emissions, as long as all other countries choose zero emissions, since a positive emission level (however small) would trigger a move of the equilibrium from the zero emission path to the $v(S)$ path from S^g to S^*.

Since the strategy function $g(S)$ by construction gives a Markov perfect equilibrium of a game with zero emissions once cumulative emissions reach S^g, the strategy function $f(S)$ must therefore define a Markov perfect equilibrium.

By varying S^g from the minimal level consistent with the zero emission path being preferred to the path $v(S)$ to the level S^*, we obtain a continuum of outcomes for the emission paths which all are supported by Markov perfect equilibria.

7. Pigouvian taxes

In the previous sections it was shown that both the open loop and the Markov perfect equilibrium have higher emissions than the full optimum. Moreover, if the number of countries and/or the initial cumulative stock of CO_2 is sufficiently high, the Markov perfect equilibrium of a symmetric game has higher CO_2 emissions than the open loop equilibrium at any $S < S^*$. In other words, the distortion is usually largest in the perfect equilibrium, in the sense that relatively more of the total emissions in this case are "early" than "late" compared with the open loop equilibrium. Intuitively, we would therefore expect that an optimal Pigouvian tax was higher (at least initially), in the Markov perfect equilibrium than in the open loop equilibrium. This issue is the topic for the present section.

Assume that the authorities commit themselves to a time path of tax rates on CO_2 emissions. With the general formulation $t(S, \tau)$ (cf. (3.12)) we thus have $t_s = 0$. The case of $t_s \neq 0$ will be treated in the next section.

Consider the general non-cooperative equilibrium (3.15) - (3.20) with some tax function $t(\tau)$. We want to see if there exists a tax function making the non-cooperative equilibrium coincide with the social optimum (given by (3.1) - (3.7)). From (3.6) and (3.19) we see that an optimal tax implies

$$\lambda_j(\tau) - (1 - \beta_j) \, t(\tau) = \lambda(\tau), \tag{1}$$

where the λ_j-development is given by (3.18) and the λ-development is given by (3.5). Consider first the open loop case, i.e. $v_{-js} = 0$. Moreover, we assume $D_j(S) = \beta_j \, D(S)$, cf. the discussion in section 2. It then follows from (3.5) and (3.18) (since $t_s = 0$) that we must have

$$\lambda_j(\tau) = \beta_j \lambda(\tau). \tag{2}$$

Combining this with (1) gives us

$$t(\tau) = -\lambda(\tau). \tag{3}$$

This equation characterizes the path of the tax rate on CO_2 emissions which makes the non-cooperative equilibrium coincide with the full optimum. Combining (3) with (3.5) and (3.8) we thus have

$$\dot{t}(\tau) = r \, t(\tau) - D'(S), \tag{4}$$

$$t(T) = \frac{D'(S(T))}{r} = \max_i R_i'(0). \tag{5}$$

The optimal tax thus rises gradually over time towards its maximal value given by (5). The growth rate of the tax is lower than the rate of interest.

We now turn to the Markov perfect equilibrium. With a time-dependent tax rate, the payoff-relevant variables for each player are τ and $S(\tau)$. In a Markov perfect equilibrium emissions from country k are thus given by a function $v_k(\tau, S(\tau))$.

When the tax is given by (3) we have $t(\tau) = -\lambda(\tau) = -\lambda_j(\tau)/\beta_j$. But this means that the term in front of v_{-js} in (3.18) is always zero. There is therefore no difference between the open loop equilibrium and the Markov perfect equilibrium for this tax path.

This tax path therefore makes the closed loop equilibrium coincide with the full optimum.

The result above is quite surprising. It was shown in Section 5 that *without* taxes the Markov perfect equilibrium usually gives higher CO_2 emissions than the open loop equilibrium (for the same cumulative emissions). Intuitively, we would therefore expect that a higher Pigouvian tax is necessary to achieve the full optimum in the Markov perfect equilibrium than in the open loop case. The result above shows that this intuition is wrong.

To understand the result above, it is useful to consider *why* the perfect equilibrium has higher CO_2 emissions than the open loop equilibrium in the absence of taxes. In both equilibria each country knows that its CO_2 emissions contribute to total cumulative emissions. In the open loop equilibrium additional cumulative emissions by definition have no effect on the time path of CO_2 emissions from other countries. In the perfect equilibrium, on the other hand, additions to the CO_2 stock resulting from a particular country's emissions tend to reduce the future emissions from other countries (for $v_{-js} < 0$[6]). This benefits the country under consideration $(\lambda_j v_{-js} > 0)$, which therefore tends to choose higher CO_2 emissions than it would have chosen had the time paths of CO_2 emissions from other countries been fixed.

When there is a CO_2 tax, it is no longer obvious that reduced future CO_2 emissions from other countries benefit a particular country. The reason is that lower future CO_2 emissions from other countries also means lower future tax revenue from other countries, part of which is redistributed to the country under consideration. With the optimal tax, the negative effect of lower future tax reimbursements (the term $\beta_j t v_{-js}$ in (3.18)) is exactly equal to the positive environmental effect of other countries reducing their future emissions (the term $\lambda_j v_{-js}$ in (3.18)). Each country therefore chooses its CO_2 emissions without taking the effect on future emissions from other countries into consideration, just like in the open loop equilibrium.

8. Non-commitment and taxation

In the previous section it was assumed that the authorities could commit themselves to a time path for the CO_2 tax. Under this assumption, we found a particular tax path which made the non-cooperative equilibrium (open loop or Markov perfect) coincide

---

[6] A similar discussion is valid for the case of $v_{-js} > 0$.

with the social optimum. In the perfect equilibrium, the optimal tax at any time depends **only** on the CO$_2$ stock S, and *not* explicitly on the date. Although there exists an optimal tax path $t(\tau)$, starting at any date with some particular CO$_2$ stock, this tax path is only optimal along the equilibrium path. *If* for some reason the CO$_2$ stock $S(\tau)$ should deviate from the original path from τ'onwards, sticking to the tax path $t(\tau)$ after τ' would no longer lead to a first best optimum. It seems unreasonable to assume that the authorities can commit themselves to a particular time path for the CO$_2$ tax. Instead, we would expect the tax path at any date to be chosen so that the non-cooperative equilibrium path (from this date onwards) coincides with the first best optimum. For the perfect equilibrium this implies that the CO$_2$ tax only depends on total cumulative CO$_2$ emissions, i.e. $t = t(S)$.

The tax given by (7.4) - (7.5), which was optimal when each country assumed $t_s = 0$, gave an increasing tax rate over time. Since S also is increasing, this means that we have $t_s > 0$. With $t_s > 0$, the term with t_s in Eq. (3.18) must be included in our analysis. If $V_j = \beta_j \Sigma_i V_i$ for all j, the tax given by (7.4) - (7.5) makes the non-cooperative equilibrium coincide with the social optimum even if each country recognizes that $t_s > 0$. If the term $V_j - \beta_j \Sigma_i V_i > 0$, country j pays more in CO$_2$ tax than it gets back. In this case country j is worse off the higher is the CO$_2$ tax. Since $t_s > 0$, country j therefore has an incentive to try to keep S low, i.e. to keep its own CO$_2$ emissions low. Loosely speaking, we therefore have the following result: Compared with the social optimum, the non-cooperative equilibrium with the tax given by (7.4) - (7.5) has less CO$_2$ emissions from countries with relatively high CO$_2$ emissions in equilibrium (i.e. $V_j/\Sigma_i V_i > \beta_j$), and more CO$_2$ emissions from countries with relatively low CO$_2$ emissions. In other words, the tax path (7.4) - (7.5), with $t_s > 0$ recognized by the players, tends to compress the distribution of CO$_2$ emissions between countries towards the distribution $(\beta_1, ..., \beta_N)$ compared with the full optimum.

References

Fershtman, C., 1989, "Fixed rules and decision rules: Time consistency and subgame perfection", *Economics Letters 30*, 191-194.

Maskin, E., and Tirole, J., 1988, "A theory of dynamic oligopoly, I: Overview and quantity competition with large fixed costs", *Econometrica 56*, 549-570.

Reinganum, J.F., and Stokey, N.L., 1985, "Oligopoly extraction of a common property natural resource: The importance of the period of commitment in dynamic games", *International Economic Review 26*, 161-173.

Selten, R., 1975, "Reexamination of the perfectness concept for equilibrium points in extensive games", *International Journal of Game Theory 4*, 25-55.

Comments by Otto Keck

This is an interesting paper with a happy result. Global emissions of CO_2 can be brought down to the social optimum by using a Pigouvian tax. Although international negotiations on establishing the tax will certainly be very difficult, the paper shows that the optimal tax leads to the same social optimum, no matter whether the dynamic model used to analyze its impact is based on open—loop strategies or on a Markov decision rule. This result is a happy one, since it removes at least one issue from the difficult negotiations between governments. One may ask the question whether this interpretation of Michael Hoel's result does not impute too much rationality to international negotiations among governments. But even for those with a less optimistic view about the rationality of international negotiations, the result is a happy one, since at least it does remove one issue from the discussions among the economists advising the governments in these negotiations: The economists at least will not quarrel whether to base their analysis of the impact of the tax on a dynamic model with open—loop strategies or on a dynamic model with Markov strategies.

As to the static model, Michael Hoel points out at several places in the paper that problems may arise when there is a country "which would not be negatively affected by the climatic changes following from increased atmospheric concentration of CO_2" (page 43, see also p. 44).

He discusses in passing the case $D_j{}'(S) \leq 0$, as throughout the rest of the paper he assumes that $D_j(S)$ is increasing and $D_j(S) \geq 0$. The latter assumption is never explicitly stated. It seems to me both restrictions are unnecessarily restrictive. If a country benefits from the greenhouse effect, it has a negative damage. Nevertheless, it can be included in the global tax agreement by having it pay a negative tax, i.e. by paying it a compensation for the benefits it foregoes by restricting its emissions. It seems to me that the static model could be extended without difficulty so as to cover also the cases $D_j(S) < 0$, $D_j{}'(S) < 0$, while keeping the convexity of the damage function.

Now to the dynamic models. The open—loop equilibrium and the Markov equilibrium both lead to the same endstate: Pollution becomes so strong that no country can gain individually from further polluting activity. This is not a surprising result, in fact it could have been found without dynamic programming. The main result is that, while without a tax, the Markov–strategy model gets to the dismal endstate quicker than the open–loop–strategy model, with the optimal tax both models lead to the same social optimum.

Although I can feel with Michael Hoel the joy he experienced when he found that fitting the optimal tax path into the Markov–model equation for the social optimum, I am concerned about the restrictions to which the result is subjected. First, the different behavior of the models for the case without tax is shown only for the symmetric case in which all countries are equal. The symmetric case excludes by definition some interesting situations, as all countries suffer and benefit equally from emissions and there is no country that is indifferent to emissions or benefits from pollution.

Second, the proposition that the Markov strategy model leads to higher emission rates than the open–loop model is valid only for the Markov model with continuous strategies. If discontinuous strategies are admitted, a continuum of emission paths may be supported by Markov perfect equilibria, as Michael Hoel points out on pages 64–66. For any cumulative emission level reached by the history of the game, a Markov perfect equilibrium can be defined in which all countries stop emissions even in the absence of a global tax.

Third, the proposition that in the case with tax both models lead to the same social optimum is arrived at with a time–dependent tax schedule. This requires that the countries commit themselves to a time path for the CO$_2$ tax and admit no possibility for revising the tax in the future. In the real world this will never happen. In the arena of international politics it is impossible for countries to commit themselves never to revise an agreement. Such a commitment will never stick. Even, if it was possible to make such a commitment stick, it would be very unwise for any country to enter it, given the uncertainties any country faces with regard to its own damage functions and revenue functions. These uncertainties are immense already for the present, they are even greater for a time span reaching decades into the future.

A realistic tax strategy, as Michael Hoel acknowledges in the revised version of the paper, cannot be an open–loop strategy. It must be a closed–loop strategy that provides for the possibility of revising the tax schedule as time moves on and more information becomes available. The fact that Michael Hoel's dynamic models of the open–loop and of the closed–loop type use an open–loop tax does in my view seriously limit the relevance of the results for real world problems.

As I said this paper is an interesting piece with a happy result. However, I think that the result is subject to restrictions which may, I am afraid, prevent the paper from being a great help to policy makers.

Chapter 3

Karl–Göran Mäler

Critical Loads and International Environmental Cooperation[1]

Abstract. Critical loads are defined as the maximum deposition of a pollutant that in the long run will not cause any changes in the receiving ecosystem. It is shown that if countries play their open Nash equilibrium strategies, in the long run they will try to approach emissions consistent with the critical loads. If they cooperate, they will also in the long run approach the same emissions but they will try to do it faster. Thus the notion of critical loads and the determination of these loads in different parts of Europe seem to promote cooperation among countries.

1. Critical loads

During the last five years, the notion of *critical loads* has been brought to the discussion on international cooperation on transboundary pollution problems. It has been thought that by introducing the idea of critical loads it would be easier to achieve cooperation that would bring about cost–effective solutions to common problems.

As critical load is basically an ecological concept and captures the idea of a sufficient small pollution load that will not give rise to long term environmental harm. Exactly how the critical load concept should be defined has not been agreed upon but provisionally it can be stated that *"critical load" means a quantitative estimate of the exposure to one or more pollutants below which significant harmful effects on specified sensitive elements of the environment do not occur according to present knowledge*, (UN, ESC, ECE 20/1 1989). It has been argued that countries should coordinate their abatement strategies in order to reduce the exposure to pollutants to the critical loads. For example, in the NO_x protocol to the Geneve Convention on Long Range Transports of Pollutants, the necessary elements to control policies based on critical loads are defined. In

[1] I am grateful to Henry Tulkens for useful comments on an earlier draft. The usual disclaimer is of course applicable.

ECE 8/1 1990, the use of critical loads for such cooperation is discussed and illustrated. It is based on estimation of the critical loads on a grid for Europe made by Chadwick and Kuylenstierna (1990). This estimation is based on the sensitivity of various ecological systems which in turn depends on soil type, land use, geological formations, rainfall.

Is there an economic rationale for this and if that is the case, what is the rationale? These questions will be discussed in this paper and some tentative answers will be given.

2. Naive interpretations

The standard model in environmental economics assumes the existence of a physical damage function

$$Y = F(Q) \tag{1}$$

where Q is the pollution load in a specified area, such as the deposition of sulphur and Y is the resulting damage measured in physical units, for example the losses in timber because of reduced growth of trees. The critical load Q^c can then be defined as the maximum level of pollution load that makes the physical damage zero, i.e.

$$F(Q) \begin{Bmatrix} > \\ = \end{Bmatrix} 0 \quad \text{if} \quad Q \begin{Bmatrix} > \\ \leq \end{Bmatrix} Q^c \tag{2}$$

However, and this is the important point that most ecologists neglect, it is not obvious that it is socially desirable to reduce the physical damage to zero. What is socially desirable depends not only on the physical damage but also on the social valuation of this damage and the social cost of avoiding the damage. There are sufficiently many examples of cases where it has been found social desirable to change the natural environment in a radical way and thereby creating substantial physical damage. The agriculture revolution about ten thousand years ago is one such a case. The use of exhaustible resources with the accompanying pollution have not seldom been socially sound. Thus the fact that the physical damage is zero at a certain pollution load has no direct normative consequences.

However, it has quite often been argued that there are threshold effects at the critical load. The physical damage function would the look like

$$Y = F(Q) = \begin{cases} 0 & \text{if } Q \le Q^c, \\ \infty & \text{if } Q > Q^c. \end{cases} \tag{3}$$

In a diagram the situation would be as in Fig. 1.

However, even in this case the valuation of the infinite physical damage must be made by society. For example, if the physical damage is infinite because a certain ecological system is irreversibly destroyed, it does not follow that the social damage measured in economic terms is infinite. This would be the case only if society regards the eco–system as absolutely essential to the performance of society. In some cases, this may be true, as would be the case if a life supporting service of the environment is in jeopardy. However, for other cases, this will surely not be the case.

Let us, however, assume that the social damage becomes infinite at a particular pollution load, that is assume that the damage function depicted in Fig. 1 represents the social damage. The pollution load Q represents the total load that comes from all emission sources, domestic as well as foreign sources.

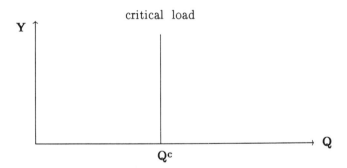

Figure 1: Physical damage function

As the damage cost is infinite at loads exceeding Q_i^c for all countries i, it follows that all countries would be interested in reducing their emission to such an extent that the total load does not exceed the critical load. We can now consider two possible cases for achieving this:[2]

i)   each country takes into account the other countries' payoff and design its best response strategy – the Nash equilibrium;

---

[2] The following discussion is based on Olsson and Mäler 1990.

ii)   countries agree to cooperate to reduce their emissions in such a way that the
        critical load objective is met in each country — the cooperative outcome.

Assume that the transport of the pollutant from one country to another can be described
by a square matrix

$$A = [a_{i,j}], \tag{4}$$

where $a_{i,j}$ indicates the proportion of the emissions in country j that ultimately will be
deposited in country i. We will for the moment assume not only that A is non—singular
but also that its inverse in non—negative. The total deposition in country i is then

$$Q_i = \sum_{j=1}^{n} a_{i,j} E_j \tag{5}$$

where E_j is the emissions in country j and Q_i is the deposition in country i.

    The Nash equilibrium outcome occurs if each country takes into account the fact
that all other countries also have interests in reducing their emissions in such a way that
their exposure to pollution is consistent with the critical load objective. In other words,
in a Nash equilibrium each country tries to minimize its abatement costs subject to the
restriction that

$$Q^c_. \geq \sum_{j \neq i}^{n} a_{i,j} \hat{E}_j + a_{i,j} E_i, \tag{6}$$

where $\hat{E}_j$ is the Nash strategy of country j. However, if the matrix $[a_{i,j}]$ is non—singular,
the Nash equilibrium will be equal to the cooperative outcome as it represents the only
emission vector that will satisfy the critical loads with equality. Thus, there will be no
gains from cooperation in this case.

    In these naive models, gains from cooperation in case we take the notion of an L—
shaped environmental damage cost curve seriously, will occur only if countries behave
irrationally in the absence of cooperation. However, the basic criticism is obviously that
we have not observed in real life any environmental damage cost function that even
approximately can be analyzed in the framework of an L—shaped damage cost curve.

    The models have been naive in the sense that they have been completely static. The
notion of critical loads refer to long term harmful effects and we should therefore go on

to more dynamic models. This will be the next topic.

3. Stock of pollutants – the case of one country

Let us keep the assumption of a transport matrix $A = [a_{i,j}]$ of the pollutants. The total annual deposition in country i is then given as before by

$$Q_i = \sum_{j=1}^{n} a_{i,j} E_j \tag{7}$$

We will maintain the assumption that the matrix A is non–singular and has a non–negative inverse. This assumption is crucial for the ensuing discussion and also excludes several environmental problems such as the emission of carbon dioxides and the greenhouse effect. In this case, it does not matter for the greenhouse effect where the carbondioxide is emitted and the matrix A would have identical columns. On the other hand, if we are interested in sulphurdioxide and nitrogeneoxide emissions and the acid rains, the assumption of a non–singular transport matrix is appropriate. Furthermore, it turns out that the transport matrix for sulphur implied by the sulphur budgets for Europe calculated by EMEP[3] has a dominant diagonal and therefore a non–negative inverse. The fact that A has a dominant diagonal reflects that a country has a major influence on its own deposition of sulphur.

Let us now assume that the actual environmental damage is not due to the annual deposition but to the accumulated net depositions of the pollutant. Let us furthermore assume that the receiving eco–system can neutralize or remove a certain amount L_i^c of the pollutant per unit of time. Thus the net depreciation of the stock of pollutants is constant over time. The net accumulation in country i is then given by

$$\frac{dY_i}{dt} = Q_i - L_i^c \tag{8}$$

This formulation is, of course, not the only one possible. The conventional formulation in capital theory is that the depreciation is proportional to the stock of pollutants. Such an assumption seems, however, misplaced in this connection. The definition of a critical

---

[3] European Monitoring and Evaluation Programme, a research programme within the United Nations Economic Comission for Europe.

load implies that there is a fixed amount of pollutants, independent of previous pollution and determined by characteristics in the receiving ecological system, than can be removed from the environment without creating any long term environmental damages. Another more interesting formulation would be to assume the existence of a stock of a buffering substance that can grow naturally, but is depleted in proportion to the pollution load. However, in this paper we will use the assumption of constant depreciation.

If we look at a single country i and assume that the damage function is $D_i(Y_i)$ and the cost of controlling emissions to the level E_i is $C_i(E_i)$, the problem for the country is to choose a time profile for the emissions so that the present value of damage and abatement costs is minimized. This can be formulated as a problem in optimal control and the optimal trajectory of the emissions can be characterized by Pontryagin's maximum principle.

$$Min \int_0^\infty e^{-r_i t} [C_i(E_i(t)) + D_i(Y_i(t))]dt$$

$$\text{(9)}$$

$$\text{subject to} \quad \frac{dY_i}{dt} = E_i(t) - L_i^c(t),$$

where r_i is the interest rate in country i.

It will turn out that the long run behavior of the optimal trajectory will be close to the emissions corresponding to the critical loads.

Let $p_i(t)$ be the current value shadow price of the stock of pollutants (i.e. the reduction in current total costs that would occur if the stock is reduced by one unit) and let H be the current value Hamiltonian. Then we have

$$H_i = C_i(E_i) + D_i(Y_i) + p_i(E_i - L_i^c), \tag{10}$$

and the necessary condition for an optimal trajectory is (if we assume an interior maximum)

$$C'_i(E_i) + p_i = 0. \tag{11}$$

Moreover, the shadow price p_i at time t is equal to the present cost of having one more unit of the pollutant or

$$\frac{dp_i}{dt} = r_i p_i - D'_i(Y_i).$$ (12)

It is obvious that there exists a unique steady state for this system, which is defined by

i) $E_i^* = L_i^c,$
ii) $p^*_i = C'_i(E_i^*),$ (13)
iii) $Y_i^* = D^{-1}(r_i p^*_i).$

It is well known that this steady state will be a saddle point and all optimal trajectories will in the long run approach this saddle point.[4] This is illustrated in Figure 2. The optimal trajectory will converge to the saddle–point at (p^*_i, Y_i^*). However, this steady state corresponds to emissions giving rise to a deposition load equal to the critical load. *In the long run, given our interpretation of the dynamics, an optimal trajectory will tend to a state characterized by the critical loads.*

Thus it seems that in the long run, the notion of critical loads may be of economic interest as it characterizes the possible steady state.

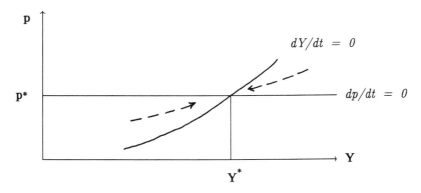

Figure 2: Steady state and optimal trajectories

4. Stock of pollutants – several countries and the open loop equilibrium

Let us now return to the n–country model discussed in Section 2 above, except that we introduce the considerations in the previous section. Let us begin by assuming that

---

[4] See f.ex. Arrow and Kurz (1970) for a discussion of this.

countries can not monitor emissions in other countries or total depositions in the own country. In this very special case, the idea of open loop strategies and open loop equilibrium are natural. Countries design their strategies for all future and will adhere to these, irrespective of what other countries do.

The open loop strategy for country i is defined from

$$\underset{E_i}{min} \int_0^\infty e^{-r_i t}[D_i(Y_i) + C_i(E_i)] \tag{14}$$

$$\text{subject to} \quad \frac{dY_i}{dt} = \sum_{j=1}^n a_{i,j} E_j - L^c \tag{15}$$

where the minimization is of course over E_i and where country i takes E_j, $j \neq i$, as given functions over time. The necessary conditions for this minimization problem are obviously the same as the one we derived for the single country optimization above, that is Eq. (11) and (12). The total dynamical systems, i.e. the system describing all countries, is therefore given by Eq. (11), (12) and (15) for each country. It is easily seen if A is non–singular, there exists a unique steady state such that total depositions in all countries equal the critical loads. Furthermore, this steady state will be a saddle point, so that the optimal trajectories will ultimately converge to the steady state. Thus, even in an open loop Nash equilibrium without any cooperation, the emissions will tend to levels that correspond to what "Nature can bear".

We can now look at cooperative behavior, still in the open loop framework. Assume then that countries have agreed to reduce their emissions in order to minimize the total abatement and damage cost.

$$Min \int_0^\infty \sum_{i=1}^n e^{-r_i t} [C_i(E_i) + D_i(Y_i)] \, dt. \tag{16}$$

It is quite easily seen that the ensuing dynamical system from the optimization problem does not admit a steady state unless all interest rates are equal. Let us then assume that all interest rates are equal to r. It then follows that there will be a unique steady state, characterized by

$$\sum_{j=1}^{n} a_{i,j} E_j = L_i^c,$$

$$C'_i(E_i) + \sum_{j=1}^{n} p_j a_{j,i} = 0, \qquad (17)$$

$$rp_i - D_i(Y_i) = 0.$$

It must be pointed out that the net present cost from the cooperative behavior may for some countries be greater than the net present cost from the open loop Nash equilibrium. Unless these countries are compensated for their extra costs, they will obviously not find it in their interest to participate in the cooperation. In the sequel we will assume that side–payments are made in order to secure that no country will loose from cooperation compared with the Nash equilibrium.

Once again, if A is non–singular, there exists a unique steady state which is a saddle point and the optimal trajectory will tend to this saddle point. This steady state equilibrium is equal to the steady state Nash open loop equilibrium only in that the emissions are equal. The stock of pollutants will differ as can be seen from the equations above. With cooperation, the stock of pollutants in each country will be less than in the Nash equilibrium. Furthermore, the speed of convergence to the steady state will also in general differ between the two solution concepts.

Thus, irrespective of whether we have cooperation or not, the emissions will in the long run tend to the levels required by critical loads, although the states of the environment will differ. This suggests that critical loads may play an important role in international negotiations on transboundary pollution problems. It is only a suggestion, as we have assumed that countries cannot monitor emissions in other countries or depositions in other countries in order to motivate open loop strategies. This has as one clear consequence that countries cannot discover cases when countries are cheating, that is deviating from an agreement. Moreover, we had to assume a particular depreciation model for the stock of pollutants and that countries discount the future in identical ways. We will study the same situation with closed loop equilibria in the next section.

5. Closed loop or feed back equilibria

We now assume that every country at each point in time receives information on emissions in other countries and on deposition in the own country. It can therefore react to changes in policies in other countries. Hence we assume that the country at each moment knows the actual state of the environment. Such an assumption defines closed loop or feedback equilibria.[5] In particular, we can think of punishment schemes for countries that deviate from agreed cooperation. Such punishment can take the form of military interventions (which have happened), trade restrictions, retaliation through environmental punishment or in some other way. Here we will limit ourselves to a rather narrow list of retaliatory strategies, namely those retaliations that can take place through variation of the emissions.

If we would have modeled the game in discrete time, we would have applied the Folk theorem[6] and concluded that the cooperative behavior coupled with suitable side—payments could be supported as a perfect Nash equilibrium if the interest rate is small enough. The same is obviously true when we have modeled the accumulation of pollutants in continuous time. Thus the open loop cooperative behavior may be agreed upon in international negotiations and this equilibrium will be stable in the sense that countries will find that their best response is to adhere to the cooperative agreement.

It should be pointed out that this closed loop or feed back equilibrium is based on the assumption that countries can monitor emissions and/or the transboundary flux of pollutants, something which up to now is not completely realistic. On the other hand, it is a more realistic assumption than the one underlying the open loop information structure.

This brief discussion indicates that an agreement on gradual emission reductions which in the long run will reduce the exposure to pollution to the critical loads, not only seems to be feasible but also credible if it is coupled with side—payment to make it worthwhile for all countries to cooperate. This conclusion is dependent of many assumptions, but perhaps the most important assumption is that the dynamics of the pollution problem can be modeled in the way that has been followed in this paper. If this modeling seems reasonable, and if different countries discount the future at the same rate, then critical loads may be quite important in international negotiations.

---

[5] See Mehlman, 1988, and Basar (ed.), 1986, for a detailed discussion of this concept.
[6] See f.e. Fudenberg and Maskin 1986.

References

Arrow, K., and Kurz, M., 1970, *"Public Investment, the Rate of Return and Optimal Fiscal Policy"*, Baltimore, Johns Hopkins Press

Basar, T., (ed.), 1986, *"Dynamic Games and Applications in Economics"*, Berlin Heidelberg, Springer Verlag

Chadwick, M., and Kuylenstierna, J., 1989, "The relative sensitivity of ecosystems in Europe to the indirect effects of acidic depositions", in Kamari et al. (eds.), *Regional Acidification Models*, Springer Verlag, Berlin Heidelberg

Fudenberg, D., and Maskin, E., 1986, "The folk theorem in repeated games with discounting or with incomplete information, *Econometrica 54*, 533–556

Economic Commission for Europe, UN Economic and Social Council, 1989, *"The Critical Loads Approach"*, EB.AIR/WG.5/R.1, restricted

Economic Commission for Europe, UN Economic and Social Council, 1990. *"Using Critical Loads as the Basis for Abatement Strategies in Europe"*, EB.AIR/WG.5/R.7, restricted

Mehlman, A., 1988, *"Applied Differential Games"*, New York, Plenum Press

Olsson, C., and Mäler, K.–G., 1990, "The cost–effectiveness of different solutions to the European sulphur problem", *The European Review of Agriculture Economics 17*, 153–166

Comments by Henry Tulkens[1]

This comment contains three points: one bearing on the general spirit of the paper, and two others on the implications of some of its assumptions as to the generality of the results.

The general spirit of Karl–Göran Mäler's interesting paper is the one of positive science: in contrast to much of the work done in environmental economics, that (too?) often rushes towards normative conclusions, the author here adopts instead an attitude that consists in searching for an implicit economic rationale for a non–economic based concept used by scientists of other disciplines dealing with environmental affairs, namely

---

[1] I should like to acknowledge englightening conversations I had with Rüdiger Pethig, Leonhard Mirman and Philippe Michel on some of the issues raised by the paper discussed here.

the one of critical load.

That economic analysis can serve other purposes than only normative ones is of course evident for analysts and theorists, but the discipline is usually very much less seen that way by practitioners and policy—oriented people. The originally of the paper in this respect is therefore to be stressed, and to be commended. One of its principal merits is, in my opinion, to draw the attention of the economist to a notion that he otherwise might be tempted to criticize as an arbitrary one, or even to ignore.

A central assertion in the paper is that non—cooperative and cooperative equilibrium outcomes are identical in terms of emissions (although not in terms of the resulting pollutants stocks). This is derived from the fact that the "transport" function (5) is formulated as a system of linear equations, with a unique solution when the matrix of its coefficients is non singular.

While the paper interestingly discusses the non singularity issue, it does not so as to the validity of the *linearity* assumption. Beyond the examples that the author gives in the paper, one might wish to know to what extent this is an important limitation of the model, in particular concerning the identity issue between cooperative and non—cooperative equilibrium emission flows. Intuitively, one would conjecture that this identity would no longer hold for non linear transport (or transfer) function. This suggests the general idea that the possibilities offered by cooperation vs. non—cooperation may depend upon the formal structure of the physical phenomena that are of concern.

A second point that one could perhaps take issue with is the specification of expression (8) in the paper, where it is assumed that the critical load level is constant, not only over time but also with respect of the level of accumulated pollutants. Although the author recognizes that alternative assumptions are conceivable, and might even be preferable, he does not discuss how the analysis would be modified — nor whether his results would still hold — if some of these alternative assumptions were made. Now, from the verbal exchanges that followed the presentation, it appeared that the form of expression (8) does matter to a large extent, because the results would not be obtained if it were specified e.g. as

$$dY/dt = Q - f(Y).$$

In addition to this formal aspect, that relates with the properties of the *economic* model, one should like to consider also the question from a technical environmental point of view, namely: is it realistic to assume constancy with respect to the stock of pollutants?

To a large extent, this is an empirical question, whose answer probably varies according to the pollutants considered. The discussion that the paper invites from this point of view lies however beyond the scope of economics: it does indeed require a detailed enquiry of the *physical* determinants of the critical load levels.

In each one of the two brief points made above, the attention has been shifted from the economic model to technical aspects of environmental phenomena. This illustrates once again, if not necessarily the modesty of the role the economist can play in this field, at least the inescapable interdisciplinary character his efforts must take for them to be relevant and fruitful.

Chapter 4

Jason F. Shogren
Kyung H. Baik
Thomas D. Crocker[1]

Environmental Conflicts and Strategic Commitment

Abstract: We examine two key aspects of strategic behavior in an environmental conflict. First, we consider the tactics of players who differ in relative strength, given that the order in which they play is endogenous. The results suggest that the weaker player (the underdog) always has an incentive to move first, while the more powerful player (the favorite) has an incentive to wait. The optimal level of self–protection is less than with either Nash equilibrium or favorite commitment, implying reduced social costs. Second, we explore the profitability of a strategic commitment where team members determine and publicly announce their optimal sharing rule before effort decisions of all the players are made. We rationalize the existence of exclusive membership in teams. Finally, the social costs of allocating resources to a conflict become greater when the team size is less than half of the number of contenders, compared to the same conflict without strategic team formation.

1. Introduction

Environmental conflicts are common. Canada and the United States debate the economic relevance of acid deposition, as do Sweden and the United Kingdom (Forster, 1989). Tennessee confronts North Carolina over the potentially toxic discharge of wastes by Champion Paper into the Pigeon River. Citizens groups and agricultural producers argue about the present and future consequences of agrichemicals such as pesticides and nitrates. Brouwer and Nijkamp (1990) note that the intensity and frequency of environmental conflicts like these seem likely to worsen because of rapid increases in overall population, urban populations, industrial development, and competing land uses.

[1] A. Dixit, J. Hirshleifer, T. Perri, and T. Sterner provided helpful comments on related work. C. Kolstad, J. Braden, and seminar participants at the University of Illinois and Iowa State University also supplied useful suggestions. Detlev Homann and a reviewer added detailed comments which have improved the paper.

These conflicts are driven by the fact that most efforts to protect one's self from environmental problems simply transfer rather than resolve them (Sterner, 1990). Tall stacks in the United States and the United Kingdom reduce their citizens' exposure by transferring pollution to Canada and to Sweden. North Carolina protects its jobs and its environment by allowing one of its major firms to ship wastes to Tennessee. The pollution from other sources which affects agriculture encourages agricultural land, fertilizer, and pesticide substitutions that produce pollution (Adams and Crocker, 1989). Private actions to minimize pollution–induced losses shift pollution to other parties. From a materials balance perspective (Kneese et al., 1970), most self–protection actions allow the mass of waste to flow into the environment, only transferring this mass through time and across space. Future generations and other jurisdictions then suffer the consequent environmental damages. Bird (1987) labels these phenomena as transferable externalities. (Also see Shogren and Crocker, 1991).

Transferable externalities create environmental conflicts. Environmental conflicts, in turn, lead to strategic behavior, the core element of any contest. Conflicts usually involve strategic commitment of self–protecting actions which can have significantly different impacts on resource allocation than traditional Nash behavior. (See for example Dixit, 1987). This paper explores some economic implications of environmental conflicts and strategic commitment. We focus on cooperative versus noncooperative behavior, endogenous timing of action, and the benefits of strategic team formation. We use a simple game–theoretic framework to demonstrate the following results:

(1) Given a transferable externality, noncooperative Nash behavior leads to economically inefficient overprotection. This contrasts the standard argument that Nash behavior will lead to underprovision of actions to reduce environmental damage.

(2) Given a transferable externality, and if the order of play between two asymmetrically powerful players is endogenous, then the more powerful player, the favorite, will find it in his advantage to allow the weaker player, the underdog, to move first. The underdog has the incentive to move first, implying no conflict in strategy. Consequently, strategic behavior between two unevenly matched contenders leads to lower social costs than does Nash behavior.

(3) Given n players, it is beneficial for some to join a team as a type of strategic commitment. Each member's expected profits are then greater than without the team. Moreover, intra–team competition is beneficial to team members. An optimal sharing rule can be set which provides an incentive to team members to increase self–protection effort, thereby increasing expected profits to the team. Note that if free entry is allowed,

however, teaming and the consequent intra–team competition results in behavior identical to Nash.

(4) When the team membership exceeds 50 percent of all players, it is desirable for the team to recruit new members. Nonmembers are not particularly interested in joining, however. This result could explain the willingness or reluctance of a player or country to sign an agreement or treaty specifying an unilateral action. It can be advantageous for a player to hold out, thereby gaining a competitive edge on the signees.

(5) The social costs of environmental conflict are lower (relative to the contest without a strategic team) if membership exceeds 50 percent of the number of players; they are higher if membership is less than 50 percent. Free entry and exit into the team results in no change in social costs relative to Nash behavior. The team may have no impact on the inefficiency associated with noncooperative protection. Regulators seeking rents by setting rules would find it advantageous to inhibit free entry into a team. Restriction on team size generates more self–protecting activities, thereby increasing the regulator's rents. If the regulator is interested in minimizing social costs, however, he should enact rules that encourage entry into the team.

The paper proceeds as follows. In Section 2, we construct an analytical framework to explore self–protection and transferable externalities given cooperative and noncooperative behavior. Sections 3 and 4 explore strategic behavior in the form of endogenous order of play and team formation. The paper concludes with a summary briefly discussing the implications for environmental policy.

2. Analytical framework

In a manner similar to Davis and Whinston (1962), Shogren and Crocker (1991) construct a framework to consider any pair of economic agents, i and j, who must confront potential economic losses from exposure to a negative externality. Let X_i represent player i's self–protection, and X_j be the same for player j. Write player i's expected damage function as

$$D_i(X_i,\ X_j) = [1 - \pi_i(X_i,\ X_j)]\, L_i(X_i,\ X_j), \tag{1}$$

where $[1 - \pi_i]$ is the ex ante probability that player i will suffer the money equivalent of the ex post loss, $L_i > 0$. The expected damage function captures the two key components of an undesirable event: the probability, $1 - \pi_i$, that the event will occur and the severity, L_i, if the event does occur (Ehrlich and Becker, 1972). Player i's self–protection is assumed to reduce his expected damages such that

$$\frac{\partial \pi_i}{\partial X_i} > 0 \quad \text{and} \quad \frac{\partial L_i}{\partial X_i} \leq 0 . \tag{2}$$

Assume a negative impact of player j's protection on player i's expected damage function

$$\frac{\partial \pi_i}{\partial X_j} < 0 \quad \text{and} \quad \frac{\partial L_i}{\partial X_j} \geq 0 \qquad (i \neq j). \tag{3}$$

Write player i's expected costs of exposure to the negative externality as $C_i(X_i, X_j)$ which include his cost of protection $P_i(X_i)$, and his expected damage function $D_i(X_i, X_j)$ such that for players i and j

$$C_i(X_i, X_j) = P_i(X_i) + D_i(X_i, X_j), \tag{4}$$

$$C_j(X_j, X_i) = P_j(X_j) + D_j(X_j, X_i). \tag{5}$$

Assume $C_i(\cdot)$ is a strictly convex function of X_i, given X_j; a similar convexity condition holds for $C_j(\cdot)$. Also assume $\partial P_i/\partial X_i > 0$ and $\partial P_j/\partial X_j > 0$.

In the Nash case where the players act noncooperatively by taking each other's self–protection measures as given, the problems of players i and j are

$$\underset{X_i}{Min}\, C_i = P_i(X_i) + D_i(X_i, X_j), \tag{6a}$$

$$\underset{X_j}{Min}\, C_j = P_j(X_j) + D_j(X_j, X_i). \tag{6b}$$

The cooperative solution requires that joint costs be minimized:

$$\underset{X_i, X_j}{Min}\, \bar{C} \equiv C_i(\cdot) + C_j(\cdot) = P_i(X_i) + P_j(X_j) + D_i(X_i, X_j) + D_j(X_j, X_i). \tag{7}$$

By comparing the first–order optimality conditions of the Nash problems (6a) and (6b) to the Pareto—optimal condition for the cooperative problem (7), Shogren and Crocker (1991) demonstrate the following proposition, (also see Sandler and Lapan, 1988).

Proposition 1: *For the case of transferable externalities, noncooperation results in over-protection.*

An observation that noncooperative, unilateral behavior can lead to inefficient resource allocation is hardly unique: Cournot (1838) cornered that market over a century and a half ago. What is important about Proposition 1 is the observation that self—protection from an externality can create yet another externality. Proposition 1 contradicts the traditional argument that private actions which ignore social cost will involve too little effort to reduce an environmental loss. Transferable externalities suggest the opposite occurs: individuals invest too much effort to reduce a loss. The reason for this difference is that the traditional case assumes abatement technology or salable output reductions always resolve the externality. In contrast, Sterner (1990) argues that most environmental policy simply transfers rather than resolves externalities. Moreover, in the absence of collectively imposed limits to the self—protection acts of individuals, heedlessness of Proposition 1 could make environmental improvements and preservations seem prohibitively expensive. Empirical research to estimate the magnitude of the inefficiencies engendered by noncooperative environmental policies should be of high priority. This research will be eased by any prior restrictions that reduce the set of stories consistent with the data. We now develop several restrictions on the manner in which these inefficiencies can change, given two strategic commitment tactics: endogenous timing and team formation.

3. Asymmetric players and endogenous strategic timing

Almost by definition, environmental conflicts involve strategy. This is especially true in conflicts between unevenly matched contenders. Because of differences in information or in endowments, players often differ in their access to self—protection opportunities. The classic favorite—underdog match—up is an example. The favorite's better access may provide him a first—mover advantage because he can commit his level of self—protection (Dixit, 1987).

This section demonstrates a fairly general case in which the favorite will never overcommit self—protection effort even if he has the opportunity to move first. If the favorite is given the opportunity to move first, he will not take it. The favorite is always better cff by waiting until the underdog has moved. Surprisingly, the underdog's best strategy is not to wait, but to make the first move. Hence, equilibrium order of play is that the underdog moves before the favorite and the favorite moves after the underdog. In this Stackelberg equilibrium with the underdog as a leader, one never observes over-commitment of effort, thereby suggesting reduced inefficiency from conflict compared with Nash behavior.

Following Tullock (1980), presume the agent i's probability of suffering or of not suffering damages can be represented by a logit function used extensively in the conflict literature such that

$$D_i(X_i, X_j) = [1 - \frac{\sigma X_i^r}{\sigma X_i^r + X_j^r}] L_i, \tag{8}$$

where r reflects the marginal cost of influencing the probability of winning. Let σ be a measure of agent i's access to self–protection relative to that of agent j. If $\sigma > 1$, then agent i has better access to self–protection opportunities than does agent j. For example, control agencies make errors in their assessments of pollution damages and control costs; pollution sufferers will use input mixes that increase the likelihood of those errors that exaggerate pollution damages. Perpetrators can do the same thing with control costs (Forster, 1989). Both sufferers and perpetrators are practicing self–protection. If $\sigma > 1$, and if the sufferer were agent i, then errors that exaggerate pollution damages would be easier to assure than would those that exaggerate control costs. If the opposite were true, then $\sigma < 1$.

For simplicity, assume that $r = 1$ in (8), $L = L_i = L_j$ and is exogenous, and $P_i(X_i) = X_i$ and $P_j(X_j) = X_j$. As with (6a) and (6b), any noncooperative Nash solution then results from agents i and j solving

$$\underset{X_i}{Min}\ C_i(X_i, X_j) = X_i + [1 - \frac{\sigma X_i}{\sigma X_i + X_j}] L, \tag{9a}$$

$$\underset{X_j}{Min}\ C_j(X_j, X_i) = X_j + [1 - \frac{\sigma X_i}{\sigma X_i + X_j}] L. \tag{9b}$$

The reaction functions, $R_i(X_j)$ for player i and $R_j(X_i)$ for player j, are

$$R_i(X_j) = \begin{cases} \dfrac{\sqrt{\sigma L X_j} - X_i}{\sigma} & \text{for} \quad 0 < X_j \le \sigma L \\ 0 & \text{otherwise,} \end{cases}$$
(10a)

$$R_j(X_i) = \begin{cases} \sqrt{\sigma L X_i} - \sigma X_i & \text{for} \quad 0 < X_i \le L/\sigma \\ 0 & \text{otherwise,} \end{cases}$$
(10b)

which are shown in Figure 1.

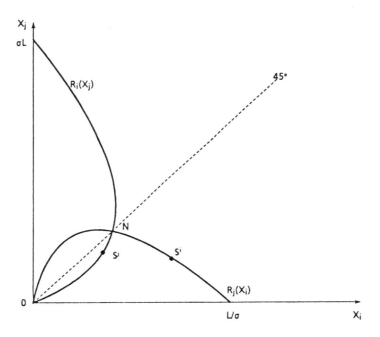

Figure 1: Reaction functions and equilibria

Nash equilibrium. The Nash equilibrium is $(\sigma L/(1 + \sigma)^2, \sigma L/(1 + \sigma)^2)$, which is represented in Figure 1 by N. With $\sigma > 1$, player i's probability of losing is less than $1/2$ in the Nash equilibrium. Then player i is called the favorite and player j the underdog. The players' expected costs in the Nash equilibrium are

$$C_i^N = L\left[1 - \frac{\sigma^2}{(1 + \sigma)^2}\right] \quad \text{and} \quad C_j^N = L\left[1 - \frac{1}{(1 + \sigma)^2}\right].$$
(11)

Favorite moves first. Suppose the favorite commits to some positive level of self–protection effort. Given the effort level of the favorite, the underdog will respond according to expression (10b). Hence, the favorite chooses an effort level which minimizes his expected costs on the underdog's reaction curve. The Stackelberg equilibrium with the favorite as a leader is $(\sigma L/4, \sigma(2-\sigma)L/4)$ for $1 < \sigma \le 2$ and $(L/\sigma, 0)$ for $\sigma \ge 2$, which is represented in Figure 1 by S^i. The players' expected costs in this Stackelberg equilibrium are

$$
\overset{si}{C_i} = \begin{cases} L[1 - \dfrac{\sigma}{4}] & \text{for } 1 < \sigma \le 2, \\ \dfrac{L}{\sigma} & \text{for } \sigma \ge 2, \end{cases} \tag{12a}
$$

$$
\overset{si}{C_j} = \begin{cases} L[1 - \dfrac{(2-\sigma)^2}{4}] & \text{for } 1 < \sigma \le 2, \\ L & \text{for } \sigma \ge 2. \end{cases} \tag{12b}
$$

Underdog moves first. Suppose the underdog commits to a level of effort. Given the effort level of the underdog, the favorite will respond according to expression (10a). Hence, the underdog chooses an effort level which minimizes her expected cost on the favorite's reaction curve. The Stackelberg equilibrium with the underdog as a leader is $((2\sigma - 1)L/4\sigma^2, L/4\sigma)$, which is represented in Figure 1 by S^i. The players' expected payoffs in this Stackelberg equilibrium are

$$
\overset{sj}{C_i} = L[1 - \frac{(2\sigma - 1)^2}{4\sigma^2}] \quad \text{and} \quad \overset{sj}{C_j} = L[1 - \frac{1}{4\sigma}]. \tag{13}
$$

From the above analysis, it is straightforward to obtain the following proposition.

Proposition 2: *If the favorite should move first, then he overcommits effort compared with the Nash equilibrium. If the underdog has the opportunity to move first, then she expends less effort relative to the Nash equilibrium.*

Proposition 2 implies that if the favorite moves first, then he will move further away from the Pareto efficient cooperative benchmark identified in Proposition 1. In contrast, if the underdog has the opportunity to move first, she will always take it, implying her effort will approach the efficient outcome of the cooperative solution. The key question we now examine is who will move first.

Consider a three–period game where in period 0 the players simultaneously decide and publicly announce whether to play in period 1 or 2, and in the next two periods the players choose effort levels. Table 1 illustrates the players' expected payoffs for the four possible combinations of period choices. If the players decide to move in the same period, the players end up with the expected payoffs in the Nash equilibrium (C_i^N, C_j^N). If the favorite decides to move in period 1 and the underdog in period 2, their expected payoffs are given by those in the Stackelberg equilibrium with the favorite as a leader (C_i^{si}, C_j^{si}).

Finally, if the underdog decides to move in period 1 and the favorite in period 2, their expected payoffs are given by those in the Stackelberg equilibrium with the underdog as a leader (C_i^{sj}, C_j^{sj}). It is straightforward to show that for the favorite $C_i^N > C_i^{si} > C_i^{sj}$ and for the underdog $C_j^{si} > C_j^N > C_j^{sj}$. Hence, the unique Nash equilibrium in period 0 is that the underdog chooses period 1 and the favorite chooses period 2. The implications of equilibrium order of moves on effort levels are summarized in the following propositions.

Proposition 3: *In equilibrium, the favorite moves after the underdog. Therefore, in an environmental conflict over a fixed loss an endogenous ordering of moves results in both players' expending smaller self–protection efforts compared with the Nash equilibrium.*

		Underdog	
		Period 1	Period 2
Favorite	Period 1	C_i^N C_j^N	C_i^{si} C_j^{si}
	Period 2	C_i^{sj} C_j^{sj}	C_i^N C_j^N

Table 1: Expected payoffs

Proposition 4: *In equilibrium, each player's effort level is decreasing in σ; that is, when confronted with the prospect of a fixed loss, the more self–protection opportunities a* *player has available relative to the other player, the less likely he is to use these opportunities.*

In terms of the economic theory of environmental conflicts, Proposition 3 suggests that the inefficiency associated with Nash behavior decreases with endogenous timing. Relative to Proposition 1, the players move closer to the cooperative Pareto–efficient outcome. Both strategies are self–enforcing in that if the underdog changes her commitment to move first it leads to higher costs. This is also the case for the favorite's commitment to wait. This result has intuitive appeal in that one often witnesses or has experienced the neighborhood bully's willingness to allow his weaker opponent the first swing. This willingness is not some distorted notion of fairness, but rather rational, calculated behavior. By moving first, the underdog expects the favorite to react in proportion to her effort, thereby she does not commit too many resources. The underdog is willing to take this chance in that the favorite does not have to spend as much effort. Both parties gain by expending less effort. [Baik and Shogren (1992) establish this in a more general framework]. Proposition 4 suggests all this effort is sensitive to the favorite's relative power. The likelihood of an upset decreases as the favorite becomes more powerful. Recognizing her opponent's new strength, the underdog reduces her effort, but still will move first. The favorite will wait, but he also expends less effort in the increasingly lopsided contest.

If the contest arena is North American public opinion, these propositions suggest at least the broad outlines of the pattern of play between Canada and the United States with respect to acid deposition–control policy. As Forster (1991) points out, the two federal governments have spent more than a decade trying to form a joint agreement to reduce emissions of acid deposition precursors, especially sulfur dioxide (SO_2). In 1984, the Canadian government chose to act independently to reduce its nationwide SO_2 emission by 50 percent. In the fall of 1990, the United States, whose sulfur dioxide emissions in the early 1980s were five times larger than Canada's and whose airborne SO_2 exports to Canada exceeded Canada's to the United States by a factor between three and eight, continues to resist taking domestic emission control actions.

4. N players and strategic team formation

This section examines a second tactic potentially important to the theory of environmental conflict: strategic team formation. In contests, we often observe two or more players uniting against common opponents. One observes such strategy in political contests where candidates implicitly unite and attack a strong front–runner. The team noncooperatively tries to derail a powerful incumbent in the early primaries knowing if they are successful they will all gain some share of his or her support. Politicians are just one example. The argument can be applied more generally to include environmental conflicts. Countries sign treaties aimed at minimizing free–rider incentives, e.g., the Montreal protocol on ozone depletion (Bohm, 1990, or Hoel, 1991). Competitive firms in industries threatened by pollution control legislation form teams to lobby against legislation and to grant stature to exaggerations of the costs and the disruptions its passage and implementation would cause, e.g., the Citizens for Sensible Control of Acid Rain (Forster, 1991). Noncooperative action with a coordinated sharing rule can prove more efficient than isolated moves.

Although the economic theory of alliances and teams has often been examined (e.g., Marschak and Radner, 1972), our model differs in that players form a team to compete with outsiders and among themselves for a rivalrous, excludable private reward. We examine noncooperative behavior where players form a team purely as a strategic move. Team formation is a tactic of strategic commitment since team–members determine and announce their sharing rule before all players decide how much effort to invest in self––protection. If the team is victorious, then each member receives some fraction of the reward based on the predetermined sharing rule. The gain the players are competing over in an environmental conflict include the damages avoided by transporting the pollution to another location. This includes domestic liability policies for industry that lead to distributing waste material in other locales or the actual movement of the polluting industry to another country.

Nash equilibrium. Consider a situation where n risk–neutral players with identical preferences compete with one another to capture a fixed gain G. Let x_i be player i's effort level in units commensurate with the loss and $\beta_i(x_i, ..., x_n)$ the probability that player i will gain G. Then player i's expected profits are

$$Max \; \pi_i^n = \beta_i(x_i, ..., x_n) \; G - x_i.$$

For analytical tractability, we assume the simplest logit form for the probability that player i will gain:

$$\beta_i(x_i, ..., x_n) = \frac{x_i}{S}, \tag{14}$$

where $\quad S = \sum\limits_{j=1}^{n} x_j.$

Given the other players' effort levels, the best response of player i is obtained from the first-order condition for maximizing the expected profits π_i^n. (Note π_i^n is convex in x_i, thereby satisfying the second order condition.) The reaction function for player i is then

$$R(X_{-i}) = \begin{cases} \sqrt{GX_{-i}} - X_{-i} & \text{for } X_{-i} \leq G, \\ 0 & \text{for } X_{-i} \geq G, \end{cases} \tag{15}$$

where $\quad X_{-i} = \sum\limits_{j \neq i}^{n} x_j.$

The Nash equilibrium is an n-tuple vector of effort levels which satisfies all players' reaction functions. Geometrically, it is the intersection of all the reaction functions. It is straightforward to obtain Lemma 1.

Lemma 1 *At the symmetric Nash equilibrium, each player's self-protection effort level is the same and is given by: $x^n = (n - 1)G/n^2$. Each player's expected profit at the Nash equilibrium is then $\pi^n = G/n^2$.*

Lemma 1 is the comparative benchmark that will be used to demonstrate the impact strategic team formation has on efficiency.

Strategic Team Formation. Consider a situation where m players $(1 < m < n)$ form a team where m is predetermined and $n \geq 3$. Assume it is costless to organize the team and that no member will breach the team agreement. We can treat the team as a single player competing to capture the gain against the rest of $(n - m)$ players. We, however, assume that the players in the team compete to take a larger share of the gain within the team. Let y_i be team-member i's effort level. If the team wins, team-member i's fractional share, σ_i, is given by

$$\sigma_i = \delta \frac{y_i}{Y} + (1 - \delta) \frac{1}{m}, \tag{16}$$

where $Y = \sum\limits_{j=1}^{m} y_j$ and δ represents the weight given to the effort-dependent sharing rule relative to the effort–independent sharing rule. The sharing rule might involve access conditions to a natural system such as a fishery that is threatened by a contagious disease. An effort–dependent rule would have each fisherman's future access vary with his contribution to the team's disease fighting effort, while an effort–independent rule can allow him to free–ride. A larger value of δ implies more emphasis is placed on effort–dependent competition.

We now examine strategic incentives for the m players to form a team using a two–stage game. In the first stage, the m players make strategic decisions about their sharing rule δ. In the second stage, after knowing the size of the team and its sharing rule, all players in the contest expend their effort levels simultaneously and independently. We consider a subgame perfect equilibrium of the game.

To solve for a subgame perfect equilibrium, we work backwards. Let x_j be the nonmember j's effort level and let H denote the total effort level expended: $H = x_1 + \ldots + x_{n-m} + Y$. The probability that the team will win is assumed to be Y/H – the ratio of the team's total effort level to the total effort level. Then the team member i's expected profit is given by

$$Max\ \pi_i^t = \sigma_i G(Y/H) - Y_i, \tag{17a}$$

and the nonmember j's expected profit is given by

$$Max\ \pi_j = G(x_j/H) - x_j. \tag{17b}$$

In the second stage, given a value of δ, each player seeks to maximize his own expected profits. The first–order condition for maximizing π_i^t is

$$\sigma_i GY(H - Y) + \sigma GH(y_1 + \ldots + y_{i-1} + y_{i+1} + \ldots + y_m) = YH^2, \tag{18a}$$

and that for maximizing π_j yields

$$G(H - x_j) = H^2. \tag{18b}$$

(The second–order conditions are satisfied in both cases.) By symmetry, we have $y_1 = \ldots = y_m = y$ and $x_1 = \ldots = x_{n-m} = x$, which imply $\sigma_1 = \ldots = \sigma_m = 1/m$ and $H = (n - m)x + my$. Then (18a) and (18b) reduce to (19a) and (19b):

$$G(n - m)x + \delta G(m - 1)\{(n - m)x + my\} = m\{(n - m)x + my\}^2 \qquad (19a)$$

and

$$G\{(n - m - 1)x + my\} = \{(n - m)x + my\}^2. \qquad (19b)$$

From (19a) and (19b), at the Nash equilibrium of the subgame which starts at the point where the values of m and δ become common knowledge, each team member's effort level $y(\delta)$ is given by

$$y(\delta) = \frac{G[m^2 - mn + n + (m - 1)(n - m)\delta] [n - m + (m - 1)\delta]}{mn^2}. \qquad (20a)$$

The corresponding effort level $x(\delta)$ of a player outside the team is given by

$$x(\delta) = \frac{G(n-m-1) - 2m(n-m)y(\delta) + \sqrt{G^2(n-m-1)^2 + 4Gm(n-m)y(\delta)}}{2(n - m)^2}. \qquad (20b)$$

The expected profit of a team member is then

$$\pi^t(\delta) = G\left[\frac{y(\delta)}{(n - m)x(\delta) + my(\delta)}\right] - y(\delta), \qquad (21a)$$

and that of a nonmember is

$$\pi(\delta) = G\left[\frac{x(\delta)}{(n - m)x(\delta) + my(\delta)}\right] - x(\delta). \qquad (21b)$$

Now in the first stage the team members determine the optimal sharing rule, δ^*, which maximizes their expected profits $\pi^t(\delta)$. Since they have perfect foresight about $\pi^t(\delta)$, they solve $\delta^* \in \text{argmax } \pi^t(\delta)$. The optimal sharing rule is characterized by Lemma 2.

Lemma 2. *At the subgame perfect equilibrium of the game, the value of δ which maximizes each team member's expected profits is given by:*

$$\delta_+^* = \frac{2mn - 2m^2 - n}{2(m - 1)(n - m)} \quad \text{or} \quad \delta_-^* = \frac{4mn - 2m^2 - 2n^2 - n}{2(m - 1)(m - n)}.$$

The value of δ_+^* is always positive under our assumption of $n \geq 3$. The value of δ_-^* is always negative. Since our results are unaffected by the choice between δ_+^* and δ_-^*, we henceforth use δ_+^* as an optimal value of δ. For notational convenience, let $\delta^* = \delta_+^*$. Note that δ^* is decreasing in m. As the team size increases, more weight is put on the effort–independent rule. This result is surprising because, as the team size increases, the optimal sharing rule decreases intra–team competition and thus increases the free rider problem within the team.

From (21a), (21b) and Lemma 2, we have equilibrium effort levels and equilibrium expected profits of the players.

Team Member	Nonmember

$$y(\delta^*) = \frac{G(2n - 2m - 1)}{4m(n - m)} \qquad\qquad x(\delta^*) = \frac{G(2n - 2m - 1)}{4(n - m)^2} \qquad (22a)$$

$$\pi^t(\delta^*) = G\left[\frac{1}{4m(n - m)}\right] \qquad\qquad \pi(\delta^*) = G\left[\frac{1}{4(n - m)^2}\right] \qquad (22b)$$

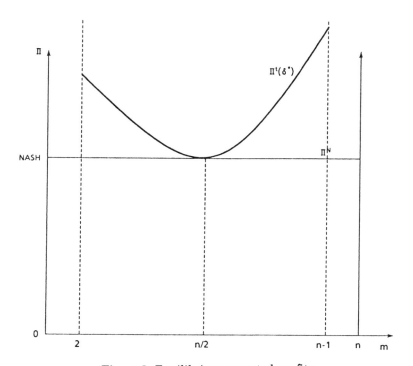

Figure 2: Equilibrium expected profits

As Figure 2 illustrates, each team member's equilibrium expected profit $\pi^t(\delta^*)$ is decreasing in m until $m = n/2$, minimized at $m = n/2$, and then increasing in m. It is maximized at $m = n - 1$.

We know from Lemma 1 that each player's equilibrium expected cost when all the players compete separately is $\pi^n = G/n^2$. We are now prepared to deduce Proposition 5 on the profitability of strategic team formation, which is also illustrated in Figure 2.

Proposition 5: *At the equilibrium, (a) if $m \neq n/2$, then each team–member's expected profit is more than the equilibrium expected profit when all the players play separately $\pi^t(\delta^*) > \pi^n$, and (b) if $m = n/2$, then $\pi^t(\delta^*) = \pi^n$.*

If the number of players in the contest is even, then forming a team strategically is always profitable except for the case where team size exactly equals half of the total number of players. If the number of players is odd, a strategic team formation of any size is beneficial to the team members. Each team member's expected profit is higher than the profit without the team. The optimal sharing rule sets intra–team competition that is actually beneficial to members. The intra–team competition between members leads to a higher probability to capture the gain when coupled with the sharing rule which provides incentive to increase self–protection effort. As Figure 2 shows, the team members can maximize their expected profits by forming a team which consists of $n - 1$ players. Notice, however, that a team of size two (the case where $m = 2$) might be most beneficial to the team members if it is costlier to organize a team of larger size, implying the possibility of multiple teams.

The above result suggests that team formation is a viable form of strategic commitment in a contest with many players. Noncooperative players have incentives to form a team in order to increase the likelihood of winning some share of the fixed reward.

Exclusive Team and Free Riding. We have seen the contenders in the contest have strategic incentives to form a team (except for the case of $m = n/2$). Another interesting question is whether or not, given a team of size m, the team members are eager to induct outsiders. A parallel question is whether or not the outsiders have incentive to join the team.

Based on (22), Figure 3 illustrates the equilibrium expected payoffs of team members and nonmembers. Lemma 3 summarizes our observations.

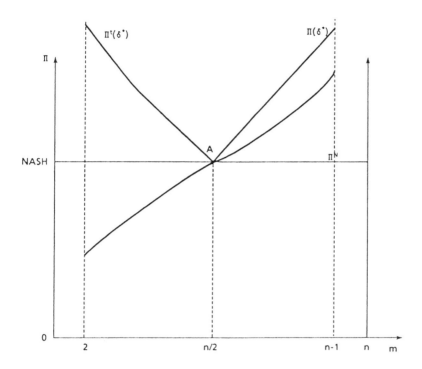

Figure 3: Equilibrium expected profits of team members $\pi(\delta^*)$ and Nonmembers $\pi(\delta^*)$

Lemma 3. *If $m < n/2$, then $\pi(\delta^*) < \pi^n < \pi^t(\delta^*)$. If $m = n/2$, then $\pi(\delta^*) = \pi^n = \pi^t(\delta^*)$. If $m > n/2$, then $\pi^n < \pi^t(\delta^*) < \pi(\delta^*)$.*

If the team size is less than half the number of all the players, each nonmember's equilibrium expected profit is less than that in the absence of the team. However, if the team size is greater than half the number of players, each nonmember's expected profit is higher than even that of a team member. Hence, to the left of point A in Figure 3, allowing a new member decreases each team member's equilibrium expected profits. If free entry is possible, then the outsiders will join until the equilibrium expected payoff of a team member is less than that of an outsider. Team formation with free entry has no effect on effort or profit levels. This is a key result suggesting that teams with free entry and exit do not reduce the inefficiencies of noncooperative behavior. In this case, the inefficiency associated with the team effort simply equals the Nash result in Proposition 1. A treaty might not mitigate the undesirable economic consequences of an environmental conflict. Therefore, it is in the team members' interests to exclude a new member. To the right of point A, the entrance of a new member increases each team member's equilibrium expected profits. However, each outsider is better off waiting for his rivals to join since $\pi(\delta^*) > \pi^t(\delta^*)$ for $m > n/2$. There is a free rider problem. Proposition 6 summarizes our arguments.

Proposition 6: *If $m < n/2$, then the team members try to block entry of a new member, while an outsider is eager to enter. If $m \geq n/2$, then an outsider has an incentive to wait for his rivals to join the team, while the team members are eager to induct outsiders.*

Proposition 6 provides insight into the willingness of a player to participate in an association or to sign a contract or treaty. Initially, it is in the player's best interest to sign an agreement specifying the sharing rule between the players. However, once a larger portion of players join the team, the outsider would not be willing to sign up, given that his expected benefit is higher as a nonsignee. The 1987 Montreal protocol on substances that deplete the ozone layer is a case in point. There are private gains that can be captured by using less expensive ozone depleting substances. As more countries agree to sign the treaty, nonsignees find it profitable not to sign since they can use these lower cost substances, be more competitive in the market, and free ride on the environmental benefits of others' costly efforts to protect the ozone layer. Unless a treaty can be perfectly enforced, there will always be a tendency for some countries to hold out.

Team Formation and Efficiency. Proposition 1 focused our attention on the efficiency consequences of an environmental contest. Valuable resources expended on noncooperative self–protection activities generate inefficiencies. Therefore, a key question is whether strategic team formation will create more or less inefficiency than in the basic model with nonstrategic Nash behavior. By using Lemma 1 and expressions (22a), the impacts of a strategic team formation on the individual and the total equilibrium effort levels are presented by Proposition 7. Notice that the total equilibrium effort level is the value of $(n - m)x(\delta^*) + my(\delta^*)$.

Proposition 7: *If $m < n/2$, then $x(\delta^*) < x^n < y(\delta^*)$, and the total equilibrium effort level with strategic team formation is higher than without the team. If $m = n/2$, then $x(\delta^*) = x^n = y(\delta^*)$, and the total equilibrium effort level with the team equals that without the team. If $m > n/2$, then $y(\delta^*) < x^n < x(\delta^*)$, and the total equilibrium effort level with the team is less than that without the team.*

Figure 4 illustrates the individual equilibrium effort levels. Each nonmember's equilibrium effort level is increasing in m, while that of each team member is decreasing in m. The later fact confirms the simple intuition that teams with more members would suffer more from the free rider problem. As the team size increases, δ^* puts more weight on the effort–independent sharing rule and thus decreases intra–team competition. Hence, the free rider problem within the team increases more rapidly. Figure 5 illustrates the effects of strategic team formation on total equilibrium effort levels. Total equilibrium effort level is decreasing in m, which is explained by the free rider problem within the team. If the team size is greater than half of the number of the contestants, rent dissipation will be lowered by the team formation.

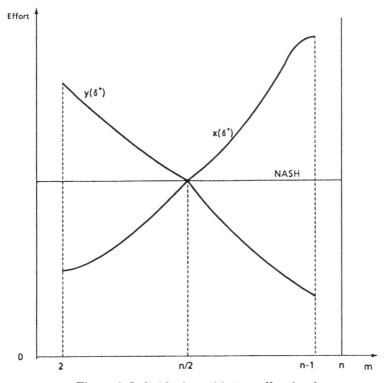

Figure 4: Individual equilibrium effort levels

5. Conclusion

Strategic behavior is a key element in any environmental conflict. We have explored two tactics of strategic commitment relative to the cooperative and noncooperative outcomes. First, we considered endogenous strategic timing. We demonstrated that in conflicts between two unevenly matched players, it is in both the favorite's and underdog's interest for the underdog to make a strategic commitment of effort. This implies that social costs of conflict between uneven players will be lower than under Nash behavior. The players will approach the cooperative outcome, thus reducing the extent of inefficient protection induced by noncooperative behavior.

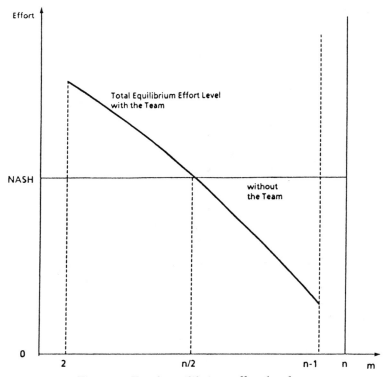

Figure 5: Total equilibrium effort levels

Second, our analysis of strategic team formation suggests that designing an optimal sharing rule among team members will lead to intra-team competition which is actually beneficial. Relative to Nash behavior, it is generally efficient to form a team. When the team size exceeds 50 percent of the contenders, it is in the team members' interest to make the team larger. Note, however, that it is more beneficial to the individual to be a nonmember and free rider. If the team size is less then 50 percent of the players, then a marginal addition to the team is not preferred by the team members. Exclusive membership guarantees higher profits for the team members.

Strategic team formation can lead to greater inefficiency, however. If the team size is less than 50 percent of the players, then the total self–protection effort level exceeds that without the team. In contrast, when the team size exceeds 50 percent of the contenders, effort levels are lower than that without the team, thus lowering the social costs associated with environmental conflicts.

Regulators interested in minimizing the inefficiencies (e.g., social welfare loss) associated with environmental conflicts could enact and enforce rules that allow free entry into the team. Rules that inhibit entry should be eliminated and new rules which encourage membership should be considered. If the regulator is self–interested, however, and attempts to obtain rents from the team members, then it is more profitable to the regulator to enact rules which inhibit free entry. Regulators who seek rents by setting rules would want to encourage exclusive team membership, thereby acquiring more personal wealth. The regulator could set up a smoke screen with an argument that by not allowing exclusive teams to expand it prohibits collusion thereby increasing social welfare. Meanwhile, the regulator is acquiring a larger level of rent.

Note we assume the sharing rule is endogenously determined by team members. The regulator, however, could use the sharing rule as a policy device to control the level of effort expended in the contest. If the regulator wanted to reduce social costs then it is optimal to restrict the sharing rule to be effort–independent $(\delta = 0)$. If the regulator wanted to generate more activity, then he should set the rule such that there is more emphasis on effort $(\delta \geq 1)$. By exogenously restricting the sharing rule, the regulator could influence the strategic behavior of team members, either in the public interest or for personal gain. To be confident, the regulator's behavior must be explicitly entered into the model. We leave this for future research.

Finally, we have not considered the situation where the outsiders form another team. In this case, we must extend our two–stage model. In the first stage, the players form two teams and set their sharing rules simultaneously and independently. In the second stage, all players expend their effort levels noncooperatively.

References

Adams, R., and Crocker, T., 1989, "The agricultural economics of environmental change: Some lessons from air pollution." *Journal of Environmental Management 28*, 295–307

Baik, K., and Shogren, J., 1992, "On strategic behavior in contests", *American Economic Review* (forthcoming)

Bird, J., 1987, "The transferability and depletability of externalities", *Journal of Environmental Economics and Management 14*, 54–57

Bohm, F., 1990, *"Efficiency aspects of imperfect treaties on global public bads: Lessons from the Montreal Protocol"*, World Bank Environmental Department Working Paper

Braden, J., and Bromley, D., 1981, "The Economics of cooperation and collective bads", *Journal of Environmental Economics and Management 8*, 134–150

Brouwer, F., and Nijkamp, P., 1990, "Modelling interactions between economic development and environmental change: A policy life–cycle interpretation", *Environment and Planning C: Government and Policy 8*, 167–178

Cournot, A., 1838, *"Researches into the Mathematical Principles of the Theory of Wealth"*, Translated by N. Bacon, New York: A. M. Kelly

Davis, O., and Whinston, A., 1962, "Externalities, welfare, and the theory of games", *Journal of Political Economy 70*, 241–262

Dixit, A. 1987, "Strategic behavior in contests", *American Economic Review 77*, 891–898

Ehrlich, I., and Becker, G., 1972, "Market insurance, self–insurance, and self–protection", *Journal of Political Economy 80*, 623–648

Forster, B., 1989, "The acid rain games: Incentives to exaggerate control costs and economic disruption", *Journal of Environmental Management 28*, 349–360

Forster, B., 1991, *"The Acid Rain Debate: Science and Special Interests in Policy Formation"*, Ames: Iowa State University Press, (in press)

Hirshleifer, J., 1988, "The analytics of continuing conflict", *Synthese 76*, 201–233

Hoel, M., 1991, "Global environmental problems: the effects of unilateral actions taken by one country", *Journal of Environmental Economics and Management 20*, 55–70

Kneese, A., Ayres, R., and d'Arge, R., 1970, *"Economics and the Environment: A Material Balance Approach"*, Washington, D.C.: Resources for the Future

Marschak, J., and Radner, R., 1972, *"Economic Theory of Teams"*, New Haven: Yale University Press

Rosen, S., 1986, "Prizes and incentives in elimination tournaments", *American Economic Review 76*, 701–715

Sandler, T., and Lapan, H., 1988, "The calculus of dissent: An analysis of terrorists' choice of targets", *Synthese 76*, 245–261

Shogren, J., and Crocker, T., 1991, "Cooperative and noncooperative protection from transferable and filterable externalities", *Environmental and Resource Economics 1*, 195–214

Sterner, T., 1990, "An international tax on pollution and natural resource deletion", *Energy Policy 18*, 300–302

Tullock, G., 1980, "Efficient rent seeking" in: *Toward a Theory of the Rent Seeking Society*, ed. J. M. Buchanan, R. D. Tollison, and G. Tullock, College Station: Texas A&M University Press

Comments by Detlev Homann

The study of transferable externalities is an important part of environmental economics because in reality pollution is often transferred from one agent to another agent (for example by building high chimneys for emissions or by transformation of waste gases to solid hazardous waste by means of filters).

In their article "Environmental Conflicts and Strategic Commitment" Shogren, Baik, and Crocker apply game–theoretic methods to analyse negative transferable externalities. This work can be divided into three parts.

In the first part, a general model with two agents is considered in which each agent can make an effort of self–protection against a negative externality. Increasing self–protecting measures of an agent lead to a decreasing probability of being influenced by the externality and to a decreasing size of damage if this agent will suffer from the externality. Such measures of an agent also have the opposite impact on the respective probability and size of damage for the other agent.

In this general framework, the cooperative solution, in which the two agents choose their efforts to minimize their joint expected cost, and the non–cooperative solution are determined. The non–cooperative solution is the Nash–equilibrium of the 2–person –game with complete information in which the agents choose their efforts of self–protection simultaneously. Non–cooperation leads to an inefficient outcome with over–protection.

In the model a cause for the externality is not given. If no agent makes an effort of protection then also each agent faces a certain expected cost because of the externality. This means that only the transfer of the externality is considered. It is reasonable to study the rise of the externality by production or by consumption, a partial abatement and a partial transfer of the externality by the causing agent (or group of agents), and the transfer of the externality among the potential sufferers in one model. Then it may turn out that the causers provide too little effort of reducing the environmental loss and that the potential sufferers provide too much effort of self–protection.

In the second part of the article, a more special model is considered. The size of the actual damage is now identical for all agents and independent of the measures of self––protection. But the probabilities of damage are dependent on these measures. The probabilities are given by different logit–functions for the different agents. According to this difference one agent (the underdog) is more likely to be damaged in the non–cooperative solution than the other agent (the favorite). In the cooperative solution no agent makes any effort of self–protection.

In this special model two leader–follower games are considered in which the leader chooses her effort before the choice of the effort by the follower. Taking her measures of self–protection the follower knows the choice of the leader. For both agents the game in which the underdog is the leader results in a lower expected cost compared with the game in which the favorite is the leader. In a leader–follower game it is important that the prescribed chronological order of the agents' moves can be enforced. Each agent must be sure that the prescribed order is the actual order of moves during the play. This means that the order is determined by technical conditions which cannot be changed by the agents or that a court must be able to enforce the chronological order in which the efforts of self–protection are chosen by the agents. The rules of a game which also include the order of moves describe the circumstances which determine the strategy sets of the players and the outcomes. If the players can simply change the rules then they are in another game in which the strategy sets contain the change of the mentioned rules.

The same consideration holds for another game which is described in the article. According to this game in the first stage each agent announces whether she will make her effort in the second or third stage. Therefore these simultaneous announcements determine whether after the first stage the agents will play a game with simultaneous choices of efforts or a leader–follower game with the underdog as leader or a leader–follower game with the favorite as leader. The analysis of the subgame–perfect equilibria of this game yields that after backward induction in the first stage it is a dominating strategy for the underdog to announce that he will choose his effort in the following stage independently of the announcement of the favorite. This is a nice result. But it must be presumed that after the first stage a court can enforce the game determined by the announcements in the first stage. The possibility to choose the order of the following moves in the first stage shows that the order is not determined by technical conditions. A court can enforce a certain order only if it can observe the efforts of self–protection. Therefore it must be publically observable at which date an agent makes an effort. This is an important restriction because often measures of self–protection are private actions which can only be identified by using special information. If this restriction can be made then it may often be the case that not only the order of making efforts but also a special choice of efforts – for example the cooperative solution – can be enforced by a court.

In the third part of the article a model which is different from the other models is analysed. There are n identical agents who simultaneously make efforts of self–protection. Depending on these efforts one agent can get a gain and for the other agents neither a gain nor a loss (apart from the provided efforts) results. The potential gain and the probability of gaining which is given by a logit function are the same for each agent. This is a very special model of a transferable externality. It can be interpreted as follows: Before the efforts all agents are influenced by a negative transferable externality. But because of the efforts one agent can transfer the externality to someone who is outside of the group of n agents. The other agents are not influenced by this transfer. They only provided their efforts without success.

In this framework it is assumed that a subset of the set of all n agents can form a team. If one team member gets the gain then it is divided among the team members according to a sharing rule which also may depend on the efforts of the members. In the considered game each team member announces a sharing rule in the first stage and in the second stage all agents make their efforts of self–protection. If the team members agree on a sharing rule in the first stage then this rule determines the sharing of the potential gain inside of the team. Non–members are single players (single "teams") who do not share their gain in the case of success.

For a given size of the team one subgame–perfect equilibrium of this game is determined. The calculation of this equilibrium shows that before the play it is commonly known which agent is a team member and which agent is a non–member. The team must be prescribed before the game is played. The team is actually formed if each team member announces the same sharing rule. In the case that different rules are announced by the members the team is not actually formed. Therefore, what is studied in this game is not so much strategic team formation but rather strategic confirmation of a prescribed team formation. In the article only one equilibrium is considered. There exist other subgame—perfect equilibria. In an equilibrium the sharing rule need not be chosen in such a way that the expected cost of a team member is minimized. A common announcement of a sharing rule by the team members yields a subgame—perfect equilibrium as long as a team member has a cost which is at least as low as the cost in the non—cooperative solution. This holds because only the agents can be players. The team as an entity cannot be a player in a game in which the agents are players in the second stage.

For describing non—cooperative strategic team formation in a model one may think of a game in which the announcements of sharing rules by all players determine a team according to the rule that players who announce the same rule are in the same team. The team is not given exogenously but each strategy tuple determines at least one team. The game may have many subgame—perfect equilibria. To analyse these equilibria it is necessary to consider also the formation of several teams at the same time. A player can deviate from an outcome in which he is a member of a team with at least 3 members by announcing the same sharing rule as a non—member. Then a new outcome with at least two teams results.

For applying the results of the analysis to the real world it is important to take into consideration the mentioned limitations of the models and also the special assumptions about the probabilities and sizes of damage resp. gain. It would be very interesting to generalize the models of the first two parts to the case of n agents and to analyse team formation in this framework. In this generalization the externality is transferred to one agent because his efforts of self—protection are not successful whereas the other agents are successful. Furthermore it would be very valuable to consider cooperative team formation in this model by means of an application of the game—theoretic concept of core.

Chapter 5

Alistair Ulph[1]

The Choice of Environmental Policy Instruments and Strategic International Trade

Abstract: In this paper I examine the question of the choice of environmental policy instruments in the context of a model of strategic international trade between countries, and I show that in such a model there is a preference for the use of standards rather than taxes as policy instruments. The paper employs a simple model of two countries who are the sole producers of a commodity sold on the world market. Production uses an input which is directly related to the emission of a pollutant, and each country has a fixed target for the emissions level it wishes to achieve. If trade is modelled as a one—shot Cournot equilibrium, the countries are indifferent about policy choice. If trade is modelled as a Stackelberg equilibrium, then both countries are better off (in terms of producer surplus) if the follower uses standards. Finally, if trade is modelled as a two—stage Cournot game in capacity and output then the choice of standards by both countries is a Nash equilibrium, and Pareto dominates the choice of taxes by both countries. These results arise from the superior commitment properties of standards.

1. Introduction

A much discussed paradox in the design of environmental policy for the control of pollution is the contrast between the recommendations of economists for the use of market—based instruments such as emissions taxes and tradeable pollution permits (on the grounds of efficiency), and the preference of policy makers for regulatory instruments such as standards or best—practice—technologies. (See e.g. Pearce and Turner (1990) for a recent debate, and Opschoor and Vos (1989) for a survey of instruments). Many possible explanations have been advanced. (See Hahn (1989) for a useful discussion). One line of argument, based within the welfare maximising framework, is that when there is imperfect information by policy makers about the costs of abatement, then under certain

---

[1] Comments by participants at the conference, and by Larry Karp and Tony Venables are greatfully acknowledged.

assumptions about marginal damage costs, the use of quantity–based instruments may be preferred to the use of price–based instruments (Roberts and Spence, 1976, Kwerel, 1977), but that is unlikely to explain all of the evidence.

A rather different approach has been the political economy approach originating with Buchanan and Tullock (1975), where they argue that the use of standards leaves polluters with higher profits than taxes, so polluters are likely to lobby for the use of such instruments. However this is open to the objection that with an appropriate set of transfers, taxes can yield the same distribution of income as standards, and still have the efficiency advantage (Yohe, 1976); indeed environmental taxes have the advantage of allowing the reduction of distortions from other taxes. (See, e.g. Ingham and Ulph, 1990).

In this paper I shall advance a rather different explanation. I will consider a situation where pollution is caused by an industrial process, and the producers are engaged in international trade. The governments of the countries concerned have set targets they wish to achieve for the pollutant within their own countries. If international trade has no strategic element to it, then I shall show that it does not matter what instruments the governments use to control pollution. But if there is a *strategic* aspect to international trade, i.e. countries can take decisions in one period which influence their market share in a subsequent period, then, *for the same level of pollution*, countries prefer to use standards rather than taxes. The intuition, rather crudely, is that the use of standards permits greater commitment by producers in the strategic trade game, and this allows the producers to earn higher surpluses. This is at the expense of consumers, but provided the consumers in the producing countries are a sufficiently small part of the total world market, the producing countries gain from the use of standards.

The structure of the paper will be as follows. In the next section I set out the basic assumptions of a two–country model of imperfectly competitive international trade in which production involves a pollutant. I then analyse, in Section 3, a non–strategic model of international trade – essentially a one–shot Cournot model – and show that it makes no difference whether governments use taxes or standards to achieve their desired levels of pollution. In Section 4 I introduce the simplest form of strategic interaction, in the form of a Stackelberg model of industry equilibrium; in this case I show that while it does not matter what instruments the leader uses, both countries are better off if the follower uses standards rather than taxes. The following section uses a symmetric move structure, analogous to Brander and Spencer (1983), by assuming that both producers can pre–commit to their use of a non–polluting input. I show that the use of standards

by both countries is a Nash equilibrium in the game of instrument choice by governments, and Pareto dominates the use of taxes by both countries. The model of this section is special in that only two factor inputs are assumed; a more general treatment of
this model can be found in Ulph (1991). In Section 6 I offer some concluding remarks.

2. The model

There are two countries, indexed $i = 1, 2$, who are the sole world suppliers of a good.
While these two countries are the sole suppliers of the good, there are other countries
who are consumers of the good; the producing countries may also be consumers of the
good. The world market for this good is represented by the total revenue functions
$R_i(q_1, q_2)$ for each producer, i, where it is assumed that

$$\frac{\partial^2 R_i}{\partial q_i^2} < 0, \qquad \frac{\partial R_i}{\partial q_j} < 0, \qquad \frac{\partial^2 R_i}{\partial q_i\, \partial q_j} < 0.$$

Since I want to focus on questions of strategic international trade in the choice of environmental policy instruments, I want to ignore the usual efficiency arguments about
taxes and standards. So I shall assume that within each country production is undertaken by a single producer using a constant returns to scale technology (which need not
be the same in each country). I shall assume that technology employs two inputs, one of
which I shall think of as energy, E_i, the other, unspecified, being denoted X_i. The assumption of only two inputs is unimportant for the next two sections, and serves only to
simplify the analysis; in the model in Section 5 it plays a substantive role; a more general treatment of that model is found in Ulph (1991). The technology will be represented
either by the production function, $q_i = f_i (E_i, X_i)$, or by the input requirement function,
$X_i = g_i (q_i, E_i)$ where

$$\frac{\partial g_i}{\partial q_i} > 0, \qquad \frac{\partial g_i}{\partial E_i} < 0, \qquad \frac{\partial^2 g_i}{\partial q_i^2} > 0, \qquad \frac{\partial g_i^2}{\partial E_i^2} > 0, \qquad \frac{\partial g_i^2}{\partial E_i\, \partial q_i} < 0.$$

Associated with the production process is a pollutant whose emission is directly proportional to the use of the energy input by the single producer in each country, and for
which there is no abatement technology (CO_2 is the obvious example). To ensure that
when comparing the effects of different instruments the same level of pollution is being

achieved, I assume that each country has agreed to limit the emission of the pollutant to a level which implies that the use of energy by its producer of the good could not exceed $\bar{E}_i$. Of course, if the use of different instruments leads to different welfare effects from trade, the countries may wish to choose different levels of emission targets. But to focus on the strategic trade question, I do not explore that question; the analysis presented here can therefore be thought of as an input to a fuller welfare analysis.

The sequence of moves will be that in the first stage the government of each country chooses its environmental policy instrument. Since energy use, E_i, and emissions are directly proportional, it will be convenient to think of policy in terms of controlling E_i, and this can be done either by setting standards (requiring the producer not to use more than $\bar{E}_i$ units of energy) or by taxing the use of energy, which will be done by setting a specific tax on energy. Since the government is assumed to have perfect information about production, it will set the tax rate so that the resulting energy use is $\bar{E}_i$, but the producers take as given the tax rate. In the absence of environmental taxes, the factor prices for energy and the other factor in country i will be P_i and W_i respectively; where it is relevant, the tax rate on energy will be denoted t_i.

In subsequent stages, producers choose their levels of inputs and output. Different models will make different assumptions about the sequence of these decisions. The following sections explore three possible structures of moves by producers.

3. Single stage Cournot model

In this section I shall assume that following the first stage, in which governments set their environmental policy instruments, there is a single second stage in which producers in each country simultaneously select their inputs and outputs.

Consider first the case where at the first stage each government has chosen to set standards. Then at the second stage producer i will take as given q_j, and choose q_i, E_i to maximise

$$\Pi_i(q_i, E_i, q_j) \equiv R_i(q_1, q_2) - W_i\, g_i(E_i, q_i) - P_i\, E_i$$

subject to $E_i \leq \bar{E}_i$. Letting λ_i denote the Lagrange multiplier on the constraint, we have the following first order conditions for producer i :

$$\frac{\partial R_i}{\partial q_i} - W_i \frac{\partial g_i}{q_i} \le 0 \qquad \text{and} \qquad q_i \ge 0, \tag{1}$$

$$- W_i \frac{\partial g_i}{\partial E_i} - P_i - \lambda_i \le 0 \qquad \text{and} \qquad E_i \ge 0, \tag{2}$$

$$\lambda_i(\bar{E}_i - E_i) = 0. \tag{3}$$

I will assume that the constraint binds strictly, so that

$$\lambda_i > 0, \qquad \text{and} \qquad E_i = \bar{E}_i$$

If at the first stage, country i had chosen instead to impose a tax t_i on energy use, then producer i would have chosen q_i and E_i (given q_j) to maximise

$$\bar{\Pi}_i(q_i, E_i, q_j) \equiv R_i(q_1, q_2) - W_i \, g_i(E_i, q_i) - (P_i + t_i) \, E_i$$

leading to first order conditions

$$\frac{\partial R_i}{\partial q_i} - W_i \frac{\partial g_i}{\partial q_i} \le 0 \qquad \text{and} \qquad q_i \ge 0, \tag{4}$$

$$- W_i \frac{\partial g_i}{\partial E_i} - P_i - t_i \le 0 \qquad \text{and} \qquad E_i \ge 0. \tag{5}$$

Since country i must ensure that $E_i = \bar{E}_i$, obviously it would set $t_i = \lambda_i$.

This establishes that the resulting Cournot equilibrium is the same whether either country uses taxes or standards. I shall assume that any taxes raised on the producer can be redistributed in a lump sum fashion, so the government is concerned only with the total producer surplus that can be earned by the industry (profit plus tax revenue). That is clearly the same in both cases, and consumer welfare will also be the same. This establishes:

Proposition 1: *If international trade is modelled as a one-shot Cournot equilibrium, then both countries are indifferent between using standards or taxes to implement their environmental policy.*

Alistair Ulph

The intuition behind this proposition is straightforward. In a one–stage Cournot model, where country i takes q_j as given, there is no strategic interaction. The choice of environmental policy instrument is then purely of domestic concern, and under the simplifying assumption of perfect information made in this model, quantity controls and price controls are equivalent.

For future reference, if a country is using standards then condition (1), holding with equality and with $E_i = \bar{E}_i$, implicitly defines producer i's *standards–based reaction function*. The slope of this reaction function is given by:

$$\frac{dq_i}{dq_j} = -\frac{\dfrac{\partial^2 R_i}{\partial q_i\, \partial q_j}}{\dfrac{\partial^2 R_i}{\partial q_i{}^2} - W_i \dfrac{\partial^2 g_i}{\partial q_i{}^2}}. \tag{6}$$

Given our assumptions, the numerator and denominator are both negative, so the standards–based reaction function is downward sloping.

If a country uses taxes, (4) and (5), holding with equality, define implicitly its *tax-based reaction* function. Its slope is given by :

$$\frac{dq_i}{dq_j} = -\frac{\dfrac{\partial^2 R_i}{\partial q_i \partial q_j}}{\dfrac{\partial^2 R_i}{\partial q_i{}^2} - W_i \dfrac{\partial^2 g_i}{\partial q_i{}^2} - Z_i{}^2 \dfrac{\partial^2 g_i}{\partial E_i{}^2}}, \tag{7}$$

where
$$Z_i = \frac{\dfrac{\partial^2 g_i}{\partial q_i\, \partial E_i}}{\dfrac{\partial g_i{}^2}{\partial E_i{}^2}}.$$

The last term in the denominator of (7) is positive, but the numerator and overall denominator are negative. Comparing (6) and (7), it can be seen that if we compare a tax–based reaction function to a standards–based reaction function at their point of intersection, the tax–based reaction function will be steeper than the standards–based reaction function (Fig. 3.1). In other words, the standards–based reaction function is more accommodating in the sense that for any given reduction in output by firm j, firm i

will expand its output less under standards than under taxes.

The rest of the paper will consider models where there is a strategic element to international trade.

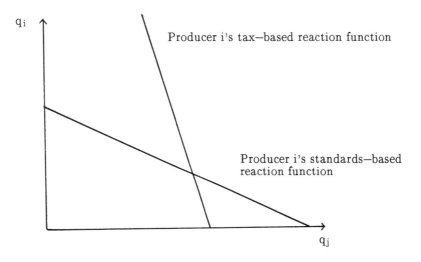

q_i

Producer i's tax–based reaction function

Producer i's standards–based
reaction function

q_j

Figure 3.1: Standards–based and tax–based reaction functions

4.Two stage Stackelberg model

As the simplest possible way of introducing a strategic element to the modelling of international trade, I assume that, following the first stage in which governments simultaneously choose policy instruments, there are two further stages. In the first of these two stages, country 1 selects its inputs and outputs, while in the second, country 2 selects its inputs and outputs. In other words, country 1 acts as a Stackelberg leader and 2 as a Stackelberg follower.

Suppose first that both countries have chosen to use standards to implement their environmental policies. Country 2's reaction function is therefore the standards–based reaction function given implicitly by (1), so the problem facing country 1, can be characterised as choosing q_1, E_1, q_2, to maximise

$$R_1(q_1, q_2) - W_1 g_1(E_1, q_1) - P_1 E_1$$

subject to $E_1 \le \bar{E}_1$ and $\dfrac{\partial R_2(q_1,q_2)}{\partial q_2} - W_2 \dfrac{\partial g_2(E_2,q_2)}{\partial q_2} = 0.$

Letting λ_1, μ_1, be the Lagrange multipliers corresponding to the two constraints we derive the following first order conditions:

$$\frac{\partial R_1}{\partial q_1} - W_1 \frac{\partial g_1}{\partial q_1} - \mu_1 \frac{\partial^2 R_2}{\partial q_1\, \partial q_2} \le 0 \qquad \text{and} \quad q_1 \ge 0, \tag{8}$$

$$- W_1 \frac{\partial g_1}{\partial E_1} - P_1 - \lambda_1 \le 0 \qquad \text{and} \quad E_1 \ge 0, \tag{9}$$

$$\frac{\partial R_1}{\partial q_2} + \mu_1 \left[W_2 \frac{\partial^2 g_2}{\partial q_2^2} - \frac{\partial^2 R_2}{\partial q_2^2} \right] \le 0 \qquad \text{and} \quad q_2 \ge 0, \tag{10}$$

$$\lambda_1 \left[\bar{E}_1 - E_1 \right] = 0. \tag{11}$$

Assuming an interior solution, we can eliminate μ_1 from (8) and (10) to obtain the condition:

$$-\frac{\dfrac{\partial R_1}{\partial q_1} - W_1 \dfrac{\partial g_1}{\partial q_1}}{\dfrac{\partial R1}{\partial q_2}} = -\frac{\dfrac{\partial^2 R_2}{\partial q_1\, \partial q_2}}{\dfrac{\partial^2 R_2}{\partial q_2^2} - W_2 \dfrac{\partial^2 g_2}{\partial q_2^2}}. \tag{12}$$

This is just the familiar condition that the slope of country 1's iso–profit curve should be a tangent to country 2's standards–based reaction function. Note also that from condition (9), if country 1 had instead chosen to use a tax policy, and set $t_1 = \lambda_1$, the outcome would be exactly the same.

Now assume that country 2 uses tax policy, but country 1 continues to use standards. Then country 2's output decisions will be given by its tax–based reaction function, and the problem of country 1 can then be characterised as choosing q_1, E_1, q_2, E_2 to maximise

$$R_1(q_1,\, q_2) - W_1 g_1(E_1,\, q_1) - P_1 E_1$$

subject to $E_1 \leq \bar{E}_1, \quad \dfrac{\partial R_2}{\partial q_2} - W_2 \dfrac{\partial g_2}{\partial q_2}(E_2, q_2) = 0, \quad$ and $\quad W_2 \dfrac{\partial g_2}{\partial E_2} = P_2 + t_2.$

Letting λ_1, μ_1, ν_1 denote the corresponding Lagrange multipliers the first order conditions are

$$\frac{\partial R_1}{\partial q_1} - W_1 \frac{\partial g_1}{\partial q_1} - \mu_1 \frac{\partial^2 R_2}{\partial q_1 \, \partial q_2} \leq 0 \qquad\qquad \text{and} \qquad\qquad q_1 \geq 0, \qquad (13)$$

$$- W_1 \frac{\partial g_1}{\partial E} - P_1 - \lambda_1 \leq 0 \qquad\qquad \text{and} \qquad\qquad E_1 \geq 0, \qquad (14)$$

$$\frac{\partial R_1}{\partial q_2} + \mu_1 \left[W_2 \frac{\partial^2 g_2}{\partial q_2{}^2} - \frac{\partial^2 R_2}{\partial q_2{}^2} \right] + \nu_1 W_2 \frac{\partial^2 g_2}{\partial E_2 \partial q_2} \leq 0 \quad \text{and} \quad q_2 \geq 0, \qquad (15)$$

$$\mu_1 W_2 \frac{\partial^2 g_2}{\partial E_2 \partial q_2} + \nu_1 W_2 \frac{\partial^2 g_2}{\partial E_2{}^2} \leq 0 \qquad\qquad \text{and} \qquad\qquad E_2 \geq 0 \qquad (16)$$

Assuming an interior solution, elimination of μ_1 and ν_1 from (13), (15), and (16) yields the condition

$$-\frac{\dfrac{\partial R_1}{\partial q_1} - W_1 \dfrac{\partial g_1}{\partial q_1}}{\dfrac{\partial R_1}{\partial q_2}} = -\frac{\dfrac{\partial^2 R_2}{\partial q_1 \partial q_2}}{\dfrac{\partial^2 R_2}{\partial q_2{}^2} - W_2 \dfrac{\partial^2 g_2}{\partial q_2{}^2} + Z_2{}^2 \dfrac{\partial^2 g_2}{\partial E_2{}^2}}, \qquad (17)$$

where Z_2 was defined in Section 3.

This is just the condition that country 1's iso–profit curve be a tangent to country 2's tax–based reaction function. Again we can see from condition (14) that if country 1 had chosen to use a tax policy rather than standards policy, and had set $t_1 = \lambda_1$ then the outcome would have been unaffected.

The comparison between the case where country 1 uses standards and taxes is shown in Fig. 4.1. Point A corresponds to the case where country 2 uses standards, point B where it uses taxes. Note that in the case where country 2 uses taxes, the tax rate will need to be chosen so that, given that the producer in country 1 produces the output

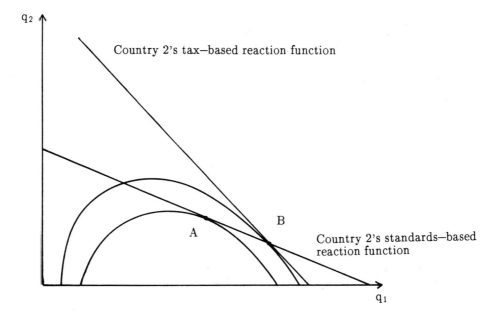

Figure 4.1: Stackelberg leadership against standards and taxes

Figure 4.1: Stackelberg leadership against standards and taxes

level corresponding to point B, the producer in country 2 uses precisely $\bar{E}_2$ units of energy. By the equivalence result of Section 3 this means that the output chosen by the producer in country 2 is at the point of intersection between the particular tax–based reaction function and its standards–based reaction function, as indicated by point B in Fig. 4.1.

If we now turn to stage 1 and consider the choice of instruments we have already shown that whatever instrument country 2 chooses, country 1 is indifferent between using standards and taxes. When country 2 uses standards we see that *both* countries will earn a higher producer surplus from the industry than when country 2 uses taxes. This follows from Fig. 2, where point A is the point on country 2's standards–based reaction function which maximises country 1's producer surplus, and point A involves more output, and hence producer surplus, for country 2 than point B.

Thus, in terms of producer surplus, both countries would prefer country 2 to use standards rather than taxes. However, under rather mild assumptions, the absolute slope of country 2's standards–based reaction function will be less than 1. So at point A the increase in country 2's output relative to point B is more than offset by the reduction in country 1's output, so overall industry output must be lower when country 2 uses standards. That will have welfare consequences for consumers in both countries (if there are any), and if both goods are close enough substitutes, consumers will be worse off. However, provided both polluting countries represent a sufficiently small part of the world market in terms of consumption (of course they account for the total world production of the good), the loss of consumer surplus will be outweighed by the gain in producer surplus. I can summarise the results of this section in the following:

Proposition 2: *If both producing countries have sufficiently small shares of the world market in terms of consumption, and international trade is modelled as a Stackelberg equilibrium, then both countries will be better off if the Stackelberg follower uses standards rather than taxes to control pollution. It does not matter what instruments the Stackelberg leader uses.*

5. Two stage Cournot model

I now consider a model in which there is a strategic aspect to international trade, but there is not the asymmetry in move structures between countries that were present in the previous section. As in the previous section, following the first stage in which the countries choose their environmental policy there are two further stages. In the first of these the producers will choose simultaneously their level of the factor X (think of this as capital), whilst in the second they choose simultaneously the amount of output they wish to produce, and hence the amount of energy they need to use. This model is analogous to that in Brander and Spencer (1983) and Spencer and Brander (1983). As indicated earlier, the assumption of only two factors is now more than just a simplifying assumption, and a more general treatment of the model in this section can be found in Ulph (1991).

As before I shall work backwards through the stages. In the final stage, if country i has chosen to use standards, then producer i chooses E_i to maximise

$$\Pi_i = R_i\Big[f_1(E_1, X_1), f_2(E_2, X_2)\Big] - P_i E_i$$

subject to $E_i \le \bar{E}_i$. Since I shall be interested in the case where the energy constraint strictly binds, so there is effectively no choice, the producer simply sets $E_i = \bar{E}_i$. If country i has chosen tax rate t_i as its instrument, then producer i chooses E_i to maximise:

$$\hat{\Pi}_i = R_i \Big[f_1(E_1, X_1), f_2(E_2, X_2) \Big] - (P_i + t_i) E_i$$

leading to first order condition

$$\frac{\partial R_i}{\partial q_i} \frac{\partial q_i}{\partial E_i} - (P_i + t_i) \leq 0 \qquad\qquad \text{with} \qquad\qquad E_i \geq 0. \qquad (18)$$

The analysis of this final stage allows us to calculate the equilibrium values of E_i as functions of X_1 and X_2, say, $E_i(X_1, X_2)$ where, in the case of standards, these take the degenerate form: $E_i(X_1, X_2) = \bar{E}_i$.

Turning to the middle stage, in which producers select their inputs X_i $(i = 1, 2)$, producer i can be thought of as choosing X_i to maximise

$$V_i(X_1, X_2) \equiv R_i \Big[f_1[E_1(X_1, X_2), X_1], f_2 [E_2(X_1, X_2), X_2] \Big]$$
$$- (P_i + t_i) E_i(X_1, X_2) - W_i X_i \qquad (19)$$

With standards , $t_i = 0$, and $E_i = \bar{E}_i$. The first order condition is

$$\frac{\delta V_i}{\delta X_i} = \frac{\partial R_i}{\partial q_i} \frac{\partial q_i}{\partial X_i} + \frac{\partial R_i}{\partial q_1} \frac{\partial q_1}{\partial E_1} \frac{\partial E_1}{\partial X_i} + \frac{\partial R_i}{\partial q_2} \frac{\partial q_2}{\partial E_2} \frac{\partial E_2}{\partial X_i}$$

$$- (P_i + t_i) \frac{\partial E_i}{\partial X_i} - W_i \geq 0 \qquad\qquad \text{with} \qquad\qquad X_i \geq 0. \qquad (20)$$

It is now necessary to consider three cases.

Case A: Both countries use standards. In this case, $\partial E_i / \partial X_j = 0$ for $i, j = 1, 2$, so, from (20), the condition for the choice of X_i is governed by:

$$\frac{\partial R_i}{\partial q_i} \frac{\partial q_i}{\partial X_i} - W_i \leq 0 \qquad\qquad \text{with} \quad X_i \geq 0, \qquad (21)$$

i.e. X_i will be chosen efficiently. Note that (21) is the same as condition (1) for the one--shot Cournot model where both countries use standards. So when both countries use standards, the outcome is the same as in Section 3. This is scarcely surprising, since, in this simple model, when country i sets standards, the choice of X_i in the middle stage completely determines its output level in the final period, so choice of X_j by country j cannot play any strategic role. It is here that the assumption of only two factors plays a crucial role.

Case B: Both countries use taxes. Assuming a strictly interior solution, the first order conditions for country i become (18) and

$$\frac{\partial R_i}{\partial q_i}\frac{\partial q_i}{\partial X_i} + \frac{\partial R_i}{\partial q_j}\frac{\partial q_j}{\partial E_j}\frac{\partial E_j}{\partial X_i} - W_i = 0. \tag{22}$$

Note that (18) is the same as condition (5) for the choice of E_i, but (22) differs from (4) because of the presence of the middle term on the LHS of (22). Thus the level of input X will be inefficiently selected. I shall discuss shortly the direction of this distortion.

Case C: One country uses standards, the other taxes. Suppose country 1 uses taxes and country 2 standards; then the first order condition for country 1 will be (18) and, using that condition and the fact that $\partial E_2/\partial X_1 = 0$, (20) becomes

$$\frac{\partial R_1}{\partial q_1}\frac{\partial q_1}{\partial X_1} - W_1 \leq 0 \qquad\qquad \text{with} \quad X_1 \geq 0. \tag{23}$$

On the other hand for country 2, $\partial E_2/\partial X_2 = 0$, so (20) becomes

$$\frac{\partial R_2}{\partial q_2}\frac{\partial q_2}{\partial X_2} + \frac{\partial R_2}{\partial q_1}\frac{\partial q_1}{\partial E_1}\frac{\partial E_1}{\partial X_2} - W_2 \leq 0 \qquad \text{with} \quad X_2 \geq 0. \tag{24}$$

So the country which uses taxes will have an efficient use of factor X, since it cannot use its choice of that factor to influence the other country's output. On the other hand, the country that uses standards will distort its choice of factor X because it thereby influences the other country's output level.

To complete the analysis of this middle stage, it is necessary to assess the direction of the distortion in the choice of X in cases B and C. That will depend on the sign of the term

$$\frac{\delta R_i}{\partial q_j} \frac{\partial q_j}{\partial E_j} \frac{\partial E_j}{\partial X_i}$$

in (22) and (24). The first two factors are respectively negative and positive, so it remains to determine the sign of $\partial E_j / \partial X_i$ in the cases where country j uses taxes. Analysis in Ulph (1991), similar to that in Brander and Spencer (1983) confirms that this term must be negative.

Returning to (22) and (24), it follows from the above that the direction of distortion is as expected, that producers who are choosing X strategically will choose a level of X where the marginal revenue product of X is below its factor price. Another way of thinking of this is that when producers choose X strategically, they act like a producer who is not acting strategically but is faced with a shadow price for X below its market price.

By totally differentiating (1) with respect to W_i it can be seen that

$$\frac{\partial q_i}{\partial W_i} = \frac{\dfrac{\partial g_i}{\partial q_i}}{\dfrac{\partial^2 R_i}{\partial q_i^2} - W_i \dfrac{\partial^2 g_i}{\partial q_i^2}} < 0$$

so that a reduction in the factor price of X_i acts to shift out country i's standards–based reaction function.

I now turn to the first stage — the choice of policy instruments by countries. I begin by considering only producer surplus. The situation can be seen from Fig. 5 (1 and 2). If both countries use standards, the outcome is essentially the one–period Cournot outcome derived in Section 2, and this is shown in Figs. 5.1 and 5.2 by point A, the intersection of the two standards–based reaction functions with producers using the true market prices W_i, $i = 1, 2$, to guide their decisions on inputs X_i. I denote by Π_i^{ss}, $i = 1, 2$, the corresponding levels of producer surplus.

If both countries use taxes than there will be a distortion in their decisions on inputs X_i; they will act as if the market price for factor X is less than W_i. This is represented in Fig. 5.1 by the standards–based reaction functions for both shifting out, intersecting at point B. It may seem odd to use standards–based reaction functions for an equilibrium when both countries use taxes, but this just reflects the result in Section 3, that there is an equivalence between taxes and standards in the one–shot Cournot equilibrium, and the effect of introducing the second period is simply captured by the distortion to the shadow price used by both producers for factor X. So through point B there will be the appropriate pair of tax–based reaction functions that characterise this equilibrium. I shall denote the producer surpluses of the two countries where both use taxes by Π_i^{tt}.

In comparing the cases where both countries use standards and both use taxes, it is clear that, in general, $\Pi_i^{tt} < \Pi_i^{ss}$. This is for two reasons; firstly output will be higher when taxes are used, reducing profits for both producers. Second, both producers are making inefficient choices of factor inputs, and hence are not producing at minimum cost. This argument will certainly apply if both producers are identical, and, by extension, if producers are not very different. There may be the case where producers are very different, and point B lies within one producer's iso–profit curve through point A. But if such situations exist, they are clearly rather extreme cases, which I shall ignore.

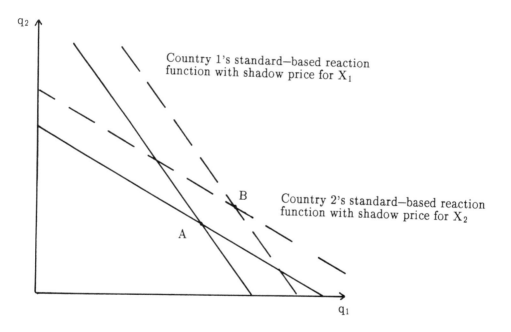

Figure 5.1: Effect of both countries using taxes rather than standards

Finally Figure 5.2 shows the outcome when country 1 uses taxes, and country 2 uses standards. The previous analysis shows that country 1 will not act strategically, so any

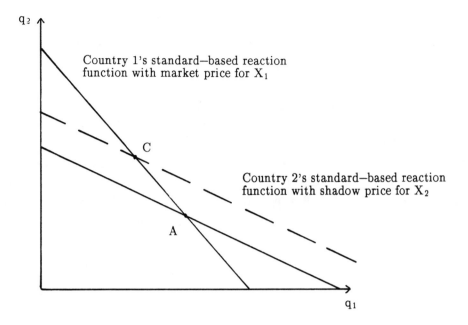

Figure 5.2: Effect of country 1 using taxes, Country 2 using standards

equilibrium must be on its original standards—based reaction function through A. Country 2 does act strategically, using a shadow price for factor X_2 below W_2, thus shifting
out its standards—based reaction function, with equilibrium resulting at point C. As in
the previous case, country 1 will actually be operating on a tax—based reaction function
through point C. Denote by (Π_1^{ts}, Π_2^{st}) the producer surpluses of the two countries
where the first superscript indicates the policy instrument that producer i uses while the
second superscript indicates the policy instrument of the other producer.

Now it is immediately clear from Figure 5.2 that $\Pi_1^{ts} < \Pi_1^{ss}$. In general it is not
possible to say much about the producer surplus for country 2, for there are three factors
at work. The move along country 1's reaction function in the direction of increased output for country 2 would lead to raising country 2's profits; if point C corresponded to
country 2 acting as Stackelberg leader against country 1's standards—based reaction
function (as in one of the cases in Section 4); then clearly it would be the case that Π_2^{st}
$> \Pi_2^{ss}$. But the other two factors offset this. First, as in the other case in Section 4,
country 2 is responding to a country using taxes not standards — so this will induce
country 2 to overexpand its output. Second country 2 is unable to precommit output,
but only factor X_2, so again there is a distortion in factor choice which means that coun-

try 2 does not minimise cost at its chosen output level.

What are the implications of the above for the choice of instruments? The fact that for any country $\Pi_i^{ss} > \Pi_i^{ts}$ means that the case where both countries choose standards is a Nash equilibrium of the first stage game. If it were the case that $\Pi_i^{st} > \Pi_i^{ss}$, then since $\Pi_i^{ss} > \Pi_i^{tt}$, it would follow that $\Pi_i^{st} > \Pi_i^{tt}$, so the case where both countries choose taxes could not be a Nash equilibrium. Even if $\Pi_i^{st} < \Pi_i^{ss}$, it is still likely that that $\Pi_i^{st} > \Pi_i^{tt}$, so that there will be a unique Nash equilibrium where both countries choose standards rather than taxes. I have not found any cases for which there exists a second Nash equilibrium where both countries choose taxes; even if such an equilibrium existed for some particular situations, our earlier analysis suggests it would be Pareto dominated by the Nash equilibrium where both choose standards.

Finally, as in Section 4, it is necessary to take account of consumer surplus as well as producer surplus. As in Section 4, the use of standards leads to lower output levels than the use of taxes, so that consumers are likely to prefer the use of taxes to standards. For cases where the consumers in the producing countries represent a small proportion of the world market for this good, the producer surplus argument will dominate. I summarise the conclusions of this section in the following proposition:

Proposition 3: *When international trade is modelled as a two—stage game in which producers commit in the first period to the level of a non—polluting input, then the use of standards by both countries constitutes a Nash equilibrium in the choice of instruments by governments, provided that the two countries represent a sufficiently small share of the world market for the good in terms of consumption.*

6. Conclusions

In this paper I have shown that by embedding the question of the choice of environmental policy instruments in the context of a model of strategic international trade, one can derive arguments which favour the choice of standards rather than taxes. I do not believe that this provides the fundamental resolution of the paradox with which I introduced this paper — the contrast between economists' recommendations and governments' actions in designing environmental policy, though I hope it is seen as an interesting line of research for further exploration.

The reason for this assessment of the paper is partly the very special nature of the model presented. Even within the framework of the model, the choice of standards rather than taxes depends on the weight to be attached to producer surplus rather than consumer surplus in overall welfare. More serious is the assumption that the government uses only one set of instruments which have to serve for both environmental and trade policy. The question clearly arises whether, as in Spencer and Brander (1983), the introduction of a separate set of instruments targetted specifically on trade (e.g. subsidies to the non–polluting input) will restore the policy indifference between environmental policy instruments that characterised the results in Section 3. Of course even if that turns out to be true, the results of this paper would still be of some interest in the context of, say, the EEC, where there may be restrictions on the use of specific trade policy instruments.

A rather different set of simplifications concerns the modelling of the pollution problem itself. For example, there is no abatement technology, and the pollution authorities have perfect information. Hahn (1989) argues that it is the simplicity of the models used by economists to discuss pollution policy (e.g. ignoring the fact that policy evolves over time) that leads to the apparent conflict between economists and policy–makers. As in other areas of economics, such as public finance, economists need to pay attention to the details of the constraints facing policy makers. I do not disagree with this view. This paper seeks only to introduce another aspect into the analysis of the choice of instruments.

Finally, the model is limited in its time structure. Another fruitful development would be to consider an infinite time horizon and study more carefully the question of the degree of commitment of inputs, along the lines developed by Karp (1990) in the context of trade policy alone. It would also be desirable to introduce an element of strategic interaction between the countries in the environmental problem itself, arising from some international externality caused by the pollutant. This would extend the analysis found, for example, in Hoel (1990) and de Zeeuw and van der Ploeg (1990).

References

Brander, J., and Spencer, B., 1983, "Strategic commitment with R&D: The symmetric case", *The Bell Journal of Economics 14*, 225–235

Buchanan, J., and Tullock, G., 1975, "Polluters profits and political response: Direct controls versus taxes", *American Economic Review 65*, 139–147 de Zeeuw, A., and van der Ploeg, R., 1990, *"International Aspects of Pollution Control"*, Working Paper, Center for Economic Research, University of Tilburg

Hahn, R.W., 1989, "Economic prescriptions for environmental problems: How the patient followed the doctor's orders", *The Journal of Economic Perspectives*, 3, 95—114

Hoel, M., 1990, *"Emission taxes in a dynamic game of CO_2 emissions"*, Memorandum 7, Department of Economics, Oslo

Ingham, A., and Ulph, A., 1990, "The economics of global warming", in: Bennett, J. (ed), *Economics and the Environment*, Australian Institute for Public Policy, Perth

Karp, L., 1990, *"A comparison of tariffs and quotas in a strategic setting"*, Working Paper, University of Southampton

Kwerel, E., 1977, "To tell the truth: Imperfect information and optimal pollution control", *Review of Economic Studies 44*, 595–601

Opschoor, J. B., and Vos, H.B., 1989, *"Economic Instruments for Environmental Protection"*, O.E.C.D., Paris

Pearce, D.W., and Turner, K., 1990, *"Economics of Natural Resources and the Environment"*, Harvester Wheatsheaf, Hemel Hempstead

Roberts, M., and Spence, M., 1976, "Effluent charges and licenses under uncertainty", *Journal of Public Economics 5*, 193–208

Spencer, B., and Brander, J., 1983, "International R&D rivalry and industrial strategy", *Review of Economic Studies 50*, 707–722

Ulph, A., 1991, *"Strategic International Trade and Environmental Policy"*, (mimeo, University of Southampton)

Yohe, G., 1976, "Polluters' profits and political response: Direct control versus taxes: Comment", *American Economic Review 66*, 981–982

Comments by Marji Lines

In this paper, Alistair Ulph reconsiders the standards vs. taxes debate over environmental policy instruments by placing it in a model of "strategic international trade". One could argue that his analysis shows rather that if the assumption of either simultaneous or instantaneous decision making is relaxed, a case can be made for choosing standards over taxes in markets which are not perfectly competitive. Whatever interpretation might be given to the structure of the models used, it is interesting to note under what conditions these standards favoring results hold, and I review below the three scenarios analyzed in the work.

The general model has two countries, each with a single firm, producing a single product with a non—polluting input X, and a polluting energy input E. Emissions are proportional to total energy use so that the countries' Authorities can set policy by either limiting energy use or taxing it. Policy is set simultaneously prior to the firms' decision stage(s). Three cases are considered.

Scenario I: *Simultaneous and instantaneous choice, that is, firms simultaneously decide both inputs and outputs.*

Here Authorities are indifferent (in that producer and consumer surpluses are the same) between standards and taxes, if taxes are set equal to the Lagrangean multiplier in the firms' maximization problems.

Two problems arise regarding the possible application of this scenario to real policy issues: the assumptions of simultaneity and "perfect information production" on the part of the Authority.

Simultaneity. Since the total revenue function of firm 1 is a function of both its own and the other firm's output (q_1, q_2, respectively), firm 1 has a constrained maximization problem that requires knowledge of q_2, which is assumed as simply given. Therefore, in the same instant, firm 1 chooses q_1 given q_2 and firm 2 chooses q_2 given q_1. It might seem a trivial point here, as the two firms supply world demand, but later the same framework is used in discussing the case where the two producers' combined output represents a small share of global supply. Who or what mechanism gives firm 1 the value of q_2? Or, if extended, how does firm i know the q_j ($j = 1$ to n, $j \neq i$)?

A solution might be to give a time dimension to the decision making problem, then q_j might be an estimate based on past values, the expected value of some probability density function. It should also be noted that, even given q_j, the maximization problem in the simplest of cases leads to nasty polynomials whose solution can only be approximated, if constant returns to scale are not assumed (that is, if $\alpha + \beta \neq 1.0$ in a typical Cobb—Douglas production function).

Perfect Information. In order for the Authority to get the energy tax right, it needs to know: the firm's production function, revenue function, and pollution coefficient, as well as the q_j, in addition to the more easily found data of input costs and product prices. It seems likely that information needs contribute at least as much to the preference Authorities demonstrate for standards as two stage decision making models. In a country with $n > 1$ firms producing with different technologies, the Authority's information requirements would be awesome indeed.

Scenario II: *Leader−follower, two stage decisions, that is, each firm chooses both inputs and outputs in the same moment, but one firm decides first.*

This would seem the most appropriate scenario, then firm 2, who decides last, takes as given q_1 and firm 1, a Stackelberg leader, maximizes profits with respect to q_1, E_1, and q_2, where q_2 is no longer given.

Using the reaction functions Ulph shows that − if consumer surplus can be considered smaller than producer surplus (the small share of world market assumption), and the relation between the two firms is a Stackelberg equilibrium − then both countries will be better off if the follower's Authority has set standards. It is irrelevant which policy instrument the leader's Authority has used. This is a direct result of breaking down the simultaneous choice problem, and might be part of the explanation of governments preference for standards−based pollution control policies.

However, it would seem that the small market share assumption weakens the assumption of interdependence in the revenue functions, that the motivation for assuming imperfect competition is diminished.

Scenario III: *Simultaneous decisions but in two stages, first both firms decide the input X, a capital like factor, then both firms decide the output, and therefore the energy input.*

This scenario seems more adapted to its original use, wherein the first stage input choice was R&D investment. It may be a rare industry which decides on its output level after having chosen and invested its capital.

If both Authorities impose standards, the choice of X determines output level and energy use, and the choice of X is the same as for Scenario I. The difference is when one or both Authorities apply taxes, then there is a distortion in the choice, away from efficiency, of X during the first stage. The direction of distortion however depends on the sign of a partial derivative which, in the case of both Authorities imposing taxes, is ambiguous. Furthermore the choice of E_1 is a function not only of X_1 and X_2, data available from the previous stage, but also of E_2 which, like q_2 in Scenario I, must be assumed given. That is, the simultaneity question remains, it is only put off to the second stage.

The results in this case are similar to Scenario II. If the two countries represent a sufficiently small share of the world market, then a Nash equilibrium exists when both Authorities impose standards.

Of the three scenarios, I find the Stackelberg leader−follower the most promising. The breakdown of simultaneity, that is, the introduction of a time dimension into the decision problem, is accomplished in a manner which could be extended to more firms and more time periods. I believe useful implications for such a research project would be had in a worked out problem, using explicit functions, for the two country case, and I suggest that this be the next step.

Chapter 6

Hans W. Gottinger[1, 2]

Economic Models of Optimal Energy Use under Global Environmental Constraints

Abstract. Part 1 of this paper presents simple control models on the use of fossil fuels and the global environmental problems caused by carbon dioxide accumulation. The reference model assumes that energy is the only productive factor in the economy and that energy use causes carbon dioxide accumulation which lowers productivity. Consumption of the single good in the economy causes a flow of utility. The policy maker acts to maximize the integral of the discounted utility stream. The single state variable is carbon dioxide concentration. Unique features of the model are the very general production function and the assumption that the pollutant does not affect utility directly.

Conditions which assure the existence of an optimal equilibrium for these models are discussed. In order to focus on policy directed changes such models are specified to be solvable numerically and applied to specific issues of interest. A specific form involves the assumption that the negative impact of carbon dioxide accumulation occurs abruptly at specific levels of atmospheric carbon dioxide.

Part 2 pursues in depth some specific aspects of optimizing economic models for fossil fuel use given carbon dioxide accumulation, e.g. technical progress, international co–operation and structural uncertainty. We develop a taxonomy of technical progress situations and show that depending on the assumptions the optimal steady state CO_2 concentration may rise or fall with increases in the steady state level of progress.

Two cases of international co–operation in controlling CO_2 accumulation are examined, the co–operative and non–co–operative case. In the non–co–operative situation the critical level is reached sooner, even though the region concerned about CO_2 always emits less carbon than in the co–operative case. Major results pertain to uncertainty. Here we show, supported by numerical examples, that a "certainty equivalent" treatment of uncertainty can lead to significantly higher than optimal estimates of the desirable level of fossil fuel use as compared to a proper full treatment of uncertainty.

[1] The contents of this paper are the author's sole responsibility. They do not necessarily represent the views of the Oxford Institute for Energy Studies or any of its Members.

[2] Acknowledgement: This is to thank O. von dem Hagen, University of Oldenburg, for checking some of the formulas, discovering some mistakes and recalculating Table 1. All remaining errors are mine.

Part 1: The CO_2 Problem in Basic Models of Optimal Use of Fossil Fuels

1. Introduction

Over the past decade there has been mounting concern that it will become increasingly difficult to reverse or adapt to climatic changes resulting from human activities.

Due to the accumulation of carbon dioxide and several trace gases the atmosphere is trapping more and more heat coming from the earth. The trapped heat is expected to cause increases in average yearly temperatures and other consequent climatic changes.

The major purpose of this essay is to contribute to better policy making through improvements in models studying the economic impacts of the carbon dioxide problem, and to show ways in which economic instruments can effectively be put to use to alleviate such a problem.

This approach differs in at least one major aspect from common studies of the climatic change problem. We focus on the analysis, control and optimization of modelling forms rather than the collection and analysis of data. More concretely, we search for optimal fossil fuel use, research and technology policies rather than predicting the future. Most studies of the problem exogenously specify technical developments and fossil fuel control policies and then predict future climatic changes. These prediction models incorporate a great deal of data and tend to be quite complex.

The advantage of an optimizing control model is increased flexibility in structural and dynamic assumptions on the economy allowing explicit 'what–if' questions to be asked about the possibility of controlling the growth in atmospheric CO_2 concentrations.

Let us start by looking at a class of single state aggregate optimal control models. They allow consideration of static production but also technical change. In the latter case we take care of the fact that very small rates of ongoing technical change can have an enormous impact because of the very long time–span associated with the CO_2 problem, that is the 100–150 years until major effects occur.

In this class of single state models, the level of atmospheric CO_2 is the only state variable. The only policy or control variable chosen is fossil fuel use. (In a follow–up paper we will explore a class of multiple state models including additional state variables, stocks of physical capital and levels of knowledge).

The simplest type of technical change is a finite or limited improvement in a technology. Because such a change is not ongoing, the model remains static and relatively easy to examine. Ongoing but uncontrolled technical change is also examined with a single state model.

Some major policy conclusions can be derived from this class of model:

(1)   One can show that depending on the assumptions regarding technical progress, the optimal steady state CO_2 concentration may rise or fall with increases in the steady state level of progress. Notably, an improved substitute for fossil fuels always reduces the long–run level of atmospheric CO_2, while an improvement in fossil fuel productivity may increase or decrease the level of atmospheric CO_2.

(2)   Solutions of a model with neutral, constant and ongoing technical progress and the basic static model are very similar. In the model with technical progress, higher levels of technical progress lead to lower long–run optimal levels of atmospheric CO_2.

(3)   We examine two cases of international co–operation in controlling CO_2 accumulation. The base case is complete co–operation between two regions in maximizing consumption with complete awareness of the CO_2 problem. This case is compared with a situation in which no co–operation takes place until a critical CO_2 level is reached. Our most important finding is that in the non–co–operative situation the critical level is reached sooner, even though the region concerned about CO_2 always emits less carbon than in the base case.

(4)   The last applications are on uncertainty. We first show that the results from studies of the optimal use of a resource which is in limited supply can be applied to the CO_2 problem. This similarity is important because the results regarding the use of limited resources are extensive and powerful. Then, using numerical examples, we show that an inappropriate treatment of risk can lead to significantly higher than optimal estimates of the desirable level of fossil fuel use.

2. Background problem on climatic change and global environmental constraints

The most prominent and widely accepted conclusions regarding atmospheric carbon dioxide are that CO_2 has increased significantly in this century and that elevated CO_2 levels once attained are extremely difficult to reduce (Rosenberg et al., 1988, Schneider, 1989).

Since 1958 continuous observation of atmospheric carbon dioxide concentrations on the Mauna Loa Mountain (Hawaii) and South Pole observatories has provided incontrovertible evidence of steadily increasing CO_2 concentrations (Rosenberg, 1986). The concentration at Mauna Loa was 316 ppm in 1959 and 345 ppm in 1985. The concentrations at the South Pole tend to confirm these findings. Current estimates suggest that the pre—industrial or nineteenth century concentration was between 280 and 305 ppm. The movement of carbon from sources to final deposition is known as the carbon cycle. The largest reservoir of carbon is in carbonate sediments such as limestone and chalk. Other significant but less stable reservoirs include: fossil fuels, living and dead plants and animals, carbonates and bicarbonates dissolved in the ocean. Huge quantities of carbon, in the form of carbon dioxide, move from the biosphere and oceans to the atmosphere and back each year.

It is widely believed that before the industrial revolution these flows were closely balanced and the atmospheric CO_2 level was relatively stable. In more recent times, though, several changes in the carbon cycle may have occurred. The wide uncertainty over the CO_2 releases from the biosphere and the absorption by photosynthesis and the oceans results in estimates of a high fraction of carbon dioxide released in fossil fuel use remaining airborne.

Because reabsorption is very low, about 0.1 per cent each year (National Research Council, 1983), if the atmospheric CO_2 concentration is raised significantly, it would probably remain high for several centuries.

While it is not disputed that the increase of CO_2 will have an impact on warming and climatic change, uncertainty about fossil energy use, the carbon cycle, and other climatic disturbances all make prediction of the future climate uncertain.

Carbon dioxide in the atmosphere affects the radiation balance of the earth, and increasing CO_2 concentrations are expected to cause a warmer climate. Carbon dioxide is relatively transparent to energy as sunlight, but reflects or traps a large portion of this energy when radiated from the earth as heat.

A recent and very important development in climatic studies is the identification of other trace gases with this same heat trapping property. The prediction of future temperatures is further complicated by diverse factors. Significant feedback effects are expected to accompany any direct effects of CO_2 heat trapping. Warming may change cloud, snow, and ice cover and alter the earth's "albedo" or brightness (Flohn, 1988).

Consequently, the reflection and absorption of energy may increase or decrease.

Uncertain major climatic disturbances are foreseen which are not connected with CO_2. Continental drift, fluctuations in the earth's orbit, solar flux variations, and volcanic dust are all natural causes of climatic change. The release of particulates and changes in land use are human activities which may impact local or regional climate.

On the basis of large–scale "general circulation models", assessed by MacCracken and Luther (1985), models without consideration of feedback processes (changing cloudiness, oceanic capture, etc.) predict a change in global average surface temperature due to doubling of CO_2 concentration in the range of 1.2 to 1.3° C. However, model predictions including feedback processes range from 1.5° C to 4.5° C in the long–run doubling of CO_2 levels. More recent models summarized by MacCracken and Luther predict a greenhouse warming with an increase of the global average surface air temperature between 3.5° C and 4.2° C.

Predictions of the effects of CO_2 on warming have changed very little since these estimates. Whereas these models are in close agreement over an increase in global average temperature they deviate in their predictions of regional climatic changes.

If such a warming occurs it would be an outstanding climatic event. If fossil fuel use continued to increase at the rate of the sixties, the earth could experience a warming during the next 50 to 150 years which would otherwise occur in a natural cycle over a period of 100,000 years.

At this point one may well wonder whether it will all matter. In fact, the overall pattern of warming, little near the equator and greater near the poles, might be viewed as beneficial. One might argue that people have adapted to changes of climate throughout their existence. Schelling (1988) makes this point very clear:

Without belittling the unprecedented nature of such climate changes ... it is fair to point out that most people will not undergo in the next hundred years changes in their local climates more drastic than the changes in climate that people have undergone during the past hundred years. No climate changes are forecast that compare with moving from Boston, Massachusetts to Irvine, California, ... The Goths and the Vandals, the Romans and the Vikings ... migrated through more drastic changes than any currently anticipated; Europeans who migrated to North and South America similarly underwent drastic climate changes.

Despite persistent uncertainties, and despite being a long–run phenomenon it will be safe to assume that warming will cause specific regional weather changes which are now highly speculative but potentially very disruptive.

Changes in world precipitation patterns may greatly disrupt agriculture and living conditions, in particular in the world's poorer regions. Because agricultural productivity depends on a union of fertile soil and appropriate rainfall, changes in precipitation patterns are of great importance. Specific regional changes will determine how damaging precipitation changes are to world food production.

Because a CO_2 induced warming would be extremely fast compared to natural cycles, the rapidity of the climatic change must be considered in addition to its absolute size. During natural climatic changes, animals and plants slowly adapt or optimize with respect to their environment. Rapid changes of almost any type in an optimized ecosystem can do much harm.

Another major concern is that a warmer earth would result in more rapid and violent fluctuations in weather patterns. Although people can adapt well to long—term weather changes, extreme weather variability is very destructive.

A possible sea level rise due to CO_2 warming has received much publicity. A rise of several meters would occur only if one of the major ice sheets (the East Antarctic, the West Antarctic, or the Greenland) disintegrated. A surge of the West Antarctic ice sheet, which would cause its disintegration in less than 100 years, has been of greatest concern, although it is considered a low probability event (Flohn, 1988). The National Research Council (1983) after reviewing various studies of the West Antarctic ice sheet, concluded that if it disappeared, the minimum time for the event would be 300 years with a rise in sea level of about two meters each hundred years.

Other possible problems due to warming include changes in the range of crop pests, greater health problems from the spread of diseases associated with tropical climates, and disruption of world fisheries.

3. Economic studies on the CO_2 problem

Two major kinds of economic studies can be identified for dealing with the CO_2 problem. The first category treats economic and economic modelling issues in the context of an integrated framework of energy—economy and climate changes, the second category applies the theory of resource use and depletion to the management of CO_2 emissions.

In what follows we provide a selected overview of those studies which yield pertinent results comparable to our own or which are of methodological interest in modelling the energy–economy–climate interactions.

A few years ago the US National Research Council (1983) compiled a detailed investigation that up to now constitutes the most extensive, comprehensive and consistent examination of the climate change problem. It uses energy–economy, climate and agricultural models to predict future impacts of carbon dioxide and trace gas accumulation. The major conclusions are that no radical actions should be taken, that increases in carbon dioxide are likely, and that more research is necessary. In this report, the developers of the energy–economy model (W. Nordhaus and C. Yohe) note that the technology development and elasticity of substitution parameters critically affect the model's results.

It should be added that the method of modelling technical change and energy substitution possibilities is also critical and controversial. The economic modelling chapters of the NRC report have been updated by Yohe (1984). The conclusions of the report have not changed significantly.

Another collaborative study, the joint MIT–Stanford study (Rose, Miller, and Agnew, 1983), is of interest because it is one of few reports which search for alternatives to increasing CO_2 and offer some positive choices. In the Edmonds and Reilly model (Edmonds and Reilly, 1983) S–shaped paths are exogenously specified for several new energy technologies. The MIT–Stanford study modifies these paths and also looks at additional technologies. It finds that the adoption of realistic CO_2 reducing technologies, while not eliminating a significant CO_2 warming could increase the CO_2 doubling time to several centuries.

In attempting to discuss optimizing strategies Nordhaus (1980) made a seminal contribution by applying simple optimization models to the qualitative and quantitative analysis of the CO_2 problem. By letting the consumption equation depend on fossil energy use he determines the appropriate tax policy to control CO_2 and makes a quantitative estimate of this tax.

In most present studies of the CO_2 problem we find that technological change and technology substitution are specified exogenously or modelled in a very simple fashion.

In this regard, the logistic (S–curve) assumption on the diffusion of new technologies has become very popular, although it lacks sufficient economic explanatory power. For example, in a study by Perry et al. (1982) an energy demand level and a fossil fuel use pattern is assumed. Fossil fuel use follows a logistic curve between the present and an assumed ultimate level of use. The rate of non–fossil energy growth needed to fill the gap between fossil energy use and assumed total energy demand is then examined. This study emphasizes the importance of analysing the investment needed in non fossil energy to fill this gap but it does not present a model of the substitution process. In the model we suggest, the substitution process is a direct result of our maximization of welfare.

Modelling the impacts of changes in energy use on the economy is a major problem. A good starting point for such considerations would be the ETA–Macro model (Manne, 1977) though it has not been used for studying the CO_2 problem. This model can be described as a multisector, forward–looking model. It examines consumption and investment policies and their impact on national welfare. National welfare is measured by discounting utility from the present to a distant horizon. ETA–Macro consists of two models: a macro–model of the whole economy and a more detailed model of the energy sector. The model seems more sophisticated in its treatment of capital and the determination of the desirable level of energy use than those economic models presently used in CO_2 analysis. However, it is limited to the USA in geographic scope which makes it unsuitable for examining international problems such as CO_2. The model has no endogenous technical progress which we consider an important feature for the analysis of CO_2. On the other hand, the model has several features which would be desirable in models of energy, economy and the environment. It is optimizing and considers costs and benefits of capital investment.

Very recently, there has been a flurry of economic modelling and assessment studies of CO_2 effects, in particular by Manne and Richels, that have appeared in the 1990 issues of the Energy Journal.

In setting up this approach we were influenced by applications of optimal control models to pollution problems (Fisher, 1981; Conrad and Clark, 1987). Such models often show different structures, e.g. pollution affecting utility or production, the pollutant acting as a stock or a flow and the way abatement activities are available.

In this specific context, we find that many models and results on the depletion of a non–renewable resource could be applied with simple modifications to the CO_2 problem. Under two assumptions the problem of fossil fuel use in the face of increasing carbon dioxide is parallel to the problem of consuming a limited resource. The first assumption is that the carbon dioxide absorption rate is sufficiently small to be ignored. The second is that CO_2 impacts follow a "step" pattern: that is, CO_2 has no impact on productivity until a critical level, M_c, is reached. Then if the CO_2 level exceeds M_c production falls to zero, or remains stagnant. One of the most serious effects in facing global warming is that of irreversibility, that is, given the accumulation of atmospheric CO_2 we will reach a critical level of the CO_2 budget where there is a point of no return (unless technologies are in place that effectively remove CO_2 from the budget). The interpretation of a critical level of atmospheric CO_2 accumulation where there is a precipitous drop of production means that we have reached the biophysical limits of growth.

An interesting treatment of endogenous neutral technical progress in a depletion model was suggested by Chiarella (1980). He proves the existence of a steady state growth path and a simple rule governing the rate of investment in research. Research investment along the optimal path should be carried out until the growth rate in the marginal accumulation of technology equals the difference between the marginal product due to an extra unit of research investment and the marginal product of capital.

A similar problem is the use of a limited non—renewable resource when the reserve of the resource is unknown. The model by Gilbert (1979) can be directly converted to a model of fossil fuel use when the critical CO_2 level is uncertain. Under the above assumptions this problem is equivalent to determining the rate of fossil fuel use when the critical concentration of atmospheric carbon dioxide is unknown. The results show that the optimal use of fossil fuel is lower when uncertainty is properly considered than when the expected values are assumed to be certain.

Deshmukh and Pliska (1980, 1983) study more complex models of the same problem. The possibility of doing exploration to find new reserves is a significant addition in their models. The parallel in the CO_2 problem is research to increase the probability of finding a technology for the removal of CO_2 from the atmosphere. Their findings imply that in the periods between discoveries or research breakthroughs, fossil fuel use and consumption fall, but if research is very successful long—run fuel use may rise.

4. Preliminary definitions and the general model

Our interest in model structure and policy options for energy policies leads us to the use of forward—looking, optimizing aggregate models. The class of models we are analysing here uses mathematical techniques of optimal control (Kamien and Schwartz, 1981). This requires: a measure of welfare or benefit as an objective function, and a definition of how policies, the control variables, affect specific aspects of the world, the state variables. A complete optimal control model of the CO_2 problem is an ideal rather than a reality, although outlining a detailed model provides a reference when examining simple models focusing on specific issues.

The basic ingredient of our model is an uncomplicated measure of welfare denoted by J. J is the sum over all time of the discounted flow of welfare. U is the utility or the flow of welfare at any instant. The social discount rate is r. Utility depends only on consumption, C. Consumption, production, and investment all have the same, single measure. Production is designated Y. There are numerous investment possibilities represented by the vector $\underline{I}$. At least two world regions are imagined and trade can occur between them. The vector of traded goods is $\underline{X}$, and the prices of the goods are in the vector $\underline{p}$. Consumption equals production minus the sum of investments in capital goods plus the returns from trade. Production depends on current inputs, capital inputs, atmospheric CO_2, and the use of imports. Current imports are not stored and affect production as a flow. Capital inputs can be accumulated and affect production as a stock, $\underline{K}$. We distinguish two types of current inputs, fossil fuels, $\underline{F}$, and all other current inputs, $\underline{E}$. Atmospheric CO_2 is a single number denoted by M. The welfare measure, J, can be expressed as

$$\underset{\underline{F},\underline{E},\underline{I},\underline{X}}{Max} \quad J = \int_{0}^{\infty} e^{-rt}\, U(C(t))dt \tag{1}$$

Production and consumption are determined by

$$C = Y - \underline{1}\,\underline{I} + \underline{p}\,\underline{X}, \tag{2}$$

$$Y = f(\underline{F},\ M,\ \underline{E},\ \underline{K},\ \underline{X}), \tag{3}$$

and $\underline{1}$ is the unit vector.

We assume that one region has the leadership in world trade, and its decisions on trade influence world prices through a vector function

$$\underline{p} = g(\underline{X}) \tag{4}$$

The regional use of fossil fuels, $\underline{F}_i$ also reacts to the trade policy, this reaction is determined by the vector function:

$$\underline{F}_i = h(\underline{X})$$ (5)

The capital stocks and the level of atmospheric CO_2 are the state variables. Knowledge is treated as a special type of capital stock which does not depreciate. The current capital stocks and the CO_2 level may affect their own rate of change through depreciation and reabsorption respectively.

The dynamics of their change are expressed as follows:

$$\frac{d\underline{K}}{dt} \equiv \dot{\underline{K}} = j(\underline{I}, \underline{K})$$ (6)

$$\frac{dM}{dt} \equiv \dot{M} = k(\underline{F}, \underline{F}_i, M)$$ (7)

The general model introduces many of the concepts to be elaborated: the importance of a welfare measure, feedback to production from increasing CO_2, changes in physical capital and knowledge, the ability to control these changes, and the impact of trade on fossil fuel consumption and production. In its general form the model is too complex to solve for relevant results; therefore, we develop a set of simple models to examine these concepts. The simplification is achieved in two ways: by reducing the number of variables and restricting the functional forms.

5. A simplified model

This model contains only the most important elements of the general optimal control model introduced in the previous section. As in the general model, the economy considered has only one consumption good, C, and a flow of utility. $U(C)$ results from consuming this good. The objective is to maximize J which equals the utility flow discounted at the rate r and integrated from the present time, $t = 0$, to infinity.

We assume that production of the good, C, depends only on the use of fossil fuels, F, and the level of carbon dioxide accumulated in the atmosphere, M. Control of fossil fuel use is the sole means of managing the economy. No decisions on investment and trade, as in the general model, are made. Thus, the assumptions are:[3]

$$J^* = \underset{F}{Max}\, J = \underset{F}{Max}\, \int_0^\infty e^{-rt}\, U(C)\, dt, \tag{1}$$

$$C = f(F, M). \tag{2}$$

We assume that production is finite at any finite level of fossil fuel use and that the production function is continuous in F.

The equation for change in the atmospheric carbon dioxide level is more specific than in the general model. We assume that each unit of fossil fuel use emits a fixed amount of CO_2 into the atmosphere; therefore, fossil fuel use and CO_2 accumulation can be measured in similar units. Finally, CO_2 leaves the atmosphere naturally at a rate proportional to the CO_2 concentration. The proportionality factor or "reabsorption rate" is β. We specify the relations which determine M:

$$\frac{dM}{dt} = F - \beta M, \tag{3}$$

$$M(0) = M_0. \tag{4}$$

This model already contains three specific (economic) assumptions. First, neither emissions nor carbon dioxide accumulation impact utility (comfort or health) directly; the impacts occur through productivity changes. Second, the accumulated CO_2 is the pollutant not the rate of CO_2 emissions, differentiating CO_2 from such pollutants as SO_2 or particulates. Third we assume a very simple equation for CO_2 accumulation. Both the retention of CO_2 in the atmosphere and its reabsorption may in fact be nonlinear and change over time. The model differs from the earlier general model in two fundamental ways: there are no opportunities for investment and there is only one world region.

Several additional assumptions pertain to utility and production. Utility increases with consumption, but at a decreasing rate:

---

[3] For the sake of notational simplicity the numbering of equations starts with (1) in each subsequent section. If an equation, say Equation (14), is refered to in the text, it is understood that we mean Equation (14) in the section where the reference is made. If in section y we refer to Equation (14) from section x (x ≠ y), we write Equation (x.14).

$$U' > 0 \qquad \text{and} \qquad U'' < 0 \tag{5}$$

where primes stand for derivatives.

Whatever the level of CO_2 accumulation, we assume that production increases with increases of fossil fuel use (close to zero) and that the rate of increase in production slows with additional fossil fuel inputs. But production declines with the accumulation of CO_2. Thus, the conditions hold with fossil energy being burnt.

$$\frac{\partial f(0, M)}{\partial F} > 0 \tag{6}$$

$$\frac{\partial^2 f}{\partial F^2} \leq 0 \tag{7}$$

$$\frac{\partial f}{\partial M} \leq 0 \tag{8}$$

$$F \geq 0 \tag{9}$$

5.1. Necessary conditions

First establish the Hamiltonian H:

$$H(F, M, \phi) = U(C) + \phi(F - \beta M). \tag{10}$$

The Hamiltonian equals the utility flow plus the current value of increasing carbon dioxide concentrations. The adjoint value ϕ represents the marginal value of increasing CO_2 concentrations. The term $\S F$ is added to form the Lagrangean L, and assures that $F \geq O$:

$$L = H + \S F. \tag{11}$$

From (11) we derive the necessary conditions

$$\frac{\partial L}{\partial F} = U' \left[\frac{\partial f}{\partial F} \right] + \phi + \lambda = 0, \tag{12}$$

$$\frac{d\phi}{dt} = r\phi - \frac{\partial L}{\partial M} = (r + \alpha)\phi - U'\left[\frac{\partial f}{\partial M}\right], \tag{13}$$

$$\lambda F = 0, \qquad \lambda \geq 0. \tag{14}$$

Since (12) implies that ϕ is less than zero, this agrees with our intuition that the value of increasing CO_2 should be negative. In order to deal with a CO_2 induced cost, we define q equal to $-\phi$, and q can be referred to as the shadow price of CO_2 emissions. We can now restate (12) and (13) as

$$U'\left[\frac{\partial f}{\partial F}\right] - q + \lambda = 0, \tag{15}$$

$$\frac{dq}{dt} = (r + \alpha)q + U'\left[\frac{\partial f}{\partial M}\right], \tag{16}$$

or

$$q = \int_{t}^{\infty} -e^{-(r+\alpha)(\tau-t)} U'\left[\frac{\partial f}{\partial M}\right] d\tau.$$

(15) and (16) are crucial conditions that lend themselves immediately to economic interpretations. (15) implies that fossil fuels are used up to the point at which the marginal contribution to utility equals the shadow price, unless fuel use is forced to zero. Unless the marginal utility is increasing, shadow price increases will drive down the use of fossil fuels. The condition in (16) is easily understood in its integral form. Increases in atmospheric CO_2 lower productivity and thus cause a disutility. The cost of CO_2 is the discounted sum of the marginal harm or disutility due to an increase in CO_2. We discount at the rate β because a unit of CO_2 emitted presently disappears at the rate of β, and we discount at r to put future losses on a present value basis.

A further necessary condition determines maxima or minima. By defining

$$U_{ff} = U'\left[\frac{\partial^2 f}{\partial F^2}\right] + U''\left[\frac{\partial f}{\partial F}\right]^2 \tag{17}$$

the necessary condition for a maximum can be stated as

$$\frac{\partial^2 H}{\partial F^2} = U_{ff} \leq 0. \tag{18}$$

5.2. Sufficient conditions

We assume that the first and second derivatives of the production function are defined. (In problems where the derivatives are not defined sufficiency must be proved by other methods)[4]. We use sufficiency conditions that require that the necessary conditions are met and that the utility function is jointly concave in M and F. The proof only applies when the state equation (3) is linear in F and M.

The definition in (17) and the two following definitions make the statement of concavity more concise:

$$U_{mm} = U' \left[\frac{\partial^2 f}{\partial M^2} \right] + U'' \left[\frac{\partial f}{\partial M} \right]^2, \tag{19}$$

$$U_{fm} = U' \left[\frac{\partial^2 f}{\partial F \partial M} \right] + U'' \left[\frac{\partial f}{\partial F} \right] \left[\frac{\partial f}{\partial M} \right]. \tag{20}$$

The concavity conditions can be stated as follows:

$$U_{ff} \leq 0 \tag{21}$$

and

$$U_{ff} U_{mm} - (U_{fm})^2 \geq 0. \tag{22}$$

From (22) to assume concavity of the utility function the second partial derivative of f with respect to M must be less than or equal to zero. This assumes that U_{mm} is less than or equal to zero. This requirement matches the assumption of many scientists that CO_2 impacts will accelerate at higher levels of CO_2. Another sufficiency condition is simply

---

[4] In finite horizon problems with a structure similar to (1)–(9) an additional necessary condition determines the value of the adjoint variable, ρ or ϕ, at the terminal time. Halkin (1974) showed that the simple condition on the adjoint variable in the finite horizon case does not extend to the infinite horizon case. However, there exist conditions on the shape of the function to be maximized and the state equation which in combination with (14), (15) and (16) are sufficient to determine an optimum.

that $q(t)$ does not get too big. This condition can be stated as:

$$\epsilon^{-rt}q(t) \to 0 \quad \text{as} \quad t \to \infty. \tag{23}$$

The condition is satisfied if q has a finite equilibrium value or if q grows at a rate less than r. The conditions in (15), (16), (21), (22) and (23) are sufficient to assume that an optimal path for the control variable has been found.

5.3. Definition and optimality of equilibrium

In the context of controlling fossil fuel use, the notion of equilibrium is interesting because it predicts the distant future, indicates the general direction of movement from the present to the long run.

The equilibrium is defined in terms of q and M. To specify the equilibrium conditions we assume that for F greater than zero that F can be found (as a function of q and M from (15) and (16)). This function is specified as $\{(q, M)$. F is constant when q and M are constant. From (3) if M is constant

$$\{(q, M) - \beta M = 0. \tag{24}$$

Equation (24) defines combinations of shadow price, q, and CO_2 concentration, M, which keep the concentration of CO_2 constant. M is greater than zero. Therefore, from (24), F is greater than zero in equilibrium.

Setting dq/dt equal to zero over time in (16) and substituting for F gives a second condition on the equilibrium

$$(r + \alpha)q + U' \left[\frac{\partial f(\psi(q, M), M)}{\partial M} \right] = 0. \tag{25}$$

(25) constitutes something like a price/damage equation. It assures that in equilibrium the higher the incremental damage of CO_2 the higher the price of fossil fuels.

If the equilibrium satisfies (15), (16), (21), (22) and (23) then it is optimal. q is finite in the equilibrium satisfying the sufficiency condition in (23). If we assume that the production function has a curvature satisfying (21) and (22) we know the equilibrium is optimal.

Equilibrium condition (25) can be restated in terms of the more familiar rate of substitution

$$-\frac{\partial f}{\partial F}\frac{\partial M}{\partial f} = \frac{dM}{df} = 1/(r + \alpha). \tag{25'}$$

Along an isoquant dM/dF, the slope of the isoquant equals the negative of the ratio in (25'). In Figure 1, the curve ab is the locus of all points such that $dM/dF = 1/(r + \beta)$ along an isoquant. These points represent an efficient balance between the marginal gains from increased emissions and losses from increased atmospheric CO_2. $1/(r + \beta)$ can be thought of as the price ratio of the value of increased fossil fuel use to decreased CO_2 levels. OC is the line along which F equals βM, the set of stationary points. The equilibrium is at the intersection of curves ab and OC in the figure. The line OC always has a steeper slope than dM/dF because r is greater than zero. Higher values of r lower dM/dF and move the equilibrium along OC. Because of the relative slopes of ab and OC, this means we move to higher levels of atmospheric CO_2 and lower levels of long–run production as r increases. Not surprisingly, a high discount rate causes us to value long–run consumption less.

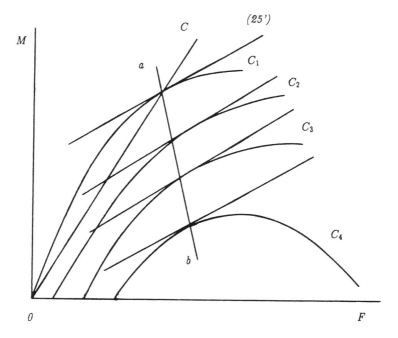

Figure 1: Solution of model

5.4. Illustration by a phase plane diagram

For conventional production functions, the equilibrium can be represented in a phase plane diagram as in Fig 1a. The phase plane diagram is a valuable tool not only because it shows the equilibrium but because it shows the changes in variables over time. In Appendix B, we precisely define the stability and existence conditions which assure that Fig 1a represents the equilibrium, that a path to the equilibrium exists, that the path is unique, and that therefore an optimal equilibrium is a long–run optimum.

Equations (24) and (25) are plotted in Fig 1a as curves AB and CD respectively. On the left–hand side of Fig 1a the curve AB lies above CD; the curves slope toward each other and intersect at equilibrium, 0. The relation between the curves results from our previous assumptions regarding the slopes of the production function, $f(F, M)$. If the shadow price is above AB, fossil fuels are relatively expensive, fossil fuel use is reduced, and the CO_2 level increases for the opposite reasons.

These movements are indicated by the small arrows in the diagram. To maintain the steady state, that is to satisfy (24), fossil fuel use must be low when the CO_2 level, M, is low and high when M is high.

Therefore, along AB when M is near zero the steady state shadow price, q, is large lowering fossil fuel use, and, at higher values of M, q is lower. Curve CD traces the "price vs harm" equation, (25). Along this line the shadow price of CO_2 emissions equals the long–run harm due to a marginal increase in CO_2 concentration. To the left of this curve, dq/dt is positive and to the right dq/dt is negative, again illustrated by the arrows. If the CO_2 concentration is low, M to the left of CD, the harm due to CO_2 is low relative to the future impacts; therefore, the shadow price of emissions is increasing. The opposite effects occur to the right of CD. With low historic levels of atmospheric CO_2, CO_2 increases have caused little harm. This implies that, at low levels of M, the marginal harm due to CO_2 is low; and to satisfy (25), the shadow price, q, must also be low. As M increases along the "price vs harm" curve, CD, q also increases. The curved arrows in the phase plane diagram describe the change in variables over time. When the equilibrium meets the sufficiency conditions noted earlier and the phase plane can be illustrated as in Fig 1a, it is optimal to choose the unique q so that the level of atmospheric CO_2 increases monotonically towards the equilibrium from levels of CO_2 less than the equilibrium. FO in Fig 1a represents such an optimal path. This means that both the shadow price, q, and atmospheric CO_2, M, increase with time. The use of fossil fuels, F, decreases monotonically, as can be seen by taking the total differential of (15).

AB: $\psi(q, M) - \alpha M = 0$ CD: $(r + \alpha)q + U'\left[\dfrac{\partial f(\psi(q, M), M)}{\partial M}\right] = 0$

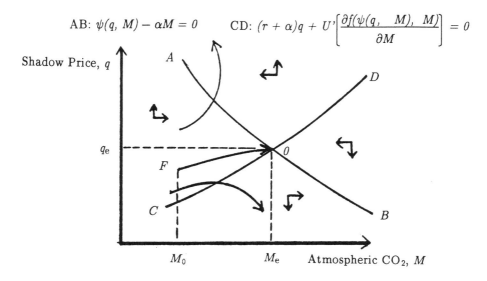

Figure 1a: Phase plane diagram

6. A discrete type impact of CO_2 emissions

In this section we analyse, as a more specific form of the model, the negative impact of CO_2 emissions that occur abruptly at specific levels of atmospheric CO_2.

In the simplest way we describe how consumption C is affected by CO_2 accumulation:

$$C = \begin{cases} f(F), & if \ M \le M_c, \\ 0, & if \ M_c < M, \end{cases} \qquad (1)$$

f being a production function with $f'(0) > 0$, $f'' < 0$ which means that, at zero fossil fuel use, fossil fuels are always productive, although they may be unproductive at higher levels of use. The basic assumption is that carbon dioxide has no impact on production until it reaches a critical level M_c. First assume that if CO_2 levels exceed M_c, production falls to zero. Hence the step function's simplicity has very drastic consequences indicating the observation that damages from CO_2 accumulation could rise rapidly at a critical level.

The necessary conditions for the basic problem when C is given by (1) are:

$$q = \begin{cases} U'f', & \text{if } M \leq M_c, \\ 0, & \text{if } M_c < M, \end{cases} \tag{2}$$

$$\frac{dq}{dt} = (r + \alpha)q, \qquad M \neq M_c. \tag{3}$$

Because the optimization is over an infinite horizon, there is no simple necessary transversality condition on the adjoining variable, q.

The problem is further complicated because the derivative of the Hamiltonian with respect to M does not exist at M_c. However, a careful analysis of the problem can determine q and F at M_c. If the function f gives a maximum at F_m and F_m is less than or equal to αM_c, there is a simple answer. Producing at the maximum for all time creates the highest possible utility. If producing at the maximum never raises M above M_c, we set q equal to zero and F at F_m. Both (2) and (3) are then satisfied. If F at the maximum of f is greater than αM_c or if f has no maximum, the solution is more complex. But it can be shown that it is always optimal to use the entire CO_2 capacity, that is burn fossil fuels in a manner which raises atmospheric CO_2 to the critical level M_c.

The analysis first determines that F equals αM_c when M equals M_c. Second, q is determined by (2), (3) and the additional necessary condition that $q(t)$ is a continuous function (except where M is constrained).

The calculation of q is simplified by finding T in the time horizon at which M equals M_c. The existence, uniqueness and finiteness of T is then proved which directly leads to the conclusion that the optimal solution exists and is unique.

The following heuristic considerations lead to this result. If M equals M_c, F must be less than or equal to αM_c; if not, M becomes greater than M_c and production drops to zero. The properties of U and f assure that (2) can be inverted and a function g, with $g(q)$ equal to F exists, which is monotonically decreasing in q. (2) further assures that q is greater than or equal to zero. (2) and (3) together assure that dF/dt is less than or equal to zero for M less than or equal to M_c. If F is strictly less than αM_c, then αM_c, or equivalently, q is strictly greater than $U'f'(\alpha M_c)$; F would remain less than αM_c for all times. Such a path is dominated by many alternative paths including F equals αM_c. Therefore, F equals αM_c when M equals M_c. This is pretty much in the spirit of Krelle's (1987) description of an ecological equilibrium though obtained from different model reasoning. These observations can be summarized in a proposition whose statement and proof is left for the Appendix A.

T is unique and exists. Assuming an optimum exists, it follows that the q_0, F and M which satisfy the necessary conditions are all unique, exist and are optimal. Figure 2 illustrates typical paths of fossil fuel use and CO_2 accumulation in the step model. M rises and F falls over time, both reach their equilibrium values at T.

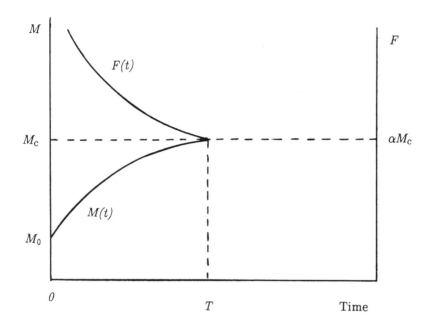

Figure 2: Illustration of paths of F and M in step model

The assumption that production falls to zero when the critical CO_2 level is reached is very extreme. We describe a model of slightly greater complexity that avoids this extreme assumption:

$$C = \begin{cases} f(F), & \text{if } M \leq M_c, \\ \beta f(F), & \text{if } M > M_c, \end{cases} \tag{4}$$

where $\beta \leq 1$.

In the previous model we did not require that f have a maximum. However, in this model we must assume a maximum of f exists or the integral in the Appendix A equation (***) is unbounded. We assume that F_m greater than αM_c maximizes f.

The necessary conditions are

$$q = \begin{cases} U'f', & \text{if } M \leq M_c, \\ \beta U'f', & \text{if } M > M_c, \end{cases} \tag{5}$$

$$\frac{dq}{dt} = (r + \alpha)q, \qquad M \neq M_c \tag{6}$$

In addition $q(t)$ must be continuous.

Again the discontinuity of production at M_c complicates the problem. However, by examining paths of q which satisfy the three necessary conditions the possible solutions can be reduced to two.

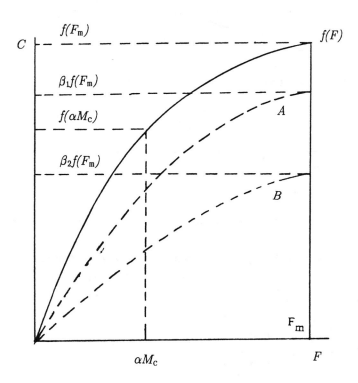

Figure 3: Two levels of CO_2 impact

If an optimum exists (5) assures that q is greater than or equal to zero; further, q is

less than or equal to $U'f'(\alpha M_c)$ as shown in the previous case. If the value of q at time zero, q_0, is zero, then (6) and continuity assure that q equals zero for all t. F equals F_m for all t, M equals M_c at some finite time, and M goes to F_m/α as t goes to infinity. If q is greater than zero, q rises exponentially until q equals $U'f'(\alpha M_c)$. q rising further is non–optimal; therefore, M must equal M_c when q equals $U'f'(\alpha M_c)$. The problem is identical to that presented in the previous case.

Consider the optimal action when M_0 equals M_c. F equals either αM_c or F_m for all time; therefore utility flow will be constant for all time at either $U(f(\alpha M_c))$ or $U(\beta f(F_m))$. The value of F which maximizes output will be optimal. If $f(\alpha M_c)$ is greater than $\beta f(F_m)$, F equals αM_c is optimal. If $f(\alpha M_c)$ equals $\beta f(F_m)$, the actions are equivalent. If $f(\alpha M_c)$ is less than $\beta f(F_m)$, F equals F_m is optimal.

Figure 3 illustrates both the production function and the optimal solution. We consider two step sizes β_1 and β_2. As illustrated by the dotted line (Curve A) and along the left axis, $\beta_1 f(F_m)$ is greater than $f(\alpha M_c)$; therefore it is optimal to use fossil fuels at F_m. As illustrated by the dashed line (Curve B and along the left axis), $\beta_2 f(F_m)$ is less than $f(\alpha M_c)$, therefore, in this second case long–run fossil fuel use is αM_c.

7. Further specification of the model

Further specification of the model allows the sensitivity analysis of particular variables. Two major results emerge: an approximation of F as a function of M and a demonstration of the importance of the productivity and efficiency in the fossil fuel sector in determining the present optimal fuel use. We specify $U(C)$ and $f(F)$ by:

$$U(C) = \begin{cases} \dfrac{C^{1-\gamma}}{1-\gamma}, & \text{if } \gamma \neq 1, \\ ln\ C, & \text{if } \gamma = 1, \end{cases} \tag{1}$$

$$f(F) = \lambda F^\delta. \tag{2}$$

These functional forms have all the properties formerly assumed for $U(C)$ and $f(F)$, lead to a simple solution, and are familiar in the economics literature. The elasticity of consumption and production with respect to fossil fuel use (i.e. the per cent change in consumption and production over the per cent change in fossil fuel use) is constant at δ, referred to as the fossil fuel productivity factor.

The utility function is sometimes referred to as the constant relative risk aversion utility function. γ is the consumption elasticity of utility or the relative risk aversion. Equation (6.2) takes the form:

$$q = \begin{cases} \delta\lambda^{1-\gamma}F^{r(1-\delta(1-\gamma))}, & \text{if } M \leq M_c, \\ 0, & \text{if } M > M_c, \end{cases} \tag{3}$$

Then using the other necessary conditions, $F(t)$, as a function of αM_c is found:

$$F(t) = \alpha M_c e^{A(T-t)} = F(0)e^{-At}, \tag{4}$$

where

$$A = \frac{r + \alpha}{1 - \delta(1 - \gamma)}. \tag{5}$$

Note that $F(t)$ is independent of the scaling factor λ.

Equation (4) for $F(t)$ can be substituted into equation (*) (See Appendix) and a simple expression in T derived:

$$\frac{\alpha}{A - \alpha}(e^{(A-\alpha)T} - 1) - 1 + e^{-\alpha T}\frac{M_0}{M_c} = 0. \tag{6}$$

A comparative statics analysis of (6) shows that: T decreases when the social discount rate or the fossil fuel productivity, r and δ respectively, increase: T increases when the consumption elasticity of utility, γ, increases; and the change in T with changes in the rate of CO_2 absorption, α, is indefinite.

The key equation is the simple approximation for F, the emissions policy, derived from (4),

$$F = A(M_c - M) + \alpha M. \tag{7}$$

This shows that unless A is much greater than α, the present policy is sensitive to all the model's parameters. A comparative statics analysis of (7) shows how the fossil fuel use pattern reacts to parameter changes within the range of interest. Highlights of the main impacts can be summed up:

- Because of the lower value of future consumption when the discount rate is high, initial fossil fuel use will increase with increases in the social discount rate.

- A higher consumption elasticity of demand, γ, tends to reduce present fossil fuel use. In general, a higher γ moves the economy to a more uniform consumption pattern. In this case, since consumption is falling, a higher consumption elasticity of demand reduces present fossil fuel use and increases future fossil fuel use.

- An increase in reabsorption, α, increases present fossil fuel use. When reabsorption is high, present emissions of CO_2 have less impact on future atmospheric CO_2 levels, encouraging higher present fossil fuel use.

- The initial use of fossil fuels increases with increases in the fossil fuel productivity factor, δ. This can be best understood by relating the fossil fuel productivity factor to the price elasticity of demand for the fossil fuel input which we call σ. σ equals $1/(1 - \delta)$, thus in this model high productivity implies high price elasticity of demand. From (6.6) the shadow price of fuels increases at a rate dependent only on the social discount rate and CO_2 reabsorption; therefore, the higher the price elasticity the more rapidly the fossil fuel use declines. A high rate of decline implies high initial use and a rapid approach to the equilibrium.

Values for T and $F(0)/M_c$ for a variety of parameter values are given in Table 1. The table shows the very significant impact which the fossil fuel productivity factor has on the optimal present level of fossil fuel use and the time to equilibrium. A high productivity factor results in very high fossil fuel use and a very short time to equilibrium. This suggests both that if the productivity is high it is not optimal to stringently restrict present fossil fuel use and that if fossil fuel productivity is low, it is important to conserve fossil fuel and delay the time at which very low levels of fossil fuel use are necessary.

8. Discussion

In these models there is a critical carbon dioxide level at which consumption and production drop to zero, and this critical level is the equilibrium level of CO_2 accumulation. Furthermore, the optimal fossil fuel use path is a declining exponential. The level of present fossil fuel use responds to parameters similarly in the models: present fossil fuel use increases with increases in the discount rate, the rate of CO_2 absorption, and the elasticity of production with respect to the fossil fuel measure. The fossil fuel use reaches equilibrium in a finite time.

$\delta(1-\gamma)$	α	r	M_c/M_0	T	$F(0)/M_c$
0.5	0.001	0.02	2	76.49	0.0248
0.95	0.001	0.02	2	12.80	0.2159
0.5	0.002	0.02	2	60.51	0.0287
0.95	0.002	0.02	2	10.79	0.2306
0.5	0.001	0.06	2	34.31	0.0658
0.95	0.001	0.06	2	5.27	0.6169
0.5	0.002	0.06	2	28.71	0.0703
0.95	0.002	0.06	2	4.64	0.6326
0.5	0.001	0.02	8	88.27	0.0408
0.95	0.001	0.02	8	14.10	0.3736
0.5	0.002	0.02	8	70.99	0.0455
0.95	0.002	0.02	8	12.02	0.3960
0.5	0.001	0.06	8	38.65	0.1117
0.95	0.001	0.06	8	5.72	1.0746
0.5	0.002	0.06	8	32.83	0.1172
0.95	0.002	0.06	8	5.09	1.0979

Table 1: T and $F(0)$ for a variety of parameter levels

Small and simple models of this kind are useful for generating ideas, supplementing large–scale models, and improving modelling approaches.

Several areas of economic research will be particularly important to CO_2. One important area is the effectiveness of research support in changing the mix of energy technologies. Another area of research is the use of market controls such as excise taxes, export limits, subsidies and cartels; to reduce or increase the use of a commodity.

The CO_2 problem should be considered in determining the type of research in the energy area which government supports. From a CO_2 perspective, economic incentives for the development of coal and oil shale are questionable. It appears that improvements in all non–fossil fuels do not necessarily lower future levels of CO_2. To displace fossil fuels, alternative non–fossil fuels must be highly substitutable. This study suggests two other factors which policy makers should be aware of when considering the economics of CO_2. As with many other environmental problems, any policies which increase the perceived discount rate will exacerbate the CO_2 problem by reducing our concern about the future. The shadow price attributed to fossil fuels by expected value economic models will be lower than the true shadow price for a risk averse society.

Part 2: Technical Change, International Co–operation, and Structural Uncertainty

9. Introduction

In this essay we pursue policy–directed applications of the simple models proposed in Part 1 for a range of three major issues: technical progress, international co–operation, and uncertainty.

Because of technical progress affecting energy production or finding mitigating strategies against CO_2 emissions (climatic engineering) the CO_2 problem may be highly sensitive to changes of technical progress parameters.

The worldwide nature of climate change, the dispersion of major fossil fuel resources, and the variation in possible effects of climate change all suggest the importance and problems of international co–operation in developing a CO_2 control policy.

Enormous uncertainty surrounds the future levels and effects of atmospheric CO_2 (Lindzen, Nierenberg et al, 1990). A specific type of uncertainty, structural uncertainty, associated with the modelling process has impacts on present optimal policies which have not been previously considered.

10. A taxonomy of technical change

The long run level of atmospheric CO_2 depends on both the degree of technical change and its form. In the following cases, technical change varies in its impacts on the productivity of inputs and the reabsorption of CO_2. We show that these differences create very different incentives for the long–run use of fossil fuels.

In an ongoing system of technical progress, the system of state equations has an additional parameter S, e.g. knowledge. Let a function of three variables represent consumption:

$$C = f(F, M, S). \tag{1}$$

In this system of equations, the existence of equilibrium, its optimality, and stability are governed by the same conditions as in the previously presented simple models.

We examine several kinds of technical change. In all cases the equilibrium is examined under the previously stated conditions (Part 1).

(1) Neutral technical progress

$$f(F, M, S) = Sh(F, M) \tag{2}$$

We refer to this as a neutral technical progress because the ratio of the partial derivative of f with respect to F and the partial derivative of f with respect to M is independent of the level of technical progress.

Examining condition (5.25') (Part 1) the constancy of this ratio under different levels of neutral technical progress assures that the long run carbon dioxide concentration is invariant.

(2) Development of non–fossil, substitutable energy

Along this line the production function represents technical progress in the development of a completely substitutable non–fossil fuel:

$$f(F, M, S) = h(F + S, M). \tag{3}$$

The equilibrium condition is the same condition as in (5.25') except that it is evaluated at $F + S$ and M:

$$-\frac{\dfrac{\partial h(F+S,\ M)}{\partial F}}{\dfrac{\partial h(F+S,\ M)}{\partial M}} = \frac{dM}{dF} = \frac{1}{(r + \alpha)}. \tag{4}$$

dM/dF is defined along an isoquant of h.

The immediate impact of the level of technical progress can be found by comparative statics or by a graphic examination of the solution. By neglecting details it shows that more technical progress reduces the equilibrium level of CO_2 and fossil fuel use.

(3) Removal of atmospheric CO_2

Removal of CO_2 changes the dynamics of CO_2 accumulation. Let S be the rate of CO_2 removal, the equation for the change in atmospheric CO_2 is

$$\frac{dM}{dt} = F - (\alpha M + S). \tag{5}$$

The equilibrium condition is then $F = \alpha M + S$, and this case parallels the previous case with a similar interpretation.

(4) Fossil fuel enhancing technical progress

Changes in fossil fuel productivity would result in a future production function:

$$f(F,\ M,\ S) = h(SF,\ M). \tag{6}$$

In equilibrium the following equation must hold along an isoquant of h

$$-S\frac{\dfrac{\partial h(SF,\ M)}{\partial F}}{\dfrac{\partial h(SF,\ M)}{\partial M}} = S\frac{dM}{dF} = \frac{1}{(r + \alpha)}. \tag{7}$$

Because the slopes of the isoquants may increase or decrease at any given value of F, the locus of points satisfying (7) may move to the right or left. The change in the equilibrium level of atmospheric CO_2 is, therefore, uncertain.

(5) Emissions Purification

Scrubbing CO_2 from emissions changes the dynamics of CO_2 accumulation as

$$\frac{dM}{dt} = \frac{F}{S} - \alpha M. \tag{8}$$

The equilibrium condition is then $F = S\alpha M$. This case corresponds to Case 4, and the same conclusion holds. The equivalence can be seen if the effects of substituting a variable F_0 equal to F/S into the production function and (8) are considered.

(6) Amelioration of CO_2 impacts (generated by forms of climatic engineering)

One representation of relieving CO_2 impacts would change the production function as

$$f(F, M, S) = h(F, M - S). \tag{9}$$

This case is similar to Case 2. Consequently, the long–run equilibrium level of CO_2 is raised with higher levels of technical progress.

A more general taxonomy is possible for production functions that are invariant under some general transformations to be called "neutral technical progress" (Sato, 1981). Such a taxonomy could translate itself into specific technology induced policies like reforestation, recovery of CO_2 from power plants, storage in the oceans, disposal in depleted gas reservoirs, energy technology substitution etc (Okken et al, 1989).

In the context of a narrower focus, e.g. energy technology substitution, very recent studies by Manne and Richels (1990), on the basis of their Global 2100 model, have given rise to assessment of a broad spectrum of CO_2 benign technologies.

11. Neutral technical change in a general model

By examining neutral technical change given exogenously in the general model we would reach the following significant conclusion: if the rest of the economy grows exponentially and the consumption elasticity of utility is constant, the equilibrium atmospheric CO_2

level declines at higher levels of economic growth.

To examine ongoing technical change additional assumptions must be made. First, we assume the production function is separable, e.g.

$$C = f(F, M, T) = h(F, M) S(t). \tag{1}$$

According to definition, this is neutral technical progress.

The necessary conditions (5.15) and (5.16) of Part 1 hold. If we differentiate (5.15) with respect to time, and let f take the form in (1) and F greater than zero:

$$\frac{dq}{dt} = \frac{\partial q}{\partial f}\frac{dF}{dt} + \frac{\partial q}{dM}\frac{dM}{dt} + \frac{\partial q}{\partial S}\frac{dS}{dt} + \frac{\partial q}{\partial U'}\frac{dU'}{dt}. \tag{2}$$

Use (5.15) and (2) to eliminate q and dq/dt from (5.16), then (5.16) turns into

$$\frac{\partial q}{\partial F}\frac{dF}{dt} + \frac{\partial q}{dM}\frac{dM}{dt} + \frac{\partial q}{\partial S}\frac{dS}{dt} + \frac{\partial q}{\partial U'}\frac{dU'}{dt} =$$

$$(r+\alpha)\, U'\frac{\partial h}{\partial F} S + U'\frac{\partial h}{\partial M} S. \tag{3}$$

In general, no equilibrium solution exists. However, when S increases exponentially with time and the consumption elasticity of utility is constant (U takes the constant relative risk aversion form), the problem is much simpler. dF/dt and dM/dt are zero in equilibrium. If η is the exponential rate of increase in S, dS/dt divided by S equals η and dU'/dt divided by U' equals $-\gamma\eta$. From (3) we derive the marginal rate of substitution between fossil fuel increases and CO_2 decreases, in analogy to (5.25'), Part 1, as

$$-\left[\frac{\partial h}{\partial F} : \frac{\partial h}{\partial M}\right] = \frac{dM}{dF} = \frac{1}{(r + \alpha - \eta(1 - \gamma))}. \tag{4}$$

If the right hand side of (4) is interpreted as the ratio of the prices of fossil fuel increases and atmospheric CO_2 decreases, the long run costs of CO_2 reductions are reduced by technical progress. We would expect such a cost reduction to cause substitution away from fossil fuel use and towards reduced CO_2 levels.

The sufficiency condition in (5.23) of Part 1 requires that the rate of increase in utility, $\eta(1 - \gamma)$, be less than the discount rate. This assures that the integral is finite and the maximum is well defined. It also assures that the slope of dM/dF will be less than the slope of the line along which αM equals F. Further, if the sufficiency and stability conditions noted in our discussion of the production function in the general model are met by h. then the equilibrium is optimal and stable.

Exponential technical progress can be added to the benchmark type model developed in Part 1. In this case the production function is

$$C = \begin{cases} F^\delta e^{\eta t}, & \text{if } M \le M_c, \\ 0, & \text{if } M > M_c. \end{cases} \tag{5}$$

By looking at the rate of change in fossil fuel use and the initial fossil fuel use, equations (5.17) and (5.22), in Part 1 are restated

$$F = F(T)\, e^{A(T-t)}, \tag{6}$$

$$F = A(M_c - M) + \alpha M. \tag{7}$$

The variable A is redefined as

$$A = \frac{r + \alpha - \eta(1 - \gamma)}{1 - \delta(1 - \gamma)}. \tag{8}$$

As we can see, the changes in F due to changes in the social discount rate, r, the fossil fuel productivity factor, δ, and the reabsorption rate, α, are as in the model without technical progress. Fossil fuel declines more slowly in this model because technical progress increases the productivity of fossil fuels. With technical progress what can we derive for the rate of growth of consumption (i.e. $(dC/dt)(1/C) = \Delta C$)?

From the present until time T when equilibrium is reached, the rate of growth in consumption is

$$\Delta C = -\frac{\delta(r + \alpha - \eta(1 - \gamma))}{1 - \eta(1 - \gamma)} + \eta. \tag{9}$$

The first term on the right is the rate of change in output from the energy sector, and the second term on the right is the rate of technical progress.

This expression can be simplified to

$$\Delta C = \frac{\eta - \delta(r + \alpha)}{1 - \delta(1 - \gamma)}.$$ (10)

When the rate of growth in the economy is positive, increases in the consumption elasticity of utility, γ, tend to increase present energy use, and thereby decrease the growth rate of consumption. When the rate of growth in the economy is negative, γ has the opposite effect.

The results can be extended and partially generalized by taking other and more complicated forms of consumption equations.

In all cases model parameters affect the rate of change in energy use in the same fashion in the models with and without technical progress.

In summary we can conclude that increases in the new parameter, η, reduce both initial energy use and the rate of decline in energy use.

Equation (10) shows whether and how consumption increases or decreases over time. Technical progress tends to make consumption grow. Reabsorption, social discounting, and high fossil fuel productivity all encourage high initial energy use and make a consumption decline more likely.

12. International co–operation

International control agreements on CO_2 emissions would require many participants. Temperature increases will impact countries in extremely varied ways, in some countries the impact may be beneficial. Thus international agreements on fossil fuel trade may be difficult to achieve. The basic premise is that critical CO_2 levels will be reached more quickly in a world without co–operation on CO_2 controls.

International co–operation on CO_2 emissions could be speeded up by acceleration of technology transfer between two countries or block of countries. If technology changes have a significant influence (or leverage) on critical CO_2 emissions, technology transfer schemes could facilitate co–operative ventures that accelerate the innovation and diffusion of technologies for enhancing global welfare.

If CO_2 emissions and possible global warming are perceived as a threat to their survival, individual countries or a group of countries may wish to unilaterally alter the international use of fossil fuels through export and import controls such as taxes and subsidies. The general relation between global pollution and international trade has only recently received considerable attention, and the suggestion to extend the mechanism of tradeable permits to global issues, such as CO_2, has just been followed up as part of the official US negotiation position on climate change (*Economist*, 1990). But the greatest part of work so far deals with local rather than transfrontier pollutants and is not particularly applicable to CO_2.

Within the class of models previously suggested we now consider the difficulties in the control of carbon dioxide emissions.

We set out from the benchmark (step) model and compare two cases: co–operative and non–co–operative, given by subscripts 'CO' and 'NC' respectively. For example, let F_{CO} refer to world emissions in the cooperative case, F_{NC} to world emissions in the non–co–operative case. q_{CO} refers to the tax or negative adjoint variable in the co–operative case, and T_{CO} to the time at which M equals M_c in the co–operative case. In the model two world regions, 1 and 2, exist. There are n and m factories in the two world regions. Let f be the production function of a single factory. The regions use F_1 and F_2 units of energy, respectively. The factories have decreasing returns and energy is used efficiently. Factories in Region 1 use F_1/n units of energy and factories in Region 2 use F_2/m units of energy. We assume a maximum level of energy use per factory, F_m, which is greater than $\alpha M_c/(n + m)$. Accordingly, we define the consumption in each region:

$$C_1 = \begin{cases} nf(F_1/n), & \text{if } M \le M_c, \\ 0, & \text{if } M > M_c, \end{cases}$$

$$C_2 = \begin{cases} mf(F_2/m), & \text{if } M \le M_c, \\ 0, & \text{if } M > M_c. \end{cases} \tag{1}$$

Co–operation is "complete" and the countries maximize the discounted sum of the consumption in the two regions being fully aware of future CO_2 effects.

The following setup describes the problem:

$$\underset{F_1, \ F_2 \ 0}{Max} \ \int_{}^{\infty} e^{-rt}(C_1 + C_2)dt, \tag{2}$$

$$\frac{dM}{dt} = F_1 + F_2 - \alpha M. \tag{3}$$

Not surprisingly, the solution is similar to that of the pure step model. The negative of the adjoint, q_{CO}, rises at an exponential rate of $(r + \alpha)$ to equilibrium at $f'(\alpha M_c/(m + n))$. The marginal product of energy in every factory equals the negative of the adjoint variable, f' equals q_{CO}. The inverse of this function, say $\Phi(q)$, determines F_{1CO} and F_{2CO}:

$$F_{1CO}(t) = n\phi(q_{CO}(t)), \quad F_{2CO} = m\phi(q_{CO}(t)). \tag{4}$$

T_{CO} is defined by

$$\int_0^{T_{CO}} e^{\alpha(T_{CO}-t)}(n + m)\, \Phi\left[f'[\frac{\alpha M_c}{m + n}]e^{(r+\alpha)(T_{CO}-t)}\right]dt - M_0 e^{-\alpha T_{CO}} = M_c. \tag{5}$$

The non–co–operative case differs considerably. Region 1 recognizes the future CO_2 impacts and controls emissions, but Region 2 is unaware of or ignores the impacts until M equals M_c. Region 2 initially burns fuel at a level mF_m such that $f'(F_m)$ equals 0.

For simplicity we assume that when M equals M_c co–operation begins and that F_{1NC}/n equals F_{2NC}/m and $F_{1NC} + F_{2NC}$ equals αM_c. Region 1 solves the following problem:

$$\underset{F_1}{Max} \int_0^\infty e^{-rt} C_1\, dt, \tag{6}$$

$$\frac{dM}{dt} = \begin{cases} F_1 + mF_2 - \alpha M, & if\ M \le M_c, \\ 0, & if\ M > M_c. \end{cases} \tag{7}$$

q_n rises exponentially at the rate $(r + \alpha)$ until equilibrium at $f'(\alpha M_c/(m+n))$. In Region 1 only, the marginal products of factories are held at q_n and emissions of these factories are equal to $\phi(q)$. F_{1NC} and F_{2NC} for $M < M_c$ are

$$F_{1NC} = n\phi(q_n(t)),$$
$$F_{2NC} = mF_m. \tag{8}$$

T_{NC} is then given by

$$\int_{0}^{T_{NC}} e^{-\alpha(T_{NC}-t)}\left\{n\phi\left(f'[\frac{\alpha M_c}{m\ +\ n}]\ e^{-(r+\alpha)(T_{NC}-t)}\right) + F_m\right\}dt - M_0 e^{-\alpha T_{NC}} = M_c. \quad (9)$$

Thus we could state the theorem.

Theorem. *A critical CO_2 emissions level is always reached in less time in the non–co–op-erative case than in the co–operative case. T_{NC} is less than T_{CO}.*

In order to prove this result, we restate (5) and (9) respectively, as:

$$\int_{0}^{T_{CO}} e^{-\alpha t}\left\{(n + m)\ \phi[f'[\frac{\alpha M_c}{m\ +\ n}]\ e^{-(r+\alpha)t}] - \alpha M_0\right\}dt + M_0 = M_c \quad (10)$$

and

$$\int_{0}^{T_{NC}} e^{-\alpha t}\left\{n\phi[f'[\frac{\alpha M_c}{m\ +\ n}]\ e^{-(r+\alpha)t}] + mF_m - \alpha M_0\right\}dt + M_0 = M_c. \quad (11)$$

Essentially the integration is now backwards in time. Because F_m is greater than $m\phi[f'(\frac{\alpha M_c}{m\ +\ n})\ e^{-(r+\alpha)t}]$ and the other terms of the integrands are equal, at each instant the integrand in (11) is greater than the integrand in (10). Since the integrand is always larger in (11), the integral must equal $M_c - M_0$ in a shorter time.

We have shown previously that $q_{NC}(T_{NC})$ equals $q_{CO}(T_{CO})$ equals $f'(\frac{\alpha M_c}{m\ +\ n})$. If we single out the specific Region 1 and let T_{NC} be less than T_{CO}:

$$q_{NC}(t) = q_{NC}(T_{NC})\ e^{-(r+\alpha)(T_{NC}-t)} > q_{CO}(T_{CO})\ e^{-(r+\alpha)(T_{CO}-t)} = q_{CO}(t), \quad (12)$$

$$n\dot\phi(q_{NC}(t)) = F_{1NC} < F_{1CO} = n\phi(q_{CO}(t)). \quad (13)$$

The emissions of the concerned region are lower in the non–co–operative case than they are in the co–operative case.

T_{NC} less than T_{CO} appears to imply that world fossil fuel use in the non–co–operative case is always higher than in the co–operative case; however, this is not necessarily true. There could be special situations identified by specific parametric configurations of the production function and other parameters, in which world emissions in the non–co–operative case are actually lower than in the co–operative case for a short initial period.

In summarizing the results, if co–operation is not feasible, regions concerned about carbon dioxide will lower emissions to compensate for regions not concerned about carbon dioxide, however, the maximum level of carbon dioxide concentration will be reached later with co–operation than without co–operation.

13. Structural uncertainty

As we have seen before, various types of uncertainties are linked with the CO_2 problem. In view of planned or perceived policy actions on national or international levels, some or most of these uncertainties are not even quantifiable. Examples include costs of new and improved technologies that could substitute for existing ones, or costs of incremental technologies that may be used to increase efficiencies and the environmental benign of existing fossil fuel use. But from the perspective of economic modelling we come across these intangible uncertainties and ask ourselves how to cope with uncertainties impacting the modelling process. We call this phenomenon "structural uncertainty". We will show that when dealing with structural uncertainty it is not enough to use expected (certainty equivalent) values of critical parameters rather a comprehensive treatment of uncertainty is called for, in view of assessing optimal present and future fossil fuel use.

First of all we observe that determinations of optimal fossil fuel use are similar in uncertainty when there is an uncertain, critical atmospheric carbon dioxide level as compared to a situation where the fossil fuel resource is uncertain. When we neglect absorption of atmospheric CO_2, the two situations are structurally equivalent in uncertainty.

The results of research on uncertain, limited natural resources are also pertinent to the CO_2 problem with minor changes in definitions.

13.1. Modelling uncertainty about critical CO_2 levels as uncertainty about a critical, limited natural resource

Let us assume first that the present level of CO_2 is M_0 and that n possible critical carbon dioxide levels, M_i, $i = 1,..., n$, exist. The prior probability that M_c equals M_i is Π_i. J_i is the maximum expected value of future fossil fuel consumption when the current level of carbon dioxide in the atmosphere is M_i.

π_{ij} is the update probability that M_c equals M_j given that M_i has been reached and is not the critical level. E denotes an expectation. J_i is defined by

$$J_i = Max \; E[\int_0^\infty e^{-rt} \; U(C) \; dt \;] \tag{1}$$

such that

$$C = \begin{cases} f(F), & if \; M \le M_c, \\ 0, & if \; M > M_c, \end{cases} \tag{2}$$

$$M(t=0) = M_i, \tag{3}$$

$$\pi_{i} = Prob\{M_j = M_c | M_i \neq M_c\} = \begin{cases} \pi_k / \sum_{j=i+1}^{n} \pi_j, & if \; k = i+1,..., n, \\ \\ 0, & if \; otherwise. \end{cases} \tag{4}$$

Let T_i be the time to move between carbon dioxide levels M_i and M_{i+1}, given by

$$\int_0^{T_i} e^{-\alpha(T_i - t)} \; F(t) \; dt = M_{i+1} - e^{-\alpha T_i} \; M_i. \tag{5}$$

This formulation is an adaptation of Gilbert's (1979) analysis of the CO_2 problem, and most of his results are pertinent to this analysis.

In view of the definition of T_i, we consider a slightly different optimization problem by considering as the value $J(M_i, M_{i+1}, T_i)$, the value obtained by moving from a CO_2

concentration of M_i to M_{i+1}, in time T_i, defined as:

$$J(M_i, M_{i+1}, T_i) = \underset{F}{Max} \int_0^{T_i} e^{-rt}\, U(C)\, dt \tag{6}$$

such that

$$C = f(F), \tag{7}$$

$$\frac{dM}{dt} = F - \alpha M, \tag{8}$$

$$M(0) = M_i \quad \text{and} \quad M(T_i) = M_{i+1}. \tag{9}$$

The results of Gilbert (1979) can be immediately transferred to the determination of optimal fossil fuel use given structural uncertainty about the critical level of atmospheric carbon dioxide. The solution algorithm for (6) requires maximization over T_i of three terms:

$$J_i = \underset{T_i}{Max} \left\{ J(M_i, M_{i+1}, T_i) + e^{-rT_i}\, [\pi_{i,\,i+1} U(C(\alpha M_{i+1}))/r = (1 - \pi_{i,\,i+1}) J_{i+1}] \right\}. \tag{10}$$

In the order of appearance the maximand consists of

(i)   the value J gained while raising the CO_2 level from M_i to M_{i+1}.

(ii)   the discounted expected value of consuming fuel at a rate that maintains the CO_2 level at M_{i+1} weighted by the probability that M_{i+1} is the critical CO_2 level.

(iii)   the discounted expected value of raising the CO_2 concentration above M_{i+1} weighted by the probability that M_{i+1} is not the critical level.

Another result is that a "certainty equivalent" critical level of CO_2 exists, i.e. M_{ce}, which produces the same initial emissions as the algorithm in (10). It can be shown that M_{ce} is greater than $E(M_c)$. If so, it follows that the calculated optimal current fossil fuel use, when probabilities are fully taken care of, is lower than the optimal current fossil fuel use when expected values are treated as certainty equivalents.

13.2. Treating structural uncertainty

We now show on the basis of the previous results that the way in which uncertainty is treated in such models can significantly alter the calculated response to CO_2. For reasons of simplicity, let us first assume that no (observable) CO_2 impacts occur and no information is gathered about CO_2 impacts until the CO_2 level reaches a threshold M_a. At that time all uncertainty regarding the future impacts of CO_2 is resolved.

This simplifies the previous model because all learning occurs at a single CO_2 level rather than at several levels.

In this form, the problem can be stated as

$$J_0 = \underset{T}{Max} \{J(M_0, M_a, T) + e^{-rt} E(J_a)\}. \tag{11}$$

T is the time at which the CO_2 level equals M_a. $E(J_a)$ is the expected utility gain after the CO_2 level reaches M_a and uncertainty is resolved. J_a does not depend on T.

From the necessary conditions, we derive

$$F(t) = F_0^{-At} \quad \text{for} \quad t \leq T. \tag{12}$$

Using (5) and (12) we determine F_0 as a function of T:

$$F_0 = \frac{(M_a e^{\alpha T} - M_0)(A - \alpha)}{1 - e^{-(A-\alpha)T}}. \tag{13}$$

The utility gained while increasing the CO_2 level from M_0 to M_a, $J(M_0, M_a, T)$ is certain and a function of T:

$$J(M_0, M_a, T) = \int_0^T e^{-rt} U(C)\, dt = \frac{F_0^{\delta(1-\gamma)}}{(1-\gamma)(A - \alpha)}(1 - e^{-(A-\alpha)T}). \tag{14}$$

The solution algorithm from equation (11) then takes the form

$$J_0 = Max_T \left\{ \frac{F_0^{\delta(1-\gamma)}}{-\gamma)(A-\alpha)} (1 - e^{-(A-\alpha)T}) + e^{-rT}E(J_a) \right\}. \tag{15}$$

To determine the maximum, the derivative with respect to T is set to zero, recalling that F_0 is a function of T:

$$\frac{dJ_0}{dT} = 0. \tag{16}$$

Thus, for (15),

$$F_0^{\delta(1-\gamma)} \left[\frac{\delta}{(A-\alpha)F_0} (1 - e^{-(A-\alpha)T}) \frac{dF_0}{dT} + \frac{1}{1-\gamma} e^{-(A-\alpha)T} \right] - re^{rT}E(J_a) = 0. \tag{17}$$

If, from (13), the derivative of F_0 with respect to T is substituted into (17), we find

$$F_0^{\delta(1-\gamma)} \left[\frac{\delta\alpha M_a}{F_0} e^{\alpha T} + \frac{1 - \delta(1-\gamma)}{1-\gamma} e^{-(A-\alpha)T} \right] - re^{rT}E(J_a) = 0 \tag{18}$$

Since we can define

$$F_a = F_0 e^{-AT} \tag{19}$$

we can simplify (18) as

$$\frac{F_a^{\delta(1-g)}}{r} \frac{\delta\alpha M_a}{F_a} + \frac{1 - \delta(1-\gamma)}{1-\gamma} = E(J_a). \tag{20}$$

(20) can be solved by numerical methods for any value of $E(J_a)$. It gives rise to a correct, appropriate treatment of uncertainty. Thus, T and the optimal present emissions can be found.

In comparing two different treatments of uncertainty, we distinguish the "certainty equivalent" case from the comprehensive treatment of uncertainty, as shown by the formulae above culminating in equation (20).

To show even more specific results we use our general benchmark model and calculate changes in present fossil fuel use under the two treatments of uncertainty for a variety of parameter settings.

Let us start with the familiar framework: M_c equals M_1 with probability π and M_2 with probability $(1 - \pi)$. The critical CO_2 level is assumed equal to the expected critical

$$M_{ca} = \pi M_1 + (1 - \pi)M_2, \tag{21}$$

where M_{ca} is the assumed certain critical level. The problem can now be treated like a deterministic problem and the results obtained in Part 1 directly apply.

In the second approach to uncertainty, we make use of the probability estimates and the algorithm developed in the previous section.

In this case, the CO_2 level certainly can increase from M_0 to M_1. $J(M_0, M_1, T)$, the value gained in this transition, is certain and is given by (14). As could be seen from (15), $E(J_a)$ represents the expected utility gathered after M_1 is reached. $E(J_a)$ is the weighted sum of the utility gained by staying at M_1 and the utility gained by going to M_2 and staying at that level of CO_2.

Let $J_s(M)$ be the utility gathered when the CO_2 level is maintained at a constant M from the present into infinity.

The following equation defines $J_s(M)$ for a general production and for the production function F^δ, in particular:

$$J_s{}'(M) = \frac{U(f(\alpha M, \ M))}{r} = \frac{(\alpha M)^{\delta(1-\gamma)}}{r \ (1 - \gamma)}. \tag{22}$$

If M_1 is the maximum level of CO_2 concentration, the utility is specified by (22) with M equals $M_$. If M_2 is the maximum level of CO_2 concentration, $J(M_1, M_2, T*)$ defined by (14), is collected going from M_1 to M_2, and $J_s(M_2)$ is collected after M_2 is reached. $T*$ is the optimal time to go from M_1 to M_2. With M_0 equal to M_1 and M_c equal to M_2, we use (6.19), Part 1, to determine $T*$:

$$\frac{\alpha M_2}{(A - \alpha)M_1} (e^{(A-\alpha)T*} - 1) + e^{-\alpha T*} - 1 = 0. \tag{23}$$

After $T*$ being defined by (23), $E(J_s)$ can now be calculated as

$$E(J_a) = \pi J_s(M_1) + (1 - \pi)\left\{ J(M_1, M_2, T_*) + e^{-rT^*} J_s(M_2)\right\}. \qquad (24)$$

In more complete, specific parametric form $E(J_s)$ is

$$E(J_s) = \frac{\pi(\alpha M_1)^{\delta(1-\gamma)}}{r(1-\gamma)} + \frac{(1 - \pi)(\alpha M_2)^{\delta(1-\gamma)}}{r(1 - \gamma)\, e^{rT_*}} [1 + \frac{r}{A - \alpha}\, (e^{(A-\alpha)T_*} - 1)]. \qquad (25)$$

To find the optimal F_0 under this full treatment of uncertainty (FTU), the above equation for $E(J_s)$ is used in conjunction with (20), the latter dealing with the simple case.

13.3. Numerical calculations

We have presented two alternatives to dealing with uncertainty and choosing the appropriate emissions level. The results show so far that emissions are higher if the "certainty equivalent" (CE) case is used. However, to determine the magnitude of the differences we have to resort to numerical examples, and we turn to this next. We did some limited calculations for specific examples presented in Tables 2 and 3.

In the first three columns of each table we list the parameters used in each run or set of calculations. In the fourth column we list the percentage increase in initial emissions when we change from the FTU case to the CE case. In the column CE appears the present optimal fossil fuel use when the expected value of M_c is assumed certain. In the final column FTU is the value of $F(O)$ when uncertainty is fully treated.

In all calculations we assume $M_0 = 1$, $\pi = 0.5$, production equals F^δ for M less than the critical level of CO_2.

In Table 2 the uncertain levels are $M_1 = 2$ and $M_2 = 4$. At this level of uncertainty the estimates of the proper emission level are close together. In Table 3 a much wider range of uncertainty is considered: $M_1 = 2$ and $M_2 = 8$. Therefore the differences in initial emission rates are more significant.

The emissions when a CE critical level of carbon dioxide is assumed are on the average over 30 per cent higher than in the case of FTU.

These examples add to the claim that an appropriate treatment of uncertainty is important in modelling carbon dioxide.

Table 2: Comparison of CE and FTU with Low Variance					
Basis : $M_0 = 1$, $M_1 = 2$, $\pi = 0,5$					
$\delta(1-\gamma)$	r	α	% change in F_0	CE F_0	FTU
0.5	0.02	0.001	12.2	0.087	0.077
0.75	0.04	0.001	7.2	0.332	0.309
0.95	0.06	0.001	0.4	2.420	2.410
0.5	0.02	0.002	5.5	0.094	0.089
0.75	0.04	0.002	4.8	0.342	0.326
0.95	0.06	0.002	1.1	2.486	2.460

Table 3: Comparison of CE and FTU with High Variance					
$\delta(1-\gamma)$	r	α	% change in F_0	CE F_0	FTU
0.5	0.02	0.001	46.4	0.215	0.134
0.75	0.04	0.001	34.2	0.825	0.584
0.95	0.06	0.001	24.3	6.105	4.780
0.5	0.02	0.002	39.6	0.230	0.154
0.75	0.04	0.002	32.1	0.850	0.615
0.95	0.06	0.002	24.1	6.210	4.880

14. Conclusions and perspectives

The choice of simple models proposed so far have been examined under three major issues: technical progress, international co–operation and structural uncertainty. We show that for this class of models depending on the assumptions regarding technical progress, the optimal steady state CO_2 concentration may rise or fall with increases in the steady state level of progress. More specifically, an improved substitute for fossil fuels always reduces the long—run level of CO_2; while an improvement in fossil fuel productivity may increase or decrease the level of CO_2.

Also we show that the solutions of a model with neutral, constant and ongoing technical progress and the general (static) model are very similar. In the model with technical progress, higher levels of technical progress lead to lower long—run optimal levels of CO_2.

By examining two cases of international co—operation in controlling CO_2 accumulation, we first considered a reference case of complete co—operation between two regions in maximizing consumption with full awareness of the CO_2 problem. This case is compared with a situation in which no co—operation takes place until a critical CO_2 level is reached. A most interesting finding is that in the non—co—operative situation the critical level is reached sooner, even though one region (concerned about CO_2) always emits less carbon than in the co—operative case. A non—intuitive situation can occur in which initial emissions of the two regions are lower in the non—co—operative case than in the co—operative case.

The final applications are to uncertainty. Here we show that the results from studies of the optimal use of natural resources in limited supply can be naturally extended to the CO_2 problem. Then, using numerical examples we show that an inappropriate treatment of structural uncertainty can lead to a significantly higher than optimal estimate of the desirable level of fossil fuel use.

Some final comments should be devoted to the general philosophy of modelling complex, highly interactive energy—environmental situations. Our task has been ambitious, namely to exhibit single type models of optimal control that are able to identify major structural parameters of the CO_2 problem as seen from an economist's perspective.

In models which optimize over an infinite horizon, future effects may change current policies, and feedback effects are always of importance. However, in these same models feedback effects may make solution much more difficult. In this class of optimizing models inclusion of feedback effects usually lowers the optimal initial use of fossil fuels. The long—run changes in fossil fuel use due to feedback effects are more uncertain and dependent on the model.

Given the uncertainty in the severity and timing of feedback effects, the sensitivity of individual models to variations in feedback effects is of much interest. In this class of models we find that current optimal fossil fuel use is significantly affected by different critical levels of CO_2.

Including optimization in models expands their applicability but may cause analytic problems and controversy. As with many social policy problems involving welfare judgments, an acceptable objective function for CO_2 control problems is difficult to define.

Any definition will seem both inadequate and overly precise and certainly will be controversial. This may be the reason we will find very few optimizing models in this area. However, such a model will not hide useful results otherwise obtained and by a carefully done sensitivity analysis may add many new insights not otherwise obtained. I concur with R. E. Lucas (1987, chap. 2) that "useful policy discussions are ultimately based on models".

Optimization raises several new issues in these models. For example, pollution impoverishes but technical progress enriches the future.

The models show that curvature of the utility function, determined by the consumption elasticity of utility in our models, tends to smooth or even out wealth over time. Without an objective function being stated, the importance of this redistribution effect in determining fossil fuel use policy can not be examined.

Appendix A: Existence and Uniqueness of the Optimal Solution

Proposition: *If f in Section 6 has no maximum or the maximum occurs at F greater than αM_c and M(0) is less than M_c, there is a unique finite time T at which M equals M_c.*

Proof. If it exists, the time at which M equals M_c, T, is defined by

$$M_e = \int_0^T e^{-\alpha(T-t)} g(q(t))\, dt + e^{-\alpha T} M_0 \qquad (*)$$

When M equals M_c or t is greater than or equal to T, q equals $U'f'(\alpha M_c)$.

From (6.3), when M is less than M_c or t is less than T, q equals $q_0 e^{(r+\alpha)t}$ where q_0 is the value of q at t equals 0. Continuity of q requires that, for an optimal path

$$U'f'(\alpha M_c) = q_0 e^{(r+\alpha)} T. \qquad (**)$$

If a q_0 and T satisfying (*) and (**) can be found the paths of q, F and M are all determined.

(**) can be solved for q_0 in terms of T. (*) can then be restated as an equation in which T is the single unknown variable. After rearranging terms:

$$\int_0^T e^{-\alpha T}\left\{g(U'f'(\alpha M_c)e^{-(r+\alpha)(T-t)}) - \alpha M_c\right\} dt - e^{-\alpha T}(M_c - M_0) = 0. \qquad (***)$$

At T equals zero the integral in (***) is zero and at T equals infinity the integral is infinity. The function is continuous, therefore, a solution exists and is finite. The derivative of the left–hand side with respect to T is positive, therefore the solution is unique.

q.e.d.

Appendix B: Existence and Stability of Equilibrium

In this appendix we show that the equilibrium solution of Section 5 holds and provide in detail the assumptions which assure our solution holds.

Several assumptions assure that a solution to (5.25') exists when F equals αM. As with the sufficiency conditions, the general existence proof is only applicable if the production function has continuous first derivatives. Continuous first derivatives assure that the left hand side (lhs) of (5.25') is continuous except in any region where $\partial f/\partial M$ equals zero. Experience has shown that CO_2 accumulation has caused little damage to date and that energy is valuable in production; therefore, we assume that at zero energy use and zero atmospheric CO_2, the marginal product of energy use is greater in magnitude that the marginal harm due to an increase in CO_2. It follows that the lhs of (5.25') is very large when F and αM equal zero.

Existence of the equilibrium is then assured if at some level of atmospheric CO_2 concentration the marginal product of energy use is less in magnitude than the marginal harm due to an increase in atmospheric CO_2, i.e. the lhs of (5.25') is less than one. This can be assured by two reasonable assumptions:

$$\frac{\partial f(0,M)}{\partial F} \leq \frac{\partial f(0,0)}{\partial F}, \qquad (A1)$$

$$\frac{\partial^{r}(\alpha M, M)}{\partial M} > \frac{\partial f(0,0)}{\partial F}, \tag{A2}$$

as M goes to infinity.

The first assumption is that the marginal product of fossil fuels is greatest at zero fossil fuel use and atmospheric CO_2 accumulation. The second condition states that, as atmospheric CO_2 increases, at some point the marginal harm is greater than the maximum marginal product of fossil fuels. More stringent assumptions, which assure that equations (A1) and (A2) are satisfied, are that the second partial derivative of f with respect to F and M are negative and that the marginal harm due to CO_2 goes to infinity.

By taking the total differential of (5.25') we can show that, if the second partial derivative of f with respect to F and M are negative, we are also assured that curve ab in Figure 1 slopes downward as shown.

Although we have discussed the conditions which show that the equilibrium is optimal and exists, we still have to show that an optimal path to the equilibrium exists. If the equilibrium is stable or, in other words, a saddle point, a unique shadow price exists for each level of CO_2 concentration which if chosen initially will cause convergence to the equilibrium along the optimal path. If the equilibrium is unstable, the equilibrium is maintained when CO_2 is initially at the equilibrium level; but no optimal path to the equilibrium exists if CO_2 starts at any other level.

Our stability analysis follows Kamien and Schwartz (1981, p 160). The proof of stability depends on the particular structure of our simple model. When F is greater than zero, (5.15) is an equation of the form $G(F, M, q) = 0$. We earlier assumed that we could express F as a function of M and q. By the implicit function theorem, this function for G exists if the partial derivative of G with respect to F does not equal zero for any F, M, and q that satisfy (5.15). The partial derivative of f with respect to F and the derivative of U with respect to C have already been assumed to be non–zero for values of F in the range of interest, therefore, the function for F in terms of q and M exists.

The next step in the stability analysis is to linearize equations (5.24) and (5.25) around the equilibrium. If the equilibrium values of M and q are designated $\bar{M}$ and $\bar{q}$, then (5.24) and (5.25) can be approximated:

$$-\left[\alpha + \frac{U_{fm}}{U_{ff}}\right](M - \bar{M}) + \frac{1}{U_{ff}}(q - \bar{q}) = 0, \tag{A3}$$

$$- \left[\frac{U_{fm}^2 - U_{ff}U_{mm}}{U_{ff}} \right](M - \dot{M}) + \left[\tau + \left[\alpha + \frac{U_{fm}}{U_{ff}} \right] \right](q - \dot{q}). \tag{A4}$$

A linear system, as in (A3) and (A4) has a characteristic equation. If the roots of the equation are real and of opposite signs, the equilibrium is a saddle point and the solution is stable. We state the derived stability condition without further discussion of the characteristic equation. For further details we refer to the discussion of stability analysis in Kamien and Schwartz (1981). If the following inequality holds, the equilibrium is stable:

$$U_{mm} + (\tau\alpha + \alpha^2)U_{ff} + (\tau + 2\alpha)U_{fm} < 0.$$

In our discussion of sufficiency we assumed that U_{ff} and U_{mm} were both negative. We again make these assumptions. The final assumption is that U_{fm} is less than or equal to zero and consequently that the equilibrium is stable. This assumption can only be true if the second partial derivative of production with respect to fossil fuel use and atmospheric CO_2 is less than or equal to zero, as can bee seen from equation (5.20). This assumption makes sure that the marginal product of fossil fuel use does not increase with increases in atmospheric CO_2. Note, the relation in (A3) may hold even if U_{fm} is greater than zero.

In our analysis of the equilibrium we have found two key conditions. First, for the equilibrium itself to be optimal, the second partial derivatives of production with respect to both fossil fuel use and atmospheric carbon dioxide must be negative, and the condition in (5.23) must hold. Second, for a simple and general proof that an optimal path to the equilibrium exists, U_{fm} in (5.20) must be negative. This implies that the second partial derivative of production with respect to fossil fuel use and atmospheric carbon dioxide must be negative. We must emphasize that these conditions are not necessary, they only allow easy proofs of sufficiency and stability. If these conditions hold and M is initially lower than the equilibrium, CO_2 increases, the shadow price increases, and fossil fuel use decreases with time until equilibrium.

References

Chiarella, C., 1980, "Optimal depletion of a nonrenewable resource when technological progress is endogenous", in: Kemp, M. C., and Long, N. V., (eds.), *Exhaustible Resources, Optimality and Trade*, North Holland, Amsterdam, 81–93

Conrad, J.M., and Clark , C.W., 1987, *"Natural Resource Economics"*, Cambridge University Press, Cambridge

Deschmukh, S.D., and Pliska, S.R., 1980, "Optimal consumption and exploration of non–renewable resources with uncertainty", *Econometrica 48*, 177–200

Deschmukh, S.D., and Pliska, S.R., 1983, "Optimal consumption of non–renewable resources with stochastic discoveries and a random environment", *Review of Economic Studies 50*, 543–554

The Economist, 1990, "Greenhouse economics", "Trading places", July 7, 19–22, 46–47

Edmonds, J., and Reilly, J., 1983, "Global energy and CO_2 to the Year 2050", *Energy Journal 4*, 21–47

Fisher, A.C., 1981, *"Resource and Environmental Economics"*, Cambridge University Press, Cambridge

Flohn, H., 1988, *"Das Problem der Klimaänderungen (The Problem of Climatic Change)"*, Wissenschaftliche Buchgesellschaft, Darmstadt

Gilbert, R.J., 1979,."Optimal depletion of an uncertain stock", *Review of Economic Studies 46*, 47–57

Halkin, H., 1974, "Necessary conditions for optimal control problems with infinite horizons", *Econometrica 42*, 267–272

Kamien, M.I., and Schwarz, N.L., 1981, *"Dynamic Optimization"*, North Holland, Amsterdam, New York

Kemp, M., 1976, "How to eat a cake of unknown size" in: Kemp, M.C., (ed.), *Three Topics in the Theory of International Trade*, North Holland, Amsterdam

Krelle, W., 1987, "Wirtschaftswachstum bei Erhaltung der Umweltqualität (Economic growth by maintaining environmental quality", in: R. Henn (ed.), *Technologie, Wachstum und Beschäftigung*, Springer, Heidelberg 757–778

Lindzen, R.S., Nierenberg, W.A., et al., 1990, "Letters to the editor: Global warming report", *Science 247*, 14–16

Lucas, R. E., 1987, *"Models of Business Cycles"*, Yrjo Johnsson Lectures, Basil Blackwell, Oxford

MacCracken, M.C., and Luther, F.M., (eds.), 1985, *"Projecting the Climatic Effects of Increasing Carbon Dioxide"*, US Dept of Energy, Office of Energy Research, Carbon Dioxide Research Division, DOE/ER–0237, Washington D.C.

Manne, A.S., 1990, "ETA–MACRO: A model of energy–economy interactions", in Charles J. Hitch (ed.), *Modelling Energy–Economy Interactions*, Resources for the Future, Washington D.C.

Manne, A.S., and Richels, R.G., "The costs of reducing U.S. CO_2 emissions further", *Energy Journal 11*, 69–78

National Research Council (NRC), Carbon Dioxide Assessment Committee, Nierenberg, (ed.), 1983, *"Changing Climate"*, National Academy Press, Washington D.
   C.

Nordhaus, W.D., 1980, "Thinking about carbon dioxide: Theoretical and empirical
   aspects of optimal control strategies", *Cowles Foundation Discussion Paper* No
   565, Oct., Yale University, New Haven, Conn.

Okken, P.A., Swart, R.J., and Swerver, S., (eds.), 1989, *"Climate and Energy"*, Kluwer
   Academic Publishers, Dordrecht

Perry, A.M., et al., 1982, "Energy supply and demand implications of CO_2", *Energy
   Journal 13*, 991–1004

Rose, D.J., Miller, M.M., and Agnew, C., 1983, *"Global Energy Futures and CO_2 Induced Climate Change"*, Report MITEL 83–015, Nov., MIT Energy Laboratory,
   Cambridge, Massachusetts

Rosenberg, N.J., 1986, "A primer on climatic change: Mechanisms, trends and projections". Renewable Resources Division, Resources for the Future, *Discussion Paper
   RR 86–04*, Aug.

Rosenberg, N.J., et al., 1988, *"Greenhouse Warming: Abatement and Adaptation"*,
   Proceedings of a Workshop, 14–15 June, Resources for the Future, Washington
   D.C.

Sato, R., 1981, *"Theory of Technical Change and Economic Invariance"*, Ch. 4., Academic Press, New York

Schelling, Thomas C., 1988, *"Global Environmental Forces"*, Energy and Environmental Policy Center, JFK School of Government, Harvard University, E88–10,
   Nov.

Schneider, St.H., 1989, *"Global Warming: Are We Entering the Greenhouse Century?"*,
   Sierra Club Books, Random House, New York

Yohe, C.W., 1984, "The effects of changes in expected near–term fossil fuel prices on
   long–term energy and carbon dioxide projections", *Resources and Energy 6*, 1–20.

Comments by Oskar von dem Hagen

Gottinger's paper addresses a "hot" topic: the emission of CO_2 by burning fossil fuels.
During the days when the final version of this comment was being prepared, the topic
dramatically attracted attention through hundreds of burning oil wells in Kuwait. At
that time the effects on climate and atmosphere were quite unpredictable.

The paper gives a good introduction to the problem[1] and an informative survey of recent economic studies in the area. The focus of the paper is a theoretical analysis of the cumulative effects of CO_2 emissions. The framework for this analysis is a single–planner dynamic optimization model. Within this framework a large number of important cases are examined:

- a single–region planning model,
- a model with a critical load of cumulative emissions,
- several models of technical progress,
- cooperation and non–cooperation in a two–region model, and
- uncertainty about the critical load.

The models and the arguments are rigorously and readably presented which makes it a pleasure to study this paper. This also leaves only a few edges to comment on or to criticize – although some of the material in part 2 is a bit sketchy. One problem is that the value of the critical load, which is also subject of Mäler's paper in this volume, is reasonably well established only for other pollutants, but not for CO_2.

The aim of this comment is to focus on two omissions from the theoretical models and to supplement the paper in this respect. In fact, the paper ignores two vital aspects of the problem:

1. There is no resource constraint mentioned in the whole paper. Only equilibria with positive levels of fossil–fuel use are examined. This – neglected – finiteness of the reserves, however, was probably one reason for the gulf war.

2. Strategic behaviour is excluded. The one model that examines non–cooperation is a plain optimal–control model, where the other region pollutes at a maximal rate.

Judging by these two omissions one could classify the paper as a "Nirvana[2]–approach".

This type of approach has a prominent place in economic theory. In fact, it is often quite helpful for understanding real–world problems. However, in the context of fossil fuels, what is omitted in this approach is probably the essence of the problem.

I am not going to present an adequate treatment of the resource constraint in the context of fossil–fuel use. This issue will be taken up by Withagen's comment. Instead, I

---

[1] A more extensive reference from a physicist's point of view is Hasselmann (1990).

am going to regard "energy" as an abstract resource with infinite, or very large, reserves. What remains is a model of public–"bad" provision which differs from other models in environmental economics because it is cumulative effect that matters here. Within this framework a few aspects of strategic behaviour will be examined.

The starting point will be the model of Part 1, Section 5. We will assume that there are n identical firms with production functions[2] $f[F^i, M]$. The output Q is sold on a world market and its normalized price is unity. Due to the global nature of the markets as well as of pollution, the regional structure of the economy is irrelevant. A firm's optimization problem is

$$\max_{F^i} \int_0^\infty e^{-rt}(Q^{\,i} - wF^{\,i})\, dt \quad \text{subject to } Q^{\,i} = f[F^{\,i}, M] \text{ and } \dot{M} = \sum_{j=1}^n F^j - \alpha M.$$

The factor price w may be zero, as in Gottinger's paper, or positive. The current–value Hamiltonian is

$$H^{\,i} = f[F^{\,i}, M] - wF^{\,i} + \phi^i(\sum_{i=1}^n F^j - \alpha M).$$

Profit maximization requires

$$f_F^{\,i} - w = -\phi^i \text{ and } \dot{\phi}^i = r\phi^i - f_M^{\,i} + \alpha\phi^i,$$

where $f_F^{\,i} = \dfrac{\partial f[F^i, M]}{\partial F^i}$ and $f_M^{\,i} = \dfrac{\partial f[F^{\,i}, M]}{\partial M}$. The equilibrium is characterized by

$$-\frac{f_F^{\,i} - w}{f_M^{\,i}} = \frac{1}{r + \alpha}. \tag{1}$$

This corresponds to Gottinger's equation (5.25'). Since this is just a comment, we are not going to worry too much about the plausibility of the symmetric open–loop Nash equilibrium used here.

---

[2] Square brackets denote function arguments, round brackets are just for grouping.

Joint profit maximization requires

$$\max_{\{F^1,\ldots,F^n\}} \int_0^\infty e^{-rt} \sum_{i=1}^{n} (Q^i - wF^i)\, dt$$

subject to $Q^i = f[F^i, M]$, $i = 1,\ldots, n$,   and $\dot{M} = \sum_{i=1}^{n} F^i - \alpha M$.

The current—value Hamiltonian is

$$H = \sum_{i=1}^{n} (f[F^i, M] - wF^i) + \phi\left(\sum_{i=1}^{n} F^i - \alpha M\right).$$

The optimality conditions are

$$f_F^{\,i} - w = -\phi,\; i = 1,\ldots, n,\; \text{and}\; \dot{\phi} = r\phi - \sum_{i=1}^{n} f_M^{\,i} + \alpha\phi.$$

The equilibrium requires

$$-\sum_{i=1}^{n} \frac{f_F^{\,i} - w}{f_M^{\,i}} = \frac{1}{r + \alpha}. \tag{2}$$

Although the public good is a stock, the difference between (1) and (2) is familiar from elementary public–good theory. A single firm ignores the negative externalities and (probably) produces too much. Joint profit–maximization, on the other hand, does take the externalities into account and this leads to the well–known Samuelson condition.

Let me illustrate the results with a numerical example. Let the single–firm production function be

$$f[F, M] = \frac{\lambda F^{\delta}}{M}.$$

The price of the resource F is zero and the other parameters are $\alpha = 0.001$, $r = 0.02$, $\delta = 0.75$, $M_0 = 1$, $M_c = 2$. These parameters are closely related to Gottinger's Table 1. To make the model more interesting, however, we allow for negative externalities below the critical load M_c. Table 1 gives the results for non–cooperative and joint profit maximization[3] for different numbers of firms. The numbers speak for themselves. There are dramatic differences in size. Furthermore, an increase in the number of firms moves the non–cooperative and the jointly optimal solution in opposite directions. This, hopefully, provides enough evidence against neglecting strategic aspects in this context.

Number of	Non–cooperation		Joint profit maximization	
firms	T	$F^i(0)$	T	$F^i(0)$
2	23.392	0.28524	29.700	0.033701
5	8.211	313.15	46.368	0.013848
10	3.946	146930000.	59.610	0.0064775

Table 1: Strategic aspects are important

References

Hasselmann, Klaus, 1990, "How well can we predict the climate crisis?", Max–Planck Institut für Meteorologie, Hamburg, mimeo

Mäler, Karl–Göran, 1991, "Critical loads and international environmental cooperation", *this volume*

Withagen, Cees, 1991, "Comment on: Economic models of optimal energy use under global environmental constraints", *this volume*

---

[3] The results were derived by backward integration of $\dot{M} = nF - \alpha M$. Denoting by F the resource input of a single firm, one obtains for the case of non–cooperation:

$$\dot{F} = \frac{-f_{FM}^i \, \dot{M} + (\alpha + r)f_F^i + \Sigma_j f_M^j}{f_{FF}^i}$$

and for the case of cooperation:

$$\dot{F} = \frac{-f_{FM}^i \, \dot{M} + (\alpha + r)f_F^i + f_M^i}{f_{FF}^i}$$

Comments by Cees Withagen

1. Introduction

In his contribution to this Conference Volume Gottinger considers the CO_2–problem in a global setting. The central question is how energy can be optimally used over time, taking into account on the one hand that energy use has a positive impact on production and therefore on social welfare, but on the other hand that the use of energy entails the emission of CO_2, increases thereby the stock of CO_2, which has a negative impact on the production possibilities. It is claimed in the first part of the paper that under some assumptions there exists a steady state which is globally asymptotically stable and a comparative statics analysis on the steady state is carried out.

I fully agree with von dem Hagen (1991) that the author addresses an important problem which is well–motivated in the introductory survey of the existing literature. But I also agree that still much more work has to be done in this area. In these comments I will briefly indicate which directions could be taken and go into the difficulties that may be encountered. Thereby attention will be paid to the explicit recognition of the fact that much of the CO_2 emissions are due to the use of fossil fuel originating from exhaustible resources. Second, since there exists no common agreement on the effect of higher CO_2 concentration on the production possibilities, it seems worthwhile to consider the case where effects on production are absent. Finally it would be interesting to cast the model into the well–known Ramsey framework, thereby introducing physical capital as a factor of production.

2. Exhaustible resources

Consider the "simplified model" of section 5.

$$Max \int_{0}^{\infty} e^{-rt} u(C) \, dt \quad \text{subject to} \quad C = f(F,M) \text{ and } \dot{M} = F - \alpha M, M(0) \text{ given.}$$

It is suggested by Gottinger that there exists a positive steady state which is globally[1] asymptotically stable. This does not hold true in general. It is for example easily seen

---

[1] Global stability is not as straightforward as suggested in the text (Appendix B). Looking at the linearized system only warrants statements about local stability.

that with Cobb–Douglas specifications of the functions involved the stock of CO_2 will eventually go to zero. This phenomenon will occur when the negative impact of M in production is of major importance, so that it is worthwhile to reduce the amount of CO_2 to zero. As a consequence also the rate of consumption will eventually approach zero. Nevertheless, even if the impact of M in the production function is not important, there is a case for the view that the optimal CO_2 level is to be zero eventually. Let S denote the stock of the exhaustible resource from which F is extracted. Then we have the additional constraint

$$\dot{S} = -F, S \geq 0, \quad S(0) \text{ given.}$$

But it is evident that a positive M is not feasible eventually, because a constant F cannot be maintained in the long run. Consequently the rate of consumption will approach zero in the long run. The conclusion is that in this type of models sustainable development is not possible.

3. No CO_2 impact on production

If the accumulation of CO_2 leads to climatic changes, it is not evident that this will negatively affect the global aggregate production possibilities. For example agriculture in some regions might benefit. So it could be interesting as an exercise to consider optimal development in the absence of any impact on production. In order to have a problem then is necessary for CO_2 to play a role elsewhere in the model. One of the possibilities is to incorporate the idea that CO_2 per se has a negative influence on social welfare because of the disutility attached to climatic changes or the disappearance of the rain forests. This can be operationalized in a number of ways. As a first shot the social welfare function can be modified as follows.

$$Max \int_0^\infty e^{-rt} \left[u(C) - D(M) \right] dt,$$

where D is a convex damage function and $C = f(F)$. If the exhaustibility is taken into account then the solution of the model will again give rise to zero consumption and zero CO_2 concentration in the long run, even in the case of a zero discount rate r. If exhaustibility is neglected, then basically Gottinger's results reappear.

4. The extended Ramsey model

One of the simplifying assumptions in the Gottinger model is that physical capital does not play a role in production. A model in which capital does enter has recently been analysed by van der Ploeg and myself (1991). It is instructive to sketch a simple version of the model and present the main results. In this version the exhaustibility of resources does not play a role and only physical capital enters into the production function. The emission output ratio is denoted by β. The damage function of the previous section will be maintained. Then the model reads as follows.

$$Max \int_{0}^{\infty} e^{-rt} \left[u(C) - D(M) \right] dt$$

subject to $\dot{K} = f(K) - \mu K - C$, $K(0)$ and $\dot{M} = \beta f(K) - \alpha M$, $M(0)$ given.

Although this is a control problem with two state variables the analysis is not too difficult. The necessary conditions are (assuming an interior solution)

$$\lambda = e^{-rt} u'(C),$$

$$-\dot{\lambda} = \lambda(f' - \mu) + \gamma \beta f'$$

$$\dot{\gamma} = - e^{-rt} D'(M) - \tau.$$

Here λ is the shadow price of capital and τ is the shadow price of the CO_2 level (obviously τ is negative). As is well-known, the modified golden rule in the pure Ramsey model yields a long run steady state for the stock of capital which satisfies $f' = \mu + r$.

In the model at hand there also exists a steady state, characterized by $\dot{K} = \dot{C} = \dot{M} = 0$. This steady state can be shown to be locally asymptotically stable due to the usual concavity/convexity assumptions. It also follows immediately that the steady state stock of capital is smaller than in the pure Ramsey model, whereas the same holds for the steady state rate of consumption. It can be shown as well that an increase of the emission output ratio decreases the steady state values. Obviously the analysis becomes much more complicated if energy from an exhaustible resource is taken into account as a factor of production. However, I do not think that exhaustibility in the strict sense of providing a finite stream of services over time imposes severe problems in reality; an alternative way to deal with energy is simply to assume (like Heal (1976)) that energy is principally plentiful but becomes more and more costly to recover due to the techniques necessary to exploit deeper ores or the investments needed for solar energy and the like. The Ramsey framework together with these observations might provide a useful vehicle to analyse the CO_2 problem. Following this type of reasoning one could study a model where capital is allocated to the production of the composite commodity and the extraction of "energy", according to a convex technology. Then the optimal development of the economy refers not only to the decision with respect to investments and consumption but also to the optimal allocation of capital. This type of models can be extended in a number of ways. One obvious example is to allow for investments in "clean technology" by making the emission output ratio dependent on the efforts directed towards causing less emissions.

5. Conclusions

The Gottinger paper raises many interesting questions, some of which have been outlined above. It seems important to me that the Ramsey model is studied in a modified setting, allowing for environmental aspects.

However, this is not the end of the story. Admittedly, looking for socially optimal solution patterns is important but the crucial issue is the insight that competitive economic systems will in general reach outcomes which, in the presence of environmental aspects, are Pareto—inefficient. Therefore, after calculating optimal consumption and production profiles, the economist is left with the challenge to devise instruments to steer the competitive economy along the optimal trajectory.

References

von dem Hagen. Oskar, 1991, "Comment on: Economic models of optimal energy use under global environmental constraints ", *this volume*

Heal, Geoffrey, 1976, "The relation between price and extraction costs for a resource with a back—stop technology", *The Bell Journal of Economics* 7, 371–378

van der Ploeg, Frederick, and Withagen, Cees, 1991, "Pollution control and the Ramsey problem", forthcoming in: *Environmental and Resource Economics*

PART TWO

MONITORING AND ENFORCEMENT

Chapter 7

Clifford S. Russell

Monitoring and Enforcement of Pollution Control Laws in Europe and the United States

Abstract. This paper concentrates on three linked matters. First, it develops the rudiments of a taxonomy of monitoring and enforcement problems based on such considerations as:

— the assumed motivation of the source
— the type of discharge situation, and
— the character of imposed requirement that is to be enforced.

Second, key dimensions of monitoring and enforcement system design are defined for the class of problems that involve individual point sources of pollution discharge, regulated with permits that specify limits on discharges per unit time, and for which there is likely to be profit in disobeying the permit terms in the absence of enforcement effort. The dimensions discussed are:

— the probability of a source's being monitored within a given period of time
— whether or not monitoring visits come as surprises to the regulated sources
— the definition of a violation, and
— the penalty of a discovered violation

Third, monitoring and enforcement of point source pollution regulation from six European nations and the United States are characterized in terms of these dimensions. While the information available for the paper is far from complete, it seems clear that there are no dramatic differences in approach among the countries. In general, the probability of being monitored is low, and something on the order of half the monitoring visits conducted in this set of countries probably involve prearrangement rather than surprise. The operational definition of violations could only be determined in a minority of cases. But in the case of United Kingdom and possibly other nations, this is so because the decision to decide whether or not to call a particular test result a violation rests with the individual inspector. The fines that *can be* imposed for a violation cover a very wide range when translated into units of a single currency; and though to make judgments about their deterrence effects one would have to know their relation to the regulated sources cost–savings from violation, prospective fines appear trivial for major dischargers in all but the U.S. and Germany.

A different future may be in the making in the United Kingdom. There the new National Rivers Authority appears to be taking the dimensions of the point–source monitoring seriously, encouraging:

— More frequent visits — with frequency choices made in relation to the probability of

discovering a violation,
- the use of surprise,
- the removal of substantial discretion in the definition of violations from local inspectors, and
- the seeking of the highest possible fines for discovered violations.

Whether this is in fact a glimpse of future policy directions or merely a flash in the pan remains to be seen.

1. Introduction

A predisposition to admire European environmental policies amounts almost to a tradition among U.S. environmental economists. This is probably traceable to the fame accorded several specific pieces of European policy that seem to pick up on the idea of using economic incentives in environmental management – e.g. the venerable pollution charging system of the *Genossenschaften* (Kneese and Bower, 1968); the newer German federal effluent charge law (Johnson and Brown, 1976); the multitude of deposit–refund systems in place across Europe for everything from bottles to automobiles (Bohm, 1981), and waste oil recycling subsidies (OECD, 1981). Therefore, one might be excused for approaching this subject with a sort of naive enthusiasm, an expectation that important contrasts between Europe and the U.S. would be found, and that Europe's approach would clearly be preferable.

At the same time, some familiarity with the difficulty of finding useful material on monitoring and enforcement policy in the U.S. made for caution. It always seems easier to find discussions of how standards are set and what policy instruments are used than it is to find out what happens to the standards where the rubber meets the road or what the chosen instruments really look like to those they are aimed at.

Why this should be so is an interesting question in its own right, especially since some of the answers that suggest themselves have implications for the search for intellectually satisfying but practically applicable monitoring and enforcement strategies. For example, one problem for the researcher in the U.S. – and, it turns out, in Europe – is that while standards may be set and policy instruments designed at the highly visible central level, the responsibility for the monitoring of continuing compliance with the resulting systems is in the hands of peripheral units – in our case, the 50 states; in Europe the nation or "land" or country or regional board. While there is some central collection of data on monitoring and enforcement activity and results, much of interest is known only within each responsible state agency, and seeking it out is difficult, time consuming, and expensive. These problems are compounded in Europe by differences in nguage, in administrative law traditions (certainly), and habits of government secrecy (probably).

A second possible explanation for the lack of a readily accessible literature on monitoring and enforcement is that the design and analysis of such systems is at once unglamorous and technically difficult. Thus, for example, building the analog for monitoring and enforcement of a regional standard setting model would require that we have not only the usual apparatus of cost and damage functions and connecting environmental quality models but also at least some sort of behavioral response function describing how each source reacts to its own and other sources' experience with the monitoring and enforcement set up. To be at all useful, such a model would further have to take account of random variations in discharge levels attributable to imperfect control of both production and treatment processes. Steady state doesn't do it here. Most models in the field usually deal only with one "representative" polluter and assume that polluter's decisions are not influenced by what happens, or does not happen, to others.

The tendency, in fact, has been for the literature on environmental economics to examine standard setting and choice of instruments on the assumption of perfect compliance. (This tendency is not a universal rule, of course. See, for example, the studies cited in Chapter 4 of Russell, et al., 1986; and, more recently, such papers as those of Cohn, 1986; Harford, 1987; Malik, 1990; Jones and Scotchmer 1990; and Russell 1990 A). Environmental Lawyers, too, have tended to avoid monitoring and enforcement technicalities in favor of grander themes such as the burden of proof in standard setting; the role of judicial review setting environmental policy; and the Constitutionality of particular policy instruments such as effluent charges. Members of both disciplines – and many others as well – tend to accept the game played by legislators at face value and to take the sizes of authorized fines for violations as evidence of seriousness of purpose, thus ignoring the other half of this particular scissors, the probability of being caught and fined at all.

Insofar as a modest amount of library searching and correspondence over the past few months can be said to represent a decent fishing expedition, it can be reported that the catch in Europe is not better than in the U.S. – and for similar reasons apparently. But it does seem that European approaches to monitoring and enforcement are broadly similar to what we know about the U.S. experience. And while there are some contrasts across the EC family of nations, and with the U.S. the most interesting lessons appear to lie in the contrast between the old and the new, as exemplified by the U.K. experience.

The remainder of this paper will follow up on these themes. First, four key dimensions of monitoring and enforcement policy will be defined and discussed. Second, the practices of six European community member nations will be characterized on those dimensions and comparisons made with the U.S.[1] As it happens, some changes currently being recommended by the National Rivers Authority are particularly interesting as attempts to break with past practice, and I shall linger over these. A brief appendix discusses the extent to which the policy of European nations in this regard can usefully be called European.

2. Differences among monitoring and enforcement problems and systems

There are several ways to try to capture the flavor of a monitoring and enforcement system. One of the most illuminating concentrates on the assumed motivation of the regulated parties. At one extreme, these parties — or at least the vast majority of them — are seen as voluntarily complying to the best of their abilities. Violations, then, become problems to be worked out in a spirit of cooperation between the responsible agency and the violators. Only a few sources consciously seek to cheat. Once these trouble makers have been identified (or have identified themselves by refusing to play the problem—solving game) they can be singled out for severe treatment. At the other end of the scale of assumptions is one that takes every regulated party to have the incentive to cheat in the absence of vigorous monitoring and swift, painful enforcement actions. More specifically, unless the expected penalty value (probability of detection and conviction times penalty) exceeds the cost savings obtainable by not complying, sources will simply violate the applicable laws and regulations. Clearly, in the case of "voluntary compliance", monitoring can be directed at the class of bad actors and penalties are imposed for remaining in that class rather than for particular measured discharges alone.

The first of these views may strike the economist as a bit odd since it seems to downplay self—interest. But it is the model that lies behind a great deal of actual system design in the world. (For example, on U.S. states see Harrington, 1981 and 1987; and, on the UK, Richardson et al., 1982). A first obvious question: Why would regulated parties "voluntarily" comply? Well, one answer is that the voluntarism is relative. That is, the parties definitely do not want to be singled out as recalcitrant — as bad guys — because

---

[1] The discussant of this paper at the symposium, Heinz Welsch of Köln University, provides some very valuable supplementary information on German practices. These will be found in his published discussion following the paper. But I have also taken the liberty of quoting from his comment.

the public relations cost of such a designation strikes them as potentially enormous. So we are not observing a denial of original sin but rather a more subtle system of sanctions than that contemplated in the straightforward picture of fines for discovered violations.[2]

A second question is, do the (limited) facts fit the voluntary compliance picture? The answer here seems to be no. For example, I reported in 1990 on U.S. problems of continuing non–compliance in air and water pollution control and the management of hazardous wastes (Russell, 1990 B). Put very briefly, and subject to the intrinsic logical problem that a lack of monitoring leaves us unable to say much of anything about compliance, such information as has been compiled in the U.S. (e.g.: from self–monitoring reports) shows patterns of widespread, long term, and substantial (in discharge terms) non–compliance with permit limitations. For example, Table 1 provides data on the extent of "significant" violations of waste water discharge permit terms by municipal and industrial discharges in the late 1970s and early 1980s based on a survey of self–reporting records by the U.S. General Accounting Office. (Significant non–compliance was taken to exist when concentration or quantity limits were exceeded by 50 percent or more for at least one permit parameter in at least four consecutive months during the 18–month reporting period studies.)

Report & Sample	Plants Self–Reporting Significant Violations[3]	
	number	percentage
1978/79: Municipal (N=242)	66	27%
1980/82: Municipal (N=272)	88	32%
Industrial (N=257)	42	16%

Table 1: Significant violations of pollution discharge permits in a U.S. sample of self–reporting sources[4]

[2] Playing the enforcement game by the voluntary compliance rules has some advantages for the individuals who are on the firing line for both parties — agency and regulated parties. Their relationship across that line can be much less stressful and unpleasant if they act as though voluntary compliance were the rule. E.g.: Richardson, et al. 1982.

[3] Note: Significant violations are defined by size of violation and number of periods the violation continued (see text).

[4] Sources: "Costly waste water treatment plants", General Accounting Office, "Waste water dischargers are not complying", reprinted from Russel, 1990 B.

Another source of a difference in system flavor is the type of regulation in question. Again to note extremes, environmental policy sometimes requires the installation of equipment (such as a particular type of stack–gas scrubber or a specific design of incinerator), or the use of "practices" that are in fact embodied in temporary structures (such as the use of dams made of hay bales to keep silt from road works out of streams). Monitoring for compliance with such requirements is a matter of looking at what is actually in place.[5] And non–compliance at a moment in time can be captured by a photo rather than a measurement.

A very different problem is posed by an upper limit on the total emissions per unit time from, say, a smoke stack. Mere inspection is not enough. Measurement, either continuous or with judicious sampling, is required. And a violation going on during time period t can only be established by measurement during t, because once the discharges have a chance to disperse and diffuse, their connection to a particular source is practically impossible to establish.

Yet another sort of problem is posed by wastes generated in small quantities and under conditions that allow them to be captured in containers. (Examples include solvents used in cleaning baths for everything from clothes to circuit boards; and the spent solutions used in electro–plating operations.) "Discharge" of such wastes in the sense of dumping them into sewers or tipping the containers into landfills, or, indeed, into woods and fields, is usually prohibited. But consider what sort of monitoring and enforcement problem this creates. Instead of measuring at one or a few obvious and well–defined points of emission, it is in principle necessary to check every vehicle leaving the premises on which the wastes are generated and, indeed, somehow checking what happens to every container that is found to depart those premises. On the other hand, so long as the wastes remain containerized, there is at least a chance that the discharger can be identified ex post by analysis of the undispersed wastes. (Even if the discharger is not so stupid as to leave a label on the containers themselves).

One last "flavor" variation might usefully be noted in the context of this symposium. Most environmental policies and most discussions of monitoring and enforcement system refer to situations in which the actions of each individual regulated party are of independent interest, though the result for the environment is determined by their col-

---

[5] This begs the questions of whether the equipment is being operated at all; operated correctly; and whether when operated correctly it does what is intended for the environment.

lective actions. This is because limitations, to be enforceable, must apply to responsible firms or public bodies or households. In certain situations, however, considerable concern is focused, or should be focused directly on the collective result. One example is the U.S. "bubble policy" in which a multi–stack industrial operation such as a refinery is allowed to minimize the costs, within limits, of meeting a total discharge from its facility. Since there is no actual "bubble", checking compliance in principle requires simultaneous measurement of the discharges from all the individual stacks included under the notional bubble. A more important example is likely to arise in the context of international treaties which assign discharge or manufacturing or use limitations to nations as a whole. To put it in crudest terms, unless each nation is also required to assign its quota to individual facilities, enforcement will be impossible, the simultaneous measurement of emissions or use at *all* facilities requiring impossibly large commitments of resources. However, such collective source regulations might be crudely monitored through use of a materials balance (for straightforward transformations such as that of the sulfur in fuels into discharged SO_2) or capacity limitations checks (for complex process chains such as those from simple hydrocarbons and a few inorganic chemicals to herbicides and pesticides, not to say chlorofluorocarbons).

With all these, and no doubt many more, choices of monitoring problems out there, for this paper to remain manageable, some lines have to be drawn. I have chosen to predicate the discussion on the problem of monitoring and enforcing restrictions on standard discharges per unit time from individual sources. (Such as SO_2 from stacks or chemical oxygen demand from waste water treatment plant outflow pipes). I assume that all (or very nearly all) sources need considerable encouragement to comply because each is tempted by potential cost savings to violate.[6] The relative and absolute importance of the following dimensions follow from these assumptions.

3. Key dimensions of monitoring and enforcement systems

Within the problem context chosen for this paper, there are four especially important dimensions of system design along which the responsible agency can make its own choices:

---

[6] This latter choice is one of degree not of a dichotomous variable. Voluntary compliance could not be presumed to occur in the total absence of monitoring or of a serious penalty, however far down the road of mutual consultation and problem solving that penalty lies.

- the probability of monitoring a source within a given period of time;
- the extent of pre–monitoring notice given the source (no notice equals "surprise");
- the definition of a violation;
- the penalty for a violation.

Together with characteristics of the dischargers' product and control processes, these choices determine the probability that a given source will choose to violate its limits rather than comply with them over any particular time period. The function through which this determination is made can be modeled in general terms by analysis on the basis of first principles. But many key elements such as the extent of risk aversion and the ease or difficulty of turning on and off control processes will be known only very imprecisely. Real advances in the design of monitoring and enforcement systems require that we study the results of alternative systems applied to at least roughly similar source populations under at least roughly similar economic conditions. But a few modestly useful observations can be made about the role of each choice dimension open to the responsible agency.

3.1. Probability of monitoring

Much of the difficulty, and therefore much of the intellectual appeal, of the monitoring and enforcement problem would disappear if precise, tamper–proof, continuous monitoring devices were always available. For pollution control purposes, some continuous monitoring devices do exist – e.g.: for particulates in stack gases, for volume and pH of wastewater – and the output of these devices can even be transmitted directly to an agency office. But all either suffer from problems of reliability or are subject to source manipulation. And so, while often required, as for new air pollution sources in the U.S., they cannot be relied on to do the whole job.[7] Self–monitoring by other than continuous, tamper–proof methods is also widely required of pollution sources. Here, all the problems of interpreting discontinuous measurements are joined to the susceptibility to tampering implicit in the "self" part of the arrangement.

Thus, visits for measurement of discharges by personnel and devices independent of the source seem to me to be necessary. And the first dimension of system design is the frequency of such visits – or the probability that a visit will occur in a particular span of

---

[7] But see the discussant's comments for a more sanguine view based on German rules and experience.

time for which the choice to comply with or violate a permit or regulation can realistically be made — commonly a day.

If the permit or regulation specifies an absolute instantaneous limit on the discharge rate then a visit and an measurement (or n measurements to reduce sample error) will reveal violation or compliance for the relevant decision period, and interpretation and planning is reasonably straightforward. If, however, the permit regulation specifies that discharges will be under some value 50 or 80 percent of the time, the problem is much harder. Indeed, if the sampling time is short and the permit time frame long, similar problems exist (e.g.: if a sample covers 30 minutes of flow and the permit terms constrain weekly discharge). Nonetheless, it is possible to translate visit frequency and corresponding time sampled into probabilities of detecting existing violations written in different ways. The decision variable, whether seen as visit frequency or desired probability of detection, is key to the functioning of the overall system.[8]

3.2. Surprise

This dimension is much more important if one views all regulated parties as both inclined toward and capable of cheating than if they are seen as intending to comply. If the parties will cheat when they can, then announced visits will produce only evidence of compliance, even if at all other times violations are occurring. This assertion implicitly assumes both that creating a violation and correcting it *can* be done on a time scale that comports with the amount of notice given and the interval between visits; and that doing so is worthwhile. At the frequencies common in both Europe and the U.S. — a few visits per year — this seems quite reasonable. If visits were daily, on the other hand, it might well not be worthwhile ever to violate. In between would be frequencies at which switching between violation and compliance would become profitable for different control processes. Because the relevant technologies differ among sources, there is no single magic number for this visit frequency.

Whether or not to surprise the parties is discussed here as a choice of the system designers in the responsible agency. But there may be legal or even Constitutional questions having to do with the right of inspectors to enter premises unannounced. In the U.S. these issues have been fought out in the contexts of several different sorts of regulation including mine safety, occupational health and safety generally, nuclear power plant

---

[8] For example, see Bethouex et al. 1978; Ellis and Lacey 1980; Gardenier 1982; Casey et al. 1983; and, Vaughan and Russell 1983.

regulation, and pollution control. I do not have an authoritative citation but have been told that in the U.S. surprise visits are always Constitutionally possible, though with recalcitrant sources they may require some advance planning by way of obtaining what is known as an *ex parte* warrant (one that can be issued in the absence of the party whose premises are to be entered). I have no idea what the fundamental laws of EC countries have to say about this, except in the case of the U.K., but can and do report on the practice in several nations in the next section.

3.3. Definition of a violation

The interplay between the definition of a violation and the frequency of measurement in producing the probability of finding a violation has already been remarked on. More broadly, but often less precisely, violations can be defined flexibly or in terms of apparent intent rather than in terms of measurements alone.[9] While taking account of intent is common in criminal law, it does have some important implications for the incentives facing regulated parties. For example, if a valid defense against having an apparent violation penalized is the claim of good intentions foiled by equipment breakdown or operator error, a variety of moral hazard is clearly created, with unknown but certainly negative implications for the environment. On the other hand, rigidly punishing every discovered excursion above permitted discharge levels could very well have its own negative pay off— the encouragement of a habit of concealment that could create the conditions for major disaster out of what might have been a containable accident.

3.4. Penalties and other responses to violations

Penalty levels authorized for discovered violations, as written into laws and regulations, mean little in themselves except in symbolic terms. Comparing authorized penalties across systems that are otherwise similar can be instructive however. Even more instructive is the comparison of actual penalties imposed. Again, to the extent data are available, the record of the past several decades in the U.S. and Europe looks similar: Average penalties per conviction have been notably low, even trivial (e.g.: Russell et al. 1986 and Richardson, et al. 1982, pp. 142 et seq.).

---

[9] For a discussion of a wide variety of considerations that can influence the violation "call", see Richardson et al. 1982.

Again, however, some distinctions are worthwhile. A very important one is among administrative, civil, and criminal penalties. The first two involve "only" money. The third can involve sending some person or persons to jail. Correspondingly heavier burdens of proof of violation generally apply as you go up this scale. A second distinction is between the total penalty for any particular violation and the marginal penalty for one more violation or one more unit of violation (an extra pound of discharge above the permitted level, for example). One expects rising marginal penalties to be part of an optimal system. It is also the case that to some extent rising marginal penalties can substitute for flexible definition of violation. If an initial (or small) violation is punished by a warning only, for example, then the source intending to comply need not be turned into a hardened cynic by one mistake. Two or three mistakes begin to look more like culpable negligence than poor luck and may be punished as such.

Finally, penalties may be related to costs saved by violation, to damages caused by violation, or to nothing but the legislature's, regulator's and judges' idea of what it takes to encourage compliance. If the penalties are cost–related, that relation has to involve a multiplier greater than one for there to be an incentive to comply, so long as the probability of detection is less than one. Penalties related to estimated damages are now quite important in the U.S. under Superfund (Comprehensive Environmental Response, Compensation and Liability Act of 1988), and the estimation of natural resource damages for this purpose has become a growth industry in environmental economics. (e.g.: Kopp & Smith 1989). But arbitrary amounts specified per violation still seem to dominate the penalty scene.

4. Some evidence on European & U.S. choices in monitoring & enforcement

Without any illusions about its completeness, though hoping it is correct so far as it goes, I have prepared Table 2 which summarizes six European national environmental monitoring and enforcement systems and that of the United States in terms of the four dimensions just discussed. The information in it has been taken principally from a draft chapter in a consultant's report, on what a firm faces in operating in Europe (ERL 1990), supplemented for the U.K. by the contents of a report from the new National Rivers Authority containing recommendations for how that agency should conduct its monitoring and enforcement activities in the future. (NRA 1990); and for the U.S. by information gathered in connections with writing a recently published chapter on this subject (Russell, 1990 B).

Unfortunately, the most striking feature of the table is undoubtedly the blanks under "Definition of Violation". Though unfortunate, this lack of information is hardly surprising. As described in detail for the U.K. in such studies as Richardson, et al., 1983; Hutter, 1988; and Hill 1982; the use of flexible definitions implies that what a violation is may vary not just by local area but even by individual inspector. And the fact that the consultants were unable to report on how violations are defined by each country suggests that this is a matter of flexibility. Admittedly, I speculate here.

Beyond this glaring problem, the following observations seem worth making. First, the probability of a monitoring visit is quite low in every country. (This probability takes a visit as involving a day, and is based on the reported visits per year in ERL, 1990).[10] The numbers for Europe cover the same orders of magnitude (.001 to .03) as similar figures in the U.S. They correspond to a range of frequencies per year of less than one to about twelve. To put this in perspective, a very simple game model of compliance, without allowing for monitoring error or for increasing marginal penalties with new offenses, implies that the fine for a discovered violation would have to be more than 30 times higher than the costs saved by choosing to violate in order to make compliance the preferred policy for the source when the probability of being monitored is 0.03.

Even the few monitoring visits commonly made each year are apparently not commonly done in a surprise fashion. Only for Belgium currently, for U.K. wastewater discharges in the future and for a subset of U.S. states can we be fairly confident that surprise is or will be used to advantage. In France, Germany, and Spain, it is unclear whether visits are pre—arranged or not. In Italy, it is clear that they are. And under existing U.K. policies, most visits to dischargers each year are pre—arranged.

As far as authorized penalties go (which is not very far, as already observed) there is wide variation. Criminal penalties are available as an environmental enforcement tool in Belgium, Germany, Italy, the U.S., and the U.K. Fines, not surprisingly, are common to all systems, but the authorized upper limits vary widely. In dollar terms, the lowest is Belgium's at $ 159 per event; the highest is Germany's at $ 65,300. Spain and Italy came in at $ 5,200 and $ 1,740 respectively, and the U.S. legislation authorizes fines up to $ 50,000 per day of violation. (Local currencies converted to dollars at rates current in September 1990.)

---

[10] For the frequencies in the Table 2 I assumed a 365—day operating year. If the parties operating only 5 days per week, the probabilities of a visit on a working day (assuming all visits occur in working days) are about 1.4 times the figures in the table.

Nations	Probability of a Visit on Any Day	Visits Surprise or Prearranged	Definition of Violations	Penalties available
Belgium	0.008	Surprise	Not available	Criminal penalties available Fines: 500 BF; doubled for 2nd violation in 2 years Other: Equipment shutdown
France	0.008	Unclear	Not available	Fines: Unspecified limits Other: Operator suspension
Germany[a]	0.01–0.03[b]	Unclear	See Discussant's paper following	Criminal penalties available Fines: Up to 100,000 DM Other: Suspension of operation
Italy	0.003	Prearranged	Not available	Criminal penalties available Fines: Up to 2 million IL Other: Suspension of operation
Spain	0.003	Unclear	Not available	Fines: Up to 500,000 SP or up to 10 times damage Other: Facility closure
United Kingdom	0.01–0.03[b]	In past: mostly prearranged[b,c] in future: potential surprise[b]	In past: at discretion of inspector In future: rigid, numerical[b]	Criminal penalties available Fines: Unspecified limits Other: Expenses of mitigation and restoration
United States	0.002–0.008[d]	Roughly half of visits are announced[e]	Generally numerical, with over correction for measurement error	Criminal penalties available Fines: Up to $ 50,000 per day and administrative penalties (latter based on costs avoided) other : Expenses of mitigation and restoration in some cases

Table 2: Summary information on six national monitoring and enforcement systems (Sources and notes of this table are listed on the next page)

Table 2 (Continued):

Sources: Environmental Resources, Ltd., 1990. Draft report *"Operating in Europe"*, London, ERL, National Rivers Authority, 1990.
Discharge Consent and Compliance Policy. London, NRA

Notes: a See the accompanying discussion by Welsch for much more detail on Germany.
      b For wastewater discharges.
      c Currently only one of several annual visits is likely to be unannounced.
      d The smaller probability applies to small sources of air pollution and the larger to large sources of water pollution.
These are means, however, and the probabilities vary systematically across states.
      e Most states maintain that they sometimes announce visits in advance and sometimes do not. About 16% of agencies surveyed by RFF (Russell, 1990B) report always announcing visits; about 20% never announce in advance.

Perhaps the most telling observation here is that the largest fine limits (Germany) go with the highest visit frequencies. Taken together, these two features of the German system suggest relatively greater seriousness of purpose, though one cannot be sure in the absence of information on surprise and violation definition, and on penalties actually levied.[11]

5. A glimpse of the future? Recommendations from the U.K.
(The "Kinnersley Report")

A general characterization of the European and U.S. monitoring and enforcement systems might fairly be drawn as follows: Infrequent, often prearranged, visits are made to measure discharges. Defining what constitutes a violation is likely to some large extent to be within the discretion of the inspector who makes the visit. When a violation is discovered, the penalty for it is likely to be fairly small, at least when measured against aggregate corporate profits. (How fines relate to cost savings from the violation is key but varies across technologies, sizes, equipment vintages, and so forth). This certainly seems fair in application to the U.K. about which this study turned up considerable detail. See, again, Richardson et al., 1982; Hutter, 1988; and Hill 1982.

---

[11]Again, see Welsch's discussion for more information on criminal prosecutions and convictions for pollution offenses, and for penalties in the form of permanently higher effluent charges.

The new guardian body for U.K. waters, the National Rivers Authority, set up when the Regional Water Authorities were privatized by the Thatcher government in 1989, setting out to change things, at least they apply to wastewater discharges. A Policy Group on Discharge Consents and Compliance, set up in July 1989, reported a year later and made a number of quite specific recommendations — and included much other language to the same effect — that will, if adopted, tighten things up considerably. (NRA, 1990). Consider the following:

Frequency:

"[Sampling Program]...frequencies must be adequate for results to provide a basis for decision and enforcement" (Recommendation 19). From the surrounding language it is clear that "adequacy" here is judged on the basis of ability to detect violations with desired probability, not on some arbitrary number of visits per year. The technical details are left to another NRA committee.

Surprise:

"The NRA should include in all relevant consents conditions indicating access and facilities required for flow measurements and the taking of samples to be done by the NRA at whatever times in the day, night or week it judges appropriate. The NRA should also encourage sampling staff to maintain the practice of making their visits unpredictable." (Recommendation 17).

Definition of Violation:

"For various reasons...absolute limits [on discharges] came to be regarded in practice as not really applying as strictly as they were stated in consents. The notion that compliance for most of the time was acceptable became widespread. A sort of spurious objectivity was often lent to this interpretation by describing the required compliance as being for '95 % of the time', long before detailed attention was given to the definition or interpretation of this formal statistical terms. This may suggest, confusingly, that discretion or opinion has a part in saying whether or not a breach of the consent has occurred, or that the results of a single sample are not to be considered alone. It also mixes informal understandings with formal legal obligations. Desirably, however, the assessment of compliance should be precise and objective ..." (Paragraph 52). "One obvious step covered in earlier chapters is to make the limits which consents set well—expressed and as free of ambiguity and misunderstanding a they can be." (Paragraph 124).

Penalties:

> "... The NRA should seek to ensure that appropriate cases are heard by the Crown Court which can impose the highest levels of penalty ..." (Paragraph 124).

An Implementation Group chaired by the NRA's chief scientist has begun meeting and will deal with implementation, taking account of collected public comment. There is no evidence at this point that any of the key recommendations highlighted in this paper will be dropped or ignored.

There are, however, several sources of misgivings about the substance of the report. The newly privatized water and sewage companies (the old Water Authorities) are especially unhappy, having been the beneficiaries of the previous ad hoc slackening.

It is clear that even if the compliance report's major recommendations are entirely reflected in regulations, there will remain substantial flexibility in the overall system. This will amount to prosecutorial discretion — what to do about a discovered violation, having regard to track record of violator, and other exacerbating or mitigating circumstances. Given that there are disadvantages to an adversarial relationship implied by formal prosecution, even this system might in fact be made to look like a "voluntary compliance" system unless central authority keeps a fairly close rein.

To sum up, the policy group, at least, is opting for changes in monitoring and enforcement policy in each key dimension that will collectively have the effect of making U.K. policy more severe, more serious if you will. It would be interesting to know, but I must admit to ignorance, whether one or more other European nations are facing up to these same issues.

6. Concluding comments

In both Europe and the U.S., and in both the worlds of policy and of environmental economics, there has been concentration on (if not obsession with) what standards (consents, permits, charges) look like and how they got that way. Very little attention has been given to the problem of motivating the parties subject to the permits or charges to comply with them. Indeed, economists have been inclined to assume the problem away by assuming compliance. Law—makers have tended to content themselves with specifying penalties for not complying, without having much to say about how much effort, how directed, would go into finding out who was and who was not complying.

This general approach is hardly unique to the environment. Indeed, it is entirely expectable, if for no other reason than that raising penalties costs legislatures nothing, while mandating monitoring probabilities or other features of the system implies spending quite obviously and directly. But there is evidence that the common approach has not served very well.

The question for the 1990s may well become, how do we do a better job of seeing our policies complied with? — How do we play the monitoring and enforcement game smarter? When that begins to happen, as it seems to have in the U.K., we can anticipate that environmental economists will be right there, as they were when benefit analysis and standard setting came center stage in the early 1980s; as they have been more recently when natural resource damages are concerned; and as they continue to be whenever the economic incentives flag gets run up anywhere.

Appendix: What is European about monitoring & enforcement policy in Europe

The answer to this question appears to be, very little. Rehbinder and Stewart (1985) make very clear that monitoring and enforcement of environmental laws and regulations, even where these have been dictated by Community directives, are not subject to Community control. While some directives are more detailed and specific than others, at some point all must result in orders to, permits for, or charges on firms, individuals, or local jurisdiction operations. Compliance with these ultimate instruments is the responsibility of the nation — and within the federal nations, of the states. "The community cannot directly enforce environmental directives against regulated firms. The enforcement of directives incorporated into national law ... is [the nations'] exclusive responsibility." (Rehbinder and Stewart, 1985, 145). Further, the Community law has only the most minimal leverage over the content of the monitoring and enforcement approaches. Procedures that do not discriminate against foreigners, are not "unreasonable", and do not completely rule out judicial review of the results of their implementation will be found acceptable if challenged in the European Court of Justice (p. 158).

Since the choice of monitoring and enforcement regime is a way to strengthen or weaken the effect of a previously chosen (or imposed) set of standards; and since this choice is quite wide open under Community law, it should not surprise us to see variations in important detail across European nations.

References

Berthouex, P.M., Hunter, W.G., and Pallesen, L., 1978, *"Monitoring Sewage Treatment Plants: Some Quality Control Aspects"*, Vol. 10, No. 4, October, 139–149

Bohm, Peter, 1981, *"Deposit–Refund Systems"*, Washington, DC, Resources for the Future.

Casey, D. Peter, Nemetz, N., and Uyeno, D.H., 1983, "Sampling frequency for water quality monitoring: Measures of effectiveness", *Water Resources Research 19, No. 5*, October, 1107–1110

Cohen, M.A., 1986, "The costs and benefits of oil spill prevention and enforcement", *Journal of Environmental Economics and Management 13, No. 2*, June, 167–188

Ellis, J.C., and Lacey, R.F., 1980, "Sampling: Defining the task and planning the scheme," *Journal of the Institute of Water Pollution Control, No 4*, 452–467

Environmental Resources, Ltd. (ERL), 1990, Draft report, *"Operation in Europe"*, London, ERL.

Gardenier, T.K., 1982, "Moving averages for environmental standards", *Simulation 39, No 2*, August, 49–58

Harford, J.D., 1987, "Self–reporting of pollution and the firm's behavior under imperfectly enforceable regulations", *Journal of Environmental Economics and Management 14, No 3*, September, 293–303

Harrington, Winston, 1981, *"The Regulatory Approach to Air Quality Management: A Case Study of New Mexico"*, Washington, DC, Resources for the Future

Harrington, Winston, 1987. *"Explaining Voluntary Compliance: Why Do Sources Comply (sort of) with Environmental Regulations in the Absence of Penalties for Non–compliance?"*, working paper from Resources for the Future

Hill, Michael, 1982, "The role of the British alkali and clean air inspectorate in air pollution control," *Policy Studies Journal 11, No. 1*, September, 165–174

Hutter, E.M., 1988, *"The Reasonable Arm of the Law: The Law Enforcement Procedures of Environmental Health Officers"*, Oxford, Clarendon Press

Johnson, R.W., and Brown, G.M. Jr., 1976, *"Cleaning Up Europe's Waters: Economics, Management and Policies"*, New York, Praeger

Jones, C.A., and Scotchmer, S., 1990, "The social cost of uniform regulatory standards in a hierarchical Government", *Journal of Environmental Economics and Management 19, No. 1*, July. 61–72

Kneese, A.V., and Bower, B.T., 1968, *"Managing Water Quality: Economics, Technology, Institutions"*, Baltimore, Johns Hopkins Press for Resources for the Future

Kopp, R.J., and Smith, V.K., 1989, "Benefit estimation goes to court: The case of natural resource damage assessments", *Journal of Policy Analysis and Management 8, No. 4*, Fall, 593–612

Malik, A.S., 1990, "Markets for pollution control when firms are non–compliant", *Journal of Environmental Economics and Management 18, No. 2*, March, 97–106

National Board of Waters, Finland, 1979, *"Final Report for the IBRD of the Research Project Carried Out in 1975–78 by the National Board of Waters"*, Helsinki NBW, Finland

National Rivers Authority, 1990, *"Discharge Consent and Compliance Policy: A Blueprint for the Future"*, London, National Rivers Authority

Organization for Economic Cooperation and Development, 1981, *"Economic Instruments in Solid Waste Management"*, Paris, OECD

Rehbinder, E., and Stewart, R., 1985, *"Environmental Protection Policy"*, Vol. 2 of a series on *Integration Through Law*, New York, Berlin, Walter de Gruyter

Richardson, G., Ogus, A., and Burrows, P., 1982, *"Policing Pollution: A Study of Regulation and Enforcement"*, Oxford, Clarendon Press

Russell, C.S., 1990 A, "Game models for structuring monitoring and enforcement systems", *Natural Resource Modeling 4, No 2*, Spring, 143–173

Russell, C.S., 1990 B. "Monitoring and enforcement", in: Portney, Paul, (ed.), *Public Policies for Environmental Protection*, Washington, DC, Resources for the Future

Russell, C.S., Harrington, W., and Vaughan, W.J., 1986, *"Enforcing Pollution Control Laws"*, Washington, DC, Resources for the Future

Vaughan, W.J., and Russell, C.R., 1983, "Monitoring point sources of pollution: Answers and more questions from statistical quality control", *The American Statistician 37, No 4*, November, 476–487

Comments by Heinz Welsch

1. The paper by Clifford Russell provides valuable insights into the structure of the monitoring and enforcement problem by defining its key dimensions, and it offers a characterization of the practices of several European nations along those dimensions. The discussion in the paper is based on two maintained hypotheses: (1) compliance with

environmental regulations is very unlikely to be completely voluntary, (2) continuous pollution monitoring is not a major option because devices suffer from reliability problems or are subject to source manipulation.

While I agree with the first hypothesis, I am somewhat more optimistic as regards the second one. Both of these views are based on evidence from Germany (or rather West Germany, for that matter), and in what follows I will briefly sketch some key features of German monitoring and enforcement practice along the dimensions introduced by Clifford Russell. In doing so I will distinguish between air pollution and water pollution as the problems encountered are different, as are the regulatory approaches. The discussion will be limited to stationary point sources. For an overview see Table 1.

2. Monitoring and enforcement of German water pollution control regulations is a matter of the states. I have no material on the actual frequency of control visits and on the question whether visits are announced or not, but it is clear that inspectors do have the right to enter premises unannounced.

German water pollution control is more instructive with respect to the definition of and the penalties for a violation than with respect to the monitoring practice. An essential element of the German water pollution regulations is the system of effluent charges. Under this system, sources of effluent have to apply for a permit which specifies instantaneous limits on the discharge of various pollutants, plus a limit on the annual effluent flow. The charges payable depend on the limits which sources request to be written into the permit.

Limits are considered violated if they are exceeded by the arithmetic mean of the five most recent measurements, provided that they do not date back longer than three years. Whenever a violation is detected, a new base for charging the source is obtained by increasing the existing limit by one half of the amount by which the maximum measured value exceeds this limit. In case of consecutive violations the maximum measured discharge becomes the new base.

Thus, the effluent charge system may be viewed as a system of flexible standards, the violation of which is defined quite unambiguously and entails a well-defined "flexible response".

3. The monitoring of sources of air pollutants is in general performed on a discontinuous basis. There are two modes of discontinuous monitoring. The first comprises control visits by agency inspectors. These visits mainly comprise an inspection of the control

	Frequency of Visits	Visits Surprise or Prearranged	Definition of Compliance	Penalty for Noncompliance
Water Pollution Control	Not available	Unclear	$0.2 \sum\limits_{i=1}^{5} x_i \leq EL$ [a]	First Violation: $EL^{new}=EL+0.5(x_i{}^{max}-EL)$ Consecutive Violations: $EL^{new} = x_i{}^{max}$
Air Pollution Control				
— Discontinuous Monitoring				
Inspections of Control Equipment	Once a year [b]	Surprise [b]	Unclear	Unclear
Metering of Emissions	Every 3 years	Prearranged	$x_i \leq EL, i \in \{1,2,3\}$	Unclear
— Continuous Monitoring	Once a year (Inspection of monitoring equipment)	Prearranged (Inspection of monitoring equipment)	• all daily averages within year $\leq$ EL • 97% of 1/2-hourly averages within year $\leq$ 1.2 EL • all 1/2-hourly averages within year $\leq$ 2.0 EL	Unclear

Notes: a) x_i = measured values, EL = emission limit. In case of effluent charge, EL provides the quantity base for determination of charge. EL's are usually instantaneous concentrations. Exception: Annual volume flow of effluent.

b) Practice in the State of Northrhine—Westfalia.

Sources: Breuer (1987), Kalmbach and Schmölling (1988), MURL (1988, 1989)

Table 1: Summary information on the German monitoring and enforcement system

equipment. According to a statement by the Ministry of the Environment of the State of
Northrhine—Westphalia visits are unannounced, except it is necessary to make sure that
certain persons are present. The ratio of visits per year to the number of facilities was
1.1 in 1988 and slightly less than 1.0 in 1989.

Thus in Northrhine—Westphalia a facility discharging air pollutants is visited roughly once a year. In addition to that it is obliged to have its emissions metered every three
years and to report the results to the control agency. A source is found in compliance if
all measured values from a sample of three are not beyond the limit value. These measurements are performed by state—approved institutes upon request by the facility, thus
not being a surprise, by definition. Nevertheless, according to an executive of one of the
major approved institutes, 10 to 20 percent of the sources are found out of compliance
because the control equipment is in bad condition. Under everyday conditions emissions
may still be higher, due to negligence of the operating personnel.

4. Since the middle of the 1980's power plants and waste incinerators are required by
law to monitor and document their emissions on a continuous basis. For other facilities
such requirements may be written into the operating license. The development of the
continuous monitoring devices now in operation in Germany has been initiated almost
20 years ago by the air pollution control agency in Northrhine—Westphalia. In this state,
which accounts for about 50 percent of the West—German power plant capacity, 3492
devices for the continuous monitoring of seven different constituents have been installed
by 1988.

With continuous monitoring, the frequency and the surprise dimension of the monitoring problem are no longer an issue. However, they are replaced by the question of
reliability, which is partly a monitoring and enforcement problem of the second order.
Part of the answer to this question is that devices must be approved by the Federal
Environmental Agency. This means that all analyzers are subject to an approval test
which is performed on the basis of standardized criteria and which consists of a laboratory test and a 3—month continuous test at a plant. Once installed and calibrated, monitoring systems are subject to an annual inspection by an approved institute. Moreover
they have to be maintained regularly, where the prescribed, type—specific maintenance
interval is determined at the approval test. Every three years the system has to be re-
calibrated. Preliminary experience in Northrhine—Westphalia in 1988 and 1989 shows
that in about 9 percent of the annual inspection visits reliability problems were detected. Problems were mainly encountered with waste incinerators, the reason being that
the highly variable pollutant content of waste makes calibration difficult. Applying con-

tinuous monitoring devices requires, of course, a definition of a violation in terms of relative frequencies. The relevant regulations specify that a source is in compliance if all of the following conditions are met:

- all daily averages within a year do not exceed the emission limit;

- 97 percent of the 1/2–hourly averages within a year do not exceed 1.2 times the emission limit;

- all 1/2–hourly averages within a year do not exceed 2.0 times the emission limit.

The necessary computations and the documentation are performed automatically by means of mini computers which must be installed in all facilities that are subject to continuous emission monitoring.

5. From the preceding discussion it follows that, out of the four key dimensions of the monitoring and enforcement problem, the definition of a violation of regulations is un- ambiguous, in the case of water pollution as well as for air pollution. So there remain the two fundamental issues of detection of and response to a violation. The corresponding problems and the approaches to them differ according to the two environmental media.

Concerning discovered violations, comprehensive data are only available for viola- tions that are subject to criminal law. It can be seen from Table 2 that the number of violations of the water pollution laws has steadily increased from 4531 in 1981 to 10529 in 1987. This is clear evidence that it would be naive to rely on voluntary compliance. For air pollution, absolute figures are in the range of 118 to 415 and show a considerable volatility. The divergence in absolute figures between the two media may be due to the fact that air pollutants, once released, are widely dispersed and much more difficult to trace back to the source than water pollutants. To me, this explanation appears to be more convincing than the assumption that potential sources of air pollutants are more inclined to comply with emission standards than sources of effluent.

A promising way of increasing the detection probability in the case of air pollution is continuous emission monitoring. Interestingly enough, the number of discovered viola- tions of air pollution laws increased sharply in 1984, but it would be speculative to relate this to the requirement of continuous monitoring introduced round about that year. Moreover, continuous monitoring is not a panacea because due to the considerable costs of continuous monitoring systems (roughly 500 000 DM for a multi–pollutant system) their application is limited to large sources. Moreover, in some cases (waste incinerators) there still seem to be reliability problems. In the case of water pollution, continuous

	Water Pollution		Air Pollution	
	Violations Subject to Criminal Law	%*	Violations Subject to Criminal Law	%*
1981	4531	15.4	163	1.8
1982	5352	14.1	148	3.3
1983	5769	12.4	118	7.6
1984	6992	11.1	415	2.9
1985	8562	11.4	406	1.7
1986	9294	9.7	338	3.6
1987	10592	9.6	406	2.0

*: Percentage of Convictions; Source: Statistisches Bundesamt (1990)

Table 2: Discovered violations of environmental laws

automatic monitoring is, as yet, hardly applicable because of the diversity and complex chemical nature of the relevant pollutants.

Regarding responses to violations, available material shows that the ratio of convictions to discovered criminal violations is quite poor. In the case of water pollution it decreased from 15.4 percent in 1981 to 9.6 percent in 1987, as shown in Table 2. In the case of air pollution the percentage is mostly in the range of 2 to 4, with quite a substantial volatility. The low percentages may partly be due to the fact that polluters could not be identified. It may also be the case that only administrative or civil penalties were imposed because the violation was due to negligence, not to intent.

An interesting example of a well–defined, flexible scheme of administrative "penalties" is provided by the German effluent charge system, which is a flexible–standard system in disguise. However, although the rule for adjusting the "penalty" base to the extent and frequency of violations seems reasonable, the amount payable per unit of pollution is so low that deterrence would be doubtful even if the detection probability were unity.

6. In conclusion, I agree with Clifford Russell that the monitoring and enforcement game is to be played smarter in the future and that this entails shifting emphasis from the raising of penalties to raising the probability of detecting violations. Continuous monitoring systems as a means to that end should be applied to the extent technically feasible and economically reasonable. Despite the priority of detecting violations, however, it is also important to design penalties and standards as flexible as possible in order to avoid unnecessary resistance to pollution control.

References

Breuer, R., 1987, *"Öffentliches und privates Wasserrecht"*, 2nd ed., München

Kalmbach, S., and Schmölling, J., 1988, *"Technische Anleitung zur Reinhaltung der Luft"*, 2nd ed., Berlin

MURL (Ministerium für Umwelt, Raumordnung und Landwirtschaft des Landes Nordrhein–Westfalen), 1988, 1989, *"Jahresbericht"*, Teil Immissionschutz, Düsseldorf

Statistisches Bundesamt, 1990, *"Umweltinformationen der Statistik"*, Ausgabe 1990, Stuttgart

Chapter 8

Wolfgang J. Ströbele

The Economics of Negotiations on Water Quality
- An Application of Principal Agent Theory[1]

Abstract: In the paper the principal–agent approach to a two–party upstream–downstream environmental problem is discussed. Negotiations between two conflicting parties can only deal on the basis of observed outcomes downstream. These are not only dependent upon the actions taken by the agent upstream but also upon some stochastic influence by nature. The formal difficulties of the approach are sketched and two special distribution functions (normal and beta) are discussed with a linear payment schedule. While for the normal–distribution (LEN–model) the solution can be given explicitly the case of the beta–distribution only allows for a numerical solution.

1. Introduction

In the following we will analyse a situation, where an upstream–downstream problem of water pollution can be solved by negotiations between two parties involved. Since we want to apply the developed methods of principal–agent theory we use the following conventions. The upstream polluting industry is the agent, whose behaviour with respect to emissions depends on her initial rights and the payoff–rule offered by the downstream party, say a drinking water company. The water company acts as the principal, who wants to induce a certain behaviour of the agent by offering a certain payment schedule, depending on the observed water quality. Following Arrow (1985, p.37), there are two necessary elements to have an interesting problem: "...(1) the agent's action is not directly observable by the principal and (2) the outcome is affected but not completely

[1] This paper grew out of a project on water resources financially supported by the Deutsche Forschungsgemeinschaft (DFG). This support is greatfully aknowledged. I also want to thank my collegues Peter Stahlecker and Dietmar Pfeifer from the University of Oldenburg and an anonymous referee for helpful discussions. The usual disclaimer concerning errors and shortcomings applies.

determined by the agent's action." In environmental economics, we generally have the special situation of *hidden action* of the agent, since the water company cannot observe the effort of the agent directly. The sources of uncertainty of nature may be found in all types of influence not attributable to the agent's action: more or less rain, longer or shorter winters, natural variations in upstream groundwater inflows etc.

Formally, this situation is modelled as a game, where the outcome (here: the water quality) is a random variable whose distribution depends on the actions taken by the upstream agent. Effort of the agent, i.e. cleaning her sewage, causes extra cost for the agent, but gives an extra utility to the principal in terms of stochastically lower water processing cost. The higher the effort, the higher the likelihood for a better water quality: The distribution function of the water quality with respect to a higher effort stochastically dominates the one with a lower effort.

The informational structure is assumed as follows: The agent knows perfectly and costlessly, what kind of action she has taken, while the principal can only have observations of the outcome of water quality. This observation may be obtained costlessly (model type A) or only by implementation of a costly monitoring system where a random sample is drawn and the water quality in the river is estimated (model type B). These two types of model reflect different ways how to obtain information with respect to water quality: In case of a water company processing the water taken from the river directly we have the case of model A: she may obtain a perfect quality information in her process without extra cost. In model B the water company has her primary sources in some underground water behind the banks so that the actual river water quality must be observed separately. In the following we assume, that both parties have the same beliefs about the probability distribution of the stochastic component, i.e. they agree upon an emission diffusion process and natural influences in the river.

As again Arrow (1985) points out, there is always some risk—sharing in the principal—agent problem. If the agent were risk—neutral, in many cases there would be a simple solution with respect to the type of contract offered by the principal and accepted by the agent. Then the "only" problem would be to enforce the contract by an appropriate monitoring system. The latter problem may be analyzed in terms of certainty equivalents, and the only uncertainty to be dealt with is the possibility of breach of contract. This type of problem was dealt with in Ströbele (1990) with respect to water pollution.

The basic ingredients of any principal—agent model are three parts and therefore three equations in sufficiently simple models:

(a)   *Maximization of the agent's utility function* with respect to his effort gives the
        first equation. Of course, this maximum depends on the payment scheme offered
        by the principal depending on the outcome, which itself depends stochastically on
        the agent's effort.

(b)   Since the agent usually has some opportunity outside the offered contract or
        simply may refuse to cooperate, there is the so—called *reservation constraint.*
        This makes sure, that the agent must not be worse off with the contract than
        with his best alternative realistic opportunity. Since most incentive schemes may
        be described by some parametric form, this constraint normally involves an addi-
        tional restriction in form of an inequality imposed on the set of feasible parame-
        ters. Often, this inequality may be assumed to hold with equality (ϵ—rule), which
        gives equation (2.4") below.

(c)   The *principal* wants to *maximise her utility function* depending on the valuation
        of the outcome net of payments to the agent (of course taking into account the
        steps (a) and (b) from above), which gives equation three.

The main formal problems in principal—agent theory arise from the simple fact that
depending on the probability distributions involved and the mixture of utility functions
of principal and agent etc. there may be a large class of simply unsolvable problems, if
"solution" should mean something explicit and interpretable in economic terms.[2]

The formal problems of an adequate modelling of the type of problems involved
especially in model of type B are quite high: the involved functions for describing costs
and (expected) benefits of the actions and payments very rapidly lead to sums of some
linear and square terms. The stochastic distributions of these types of functions already
pose very severe problems. For example, imagine the modification by introduction of
control cost in the "LEN—Model" of Spremann (1987) along the lines discussed in Ströbele (1990). This generates a sum of a term with a normal distribution and a term with
a χ^2—distribution, which cannot be handled easily any more. Even the seemingly rather
elementary calculation of the agent's participation constraint proves unsolvable for very
simple structures. So a choice has to made between a "realistic" model, that cannot be

---

[2] Therefore some papers come to the construction of "payments in terms of *utils*" (Cp.
for instance C.S. Kanodia (1985)). Of course, this helps to circumvent the formal problems, but it is difficult to imagine, how that should be worked out in a contract, since
the effective amount of "utils" is dependent on the agent's effort, which is not observable by the principal, to have an interesting problem.

olved and a "nice" model, where at least something can be calculated. The economist may find consolation in Arrow's evaluation of agency theory, where he states "... there is a pressure for simple contracts ..." in real life (Arrow, 1985, p.49).

The most common approach in principal–agent theory *assumes* as the relevant probability distribution the *normal distribution*. This is done, since in this case the solution of the three basic equations can be found under some reasonable assumptions concerning the utility functions. One type of this class of model will be presented in the following. It is a modification of Spremann's LEN–model with respect to environmental economics, where we assume, that the principal is no longer risk–neutral but has some constant (absolute) risk–aversion, which seems more realistic.

Of course, there are some well–known objections to this type of popular distribution function. Especially with respect to water quality it may be much more appropriate, to use some kind of distribution function, that has all its positive mass on a given bounded closed interval between "dead water" and "drinking water quality". This type of distribution not only allows for a good interpretation, but also has some advantages in terms of mathematical analysis. In the following a special *beta–distribution* will be looked at.

In both cases we will apply sufficiently simple utility functions. In both models it will be taken as a linear approximation from the so–called HARA–class of functions (hyperbolic absolute risk aversion), where the Pratt–Arrow index of risk aversion is described by

$$r(z) = -\frac{U''(W)}{U'(W)} = \frac{1}{a + bW}. \tag{1}$$

In case that $b = 0$ in (1.1) we have the exponential utility function

$$U(W) = -\frac{1}{a} e^{-\frac{1}{a} \cdot W}. \tag{2}$$

In case that $a = 0$ we have the popular isoelastic utility function.[3]

We will use as utility function the approximation in the so–called μ–σ–approach: The mean value of the outcome is positively appreciated, the variance supports utility in

---

[3] Cp. Bamberg/Spremann, p. 207. Modelling of the theory of natural resources with an isoelastic utility function without uncertainty was extensively done in Ströbele (1987).

a non–positive way depending upon the degree of risk aversion.

2. The basic model structure of a modified LEN–model

The model will be described by the following components:

(1)   Water quality measured in units of "cleanness" is a linear function of abatement
       effort x and a stochastic term ω.

(2)   Feasible payment schemes are *linear functions* of (observed) water quality
       $y = x + \omega$. The slope s and the fixed payment r determine the actual incentive
       for a certain behaviour of the agent.

(3)   Both the *utility function* of the agent (upstream industry) and the principal
       (downstream water company) are $(\mu$–$\sigma)$–approximations of exponential utility
       functions with different parameters $\alpha = 1/a$ and $\beta = 1/b$ describing the constant
       absolute risk aversion of both parties. The independent variable in the agents
       utility function is her wealth, which is a composite of payments and abatement
       costs. The utility of the principal depends on the water quality net of payments
       to the upstream industry. As was shown in Bamberg/Spremann (1981) the case
       of (almost) risk neutrality can then be modelled by assuming either α or β as
       "very small".

(4)   The probability distribution of ω is *Normal* with mean zero and a constant stand-
       ard deviation σ.

(5)   Abatement costs are a square function of abatement effort q.

The specifications (1), (2) and (4) imply that the stochastic components of net wealth of
the two parties are normally distributed. As was shown in Bamberg/Spremann (1981)
the assumption (3) implies that approximations to the certainty equivalents may be
expressed as expected value minus half the variance times the risk aversion parameter.
This gives the following equations for the model: The *agent's wealth*, which is industry's
received payment minus abatement costs, is given by[4]

---

[4] For the sake of notational simplicity the numbering of equations starts with (1) in each
subsequent section. If an equation, say Equation (14), is refered to in the text, it is understood that we mean Equation (14) in the section where the reference is made. If in
section y we refer to Equation (14) from section x (x $\neq$ y), we write Equation (x.14).

$$W_A(x, r, s) = r + sy - x^2 = r + s(x + \omega) - x^2 \tag{1}$$

x: abatement intensity

$x + \omega = y$:   observed outcome downstream

$r + (x + \omega)s$:   payment of principal to agent

x^2:   abatement cost

Observe, that abatement costs are not stochastic: the effort x is well known and certain for the agent. The certainty equivalent of the agent's utility U with respect to (1) is derived from her utility function:

$$\tilde{U}(x, r, s) = E(W_A) - \frac{\alpha}{2} Var(W_A) = r + sx - x^2 - \frac{\alpha}{2} s^2 \sigma^2 \tag{2}$$

Maximization with respect to effort x yields the best response of the agent:

$$\frac{d\tilde{U}}{dx} = s - 2x = 0 \tag{3}$$

which gives

$$x^* = \frac{s}{2} \tag{3'}$$

The agent's reservation constraint demands

$$\tilde{U}\left[\frac{s}{2}, r, s\right] \geq m \tag{4}$$

if

$$r + \frac{s^2}{2} - \frac{s^2}{4} - \frac{\alpha}{2}s^2\sigma^2 \geq m. \tag{4'}$$

Following the standard ϵ–rule, we may argue with equality in (4'):

$$r = m - \frac{s^2}{4}(1 - 2\alpha\sigma^2). \tag{4''}$$

Utility of the principal is derived from the availability of "clean water" measured by the variable $y = x + w$ net of payments to the agent:

$$W_p(x, r, s) = (1 - s)(x + w) - r. \qquad (5)$$

Making use of equations (3') and (4") we have as net utility

$$\tilde{V} = E(W_p) - \frac{\beta}{2}Var(W_p) = (1 - s)\frac{s}{2} - m + \frac{s^2}{4}(1 - 2\alpha\sigma^2) - \frac{\beta}{2}(1 - s)\sigma^2. \qquad (6)$$

Maximization of $\tilde{V}$ with respect to s (due to (4") r depends on s and is no longer an independent variable !):

$$\frac{d\tilde{V}}{ds} = \frac{1}{2} - s + \frac{s}{2}(1 - 2\alpha\sigma^2) + \beta(1 - s)\sigma^2 = 0. \qquad (7)$$

The necessary condition (7) describes the optimal choices of parameters s and r and the resulting action x of the agent as

$$s^* = \frac{1 + 2\beta\sigma^2}{1 + 2(\beta + \alpha)\sigma^2} \qquad (8)$$

which is equivalent to

$$s^* = 1 - \frac{2\alpha\sigma^2}{(1 + 2(\alpha + \beta)\sigma^2)}, \qquad (8')$$

$$r^* = m - \frac{(1 - 2\alpha\sigma^2)(1 + 2\beta\sigma^2)^2}{4(1 + 2(\alpha + \beta)\sigma^2)^2}, \qquad (9)$$

$$x^* = \frac{1 + 2\beta\sigma^2}{2(1 + 2(\alpha + \beta)\sigma^2)}, \qquad (10)$$

which is equivalent to

$$x^* = \frac{1}{2} - \frac{\alpha\sigma^2}{(1 + 2(\alpha + \beta)\sigma^2)}. \tag{10'}$$

One immediately obtains

$$\frac{dx^*}{d\alpha} < 0 \quad \text{and} \quad \frac{dx^*}{d\beta} > 0. \tag{11}$$

This result is quite plausible, since the higher the risk aversion of the principal (i.e. the water company), the higher her willingness to give higher monetary incentives to the agent (i.e. the industry) for abatement via a higher s^*. This latter argument can also be read directly from (8'). On the other hand, we have: The higher the risk aversion of the agent, the less she demands in terms of variable incentives via s^* and the more she wants to receive as a fixed payment.[5]

Case I: Agent almost risk neutral

In case that the principal, i.e. the water company downstream, is risk averse, but the industry upstream is almost risk neutral (i.e. we have α almost zero), the payment scheme will almost look like

$$P(x + \omega) = m - \frac{1}{4} + x + \omega, \tag{12}$$

$$x^* = \frac{1}{2}, \tag{13}$$

which is the standard result in case of a risk neutral agent, who is willing to take all the risks imposed by nature. Of course, in this special case, the resulting abatement intensity is independent of the risk aversion of the water company.

If the economy as a whole were risk neutral, we would obtain the allocation (13) as the optimal outcome.

---

[5] This is a standard argument of principal–agent theory applied also to the labour market.

Case II: Both agent and principal risk—avers

If the principal is almost risk—neutral, then we have the standard results described in Spremann (1987). In environmental economics we must assume, that also the principal may be extremely risk averse, i.e. the parameter β may be much higher than the parameter α. Then we interpret the equations above as follows:

Even if the risk—aversion of the agent is positive, a "very high" β leads to an allocation near to $x^* = 1/2$ and the steepest possible payment schedule. On the other hand, there is no way to reach an allocation of $x \leq 1/2$. The allocation and the incentive scheme is then similar to the case with a risk—neutral agent.

Remarks: The *reservation level m* heavily determines the *distribution* between the two parties but neither the optimal allocation (10) nor the steepness of the optimal incentive scheme (8). The interpretation of "m" as a *"lobbying variable"* is obvious: The primary rights to pollute or not to pollute determine the loads that have to be born by the two parties involved. If, for example, the industry has the legal right to pollute the river only up to a certain maximum standard, then the reservation constraint parameter m would be determined by the abatement cost that the industry has to bear in any case even without negotiations with the downstream water company. If, on the other side, the industry has the right to pollute whatever it likes, then m would be zero or even positive, reflecting a potential option value of future polluting activities from the point of view of industry.[6]

If the river has *some self—cleaning properties*, i.e. only a fraction $\gamma \cdot x$ with $\gamma < 1$ will be the net improvement of water quality downstream, this may be dealt with as being formally equivalent with an *increase in σ^2*. Thereby the share of uncertainty in the water quality outcome, that the principal cannot disclose, is increased.

3. The basic model with a beta—distribution of water quality depending on abatement intensity

A much more adequate description of water quality management problems may be obtained by the following type of model. We assume, that the water quality in the down-

---

[6] Here one might imagine a potential future research connection with aspects of public choice theory.

stream area can take any value between 0 and 1: $y = 0$ would mean, that the water is "dead", $y = 1$ would mean, that the water may be taken directly as drinking water, i.e. it is perfectly clean. The upstream polluter may abate a certain amount of her sewage. If her cleaning effort x were zero, there would be a high probability for poor water quality and even some probability for almost "dead" water. If on the other hand, her abatement intensity x is "very high", the probability for poor water quality near zero will be almost zero and a reasonably good water quality may be expected.

This heuristics may be modelled as follows: Water quality y (measured downstream) is a stochastic variable with a β–distribution with parameters $(2, x)$, where x denotes the abatement effort of the upstream industry. How this distribution looks like with different parameters x is shown in Figure 3.1. The choice of a special class of β–distribution (first parameter fixed at $p = 2$) is not a drastic cut with respect to general arguments, but allows for some analytical simplifications.

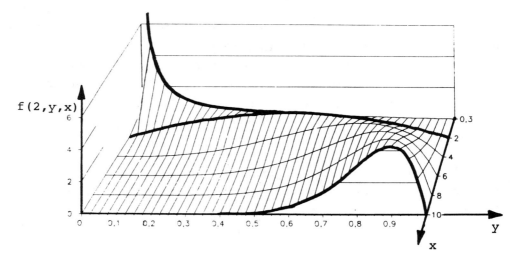

Figure 3.1: β–distribution with different x

$$f(2, y, x) = x(x + 1)(y^{x-1} - y^x) \tag{1}$$

For reasons of convenience we will abbreviate (1) by writing $f(y)$, when the parameter x is given. The *expected water quality* then depends on x and is given by

$$E(y) = \frac{x}{2 + x} = 1 - \frac{2}{x + 2}. \tag{2}$$

As argued above, we have $E(y) = 0$ if there is absolutely no abatement $(x = 0)$ and $E(y) = 1$ if abatement effort x is "very large".

The *variance* of the β—distribution is given by

$$Var(y) = \frac{2x}{(x + 2)^2(x + 3)}. \tag{2'}$$

As is well known, the variance of the β—distribution varies with the parameter x. In economic terms this means, that there may be two outcomes with rather low variance: if the abatement intensity is near to zero, then a "bad" water quality outcome will be almost sure with low variance. For sufficiently high x—values[7] we have: the higher the abatement effort of the industry upstream, the lower also the variance of the possible outcomes in terms of water quality downstream. Not only the expected value $E(y)$ in (2) is then improved by increasing x, but also the risk of "very bad" results diminishes. If the principal is risk—avers, that should have direct consequences for the payment scheme offered and the risk sharing involved in the contract.

It is obvious that this class of distribution allows for a *better interpretation* of many real life problems than the Normal—distribution with its constant variance and its shifting on the real axis without limits for the possible outcomes. Of course, one pays a price in terms of analytical easiness for handling the model.

The dependency of $E(y)$ upon abatement effort x is shown in Figure 3.2.

The payment scheme offered by the principal will again be modelled by a linear scheme

$$P(y) = r + sy. \tag{3}$$

This scheme may not be the "best" in terms of the optimal incentive mechanism (where the comparison is made strictly in terms of the formal model being the one "real" world) but it may prove as being practical and workable.

Since we assume that the abatement cost is a square function in x, the net position

---

[7] Here: x above $\tilde{x} = 1.1375$

of the agent is given by

$$W_A(x, r, s, y) = P(y) - bx^2. \tag{4}$$

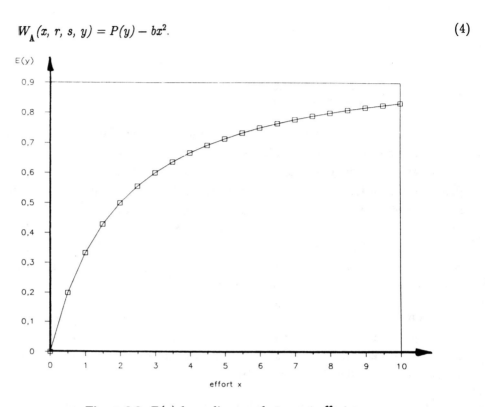

Figure 3.2: $E(y)$ depending on abatement effort x

To obtain a sufficiently simple model, we again assume that the agent has some $(\mu - \sigma)$-quadratic (expected) utility function (allowing for a simple approximation of her risk aversion):

$$U(W_A) = E(W_A) - \frac{\alpha}{2}Var(W_A) + const. \tag{5}$$

$\alpha > 0$ makes sure, that the agent is risk–avers. As in the LEN–model above, the agent's reservation constraint can simply be met by a sufficiently high basic payment of the principal. If a contract is possible from the principal's point of view, then the allocation is mainly determined by the payment weights concerning the mean outcome and the risk parameters. Here, calculating the agent's utility with the β-distribution is made "easy" by the general formula :

$$\int_0^1 (y^\gamma q(q+1)(y^{q-1}-y^q))dy = \int_0^1 (q(q+1)(y^{\gamma+q-1}-y^{\gamma+q}))dy$$

$$= \frac{q(q+1)}{(\gamma+q)(\gamma+q+1)} \cdot \int_0^1 ((\gamma+q)(\gamma+q+1)(y^{\gamma+q-1}-y^{\gamma+q}))dy \qquad (6)$$

$$= \frac{q(q+1)}{(\gamma+q)(\gamma+q+1)}.$$

Therefore the agent's expected net utility above the constant reservation level is given by

$$\tilde{U} = \frac{s\,x}{x+2} - bx^2 - \frac{\alpha}{2} \frac{2s^2 x}{(x+2)^2(x+3)}. \qquad (7)$$

Similarly we may formulate the principal's problem. If her utility function is of the same type as the agent's with risk aversion parameter β instead of α, then we have

$$U(W_p) = E(W_p) - \frac{\beta}{2} Var(W_p) + const. \qquad (8)$$

Even for the case of an almost risk—neutral agent (with α almost near to zero), the derivation of the necessary conditions proves to be rather difficult. Therefore a numerical solution will be discussed. Observe first, that the reservation constraint can formally be "ignored" for the optimization, since it changes only the constant level of initial utility of either of the two parties. This stems from the assumed utility function (8) and (5). The algorithm requires a more detailed discussion than what can be given here[8]. Therefore the results are summarized as follows:

---

[8] See Stahlecker, Ströbele (1991).

Risk–aversion		s^*	x^*
$\alpha = 0$	$\beta = 0$	1	0.2056
$\alpha = 0.1$	$\beta = 0$	0.9653	0.1976
$\alpha = 0.1$	$\beta = 0.1$	0.9664	0.1978
$\alpha = 0.25$	$\beta = 0.1$	0.9227	0.1875
$\alpha = 1.00$	$\beta = 0.25$	0.9385	0.1901

Table 3.1: Different solutions of the principal–agent–model with beta–distribution

Obviously, the higher the risk aversion of the agent, the flatter is the payment schedule. This result looks very similar to the LEN–model, which may lead to the conclusion, that some kind of linear incentive scheme may prove helpful and workable for real life problems even if the "true" distribution function is not known exactly.

4. Possible extensions

There may be some interesting modifications of the above analysis.

Monitoring costs put an additional problem into the already complex structure. If the principal must bear some control cost we have quite a new game with similarities to statistical quality control. The problems of enforceable contracts in face of eventually "high" monitoring cost are a special issue.

On the other hand, if observation of water quality is relatively easy, then another complication may arise. The agent may make use of her informational advantage with respect to water quality and environmental conditions by choosing her *emissions depending on the* estimated *state of nature*. Since she may observe the natural oscillations in water conditions directly, she can choose a certain schedule of abatement or emissions. This may happen for example by storage of sewage over some days (if it is less costly than abatement; which mainly depends on the amount of waste water that has to be stored temporarily) and emissions, when the state of nature is more favourable.

Some kind of *public choice* concept may be applied to model lobbying activities of the parties for a better initial endowment of property rights. The analysis above has shown the possible distributive aspects of such activities.

At last, one should mention that the analysis above does not contain an explicit *time aspect*. Since there is no variable as "trust" or experience with certain payment schedules real life problems may be handled with by some learning—by—doing procedure. The principal—agent—theory with renegotiation is a complex field which is not yet applied widely to environmental economics[9].

References

Arrow, J.K., 1985, "The economics of agency", in: J.W.Pratt, R.J.Zeckhauser (eds.), *Principals and Agents*, Boston, 37—51

Bamberg, G., and Spremann, K., 1981, "Implications of constant risk aversion", *Zeitschrift für Operations Research 25*, 205—224

Dye, R.A., 1986, "Optimal monitoring policies in agencies", *The Rand Journal of Economics 17*, 339—350

Fudenberg, D., Holmström, B., and Milgrom, P., 1990, "Short—term contracts and long—term agency relationships", *Journal of Economic Theory 52*, 194—206

Groves, T., 1982, "On theories of incentive compatible choice with compensation", in: Hildenbrand (ed.), *Advances in Economic Theory*, Cambridge, Ch.1.

Harris, M., and Townsend, R.M., 1981, "Resource allocation under asymmetric information", *Econometrica 49*, 231—259

Holmström, B., 1982, "Moral hazard in teams", *Bell Journal of Economics 13*, 324—340

Kanodia, C.S., 1985, "Stochastic monitoring and moral hazard", *Journal of Accounting Research 23*, 175—193

Jensen, M.C., and Meckling, W.H., 1976, "Theory of the firm: Managerial behaviour, agency costs and ownership structure", *Journal of Financial Economics 3*, 305—360

Jewitt, I., 1988, "Justifying the first—order approach to principal—agent problems", *Econometrica 56*, 1177—1190

Linder, S.H., and McBride, M.E., 1984, "Enforcement costs and regulatory reform: The agency and firm response", *Journal of Environmental Economics and Management 11*, 327—346

---

[9] See for instance Fudenberg, Holmstöm and Milgrom (1990).

Milgrom, P.R., 1981, "Good news and bads news: Representation theorems and applications", *Bell Journal of Economics 12*, 380–391

Rees, R., 1985, "The theory of principal and agent, Part I", *Bulletin of Economics Research 37*, 3–26

Rees, R., 1985, "The theory of principal and agent, Part II", *Bulletin of Economics Research 37*, 70–90

Rogerson, W., 1985, "The first–order approach to principal–agent problems", *Econometrica 53*, 1357–1368

Ross, S.A., 1973, "The economic theory of agency: The principal's problem", *American Econ. Review P&P 63*, 134–139

Shavell, S., 1979, "Risk sharing and incentives in the principal and agent relationship", *Bell Journal of Economics 10*, 55–73

Spremann, K., 1987, "Agent and principal", in: G.Bamberg, K.Spremann (eds.), *Agency Theory, Information, and Incentives*, Heidelberg, 3–37

Stahlecker, P., and Ströbele, W.J., 1991, "On Some Classes of Solvable Principal–Agent–Problems", *Discussion Paper Institute of Economics* – University of Oldenburg, V–69–91

Ströbele, W.J., 1990, "Institutional Arrangements for Transfrontier River Pollution", *Discussion Paper Institute of Scarcity* – University of Oldenburg, V–62–90; to appear in H.Siebert (ed.), *Environmental Economics – The International Dimension*, (1991)

Ströbele, W., 1987, *"Rohstoffökonomik"*, München (The Economics of Natural Resources)

Weimann, J., 1990, *"Umweltökonomik"*, Berlin et al.

Comments by Günter Knieps

Environmental pollution is a generally recognized source of market failure. Without proper adjustment of externality levels, market equilibria will not achieve Pareto optimality. On the one hand, there is a large scope for the establishment of state interventions, which may deal with such a market failure, for example Pigouvian tax, emission standards or administrative regulation. On the other hand, private initiatives such as bargaining may also contribute to solve the externality problem. A negotiation model of pollution abatement and compensatory payments must specify which parties are involved, their available actions and which outcome within the model will result from strategic interaction. In the language of game theory, firstly a formal game must be specified, secondly a hypothesis concerning the proper solution concept must be formed, and thirdly the efficiency properties of the predicted outcome must be investigated.

1. The negotiation game on water quality

Ströbele (1991) analyzes a situation, where an upstream—downstream problem of water pollution has to be solved by negotiations between only two parties involved. Whereas the upstream polluting industry knows perfectly and costlessly what kind of action she has taken, the water company can only have observations of the water quality which is affected but not completely determined by the agent's action. The water company acts as the principal, who wants to induce a certain behaviour of the agent by offering a certain payment schedule depending on the observed water quality. This scenario makes it possible to apply the in meantime well—developed principal—agent theory, although unlike in traditional principal—agent—relationships neither the upstream polluter, nor the downstream water company can be viewed as a subordinate of the other. Focussing only on two parties negotiating on water quality seems quite restrictive because the power to tax the polluter (e.g. Blankart 1988) cannot be considered explicitly in such a framework. Moreover, as soon as the polluting industry consists of a large number of participants (e.g. agriculture) the postulated small number case is no longer convincing.

2. The proper solution concept

If only two parties are involved one might (perhaps quite naively) conjecture that a cooperative bargaining solution in the spirit of the Coase (1960) 'Theorem' would occur. Such bargaining might not only focus on the ex post production decision of the polluting industry and the payment schedule of the water company but *simultaneously* include the size of sunk investments in both upstream and downstream firms (e.g. Kleindorfer, Knieps 1982). Of course, if no costs would be sunk the problem could be solved by simply exchanging the location of polluting industry and water company. Independent of the allocation of property rights to pollute this simple solution would occur because transaction costs of bargaining on the location of investments between only two parties are negligible.

However, the drive of Ströbele's negotiation problem comes from the information structure assumed. Whereas the downstream water company can only observe actual water quality (depending on pollution and some random factor) the upstream firm knows the actual level of pollution, coming from his production process. Some of the existing literature recognizes information and monitoring costs as an abstract source of transaction costs for which strategic aspects are of particular importance. It appears as one of the main virtues of the noncooperative approach applied by Ströbele that it permits such situation to be handled.

3. Outcomes of the negotiation game

The first question is whether the noncooperative negotiation game on water quality has one or more optimal outcomes (Nash equilibria). The major part of Ströbele's paper addresses this question: explicitly analyzing the impact of risk aversion of the firms involved. In doing so, he makes rather specific assumptions, both on the utility functions of the parties involved as well as on the relevant probability distributions of water quality. The optimal solution has been calculated for the unrealistic case of normal distribution. For the more realistic case of a beta–distribution the derivation of the necessary conditions proved to be rather difficult, even for the case of an almost risk neutral agent. Therefore, only a numerical solution has been discussed.

Although the derivation of optimal outcomes seems already a complex task, nevertheless the question remains concerning the efficiency properties of the solutions derived. In fact, the original principal–agency literature (e.g. Ross, 1979) tried to characterize the family of Pareto–efficient fee schedules. However, in contrast to cooperative solution concepts where efficiency remains a matter of definition, noncooperative Nash equilibria need not lead to an (ex post) efficient outcome. To give Nash equilibria a chance of being efficient, steps of the bargaining procedure must explicitly be included. As has been shown by Schweizer (1988, pp. 258 f.), efficiency can be restored, if the utility level associated with the unformed party's outside option does not depend on the informed party's private information. In Ströbele's model a reservation level may not only be defined for the upstream polluting firm but also for the downstream water company. If the primary allocation of property rights are enforcing minimal standards of observed water quality, the water company's threat point does not depend on unobservable pollution. One might therefore expect that an efficiency result occurs also in the water quality negotiation game. Obviously, this would require a reformulation of the bargaining model into a sequential game (e.g. Kreps, Wilson 1982).

References

Baumol, W.J., and Oates, W.E., 1988, *"The Theory of Environmental Policy"*, 2d. Ed., Cambridge University Press

Blankart, C.B., 1988, "Umweltschutzorientierte Sonderabgaben und ihre Alternativen", A. Der Wasserpfennig aus ökonomischer Sicht, in: K. Schmidt (Ed.), *Öffentliche Finanzen und Umweltpolitik I*, Duncker & Humblot Berlin, 51–65

Coase, R., 1960, "The Problem of Social Cost", *Journal of Law and Economics 3*, 1–44

Kleindorfer, P., and Knieps, G., 1982, "Vertical Integration and Transaction–Specific Sunk Costs", *European Economic Review 19*, 71–87

Kreps, D.M., and Wilson, R., 1982, "Sequential Equilibria", *Econometrica 50*, 863–894

Ross, St.A., 1973, "The Economic Theory of Agency: The Principal's Problem", *American Economic Review P.a.P. 63*, 134–139

Schweizer, U., 1988, "Externalities and the Coase Theorem: Hypothesis or Result?", *Journal of Institutional and Theoretical Economics 144*, 245–266

Ströbele, W.J., 1991, "The Economics of Negotiations on Water Quality – An Application of Principal Agent Theory", *this volume*

Chapter 9

Rudolf Avenhaus[1]

Monitoring the Emission of Pollutants
by Means of the
Inspector Leadership Method

Abstract. The decision theoretical analysis of monitoring point sources of pollution is the subject of this paper. Its goal is to develop a general method which puts the competent monitoring agency into a position to find appropriate decision procedures for this purpose. At the beginning of the paper the problem is discussed qualitatively; in particular, two possibilities are mentioned: Either the agency takes the data reported by the pollution emitting plant as the basis for its procedure, or it uses exclusively its own findings. Thereafter, the idealized monitoring problem is formulated in decision theoretical terms.

Two simple game theoretical models are analyzed: The simultaneous game in which both players act independently and without knowing the other's intentions, and the inspector leadership game, in which the inspector announces his strategy to the inspectee in a credible way. The inspector leadership game is considered to be more appropriate than the simultaneous game for the application under consideration. The paper proceeds by generalizing the inspector leadership game such that the inspectee has an extended set of strategies, and the connection with statistical decision theory is established. An example of a specific application completes the paper.

1. Monitoring point sources of pollution

The following example serves to illustrate the problem of controlling the compliance with regulatory limits on the emission of pollutants from a point source: Consider some industrial or technical installation for which licensing authorities have allowed the emission of some given amount of pollutants per unit of time into the environment, for instance, into a nearby river or the atmosphere. We assume that the installation produces more pollutants than can in this way legally be disposed of, and that its further treat-

---

[1] The author would like to thank Dr. M. Canty, Kernforschungsanlage Jülich, for very valuable suggestions and improvements of the original manuscript.

ment is costly so that an economic incentive exists to exceed the allowed emission thresholds. Consequently, the licensing authority is obliged to verify the observance of the emission standards.

Generally, one may assume that the facility measures its own emissions — according to Russell (1990) this is required in most States in the USA for all sources discharging into the water or the atmosphere. The task of the control authority is to verify the reported data, at least on a sampling basis. This can be done in one of two ways: Either the authority accepts the data as being correct, and need then only confirm that they concur with the allowed levels, or a deliberate falsification of data by the facility is considered credible, in which case independent measurements have to be carried out to check the validity of the reported data.

An example of the former possibility, which actually led to court action, is illustrative here (Schuster 1986). A facility reported approximately 44,000 measurements concerning several discharge canals to the water authority in charge. Of these 12,000 were evaluated with regard to acidity and other parameters. In 127 cases the allowed concentrations were found to have been exceeded. The courts were required to decide whether these 0.3 % higher concentration values which in fact said nothing about the actual amount of pollutant discharged constituted a mere irregularity or a punishable offense.

If deliberate falsification with the intention of concealment of a violation cannot be excluded, the authority, as already pointed out, will launch independent measurements and either compare these with the reported data or, ignoring the reported data altogether, draw its own conclusions as to the compliance with its emission standards. (e.g., Chapman, El–Shaarawi, 1989).

In either case, this procedure presents new difficulties: It is not possible for the authority to perform continuous monitoring at all emission sources; rather, it can only set up its measuring devices at a few selected points along a river or in the atmosphere. Therefore, pollutant propagation models have to be devised with the help of which conclusions regarding the source strengths can be drawn.

A large number of stochastic and deterministic models of this type have been developed for water and airborne pollutants in recent years, where the latter of course take into account meteorological conditions. (See, for example, Jakeman et al., 1985, Wathern et al., 1986, Simpson et al., 1987, Jaeschke et al., 1989). Welsch (1990) has recently given an overview of such models as well as their relation to questions of economics and measurement technology. We will not delve further into these complex matters in the following, but rather assume that the control authority is indeed in a position to draw statistical conclusions with regard to pollutant emission from point sources under its jurisdiction.

A further problem that one must take into account is that an operator intending to circumvent the allowed thresholds will act in such a way as to reduce his chance of detection to a minimum. As a consequence the classical statistical evaluation techniques of quality and process control for which the "adversary" is inanimate technology are largely irrelevant: game theoretical methods are called for.

If the control authority's measurements only serve the purpose of verifying the correctness of the polluter's own measurements, then there exists a certain similarity with the auditing problem which has been dealt with extensively in the economics literature. (For example, Arkin, 1974).

In a somewhat general sense one can find similar questions treated under the heading "principal agent problems". (Kanodia, 1985, Dye, 1986). The "agent" carries out actions that the "principal" is not in a position to control directly and which influence the financial means which are to be in some way divided among the two parties. Examples are insurance companies which cannot control exactly how prudently its customers behave, and the management of firms that cannot continuously monitor their employees. The essential difference to the considerations in the present work is that, in general, the "principal agent problem" does not permit a clear distinction between legal and illegal behavior.

The subject of this paper is the game theoretical and statistical analysis of the control of point sources of pollution with the aim of developing general decision procedures for the monitoring authority. To this end, the next section formulates an idealized control problem from the point of view of decision theory. Thereafter, two simple game theoretical models are analyzed, the "simultaneous" game in which both players act independently and without knowledge of the other's actions, and the "inspector leadership" game, in which the inspector announces his strategy to the inspectee. Since the inspector leadership game is considered more appropriate than the simultaneous game for the problem at hand the fourth section proceeds to generalize it by introducing an extended strategy set for the inspectee and by establishing the links to the theory of statistical testing. The paper concludes with a practical example and some remarks concerning sequential aspects of the control problem.

2. Decision theoretical formulation of the problem

In order to be able to analyze quantitatively the monitoring problem sketched in the previous section, we have to know the agreed rules and the information structure for each possible procedure. In addition, we have to model the statistical and game theoretical aspects of the problem.

In simplified form, the monitoring procedure may be characterized by the following four activities which are carried through alternatively by the responsible monitoring agency (the "inspector") and by employees of the inspected technical plant (the "inspectee").

i)   According to the agreement with the inspector, the inspectee promises not to release more than the amount μ_0 of pollutants per unit of time.

ii)   The inspector announces to the inspectee in a credible way that he will monitor the releases, and he informs the inspectee what procedure, including the false alarm probability, he will choose.

iii)   The inspectee decides either to keep his emissions within the limits of the agreement, or to release in the ith unit of time the amount $\mu_0 + \mu_i$, $i = 1,2,...,$ of pollutants, such that the total additionally released amount in the reference time period (e.g., one year), is $\mu = \Sigma_i\mu_i$. Obviously, the inspectee does not tell the inspector whether or not he will act legally, i.e., in accordance with the terms of the agreement, and if not, what will be the size of the total emission μ. The inspector, on the other hand, will consider some value of μ as intolerable or "critical", and he will use a procedure such that illegal releases of that size will be detected with highest possible probability.

iv)   The inspector performs his monitoring procedure, i.e. he performs his measurements, and decides with the help of a test of significance whether or not the inspectee behaved legally during the reference time under consideration.

Let us assume now that the emissions X_i, $i = 1,..., n$, measured by the inspector per unit of time can be considered as random variables, the distributions of which — especially their variances — are known to both the inspector and the inspectee. It should be emphasized that these distributions do not reflect only the uncertainties of the measurements but possibly also the stochastic dispersion model with the help of which the amount of emissions from the point source are determined from the measurements, which may be performed at different locations. Two hypotheses describe the statistical aspect of the monitoring problem.

Definition 1. *Consider the random variables* X_i, $i = 1,..., n$, *whose distributions – up to the expected values – are known to both inspector and inspectee. Under the null hypothesis* H_0, *the expected values of the random variables* X_i *are* μ_0,

$$H_0 : E_0(X_i) = \mu_0 \qquad\qquad for\ i = 1,...,\ n \qquad\qquad (1a)$$

and under the alternative hypothesis H_1 *the expected values of the random variables* X_i *are* $\mu_0 + \mu_i$,

$$H_1 : E_1(X_i) = \mu_0 + \mu_i \geq \mu_0 \quad for\ i = 1,...,\ n \quad \sum_i E_1(X_i) = n\mu_0 + \mu > 0. \quad (1b)$$

If the inspectee decides to act illegally, then he will use that strategy which minimizes the chance of the inspector to decide H_1 being true, i.e. to detect the illegal behavior. In turn, the inspector will use that decision procedure which detects with greatest probability – or, even more, deters the inspectee from – illegal behavior. These two strategies can only be determined with the help of an appropriate game–theoretical model.

For this purpose, we have to introduce the payoffs to both inspector and inspectee for all possible results of the monitoring procedure.

Definition 2. *The payoffs to the inspector as player 1 and to the inspectee as player 2 are given by the following table:*

1 \ 2	H_1	H_0
reject H_0	$(-a,\ -b)$	$(-e,\ -f)$
reject H_1	$(-c,\ +d)$	$(0,\ 0)$

(2a)

Here, the payoff parameters (a,..., f) satisfy the conditions

$$(a,..., f) > (0,..., 0), \quad e < a < c, \quad f < b. \tag{2b}$$

The inequalities $0 < a < c$ reflect our assumption that the inspector's highest priority is to deter the inspectee from illegal behavior, but that he naturally prefers detection of illegal behavior to non–detection. Furthermore, we assume that a false alarm causes losses to both players even though it may be clarified in a further activity which is not modelled here. However, we assume that these losses are smaller than the loss entailed by a justified alarm, since otherwise there would be no incentive for legal behavior on the part of the inspectee $(f < b)$ and since illegal behavior of the inspectee is in any case worse than legal behavior from the inspector's point of view $(e < a)$.

Moreover, one may give good reasons in favor of the hypothesis that the inspectee's payoff depend on the amount of illegal discharge of pollutants for payoffs in case of the inspectee acting illegally which do depend on the size of the illegal action. This hypothesis has not been considered here since only this way, for a given false alarm probability, the independence of the optimal inspection strategies of the payoff parameters can be achieved — as the third theorem in the fourth section demonstrates. Substantially, we justify our assumption with the remark given under ii) at the beginning of this section that all payoffs are defined for an illegal action of size μ which is considered intolerable by the inspector.

It should be mentioned that the costs of the monitoring procedure are not part of the payoff to the inspector. They are parameters of the model which are not explicitly spelled out in the present paper. Game theoretical models, in which the control costs are explicitly taken into account, were analyzed, e.g. by Russell (1990).

Finally, it should be mentioned that we can set one of the payoff parameters of both players equal to one implying that we have to consider four parameters only. We maintain, however, the form given by (2) for two reasons: firstly, it is more illustrative — one can imagine the parameters to have dimensions, and secondly, a generalization, e.g. with respect to incomplete information, (see Section 3), would require this procedure anyhow.

3. Comparison of the solutions of the simple "simultaneous" and "leadership" games

In this section we assume that the inspection procedure is fixed up to the value of the false alarm probability α (probability of the error first kind), and that the inspectee chooses in case of illegal behavior a fixed illegal strategy — in our case $(\mu_1,..., \mu_n)$ — which leads to the probability of no detection $\beta(\alpha)$ (probability of the error second kind).

If the inspector does not announce his strategy, i.e. the value of α to be chosen, then one obtains the simple 'simultaneous' non–cooperative two–person game, the extensive form of which is represented in Figure 3.1.

The inspector chooses the value α of the false alarm probability without announcing this to the inspectee. The inspectee chooses H_1 with probability t and H_0 with probability $1 - t$. Chance (Z) decides if alarm (A) is given or if not $(\bar{A})$, where $1 - \beta = prob(A \mid H_1)$ and $\alpha = prob(A \mid H_0)$. The encircled area in Figure 3.1 is the information set of the inspectee. The payoffs $(a,..., f)$ to I and O have to satisfy the conditions (2.2b)[2].

If the inspectee acts illegally with probability t, then the expected payoffs to the two players are given by

$$(I(\alpha, t), O(\alpha, t)) = (((a - c)\beta - a + e\alpha)t - e\alpha, ((b + d)\beta - b + f\alpha)t - f\alpha). \qquad (1)$$

---

[2] For the sake of notational simplicity the numbering of equations starts with (1) in each subsequent section. If an equation, say Equation (14), is refered to in the text, it is understood that we mean Equation (14) in the section where the reference is made. If in section y we refer to Equation (14) from section x (x ≠ y), we write Equation (x.14).

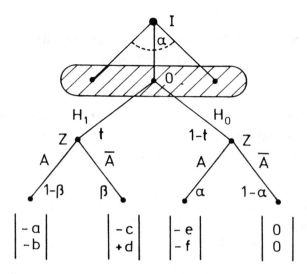

Figure 3.1: Extensive form of the simple simultaneous non–cooperative two–person game between inspector *(I)* and inspectee *(O)*.

Therefore, the inspectee decides

$$t = \left\{ \begin{array}{c} 0 \\ 1 \\ arbitrary \end{array} \right\} \quad \text{for } (b+d)\beta - b + f\alpha \left\{ \begin{array}{c} < \\ > \\ = \end{array} \right\} 0. \tag{2}$$

Under the assumptions "$\beta(\cdot)$ convex, $\beta(0) = 1$, $\beta(1) = 0$" the equation

$$(b+d)\beta - b + f\alpha = 0 \tag{3}$$

has exactly one solution as illustrated in Figure 3.2.

Therefore, we can write (2) also as

$$t = \left\{ \begin{array}{c} 0 \\ 1 \\ arbitrary \end{array} \right\} \quad \text{for } \alpha \left\{ \begin{array}{c} > \\ < \\ = \end{array} \right\} \alpha^*, \tag{4}$$

where α^* is the unique solution of (3).

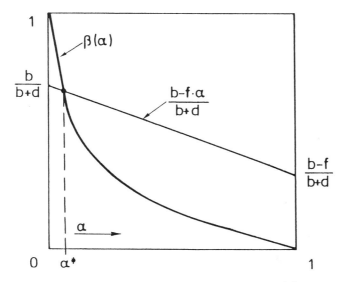

Figure 3.2: Graphical solution of equation (3).

The solution of the game given by Figure 3.1 is formulated as

Theorem 1. *(Avenhaus and Frick 1977) Under the assumption that $\beta(\cdot)$ is convex and differentiable, and $\beta(0) = 1$, $\beta(1) = 0$, the equilibrium point (α^*, t^*) of the non–cooperative two–person game is given by the solution α^* of equation (3) and by*

$$t^* = e/(e + (a - c)\frac{d}{d\alpha}\beta(\alpha^*)). \tag{5}$$

Proof. We have to show that (α^*, t^*) satisfies the equilibrium conditions

$$I(\alpha^*, t^*) \geq I(\alpha, t^*) \quad \text{for } \alpha \in [0, 1]$$

$$O(\alpha^*, t^*) \geq O(\alpha^*, t) \quad \text{for } t \in [0, 1],$$

where the payoffs $I(\alpha, t)$ and $O(\alpha, t)$ are given by (1). The second condition is identically fulfilled for any $t \in [0,1]$, if we use (3) with $\alpha = \alpha^*$. The first inequality, explicitly given by

$$((a - c)\beta(\alpha^*) - a + e\alpha^*)t^* - e\alpha^* \geq ((a - c)\beta(\alpha) - \alpha + e\alpha)t^* - e\alpha$$

for $\alpha \in [0,1]$ is equivalent to the condition that the maximum of the function of α given by

$$((a - c)\beta(\alpha) - a + e\alpha)t^* - e\alpha$$

is obtained at the point $\alpha = \alpha^*$. A necessary condition for this condition to be satisfied is

$$((a - c)\frac{d}{d\alpha}\beta(\alpha^*) + e)t^* - e = 0,$$

which means that (3) must hold. From the conditions for $\beta(\cdot)$ we conclude that this stationary point is in fact the unique maximum.   □

This theorem shows that the equilibrium false alarm probability depends only on the payoff parameters of the inspectee, a fact which is important for applications since the payoff to the inspector, in general, cannot be easily estimated. Furthermore, this theorem shows that in equilibrium the inspectee chooses illegal behavior with positive probability t^*.

Let us now consider the case that the inspector announces to the inspectee his strategy, i.e. the value of α to be chosen by him in a credible way. The extensive form of this game is represented graphically in Figure 3.3. The inspector chooses the value α of the false alarm probability and announces this to the inspectee. Compare the form of the information sets of the inspectee with those given in Figure 3.1! The rest of the game is the same as that of the game given by Figure 3.1.

According to the previous argumentation, the inspectee chooses

$$t(\alpha) = \left\{\begin{array}{c} H_0 \\ H_1 \\ arbitrary \end{array}\right\} \quad \text{for } \alpha \left\{\begin{array}{c} > \\ < \\ = \end{array}\right\} \alpha^*, \tag{6}$$

where α^* is again the solution of equation (3). Accordingly, the payoff to the inspector is

$$I(\alpha,t(\alpha)) = \left\{\begin{array}{c} -e \cdot \alpha \\ -a + (a - c) \cdot \beta \\ any \ convex \ combination \end{array}\right\} \quad \text{for } \alpha \left\{\begin{array}{c} > \\ < \\ = \end{array}\right\} \alpha^*, \tag{7}$$

which is illustrated in Figure 3.4.

In this game, however, the inspectee's equilibrium behavior is not the same as in the simultaneous game:

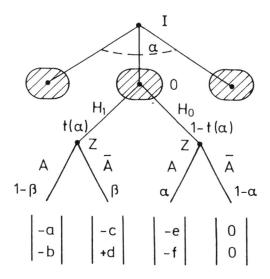

Figure 3.3: Extensive form of the simple inspector leadership game between the inspector *(I)* and the inspectee *(0)*.

Theorem 2. *(Avenhaus and Okada 1988) The equilibrium $(\alpha^*, t^*(\alpha))$ of the simple inspector leadership game given by Figure 3.3 is given by the solution α^* of equation (3), as well as by*

$$t^*(\alpha) = \left\{ \begin{matrix} H_0 \\ H_1 \end{matrix} \right\} \quad for \ \alpha \left\{ \begin{matrix} \geq \\ < \end{matrix} \right\} \alpha^*, \tag{8}$$

Proof. We have to show that (α^*, t^*) satisfies the equilibrium conditions

$I(\alpha^*, t^*) \geq I(\alpha, t^*)$ for $\alpha \in [0, 1]$

$O(\alpha^*, t^*) \geq O(\alpha^*, t)$ for all $t: [0, 1] \rightarrow \{H_0, H_1\}$,

where the payoffs $I(\alpha, t)$ and $O(\alpha, t)$ are given by (7) and by

$$O(\alpha,\ t) = \left\{ \begin{array}{l} -f\alpha \\ -b + (b - d)\beta \\ arbitrary \end{array} \right\} \qquad \text{for } \alpha. \left\{ \begin{array}{l} > \\ < \\ = \end{array} \right\} \alpha^*.$$

The first inequality is equivalent to

$$-e\alpha^* \geq \left\{ \begin{array}{l} -e\alpha \\ -a + (a - c)\beta \end{array} \right\} \qquad \text{for } \alpha \left\{ \begin{array}{l} \geq \\ < \end{array} \right\} \alpha^*,$$

which is fulfilled because of the relations (2.2b) between the payoff parameters. This can be seen in Figure 3.3. The second inequality is equivalent to

$$-f\alpha^* \geq \left\{ \begin{array}{l} -f\alpha^* \\ -b + (b + d)\beta(\alpha^*) \end{array} \right\} \qquad \text{for } t(\alpha^*) = \left\{ \begin{array}{l} H_0 \\ H_1 \end{array} \right\},$$

which is fulfilled because of (3).   □

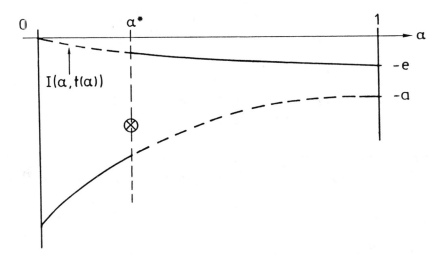

Figure 3.4: Payoff to the inspector according to (3.7). The point ⊗ denotes the equilibrium payoff of the simultaneous game.

In contrast to the situation in the simultaneous game, the inspectee acts legally in equilibrium in the leadership game, even though the equilibrium strategy of the inspector is the same as in the simultaneous game, and even though in equilibrium the payoff to the inspectee is the same for legal and illegal behavior; we call this property the knife—edge-

−property of the solution. It should be mentioned that the equilibrium payoff to the inspector is larger in case of the leadership game, since according to (5) $t*$ is smaller than one (see also Figure 3.4). Also, it should be mentioned that the knife–edge–property can be avoided if one models the game as a game with incomplete information where, e.g. the payoff to the inspectee in case of undetected illegal action is not known precisely to the inspectee (Avenhaus and Okada, 1988).

The leadership principle was discussed in economics first by v. Stackelberg (1934). In connection with inspection problems it was first used by Maschler (1966/67) who, however, did not take into account false alarms which, as we saw, are constituent for the possibility of inducing the inspectee to legal behavior.

4. The general inspector leadership game and the Neyman–Pearson lemma

We consider now the general inspector leadership game the extensive form of which is represented graphically in Figure 4.1. The set of strategies of the inspectee, on the one hand, no longer consists of two strategies only representing legal and illegal behavior respectively. The single option of illegal behavior is now substituted by a set of illegal strategies. In our example, we have

$$\Psi = \{(\mu_1,..., \mu_n) : \mu_i \geq 0 \text{ for } i = 1,..., n, \ \Sigma_i\mu_i = \mu\}. \tag{1}$$

The set of strategies of the inspector, on the other hand, no longer consists only of the set of false alarm probabilities, but of the set Φ of all possible decision procedures.

For reasons to be discussed below, we decompose the inspection strategy ϕ in such a way that the inspector first announces the value of the false alarm probability, and then the decision procedure for a given value of α. By definition, the choice of $\phi(\alpha)$ will result in a false alarm probability α if the inspectee behaves legally; the set of these decision procedures is called Φ_α. The set Φ of all decision procedures then is the union of all Φ_α,

$$\Phi = \bigcup_{\alpha \in [0, 1]} \Phi_\alpha. \tag{2}$$

As illustrated in Figure 4.1, the inspector chooses first the value α of the false alarm probability and then his inspection strategy $\phi(\alpha)$ for given α and announces both to the inspectee. The inspectee chooses H_1 with probability t and H_0 with probability $1 - t$. In the first case he chooses the illegal strategy $\psi \in \Psi$. Chance (Z) decides if alarm (A) is given or if not $(\bar{A})$, where $1 - \beta = prob(A|H_1)$ and $\alpha = prob(A|H_0)$. The payoffs $(a, ..., f)$ to I and O satisfy the conditions (2.2b).

We formulate the solution of this general inspector leadership game as a theorem, the proof of which is given in the quoted literature.

Theorem 3. Let Φ_α be the set of inspection strategies $\phi(\alpha)$ resulting in a false alarm probability α, in the general inspector leadership game the extensive form of which is given in Figure 4.1, and let the set Φ of all inspection strategies be given by (2). Furthermore, let Ψ be the set of all illegal strategies ψ of the inspectee. Let $\beta(\alpha)$ be defined by

$$\beta(\alpha) = \min_{\phi(\alpha) \in \Phi_\alpha} \max_{\psi \in \Psi} \beta(\phi(\alpha), \psi). \tag{3}$$

Let the function $\beta(\cdot)$ be convex, with $\beta(0) = 1$, $\beta(1) = 0$. Then this game has a perfect equilibrium $(\alpha^*, \phi^*; t^*, \psi^*)$ with $\alpha^* \in [0, 1]$, $\phi^*: [0, 1] \to \Phi$ and $t^*: \Phi \to [0, 1]$, $\psi^*: \Phi \to \Psi$ if and only if

$$\phi^*(\alpha) = arg \min_{\phi(\alpha) \in \Phi_\alpha} \max_{\psi \in \Psi} \beta(\phi(\alpha), \psi) \qquad \text{for all } \alpha \in [0, 1]; \tag{4}$$

α^* is the unique solution of the equation

$$-t + (b + d)\beta(\alpha^*) + f\alpha^* = 0$$
$$\tag{5}$$

and satisfies $0 < \alpha^* < 1$, and furthermore

$$t^*(\phi(\alpha)) = \begin{Bmatrix} 0 \\ 1 \end{Bmatrix} \quad \text{for} \quad -b + (b + d)\beta(\phi(\alpha)) + f\alpha \begin{Bmatrix} \leq \\ > \end{Bmatrix} 0, \tag{6}$$

$$\psi^*(\phi(\alpha)) = arg \max_{\psi \in \Psi} (\phi(\alpha), \psi), \tag{7}$$

where $\beta(\phi(\alpha))$ is given by

$$\beta(\phi(\alpha)) = \max_{\psi \in \Psi} (\phi(\alpha), \psi). \tag{8}$$

Proof. See Avenhaus and v. Stengel (1990).   □

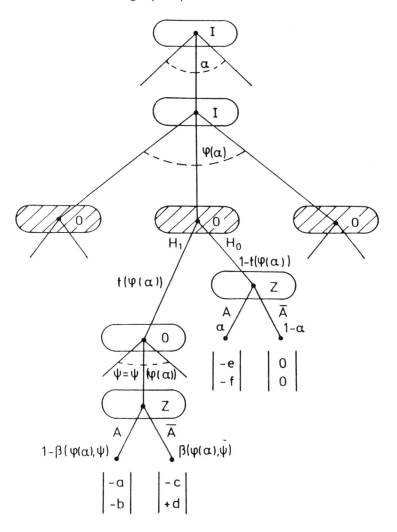

Figure 4.1: Extensive form of the general inspector leadership game between the inspector *(I)* and the inspectee *(O)*.

Let us reemphasize that the inspectee behaves legally in equilibrium as for the simple inspector leadership game, in contrast to the game where the inspector does not announce his strategy.

For practical applications, it is important that for a fixed value of the false alarm probability α the optimal strategies ϕ^* and ψ^* of both players are determined by means of optimization of the probability of non–detection β, and that they do not depend on the payoff parameters of both players. The payoff parameters, and only those of the inspectee, enter only into the equilibrium value of the false alarm probability α^*; this value is the solution of equation (4.5) which corresponds to the determinant (3.3) of the optimal false alarm probabilities for the simple games if we interpret $\beta(\alpha)$ in an appropriate way.

There is another reason why the decomposition of the inspection strategy is very important for applications. For a given value of the false alarm probability α the optimal inspection strategy $\phi^*(\alpha)$ represents a statistical test procedure which can be determined with the help of the fundamental Neyman–Pearson lemma (See, e.g. Lehmann, 1959). This will be briefly explained below. (For more details see, e.g. Avenhaus, 1986). An application will be presented in the next section.

A statistical hypothesis is called simple if it uniquely determines the distribution of the random variable which is used for the decision for this hypothesis. Now the Neyman–Pearson lemma provides a method to construct a procedure for a decision between two simple hypotheses such that the error second kind probability β is minimized for a given value of the error first kind probability: Let $f_0(x_1,..., x_n)$ and $f_1(x_1,..., x_n)$ be the densities of the random variables under consideration for the two hypotheses. Then the critical area of the test, i.e. the set of observations which leads to the rejection of H_0, in our case to an alarm, is given by

$$\{(x_1,..., x_n): f_1(x_1,..., x_n)/f_0(x_1,..., x_n) > \lambda\}$$

where λ is determined by the error first kind or false alarm probability α.

In our case these two hypotheses are H_0, i.e. legal behavior of the inspectee, and H_1, i.e. illegal behavior of the inspectee with well defined illegal strategy ψ. Therefore, the Neyman–Pearson lemma provides the decision rule $\phi^*(\alpha, \psi)$ for given false alarm probability α and illegal strategy ψ.

This procedure, however, requires knowledge of the well–defined illegal strategy ψ as part of the alternative hypothesis, in order to determine $\phi^*(\alpha, \psi)$ and, therefore, the minimized probability of non–detection β. Even if this probability is maximized subsequently for all possible choices of ψ, with the result

$$\beta(a) = \max_{\psi \in \Psi} \quad \min_{\phi(a) \in \Phi_\alpha} \quad \beta(\phi(a), \psi),$$

this procedure involves the wrong sequence of the two optimization processes, namely "maxmin" instead of "minmax" as required by Theorem 3. This difficulty disappears if the non–cooperative zero–sum game $(\Phi_\alpha, \Psi, 1-\beta)$ has a saddlepoint: In this case $\beta^*(\alpha) = \beta(\alpha)$ is the required guaranteed minimal probability of non–detection.

5. Application

In order to illustrate the results presented so far, we consider an idealized example which had already been sketched in the second section: A technical plant (again called inspectee) may release the amount μ_0 of pollutants to the water of a nearby river per unit of time; its own measurements of these releases are X_i, $i = 1,..., n$, in the reference time under consideration. Not far from this point source of pollutants, the monitoring agency in charge (again called the inspector) has established a measurement system, and it is assumed that the corresponding measurements Y_i, $i = 1,..., n$, permit a reliable inference about the correctness of the data reported by the inspectee. Both sets of measurements are assumed to be realizations of independently and identically normally distributed random variables the variances of which, $var(X_i) = \sigma_x^2$, $var(Y_i) = \sigma_y^2$, $i = 1,..., n$, are known to both parties, inspector and inspectee.

The objective of the decision procedure to be discussed here is to decide with the help of the inspector's measurements, if the data reported by the inspectee are correct within the limits of the uncertainty of the measurements and the afore mentioned dispersion model, or if the data might be falsified. For this purpose, the inspector forms the differences $Z_i = X_i - Y_i$, $i = 1, ..., n$, and tests with their help the two hypotheses

$$H_0: E_0(Z_i) = 0, \qquad i = 1,...,n$$

$$H_1: E_1(Z_i) = \mu_i > 0, \qquad i = 1,...,n, \qquad \Sigma_i \mu_i = \mu \qquad (1)$$

for the independently and identically normally distributed random variables Z_i with the variances

$$var(Z_i) = \sigma_x{}^2 + \sigma_y{}^2 = \sigma^2, \qquad\qquad\qquad\qquad i = 1,...,n. \qquad\qquad (2)$$

According to Theorem 3, we are looking for the test procedure $\phi \in \Phi_\alpha$, which minimizes, for a given false alarm probability α, the probability of non–detection β. We formulate the result of the analysis as

Theorem 4. *Given the two–person zero–sum game $(\Phi_\alpha, \Psi, 1 - \beta)$, where $\phi(\alpha) \in \Phi_\alpha$ is a test procedure for the decision between the two hypotheses (1). The equilibrium point of this game is given by the test procedure $\phi^*(\alpha)$ which is characterized by the critical area*

$$\{(z_1,..., z_n): \Sigma_i\, z_i > \sqrt{n}\cdot \sigma \cdot U(1 - \alpha)\} \qquad\qquad (3)$$

and by the (illegal) equal distribution strategy

$$\psi^* = (\mu/n,..., \mu/n); \qquad\qquad (4)$$

the minimal guaranteed probability of non–detection is

$$\beta^* = \Phi\left[U(1 - \alpha) - \frac{\mu}{\sqrt{n}\sigma}\right], \qquad\qquad (5)$$

where $\Phi(\cdot)$ is the Gaussian or standard normal distribution and $U(\cdot)$ its inverse. (Φ should not be confused with the strategy set given by (4.2)!)

Proof. We have to show that the saddlepoint criterion

$$\beta(\phi^*(\alpha), \psi) \le \beta^*(\alpha) \le \beta(\phi(\alpha), \psi^*)$$

is fulfilled.

Lefthand side: Because of $E_1(\Sigma_i Z_i) = \mu$, $\Sigma_i Z_i$ is a $(\mu, n\sigma^2)$–normally distributed random variable. We get therefore

$$\beta(\phi^*(\alpha), \psi) = prob(\Sigma_i Z_i < \sqrt{n}\sigma U(1 - \alpha)) = \Phi\left[U(1 - \alpha) - \frac{\mu}{\sqrt{n}\sigma}\right].$$

Righthand side: Under the two hypotheses and for $\psi^* = (\mu/n,..., \mu/n)$ the densities of the random variables are of the form

$$f_0(z_1,..., z_n) = \prod_{i=1}^{n} \frac{1}{\sqrt{2\pi}\sigma} \cdot exp\left[-\frac{z_i^2}{2\sigma^2}\right]$$

$$f_0(z_1,..., z_n) = \prod_{i=1}^{n} \frac{1}{\sqrt{2\pi}\sigma} \cdot exp\left[-\frac{(z_i - \mu/n)^2}{2\sigma^2}\right].$$

Therefore the critical area of the best test is, according to (4.9),

$$\{(z_1,..., z_n): f_1(z_1,..., z_n)/f_0(z_1,..., z_n) > \lambda\}$$

or, if we manipulate the inequality appropriately,

$$\{(z_1,..., z_n): \Sigma_i z_i > \lambda'\},$$

where λ resp. λ' have to be determined in such a way that the false alarm probability has the desired value. This leads immediately to the assertion.   □

This theorem says that in equilibrium the inspector performs the so-called D-test, i.e. he uses the sum of the differences of reported and independently generated data as test statistic. Interestingly enough, this test has the property that it leads, for each illegal strategy of the inspectee (1), to the same probability of non-detection. Nevertheless, the equilibrium strategy of the inspectee is not arbitrary, but well defined and given by (4). This is a typical property of equilibria of this kind.

So far we have assumed that the inspector verifies all data of the inspectee with the help of corresponding independent measurements. This may be too expensive, however. Therefore, one can imagine that the data of the inspectee are only verified with the help of an appropriate random sampling scheme. In this case the statistical analysis is much more complicated. It turns out that, for small total falsification, the D-statistic and the equal distribution of the falsification of the reported data are indeed optimal, but that for large total falsification neither the D-statistic nor the equal distribution of the falsification are optimal, (Avenhaus, Battenberg, Falkowski, 1991).

If the uncertainty of the measurements or estimates of the inspectee and of the inspector are large, then one can imagine quite another illegal strategy. The inspectee does not falsify data, but increases the releases of pollutants in the limits of the uncertainty beyond the agreed standard. In such a case, the inspector will either not perform any data comparison, but only check whether or not the sum of his measurements is significantly larger than permitted, or he will perform the comparison and, thereafter, check with the help of the inspectee's data whether or not the releases are too large. Naturally, in the latter case also a combined strategy of the inspectee is possible.

In general, it cannot be easily decided which of the two procedures of the inspector leads, in case of optimal behavior of the inspectee, to a higher detection probability, since the resulting optimization problems do not lend themselves to analytical treatment. Since a detailed presentation of these problems would be beyond the scope of this paper, two special cases are treated in the Annex.

6. Concluding remarks

In all deliberations of the previous sections we had assumed that data on emissions of pollutants of, e.g. a technical plant (the "inspectee") are collected by a responsible monitoring agency (the "inspector") during some reference time, e.g., one year, and that they are evaluated in such a way that at the end of this reference time a decision on the inspectee's behavior can be made. The criterion for the optimization of the decision procedure to be used was the probability of detection for a given value of the false alarm probability.

Standards of pollutants emissions from point sources can be defined in two different ways: On the one hand, it may delineate upper bounds for total emissions during a longer period of time ignoring any short—term peaks within that period. On the other hand, standards in the sense of upper emission bounds may apply to all "points in time" (very short time periods). (e.g. Simpson et al., 1987). It is obvious that a violation of the latter standards should be detected as fast as possible.

Modelling time dependent monitoring procedures leads into much more difficult analytical problems. A "quality control approach" which did not take into account the possibility of strategic behavior of the inspectee was presented by Vaughan and Russell in 1983. In particular one has to formulate time dependent payoff parameters, since the interests of both sides — inspector and inspectee — in earlier or later detection of unauthorized emissions have to be taken into consideration.

Assume that the payoffs to both parties can be discounted appropriately and consider sequential game theoretical inspector leadership models, in which both parties fix their strategies at the beginning of the game in such a way, that they do not take into account information obtained during the game. The analysis of such games shows that as a criterion for the optimization of the strategies of both parties the average run length under the alternative hypothesis H_1, i.e. the expected time between illegal behavior and detection should be used, with the average run length under the null hypothesis H_0, i.e., legal behavior, as boundary condition. This means that the error first and second kind probability criteria have to be replaced by the average run length criteria.

For practical applications this is a satisfying result; in fact, these criteria were used for other safeguards problems, e.g. industrial process control, on the basis of heuristic arguments, (e.g. Wetherill, 1982). A disadvantage is that the analysis cannot be continued in the same, theoretically convincing way as in the stationary case since for sequential test problems there is no equivalent to the Neyman–Pearson lemma. Therefore, one can only formulate heuristic procedures by selecting plausible test procedures for given illegal strategies, and compare them by using the run length criteria. Interestingly, the so–called CUSUM–test by Page (1954) seems to have, in the area of monitoring point sources of pollution, a similar importance (e.g. Wathern et al., 1986) as in the industrial quality and process control area.

Appendix: Comparison of two different monitoring procedures

Problem formulation

A technical plant (again the "inspectee") is authorized to release per unit of time some amount of pollutants into a nearby river. A competent monitoring agency (again the "inspector") controls with the help of randomly sampled, independent measurements, whether or not the real releases are larger than the permitted ones.

We consider two different procedures: The first one is that the inspector uses only his own measurements, i.e. the inspector decides only on the basis of his own measurements whether the real releases were, in a given reference period of time, below the agreed standards.

The second procedure is that the inspectee reports the releases regularly, and that the inspector compares his own measurements with the reported ones in order to decide whether the reported data are credible. If this test does not lead to an alarm, then the inspector uses the reported data of the inspectee in order to decide whether the real releases were below the agreed standards.

Two different sets of "illegal" strategies correspond to these two procedures, if the inspectee really wants to release more pollutants than permitted. In the former case, the inspectee simply hopes that the test procedure, based on the uncertain measurements of the inspector, will not detect his illegal releases. In the latter case, the inspectee falsifies the reported data and hopes that the inspector's comparison of the reported with the independently sampled data will not detect this falsification.

The question arises which of the two procedures will result in a higher probability of detection for a given total amount of pollutants to be released within a reference time.

One reported, one independently generated measurement

We consider one single emission of pollutants. Without loss of generality we assume that the authorized releases are zero and that the inspectee in the illegal case tries to release the amount $\mu > 0$ of pollutants.

The measurement Y performed by the inspector is assumed to be a normally distributed random variable with variance σ_y^2 and expected value

$$E_0(Y) = 0 \qquad\qquad H_0 \text{ (legal behavior)}$$
$$\text{for} \qquad\qquad\qquad\qquad\qquad\qquad (A.1)$$
$$E_1(Y) = \mu > 0 \qquad\qquad H_1 \text{ (emission } \mu).$$

The probability of detection for the first procedure then is given by

$$1 - \beta_1^{11} = \Phi\left(\frac{\mu}{\sigma_y} - U(1-\alpha)\right), \qquad\qquad (A.2)$$

where α is the given false alarm probability, $\Phi(\cdot)$ the Gaussian or standard normal distribution and U its inverse.

In case of the second procedure the inspectee reports the amount X of emissions which represents a normally distributed random variable with variance σ_x^2. The inspector therefore compares first his own value with the reported one and decides then if the reported value is significantly greater than zero. In the illegal case of the emission μ the inspectee will report a value which is smaller by μ_1 than the real one so that the inspector has to decide between the two hypotheses for the expected values of $Y - X$ and X,

$$E_0 \begin{bmatrix} Y - X \\ X \end{bmatrix} = \begin{bmatrix} 0 \\ 0 \end{bmatrix} \qquad H_0 \text{ (legal behavior)}$$

for (A.3)

$$E_1 \begin{bmatrix} Y - X \\ X \end{bmatrix} = \begin{bmatrix} \mu_1 \\ \mu - \mu_1 \end{bmatrix}, \ 0 \le \mu_1 \le \mu \qquad H_1 \text{ (emission } \mu)$$

The covariance matrix of this random vector is

$$\Sigma = \begin{bmatrix} \sigma_x^2 + \sigma_y^2 & -\sigma_x^2 \\ -\sigma_x^2 & \sigma_x^2 \end{bmatrix} = \sigma_x^2 \begin{bmatrix} 1 + a^2 & -1 \\ -1 & 1 \end{bmatrix}, \qquad a^2 = \frac{\sigma_y^2}{\sigma_x^2}. \quad (A.4)$$

The Neyman–Pearson test for this decision problem is characterized by the test statistic

$$(Y - X,\ X) \cdot \Sigma^{-1} \cdot \begin{bmatrix} \mu_1 \\ \mu - \mu_1 \end{bmatrix} \qquad (A.5)$$

and leads to the probability of detection

$$1 - \beta_2^{11} = \Phi\left(\sqrt{\mu' \cdot \Sigma^{-1} \cdot \mu} - U(1 - \alpha)\right), \qquad (A.6)$$

where $\mu' = (\mu_1, \mu - \mu_1)$ and Σ^{-1} the inverse of Σ. Now the inverse Σ^{-1} is given by

$$\Sigma^{-1} = \frac{1}{\sigma_y^2} \begin{bmatrix} 1 & 1 \\ 1 & 1 + a^2 \end{bmatrix}. \qquad (A.7)$$

Therefore we have

$$\mu' \cdot \Sigma^{-1} \cdot \mu = \frac{1}{\sigma_y^2} (\mu^2 + (1 - a^2)(\mu - \mu_1)^2). \qquad (A.8)$$

The probability of detection (A.6), thus, is minimized by

$$\mu_1^* = \mu, \tag{A.9}$$

and the guaranteed probability of detection is the same as that of the first procedure, which is given by (A.2). According to (A.5) and (A.7), the test statistic is

$$(Y - X,\ X) \cdot \Sigma^{-1} \cdot \begin{bmatrix} \mu \\ 0 \end{bmatrix} \sim Y \tag{A.10}$$

which can also be taken from the guaranteed probability of detection. In other words, we are again led to the first procedure. Interestingly enough, the optimal illegal strategy is, according to (A.9), a pure data falsification strategy even though, according to (A.10), the inspector does not take any notice of the reported datum.

n reported, $k(< n)$ independently generated measurements

Now we consider n possible releases of pollutants and $k(< n)$ measurements of the inspector. Without loss of generality we assume again that the authorized releases are zero.

Under explicit limitation of generality we now assume that in the illegal case the inspectee tries to release n–times the amount μ/n of pollutants. The measurements Y_i, $i = 1,...\ k$, performed by the inspector are independently and identically distributed random variables with variance σ_Y^2 and expected value

$$
\begin{aligned}
E_0(Y_i) &= 0 & &H_0 \text{ (legal behavior)} \\
& & \text{for} & \\
E_1(Y_i) &= \mu/n > 0 & &H_1 \text{ (total emission } \mu)
\end{aligned}
\tag{A.11}
$$

For the first procedure the application of the Neyman–Pearson lemma gives the test statistic

$$Y = \frac{n}{k} \sum_{i=1}^{k} Y_i \tag{A.12}$$

and the probability of detection

$$1 - \beta_1^{nk} = \Phi\left(\frac{\sqrt{k}}{n} \cdot \frac{\mu}{\sigma_y} - U(1-\alpha)\right).$$ (A.13)

In case of the second procedure the inspectee reports the measured values X_i, $i = 1,...,$ n, which are independently and identically normally distributed random variables with covariance σ_x^2. The inspector compares his own measured values Y_i, $i = 1,..., k$, with the reported values X_i, $i = 1,..., n$, and decides whether or not the reported values are significantly greater than zero. Again, under explicit limitation of generality, we assume that the two corresponding test statistics are

$$D = \frac{n}{k} \sum_{i=1}^{k} (Y_i - X_i) \qquad \text{and} \qquad S = \sum_{i=1}^{n} X_i,$$ (A.14)

where in case of the first statistic the corresponding reported and independently generated data have to be subtracted. In the illegal case of total releases μ the inspectee will report the sum of all values too small by an amount μ_1 such that the inspector has to decide between the two hypotheses

$$E_0\begin{bmatrix} D \\ S \end{bmatrix} = \begin{bmatrix} 0 \\ 0 \end{bmatrix} \qquad\qquad H_0 \text{ (legal behavior)}$$

$$\text{for} \qquad\qquad\qquad \text{(A.15)}$$

$$E_1\begin{bmatrix} D \\ S \end{bmatrix} = \begin{bmatrix} \mu_1 \\ \mu - \mu_1 \end{bmatrix}, \quad 0 \le \mu_1 \le \mu \qquad H_1 \text{ (total emission } \mu)$$

We justify this statistical model with the arguments that, under assumptions (A.11) and $E_1(X_i) = (\mu - \mu_1)/n$, $i = 1,..., n$, both these statistics are unbiased estimates of μ_1 and $\mu - \mu_1$ and, furthermore, that they are Neyman–Pearson test statistics for the two corresponding single tests.

Now the variances of D and S and their covariance are given by

$$\sigma_D^2 = \frac{n^2}{k}(\sigma_y^2 + \sigma_x^2), \qquad \sigma_S^2 = n\sigma_x^2, \qquad cov(D, S) = -\sigma_S^2$$ (A.16a)

therefore, the covariance matrix of the random vector (D, S) is

$$\Sigma = \begin{bmatrix} \sigma_D^2 & -\sigma_S^2 \\ -\sigma_S^2 & \sigma_D^2 \end{bmatrix} = \sigma_S^2 \begin{bmatrix} a^2 & -1 \\ -1 & 1 \end{bmatrix}, \qquad a^2 = \frac{\sigma_D^2}{\sigma_S^2}. \tag{A.16b}$$

The Neyman–Pearson test for this decision problem is characterized by the test statistic

$$(D, S) \cdot \Sigma^{-1} \cdot \begin{bmatrix} \mu_1 \\ \mu - \mu_1 \end{bmatrix} \tag{A.17}$$

and leads to the probability of detection

$$1 - \beta_2^{nk} = \Phi\left[\sqrt{\mu' \cdot \Sigma^{-1} \cdot \mu} - U(1 - \alpha)\right], \tag{A.18}$$

where $\mu' = (\mu_1, \mu - \mu_1)$ and Σ^{-1} the inverse of Σ. Now the inverse Σ^{-1} is given by

$$\Sigma^{-1} = \frac{1}{\sigma_D^2 - \sigma_S^2} \begin{bmatrix} 1 & 1 \\ 1 & a^2 \end{bmatrix}, \tag{A.19}$$

therefore we have

$$\mu' \cdot \Sigma^{-1} \cdot \mu = \frac{1}{\sigma_D^2 - \sigma_S^2} (\mu^2 + (a^2 - 1)(\mu - \mu_1)^2). \tag{A.20}$$

The probability of detection (A.18) is minimized with respect to μ, because of $a^2 > 1$ by

$$\mu_1^* = \mu \tag{A.21}$$

and the guaranteed probability of detection is

$$\min_{\mu_1} (1 - \beta_2^{nk})) = \Phi\left[\frac{\mu}{\sqrt{\sigma_D^2 - \sigma_S^2}} - U(1 - \alpha)\right]. \tag{A.22}$$

The corresponding test statistic is with (A.17)

$$(D, S) \cdot \Sigma^{-1} \cdot \begin{bmatrix} \mu \\ 0 \end{bmatrix} \sim D + S, \tag{A.23}$$

for $k = n$ we have with (A.14)

$$D + S = \sum_{i=1}^{n} Y_i.$$

In this case the inspector uses only his own data for the test.

For $k < n$ we have with (A.16a)

$$\sigma_D^2 - \sigma_S^2 - \frac{n^2}{k} \sigma_Y^2 = n\sigma_x^2 (\frac{n}{k} - 1) > 0,$$

which means that for $k > n$ the probability of detection (A.22) is smaller than that given by (A.13). This, in turn, means that the first procedure is better than the second one.

Final remark

Obviously, we cannot conclude from the two special cases considered here that the first procedure is better or equal to the second one in all cases: In the general case already the analysis of two reported data and one inspector measurement leads to optimization problems which can hardly be solved analytically. Hence the analysis does not allow for a general comparison between the two procedures.

In addition, it should not be forgotten that there are not only "statistical" criteria, like the probability of detection. There may be other, e.g. administrative reasons which justify the preference of one of the two procedures, even though the corresponding probability of detection is smaller than that of the other one.

7. References

Arkin, A., 1974, "*Handbook of Sampling for Auditing and Accounting*", 2nd Edition, McGraw Hill, New York

268   Rudolf Avenhaus

Avenhaus, R., and Frick, H., 1977, "Analyse von Fehlalarmen in Überwachungssystemen mit Hilfe von Zwei–Personen Nichtnullsummen–Spielen", *Operations Research Verfahren 26*, 629–639

Avenhaus, R., 1986, *"Safeguards Systems Analysis"*, Plenum Publisher, New York and London

Avenhaus, R., and Okada, A., 1988, "Inspector leadership games with incomplete information", *Discussion Paper 17 of the Zentrum für Interdisziplinäre Forschung* an der Universität Bielefeld, July

Avenhaus, R., Battenberg, H.P., and Falkowski, H.J., 1991, "Optimal data verification tests", *Operations Research*, in print

Avenhaus, R., and v. Stengel, B., 1991, "Verification of attributes and variables: Perfect equilibria and inspector leadership", in: *Defense Decision Making, Analytical Support for Arms and Crisis Management*, by R. Avenhaus, M. Rudnianski, J.–C. Karkar. (eds.), Springer Verlag, Berlin, Heidelberg, in print

Chapman, D.T., and El–Shaarawi, A.H., (eds.), 1989, *"Statistical Methods for the Assessment of Point Source Pollution"*, Kluwer Academic Publishers, (Reprinted from Environmental Monitoring and Assessment, Vol. 13, Numbers 2–3)

Dye, R.A., 1986, "Optimal monitoring policies in agencies", *Rand Journal of Economics 17*, No. 3, 339–350

Jaeschke, A., Geiger, W., and Page, B., (eds.), 1989, *"Informatik im Umweltschutz"*, Informatik–Fachberichte 228, Springer Verlag, Berlin, Heidelberg, Teil C

Jakeman, A.J., and Simpson, R.W., 1985, "Assessment of air quality impacts from an elevated point source", *Journal of Environmental Management 20*, 63–72

Kanodia, ,Ch.S., 1989, "Stochastic and moral hazard", *Journal of Accounting Research 23*, No. 1, 175–193

Lehmann, E.L., 1959, *"Testing Statistical Hypotheses"*, J. Wiley, New York

Maschler, M., 1966, "A price leadership method for solving the inspector's non–constant–sum game", *Nav. Res. Logistics Quarterly 13*, 11–33

Maschler, M., 1967, "The inspector's non–constant–sum game: Its dependence on a system of detectors", *Nav. Res. Logistics Quarterly 14*, 275–290

Page, E.S., 1954, "Continuous inspection schemes", *Biometrika 41*, 100–115

Russell, C.S., 1990, "Game models for structuring monitoring and enforcement systems", *Natural Resource Modeling 4*, Number 2, 143–173

Russell, C.S., 1990, "Monitoring and enforcement", in: *Public Policies for Environmental Protection*, Paul R. Portney (Ed.), Resources for the Future, Washington, D.C.

Schuster, P., 1986, "Die Rolle behördlicher Gestattungen in der Strafrechtspraxis", in: *Umweltschutz und Umweltkriminalität*, H.–D. Schwind und G. Steinhilper (Eds.), Kriminalistik–Verlag, Heidelberg, 51ff.

Simpson, R.W., Miles, G.M., and Taylor, J.A., 1987, "An air pollution emissions control strategy to avoid violations of both short— and long—term health standards for particulate levels", *Journal of Environmental Management 24*, 53–70

v. Stackelberg, H., 1934, *"Marktform und Gleichgewicht"*, Springer, Berlin

Vaughan, W.J., and Russell, C.S., 1983, "Monitoring point sources of pollution: Answers and more questions from statistical quality control", *American Statistician 37 (4)*, 476–487

Wathern, P., and Young, S,.N., 1986, "Use of cumultative sum analysis to assess policy impacts on the river Ebbw, Wales", *Journal of Environmental Management 23*, 139–148

Welsch, H., Eiß, H., and Funk, C., 1990, *"Meßtechnik und Umweltpolitik – Entwicklungstendenzen und umweltpolitische Bedeutung der Umweltüberwachung und —modellierung"*, Report of the Energiewirtschaftliches Institut an der Universität Köln, July

Wetherill, G.B., 1982, *"Sampling Inspection and Quality Control"*, Chapman and Hall, London and New York, 2nd edition

Comments by Till Requate

Avenhaus's paper addresses an important issue which has often been neglected or simply "assumed away" in the literature of environmental economics. Most authors concerned with taxation of pollutants, emission permit trading, or just imposing upper bounds on pollutant levels simply assume perfect compliance.

In reality, however, there is a conflict between polluting firms which would like to emit pollutants in excess of the permitted level in order to save abatement costs and the authorities which are interested in maintaining the allowed level. Avenhaus models this conflict by setting up several games which differ in timing as well as in the choice of the strategy spaces.

The first game is a simultaneous move game. The inspecting authority (simply called the inspector in the remainder of this comment) uses a fixed monitoring procedure which is common knowledge to both players. The inspector's strategic variable is an error probability α (in terms of statistics, this is a type I error) for triggering a false alarm although the polluting firm (in the following simply called the firm) acts legally. The firm, on the other hand, plays mixed strategies on the set of actions {"acting legally", "acting illegally"}. Acting illegally means that the firm chooses a fixed vector of excess pollutants $\psi = (\mu_1, ..., \mu_n)$, which is also common knowledge. The alarm probability α, chosen by the inspector, generates a probability β for the firm not to get detected in the case of illegal behavior. Since illegal behavior can only be detected by inspection, we can say that the inspector implicitly chooses mixed strategies on the set of actions {"inspection", "no inspection"}.

The simultaneous move game has a unique equilibrium (in mixed strategies) with an alarm probability α^* lying strictly between zero and one. The firm, on the other hand, behaves illegally with positive probability (but less than one).

Next, Avenhaus considers a sequential move game which differs from the first one only in timing and, therefore, in information. The inspector takes the role of a leader. That is, he chooses an alarm probability and reveals it to the firm. Even so, the game remains a game of imperfect information since the firm does not know whether it will be inspected or not. Knowing α, and therefore β, the firm decides to act legally or illegally. This sequential move game also has a unique equilibrium point where the inspector chooses the same alarm probability α^* as in the simultaneous move game. The firm, on the other hand, behaves legally. More precisely, the firm's equilibrium strategy is a mapping from $[0, 1]$ (alarm probabilities) to {"legal", "illegal"} with

$$\phi^*(\alpha) = legal \qquad \text{if } \alpha \geq \alpha^*,$$
$$\phi^*(\alpha) = illegal \qquad \text{if } \alpha < \alpha^*.$$

This might seem to be somewhat surprising at first glance. The point is, once the inspector has chosen α^*, the firm is indifferent between acting legally and illegally like in the simultaneous move game. So it could flip a coin for what to do. If it did so, however, it would play mixed strategies, acting illegally with positive probability. But this is, of course, not an equilibrium in the leadership game. For, anticipating a (proper) mixed strategy by the firm in the subgame, the inspector would better choose $\alpha^* + \epsilon$. This means that if the inspector is not quite sure about the firm's mood in case that the firm is indifferent between several actions in the subgame, the inspector should choose $\alpha^* + \epsilon$ anyway in order to enforce legal behavior. We may conclude that an ϵ–equilibrium may be a better solution concept for this game rather than a Nash–equilibrium. (This may be a further example for the hypothesis that a unique Nash equilibrium is not always self–enforcing.)

It is important to notice that the model implicitly contains the assumption that the firm can perfectly observe α^* after the inspector has made his move, in other words, the inspector can credibly reveal his alarm probability, which in turn generates the probability that illegal behavior will not be detected. To me, it is not quite clear how this can be done. If it is *not* possible to reveal the alarm probability, however, and if the firm has good reasons to believe that the inspector is bluffing, it may prefer to act illegally after knowing the alleged value of α.

If α cannot be revealed credibly at once, there could be need of a dynamic model, in which the inspector can build up reputation to make the polluting firms believe in his alarm probability α^*. Another possible way to deal with this problem may be the signaling game approach developed by Güth and Pethig [this volume].

In the third game, set up in Section 4 of his paper, Avenhaus allows the firms not only to choose a probability of behaving legally or illegally. They may also choose among different illegal strategies $\psi = (\mu_1,..., \mu_n)$, $\mu_i \geq 0$ and $\Sigma_i \mu_i = \mu > 0$. However, μ is taken as fixed and common knowledge. The firm can only decide how to split up μ into n parts in order to minimize the probability of not getting detected. It is not quite clear from the paper what the interpretation of ψ is. In the set–up of the model, the author calls it *real* amounts of excess pollutants. In the introduction and also in the example of Section 5, he is talking of (possibly falsified) data of emitted pollutants, transmitted to the inspector by the firm. With this interpretation, however, there would also be need of a strategic variable which denotes *real* amounts of pollutants since these real amounts rather than the falsified data of them have an impact on the results of the inspector's inquiry. To keep the model consistent, I would consider ψ as *real excess pollutants*. (We will return to this problem when discussing the Appendix a few lines below).

Also the *inspector* has an enlarged strategy space. Besides choosing α he can choose a particular monitoring procedure ϕ. In terms of statistics, for a fixed α, the inspector may choose a *best test* which minimizes the firm's probability not to get detected in case of acting illegally. The timing of the game is leader/follower again, that is, the inspector moves first, selecting α and a procedure (a test) $\phi(\alpha)$. Knowing α and ϕ, the firm selects a probability of acting illegally and an amount of excess pollutants (or only alleged data of those?) to be emitted in each period. However, the payoff structure of this game is the same as in the first two games. In particular, the payoff d, received by the firm if its illegal behavior has not been detected, is independent of $\psi = (\mu_1,..., \mu_n)$, the vector of excess pollutants.

The main result about this game is that in equilibrium the inspector chooses an alarm probability $0 < \alpha^* < 1$, and the firm behaves legally. Moreover, the inspector chooses a monitoring procedure ϕ^* which minimizes the probability for the firm of not getting detected given the firm maximizes this probability by choosing the best illegal strategy.

The assumption that d is independent of ψ seems to be a shortcoming of the model. It is much more natural to assume that a firm has a certain abatement cost C, with C' < 0 and $C'' > 0$, that is, higher emission levels induce lower abatement costs, und marginal abatement costs are decreasing in emission levels. In such a model the firm would choose emission levels $\psi = (\mu_1,..., \mu_n)$ and μ, such that $\mu = \Sigma_i\mu_i$, which minimize

$$C(\mu_0 + \mu) + [1 - \beta(\phi(\alpha),\psi)] \cdot K \qquad \text{or even} \qquad \overset{n}{\underset{i=1}{\Sigma}} C_i(\mu_0 + \mu_i) + [1 - \beta(\phi(\alpha), \psi)] \cdot K,$$

where K is a constant denoting a penalty to be paid in case of being detected. In a more sophisticated model, K could also depend on μ. By this kind of cost function, the firm's payoff depends heavily on its specific illegal strategy! At the end of Section 2, the author justifies the assumption that the payoff to the firm does not depend on the amount of excess pollutants in case of illegal behavior by arguing that with respect to applications it will be important that the optimal strategy of the inspector does not depend on the payoff to the firm. In reality, however, this assumption will rarely be satisfied, and the range of applications would be small.

In the Appendix, Avenhaus sheds some light on the interpretation of the illegal strategies. He compares two kinds of monitoring procedures combined with two kinds of illegal behavior. The *first* one consists of direct monitoring, that is, the inspector makes his own measurements. The firm's illegal behavior consists of polluting in excess of the allowed level. In the *second* one, the firm gives own data of its emitted pollutants to the inspector, the inspector compares these data with own data taken by monitoring the firm. So the firm's illegal strategy consists of falsifying data *and* of emitting pollutants in excess. The author shows that, for two special cases, the direct observation is better than taking (possibly falsified) data from the firm. *To me*, this is an argument in favour of dropping the *falsifying−data−story*. The question is, however, what do we want, a descriptive or a normative theory of monitoring firms? For, in reality, monitoring authorities, indeed, seem to gather data by the firms even if this is worse than relying only on direct observations, as Avenhaus shows in the appendix. For normative reasons as well as for the consistency of the model, however, one should interpret the illegal strategies of Section 4 as *real* amounts of excess pollutants.

Let me stress that, despite some critical remarks, I think this paper yields an important step towards the problem of monitoring emissions of pollutants, combining game theory with methods from statistics. With respect to further research, it could be a challenging task to extend these methods to models where firms pay emission taxes on pollutants. Strictly speaking, there is no room for illegal behavior in such models. Nevertheless, there is a monitoring problem.

Chapter 10

Werner Güth and Rüdiger Pethig[1]

Illegal Pollution and Monitoring of Unknown Quality
– A Signaling Game Approach –

Abstract: In this paper a game model is considered whose strategically interacting a-gents are a polluting firm that can save abatement costs by illegal waste emissions and a monitoring agent (controller) whose job it is to prevent such pollution. When deciding on whether to dispose of its waste legally or illegally the firm does not know for sure whether the controller is sufficiently qualified and/or motivated to detect the firm's illegal releases of pollutants. The firm has the option of undertaking a small–scale (de-liberate) "exploratory pollution accident" to get a hint about the controller's qualifica-tion before deciding on how to dispose of its waste. The controller may or may not re-spond to that "accident" by a thorough investigation thus perhaps revealing his or her type to the firm. It is this sequential decision process along with the asymmetric distri-bution of information that constitutes a signaling game whose equilibrium points may but need not signal the type of the controller to the firm.

In Part I of the paper the formal introduction of the game model is followed by an extensive discussion of four different equilibrium scenarios which are non–degenerate submodels whose (generic) equilibria are considered typical and especially interesting for the monitoring issue at hand. Having set up a rather complex game model the price to be paid is (as in many applications in other fields) the multiplicity of equilibria – even within one and the same equilibrium scenario. This multiplicity clearly weakens the predictive capacity of the model. To overcome it Part II addresses concepts of equilibri-um refinement and selection on a fairly technical level. It is shown that the set of equi-libria is reduced – not to a singleton, though – by applying the refinement concept of uniformly perfect pure strategy equilibria. Unique solutions are obtained by reference to the equilibrium selection theoretic concepts of cell and truncation consistency, of payoff dominance and of risk dominance.

[1] Comments by participants at the conference and by an anonymous referee are gratefully acknowledged.

1. Introduction

Pollution is typically a public bad since it results from the economic activities of some agents but bothers a large number of individuals in the society. Correspondingly, preventing pollution is a public good. When exploring pollution one can therefore rely on results in the literature on public goods (Blümel, Pethig, and von dem Hagen, 1986).

Most studies in the public goods literature assume that some public authority is in the position to impose the rules according to which self–interested individual agents interact (e.g. Hurwicz, 1973). Such set of rules is usually called a *mechanism,* i.e. a *strategic game.* This approach could be used to design some reasonable legal rules to prevent river or air pollution, to limit the noise level of factories, trucks etc. Other studies (like Güth and Hellwig, 1986 and 1987, as well as Rob 1989) rely on private supply of public goods, i.e. the economic agents themselves decide whether one of the proposed mechanisms for providing the public good will be implemented or not.

Some of the studies mentioned above deal explicitly with the crucial fact that people have private information about how they are really affected by public goods or pollution, respectively. Privacy of information means that the public authority or the private agent does not know the utilities which their potential customers can obtain from the proposed mechanism. The usual approach to take care of this information deficit is the *revelation principle* (for instance Myerson 1979). According to the revelation principle one can find an allocation equivalent, incentive compatible direct mechanism for every possible public goods mechanism. A *direct mechanism* is a normal form game with payoffs determined by the true preferences and all possible preferences as strategies. A direct mechanism is *incentive compatible* if the vector of true preferences is an equilibrium point.

The revelation theorem states that for any equilibrium of any public goods mechanism there exists an incentive compatible direct mechanism for which general truth telling implies the same economic results. When looking for the possible results, e.g. some (welfare) optimal mechanism, one can therefore limit one's attention to incentive compatible direct mechanisms with general truth telling as the solution. One could say that the revelation theorem offsets the need to solve games with incomplete information.

The price one has to pay for using the revelation principle is that the result, e.g. the (welfare) optimal mechanism, is very sensitive to changes of the game structure. If, for instance, beliefs concerning private preferences change, one usually will have to rely on a different mechanism. This certainly contradicts the actual practice where one mechanism is used for many different situations which often enough were not envisaged when implementing the mechanism. A way to design mechanisms which are more robust to environmental changes is to look for mechanisms providing reasonable results for a large subset in the set of all possible preference profiles (Wilson, 1986).

Although incomplete information is also a crucial aspect of our model, we do not consider a problem of mechanism design by relying on the revelation principle. We rather introduce what we consider a natural *model of asymmetric information* and focus attention on how its results are influenced by the information deficits. Furthermore, we do not look at pollution in general but only at *illegal pollution*. More specifically, it is assumed that there exists already a set of rules, a legally codified mechanism, but polluters have an incentive to violate these rules.

Difficulties or even failures to enforce regulatory rules are not an exclusive problem in the area of environmental policy, of course. They rather seem to be widespread if not ubiquarian, since "violators" of rules can safely be expected whenever a piece of legislation passes the parliament. Not all enforcement deficits have the same empirical significance, however. In many areas it may be a good approximation to proceed on the assumption of perfect compliance — or, equivalently, on the assumption of complete and costless enforcement. Russell argues in the present volume that this used to be the mainstream proposition of environmental economists as well. But in recent years much evidence accumulated pointing to considerable discrepancy between the paper form of environmental law and the true state of the environment. In Germany as in other countries the lack of enforcing existing environmental regulations has become a decisive issue in recent time. Hansmeyer (1989, p.75) considers the notion of "enforcement deficit" (in German "Vollzugsdefizit") a much conjured catch—word. It also became evident, that incomplete enforcement does not seem to be a transitory but rather a persistent phenomenon the explanation of which must be based on analysing the strategic interactions of the parties involved.

In the model to be set up in the present paper the strategically interacting agents are (i) the polluters who can save considerable costs by disposing waste illegally and (ii) the controllers who are hired to prevent illegal waste disposal. The issue of who controls the controllers which is considered relevant in the public choice literature on bureaucracy would suggest to also consider the interactions between controllers and their supervisors (e.g. Pethig, 1991). But this is beyond the scope of the present paper. Given this limitation, our study can therefore be seen as a contribution to the game theoretic tradition of *strategic inspection analyses* (Maschler, 1966; Avenhaus, 1990; Avenhaus, Okada, and Zamir, 1991). Compared to such previous studies we explore a much more complex situation with multiple equilibria which is also the reason why we have to rely on a different game theoretic methodology.

For the sake of simplicity we assume that there is just one potential violator, a *firm* whose production process yields waste which can be legally disposed of only at high costs, and a simple *monitoring agency* called the *controller*. Detecting the source of illegal waste disposal is rather difficult and requires a lot of expertise which the agency may or may not have. When deciding on whether to dispose of its waste legally or illegally the firm does not know for sure whether the controller is qualified enough to detect illegal waste disposal, i.e. we assume asymmetric information concerning the qualification of the agency.

To be more certain about the qualification of the agency the firm has the option of undertaking a small–scale "exploratory" discharge of pollutants called *exploratory (pollution) accident* hereafter. Since a thorough investigation of this accident will be more costly for an unqualified agency than for a qualified one, this might yield a hint about the controller's qualification before deciding on whether to dispose of the waste legally or illegally. Because of the *sequential decision process* and the firm's information deficit concerning the controller's qualification our model is a *signaling game* with equilibria signaling the type, respectively the qualification of the monitoring agency.

In spite of its specific assumptions our game model defines a rather large class of sequential games with three subsequent decision stages, not including the fictitious initial chance move representing the firm's incomplete information concerning the qualification of the agency. In Section 2 the game model is formally introduced. Equilibrium scenarios, i.e. typical or especially interesting results of generic equilibria, are discussed in Section 3. To derive more specific results we apply the refinement concept of uniformly perfect pure strategy equilibria (Section 4) and equilibrium selection theory (Section 5). Finally the results are summarised and some potential lines of future research are indicated.

PART 1: EQUILIBRIUM SCENARIOS
WITH POOLING AND SIGNALING BEHAVIOR

2. The game model

For the sake of simplicity we consider a situation where one single *firm f*, e.g. a major factory, can save considerable costs by discharging waste illegally instead of abating it as required by law. As an example imagine a chemical factory which can simply release toxic waste into a water course. Other examples are illegal disposal of dangerous substances on declared or undeclared waste deposits, illegal release of waste in international waters for saving transportation costs, release of toxic smoke etc.

In order to prevent firm *f* from illegal pollution the government has hired a *controller c* whose task is to detect illegal pollution. In the case of river pollution controller *c* would be, for instance, a water protection agency. Usually, jobs in such agencies are poorly paid as compared to jobs in private industries, especially if sophisticated techniques and a lot of expertise are required to prove that firm *f* has caused the pollution. Therefore it is open to question, of course, whether controller *c* is really fit to detect a polluter. Another reason to cast doubt on *c*'s qualities is shirking, i.e. controller *c* may not find out a polluter simply because he does not care about his duties but rather prefers to have some leisure time during his official working hours, instead. These arguments lead us to assume that *firm f is not sure about controller c's qualification* for detecting illegal pollution.

First of all, the controller is of course hired to detect regional (or local) increases in ambient pollution resulting from illegal releases of pollutants. But it is also his task to find out the (point) source of pollution which caused that increase, i.e. he has to trace back the pollution to the illegal polluter. As argued above, in both cases the controller's success depends on his expertise and/or determination and effort in doing his job. To simplify the subsequent analysis we assume, however, that (local) detrimental increases of ambient pollution are always detected by the controller. Hence potential polluters such as firm *f* are only uncertain about the controller's ability to identify them as the source of pollution.

In game theoretic terminology this means that our game model is one of asymmetric incomplete information since only controller *c* himself knows his own qualification to prove the discharge of pollutants by firm *f* whereas firm *f* has only probabilistic beliefs concerning c's prospects of finding out illegal behavior. In order to keep things simple we will distinguish only *two types* of controller c, as expected by f: *type e*(xpert) and *type n*(on–expert). Firm f expects type e with probability $w \in (0, 1)$ and type n with the complementary probability $1-w$. Firm f's beliefs are assumed to be common knowledge.

To capture firm f's information deficit about c's type we introduce a *fictitious initial chance move* whose result is type e with probability w and type n with probability $1-w$ respectively. While c learns about the result of the chance move, firm f only knows the probabilities for the two possible results. As a result of this fictitious initial chance move f's incomplete information concerning the type of its opponent is transformed into strategically equivalent imperfect information. With the fictitious initial chance move we obtain a game with complete but imperfect information.

In Figure 2.1 the fictitious initial chance move is the first move at the origin o (the top decision node) of the game tree. Player 0 is the chance player since at decision nodes of this player the choice behavior is determined not strategically but according to predetermined probabilities. That the result of this move is revealed to the existing type e or n of controller c but not to firm f can be seen from the information conditions of these players at later moves as graphically illustrated by their information sets. An *information set* of player i is a set of decision nodes where i has to decide. When deciding player i only knows that he is at one of the decision nodes in the information set but he doesn't know at which one exactly. Graphically the information sets in Figure 2.1 are illustrated by encircling all decision nodes belonging to the same information set.

After the fictitious initial chance move firm f – not knowing the chosen type of controller c – can initiate an exploratory small pollution "accident" with the intention to trigger an investigation of its production facilities by the controller in which the firm expects to learn whether controller c is of the $e-$ or the $n-$type. This is f's *decision I* in Figure 2.1. Decision I implies that the firm deliberately and unlawfully discharges pollutants for the purpose of checking controller c's ability and/or reluctance to detect the source of that "accidental" spill over. The main idea of such a move of firm f is to take advantage of the fact that due to their different qualification it is more difficult for the non–expert n than for the expert e to find out whether harmful pollutants have been discharged by firm f or not. In the case of river pollution one can, for instance, imagine the release of non–toxic but easily observable waste water whose chemical substances are difficult to determine. The decision not to embark on such an exploratory discharge is denoted by $\bar{I}$.

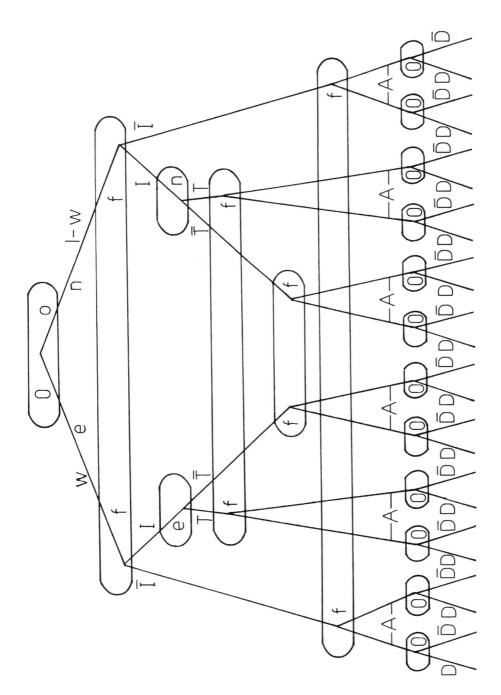

Figure 2.1: The game tree of the game model

Suppose decision $\bar{I}$ has been taken. Then firm f has to *choose the level $A \in [0, \bar{A}]$,
$\bar{A} > 0$, of illegal waste release* without any further hint about c's qualification. In other
words, when deciding on A, firm f can only rely on its a priori beliefs as expressed by the
probability parameter w. In Figure 2.1 we have graphically illustrated by the line '$-A-$'
that the level A of illegal waste disposal is a continuous variable.

In case of I the actually chosen type of controller c can decide whether to investigate
the "accident" thoroughly (the *decision T*) or not (the *decision $\bar{T}$*). It is assumed that
both types have the ability to thoroughly investigate the spill over although such an
investigation is more costly for n than for e. After the investigation firm f is informed
about the result, i.e. firm f learns about the decision T or $\bar{T}$ before the game continues.

When deciding about A, firm f therefore knows in case of I whether controller c has
chosen T or $\bar{T}$. But it still does not know the result of the initial chance move. It is because of this information condition that our model is a *signaling game*. Suppose the two
types react differently to the exploratory accident I, for example, e chooses T and n
chooses $\bar{T}$ (signaling behavior). Then firm f can infer from its observation T or $\bar{T}$ whether c's true type is e or n. This situation exhibits the typical structure of signaling games
which require asymmetric information and a sequential decision process with earlier
decisions of the more informed players allowing the less informed players to make inferences. Observe, however, that if both types of controller c do not react differently to the
exploratory accident (pooling behavior), then firm f does not know c's qualification
when choosing A in the interval $[0, \bar{A}]$.

After firm f's choice of A it is stochastically decided whether in case of $A > 0$ firm f
is detected as the illegal polluter (the *chance move D*) or not (the *chance move $\bar{D}$*). The
probability for the result D is denoted by $W(A, t)$ with $A \in [0, \bar{A}]$ and $t \in \{e, n\}$ i.e., the
detection probability of illegal pollution depends on the amount A of illegal pollution
and on controller c's qualification. A simple probability function $W(A, t)$ satisfying the
two obvious requirements,

$$W(\bar{A}, t) > W(A, t) \ for \ \bar{A} > A \ and \ t = e, n \quad and \tag{1}$$

$$W(A, e) > W(A, n) \text{ for all } A \in (0, \bar{A}),\tag{2}$$

is the linear probability function

$$W(A, t) = \begin{cases} MA/\bar{A} & \text{for } t = e, \\ NA/\bar{A} & \text{for } t = n, \end{cases} \quad \text{with} \tag{3}$$

$$0 < N < M < 1.\tag{4}$$

This completes the interpretation of the game tree as graphically visualised in Figure 2.1. We refrained from including the probabilities $W(A,t)$ and $1-W(A,t)$ for the final chance moves D and $\bar{D}$ in Figure 2.1 in order not to overburden the graphical presentation of the game decision process and the information conditions.

As for the description of the game model, it only remains to specify how firm f and the two types e and n of controller c *evaluate* the different plays. We follow the usual convention of assigning to a non—existing type of a player the payoff of its existing type.

In case of no exploratory investigation, $\bar{I}$, and in case of "I and $\bar{T}$" the controller has not invested in special work effort so that his cost of effort can be neglected.

Illegal pollution is often detected because of its disastrous environmental consequences, e.g. dead fish in case of illegal river pollution. But it is quite a different problem to find out the polluter — which is assumed to be the controller's job. How good this job is done depends on the controller's qualification and incentives which in turn are largely determined by his or her payoff. In what follows the elements constituting this payoff are successively described.

First we assume that tracing illegal waste disposals back to the polluter will promote the controller's career. This has an impact on the payoff u_t of both types $t = e$ and $t = n$ of controller c. In case of $A > 0$ the payoff level u_t of type t is simply the probability $W(A,t)$ of being able to prove that firm f has caused the pollution. The payoff u_t for $A = 0$ should not be smaller than the payoff in case of a detection. Therefore we assume $u_t = 1$ for $A = 0$. To formalise this hypothesis, define

$$\delta_A = \begin{cases} 1, & \text{if } A > 0, \\ 0 & \text{otherwise.} \end{cases}$$

With the help of the variable δ_A type t's payoff for $\bar{I}$ and $(I, \bar{T})$ can be expressed as

$$u_t = 1 - \delta_A + W(A,t) \qquad \text{for } t = e,\, n. \tag{5}$$

After I and T occurred type t's payoff is the difference of the payoff in (5) and the cost of a thorough investigation of the exploratory accident:

$$u_t = \begin{cases} 1 - \delta_A + W(A,t) - H & \text{for } t = n, \\ 1 - \delta_A + W(A,t) - L & \text{for } t = e, \end{cases} \tag{6}$$

where the assumption

$$H > L > 0 \tag{7}$$

reflects the higher qualification of the expert e as compared to the non–expert n. The inequalities (7) may be alternatively or complementary interpreted to reflect n's greater disutility from working.

Define in addition

$$\delta_I = \begin{cases} 1, & \text{if } f \text{ chooses } I, \\ 0, & \text{if } f \text{ chooses } \bar{I}, \end{cases} \quad \text{and} \quad \delta_T^t = \begin{cases} 1, & \text{if } t \text{ chooses } T, \\ 0, & \text{if } t \text{ chooses } \bar{T}. \end{cases}$$

With the help of this notation the payoff functions (5) and (6) can be comprehensively written as

$$u_t = \begin{cases} 1 - \delta_A + W(A,t) - \delta_I \delta_T^t H & \text{for } t = n, \\ 1 - \delta_A + W(A,t) - \delta_I \delta_T^t L & \text{for } t = e. \end{cases} \tag{8}$$

For the firm,

$$K'(A) = p + FA \quad \text{with } F \geq 0 \text{ and } p > 0 \tag{9}$$

is the *cost per unit of waste* by which legal disposal exceeds the cost level of illegal disposal. The assumption $p > 0$ means that illegal disposal is always cheaper. If F is posi tive, the discrepancy between legal and illegal disposal increases with the amount of waste which is illegally disposed. The cost advantage $A \cdot K(A)$ of illegal waste disposal equals the firm's abatement cost which has to be juxtaposed to the *fine* $B + PA$ with $P > p$ to be paid in case of detection. We suppose that the fine P per unit of illegal disposal is independent of the amount A since most such per unit fines do not depend on amounts. The fine $B \geq 0$ does not depend on A and hence expresses that part of the penalty which is caused by any detected illegal waste disposal. In case of $\bar{I}$ firm f's payoff u_f is therefore

$$u_f = (p + FA)A - W(A,t)(B + PA) \tag{10}$$

with $P > p > 0$ and $F \geq 0$. Let $C \geq 0$ denote the costs of firm f to induce and perform the exploratory accident I and $E \geq 0$ firm f's costs implied by the thorough investigation T of such an accident. In case of I and $\bar{T}$ the cost C, and in case of I and T the cost $C+E$, have to be subtracted from the payoff level in (10). With the help of the variables δ_I and δ_T^t firm f's payoff function can therefore be summarised by

$$u_f = (p + FA)A - W(A,t)(B + PA) - \delta_I(C + \delta_T^t E) \quad \text{with} \tag{11}$$

$$P > p > 0,\ F \geq 0,\ C \geq 0,\ E \geq 0,\ B \geq 0. \tag{12}$$

The game tree in Figure 2.1 supplemented by the probability assignment (3) and by the payoff functions (8) and (11) defines our *game model*. Of course, all these structural relationships do not define just a single game but rather a multi–dimensional class of games with parameters $\bar{A}$, B, C, E, F, H, L, M, N, P, p, and w which can vary in certain (half–)intervals. Denote by $\Omega \subset \mathbb{R}^{12}$ the set of all feasible parameter values, the *parameter space* of our game model.

Some subregions in this parameter space Ω will have obvious results. Nevertheless, to solve all games in this large parameter space is certainly beyond the scope of this paper. Therefore we will not explore all subregions in the same systematic way but restrict the most advanced game theoretic exercise to some subregions of this large parameter space that we consider to be especially interesting.

3. A gallery of equilibrium scenarios

Game theoretic studies of real–life decision problems are often attempts to provide consistent explanations of observed behavior, especially if the observed behavior appears to
be paradoxical at first sight. A naive observer might be surprised, for instance, that
there is a lot of littering on highways in spite of the fact that it would be much cheaper
to dispose garbage properly and that one finally has to pay for the more expensive clean
up, either via higher road tolls or tax rates. But a game theoretic analysis may show
that the situation is actually a *prisoner's dilemma game* with littering (resembling con-
fessing of the prisoners) as a unique dominant strategy in spite of the inefficiency which
it implies. This illustrates the purpose of game theoretic studies as attempts to resolve
cognitive dissonance about seemingly paradoxical observed behavior which becomes
more understandable if one can find a game model, reflecting the main strategic aspects,
whose equilibrium result is consistent with the observed behavior.

This way of using game theoretic models, namely to provide consistent explanations
for observed behavior, has been called the *method of equilibrium scenarios* (Güth, 1984;
Avenhaus, Güth, and Huber, 1991; as well as Gardner and Güth, 1991). According to
the method of equilibrium scenarios one does not determine all equilibria of a game
model but only those whose implied play corresponds to some really observed behavior.
An *equilibrium (point)* is a strategy vector $s^* := (s_1^*, ..., s_n^*)$ specifying a strategy s_i^* for
every player i, such that no player i can profitably deviate unilaterally. To put it differently, for all players i and all alternative strategies s_i of i one must have[2]

$$u_i(s^*) \geq u_i(s_1^*, ..., s_{i-1}^*, s_i, s_{i+1}^*, ..., s_n^*), \tag{1}$$

where u_i is player $i's$ payoff function which is transformed from the set of end
points/plays to the set of strategy vectors in the usual way. The strategy vector s^* is
called an *equilibrium scenario* if there exists a *full–dimensional subspace* Ω' of the parameter space Ω such that s^* is an equilibrium point for all games in Ω'. In other words,

---

[2] For the sake of notational simplicity, the numbering of equations starts with (1) in each
of the subsequent sections. If in some section of the present paper we make a reference in
the text to an equation by writing, say, 'Equation (14)', then it is understood that we
mean Equation (14) of the very same section where this reference appears. On the other
hand, if we wish to refer to Equation (14) from Section X in the text of Section Y, X ≠
Y, then we write 'Equation (X.14)'.

for s^* to be an equilibrium scenario there has to exist a generic game with s^* as an equilibrium.

The method of equilibrium scenario is most useful for very complex game models like the game model described in Section 2, for which a more thorough game theoretic analysis is often practically impossible. This is especially true if one is more interested in exploring certain kinds of equilibria than in determining all possible equilibrium results.

We will not check the equilibrium condition for the normal form with players f, e, and n. We rather check it for the so–called *agent normal form* (Selten, 1975, as well as Güth and Kalkofen, 1989), where there are as many players as information sets of personal players. For the case at hand this means that we have four F–players rather than a single firm f, namely the F–player who decides between I and $\bar{I}$ as well as the three F–players choosing A after $\bar{I}$, T, and $\bar{T}$. These four F–players are called the *agents of firm f*. Formally the agent normal form is a normal form game with all agents of all (normal form) players as players whose strategies are the moves in their information set and whose payoffs are those of their (normal form) player. In our game model the agent normal form has 6 players, namely the 4 F–players in addition to players e and n.

The basic idea of the agent normal form is that a given player's decision in one of his information sets should only be governed by the future consequences of his move, i.e. what one will do in such a situation is determined by what one can still achieve and not by what one initially tended or promised to do. What we exclude is therefore that a player can threaten to behave non–optimally later. Thus the agent normal form relies on decentralised decision making of local players. See Güth (1990) for a discussion of the various notions of a player.

In order to describe equilibrium scenarios based on the agent normal form it is convenient to introduce the following pieces of notation. We denote a strategy vector by

$$s = (s_f, s_e, s_n) \qquad (2)$$

with component s_f, s_e, and s_n being the strategy of firm f, type e, and type n of controller c, respectively. Firm f's strategy has to specify the choice δ_I (with $\delta_I = 1$ meaning the move I and $\delta_I = 0$ meaning move $\bar{I}$) as well as the choice of A for its three later information sets. Both types of controller c have only to decide between $\delta_T^t = 1$ (the move T) and $\delta^t_T = 0$ (the move $\bar{T}$). Therefore the strategies s_e and s_n are completely described by the move δ^e_T and δ^n_T of the two types of c. With this notation firm f's strategy s_f can be described as

$$s_f = (\delta_I, A \mid \delta_I \delta^t_T = 1, \; A \mid \delta_I (1-\delta^t_T) = 1, \; A \mid \delta_I = 0) \tag{3}$$

where $'A \mid *'$ stands for the level of A chosen after the previous moves described by $'*'$. For the sake of notational simplicity we will often write

$$s_f = (\delta_I, A_1, A_2, A_3) \tag{3'}$$

instead of (3) and correspondingly

$$s = ((\delta_I, A_1, A_2, A_3), \delta^e_T, \delta^n_T) \tag{2'}$$

for the strategy vector s.

3.1. Pooled shirking and illegal waste disposal: 'polluter's paradise scenario'

It certainly is not an unrealistic situation that both types of controller c are shirking and that firm f will react to this by maximal illegal pollution $A = \bar{A}$. This situation is described by the strategy vector

$$s^a := ((0, \bar{A}, \bar{A}, \bar{A}), 0, 0). \tag{4}$$

This strategy vector (4) describes a situation in which firm f does not invest into an exploratory accident $(\delta_I = 0)$. Therefore the response of controller c to a (hypothetical) accident is irrelevant but the reactions $\delta^e_T = \delta^n_T = 0$ as reported in s^a to that hypothetical situation indicate, of course, the controller's reluctance to investigate: If an exploratory accident would have had occurred, both types of c would not have reacted by a thorough investigation. In fact, according to s^a the enforcement of the zero-emission rule is so ineffective that the firm ignores the legal constraint completely: Not only doesn't it consider it worthwhile to explore the controller's type, but regardless of previ ous moves firm f finds it even advantageous to choose the maximum amount of emis-

sions $\bar{A}$ — based on its a priori beliefs about the controller. If s^a can be shown to be an

equilibrium for a full–dimensional parameter region, it characterises doubtlessly a "pol-

luter's paradise scenario".

In order to demonstrate that s^a is, indeed, a scenario we first show that it is an

equilibrium. For s^a to be in equilibrium the following condition must be satisfied for all

levels $A \in [0, \bar{A}]$:

$$(p + F\bar{A})\bar{A} - [wM + (1{-}w)N](B + P\bar{A}) \geq (p + FA)A - [wM + (1{-}w)N]\frac{A}{\bar{A}}(B + PA)$$

or $\quad p(\bar{A}{-}A) + F(\bar{A}^2{-}A^2) \geq [wM + (1{-}w)N][B(1 - \frac{A}{\bar{A}}) + P(\bar{A} - \frac{A^2}{\bar{A}})].$ (5)

Inequality (5) requires that the lower risk of detection by choosing smaller levels A

$< \bar{A}$ of illegal disposal must be (over)compensated by the increase of disposal costs. No

other conditions have to be satisfied for two reasons: firstly, an exploratory accident

does not pay if both types of controller c react in the same way and therefore do not

signal their qualification and secondly, the decisions δ_T^e and δ_T^n do not matter in case of

$\delta_I = 0$.

For $\bar{A} > A$ inequality (5) can be simplified to

$$\frac{\bar{A}(p + F(\bar{A} + A))}{B + P(\bar{A} + A)} \geq wM + (1{-}w)N.$$ (5')

The term on the right hand side of (5') is the a priori detection probability for $A = \bar{A}$ as

expected by firm f. The left hand side of (5') is a relation of the cost advantage and the

penalty for illegal waste disposal. Due to (2.12) the left hand side of (5') is strictly posi-

tive. Thus there exists a full–dimensional non–empty sub space Ω^a of the 12–dimen-

sional parameter space Ω of games, described in Section 2, such that s^a is an equilibrium

in all games with a parameter vector $\omega = (\bar{A},B,C,E,F,H,L,M,N,P,p,w)$ in $\Omega^a \subset \Omega$.

The most dramatic examples of the polluter's paradise equilibrium scenario s^a seem to be the nuclear power plants in their early development. Before the uprise of the anti–nuclear or green movement such plants were neither regularly turned off in case of small accidents (although this caused environmental problems as, for instance, radioactive cooling water and radioactive steam and increased the risk of major accidents), nor did the control agencies always pay attention to such accidents. By now nuclear power plants are monitored much more intensively so that even minor accidents induce an immediate stop of the process followed by a thorough investigation of the event.

An empirical situation where s^a still seems to be an equilibrium scenario is the pollution of national and international waters. Here the detection probability of illegal polluters, even of major emissions such as the release of oil into a river, is still too small to prevent illegal disposal. Partly, this might be due to the fact that detection techniques are not well developed as is the case, for instance, when ships release oil into rivers. Moreover, fines for detected polluters are often too low to be deterring. But certainly to some extent it may also be the shirking of water authorities and water police departments that must be held responsible for very low detection rates.

Observe, however, that in the polluter's paradise scenario the controller's qualification cannot be blamed for the complete breakdown of enforcement (provided that society doesn't have at its disposal controllers who are better qualified than type e of controller c), since even type e of controller c cannot cope with his or her task. Suppose, the probability of detection cannot be improved (i.e. for fixed w, M, and N) and the abatement costs of firm f (as characterised by the parameters p and F) are exogenous. Then the right hand side of (5') and the numerator of the term on the left hand side of (5') cannot be manipulated. Consequently any escape from "polluter's paradise" must rely on raising the fine for unlawful emissions thus increasing the denominator of the term on the left hand side of (5') until the inequality sign is reversed.

3.2. Exploratory accidents and illegal waste disposal
due to unqualified control: 'signaling scenarios'

Signaling takes place when $\delta_I = 1$ is followed by $\delta_T^e = 1$ and $\delta_T^n = 0$, since in that case after the move T, firm f would conclude that controller c is of the e–type whereas the move $\bar{T}$ signals the n–type. We consider two strategy vectors implying such a behavior:

$$s^b := ((1, 0, \bar{A}, 0), 1, 0) \quad \text{and} \tag{6}$$

$$s^\beta := ((1, 0, \bar{A}, \bar{A}), 1, 0). \tag{7}$$

Observe first that s^b and s^β differ only in that $A_g = 0$ in s^b, but $A_g = 1$ in s^β. The interpretation of this difference is that if the firm is asked to choose its emissions based on its a priori beliefs about controller c, then it would not emit at all in situation s^b while it would choose the maximum emission level $\bar{A}$ in situation s^β. But in both situations firm f prefers to launch an exploratory accident rendering the value of A_g irrelevant.

As a reaction to $\delta_I = 1$ the two types of controller c exhibit signaling behavior in that the expert launches an investigation $(\delta_T^e = 1)$ but not the non–expert $(\delta_T^n = 0)$. After this signal of the controller's type, firm f responds in both situations s^b and s^β as follows: If the controller turned out to be the expert, firm f abides completely to the law: $A_1 = 0$; but if the controller turned out to be the non–expert, firm f chooses to completely ignore the law: $A_2 = \bar{A}$.

Hence the polluter is extremely sensitive in his or her reaction to the controller's qualification. We now want to prove that s^b and s^β are equilibrium scenarios of our game model. For s^b to be in equilibrium for all $A \in [0, \bar{A}]$ one must have

$$(p + F\bar{A})\bar{A} - N(B + P\bar{A}) \geq (p + FA)A - N\frac{A}{\bar{A}}(B + PA), \tag{8}$$

$$(p + FA)A \leq M\frac{A}{\bar{A}}(B + PA), \tag{9}$$

$$(p + FA)A \leq [wM + (1-w)N]\frac{A}{\bar{A}}(B + PA), \tag{10}$$

$$(1-w)[(p + F\bar{A})\bar{A} - N(B + P\bar{A})] \geq C + wE, \tag{11}$$

$$H + N \geq 1 \geq L + M. \tag{12}$$

The first three inequalities ensure that firm f cannot gain by choosing a different disposal level $A \in [0, \bar{A}]$ in the three information conditions $(I, \bar{T})$, (I, T), and $(\bar{I})$, which can equivalently be expressed by $\delta_I(1-\delta_T^t) = 1$, $\delta_I\delta_T^t = 1$, and $\delta_I = 0$. Condition (11) implies the choice of I to be better than that of $\bar{I}$ for strategy vector s^b. The left hand side [right hand side] inequality in (12) is the best reply condition for $t = n$ $[t = e]$. For

$\bar{A} > A$, condition (8) can be simplified to

$$\frac{\bar{A}[p + F(\bar{A} + A)]}{B + P(\bar{A} + A)} \geq N. \tag{8'}$$

Obviously, this condition is similar to (5'). Due to $M > N \geq 0$ and $w \in (0, 1)$, inequality (9) holds for a certain level $A > 0$, whenever this is true for condition (10). Thus to prove that s^b is an equilibrium scenario we only have to demonstrate that conditions (8'), (10) (11), and (12) can be simultaneously satisfied in a non–degenerate parameter region.

Owing to $\bar{A} > 0$ and $P > p > 0$ the left–hand side of (8') is well–defined and positive. Since the condition $H > 1 > L + M$ is consistent with the parameter restrictions (2.7), conditions (8') and (12) can be simultaneously satisfied by choosing N (≥ 0) sufficiently small. For rather low values of $N \geq 0$ inequality (11) is obviously true for low parameter values $C \geq 0$ and $E \geq 0$. For $A > 0$ condition (10) can be rewritten as

$$wM + (1-w)N \geq \frac{\bar{A}(p + FA)}{B + PA}. \tag{10'}$$

Since the left hand side of (10') can be chosen near to 1 by choosing w and M near to 1, it suffices to show that the right hand side of (10') can be generically smaller than 1. This is obviously true if B, the part of the fine not depending on A, is sufficiently large.

Since all conditions stated so far are mutually independent, s^b *is demonstrated to be an equilibrium scenario.*

The equilibrium conditions for s^β are (5) [replacing (10)], (8), (9) , (12), and

$$w[M(B + P\bar{A}) - E - (p + F\bar{A})\bar{A}] \geq C \tag{13}$$

[replacing (11)]. To satisfy (13) assume the parameters $E, \bar{A}$, and C to be so small that the coefficient $[\cdot]$ of w is positive and that the left hand side of (13) is larger than C. Similarly, sufficiently small values of w and $N \in (0, M)$ ensure that (5) holds. As before it is possible to choose $\bar{A}p < B$ and $F\bar{A} < P$ such that the condition

$$\frac{\bar{A}(p + FA)}{B + PA} < M \qquad (9')$$

can be satisfied for $M \in (0, 1)$. Except for (9') and the requirement $H > 1 \geq L + M$ all our conditions are mutually independent. $1 \geq L + M$ is clearly compatible with (2.4) and (2.7) because for every $M \in (0, 1)$ there is $L \in (0, 1)$ to satisfy this inequality. Thus all our conditions can be simultaneously satisfied for a non—degenerate parameter region which proves that s^{β} is also an equilibrium scenario of our game model.

The illegal release of waste water, or chemical substances, or oil into water resources are important examples of detrimental waste disposal in case of 'unqualified control'. Unlawful polluters can take advantage of the darkness and/or of poorly controlled parts of the river system, and one can well imagine polluters starting with the emission of minor amounts, as modeled by our 'exploratory accident I'. They may then be encouraged to choose larger amounts and in some cases even more dangerous substances if they experienced that their first unlawful action did not cause a thorough investigation. It is this reinforcement of illegal behavior which causes so dramatic environmental damage if unqualified control cannot be excluded.

Since in both "signaling equilibrium scenarios" s^{b} and s^{β} firm f reacts sharply on which type of controller c is revealed, it is exclusively the controller's insufficient qualification which has to be blamed for any enforcement deficit. In fact, as far as these scenarios provide an adequate characterisation of the empirical situation, the enforcement problem could be easily solved by firing all non—expert controllers. Observe, however, that this recommendation leads us to the issue of controlling the controllers which is beyond the scope of the present paper.

3.3 Absence of illegal pollution due to efficient control: "controller's paradise scenario"

All strategy vectors with the consistent choice of $A = 0$ by firm f can easily be shown to be equilibrium scenarios since one can always prevent illegal pollution in our model by assuming sufficiently large fines and/or high detection probabilities. To design a more interesting scenario in which no illegal pollution takes place consider

$$s^{c} := ((0, 0, \bar{A}, 0), 1, 1). \qquad (14)$$

According to the strategy vector (14) both types of controller c would launch an investigation if an (exploratory) accident should occur, in which case it would be optimal for the firm not to pollute at all $(A_1 = A_3 = 0)$. Owing to the controller's types' pooling behavior the firm is not interested to choose I in the first place. But even then, monitoring and fines are so effective that zero pollution $(A_3 = 0)$ is the firm's best strategy. Such a situation is, in fact, the "controller's paradise".

For s^c to be in equilibrium the following condition must hold for all $A \in (0, \bar{A}]$:

$$wM + (1-w)N \geq \frac{\bar{A}(p + FA)}{B + PA}. \tag{15}$$

For the two types e and n of controller c no equilibrium condition has to be imposed since due to the move $\bar{I}$ by firm f their decision does not matter. But for s^c to be a perfect equilibrium (Selten, 1975, and Section 4.2 below) one must also require in addition to (15)

$$1 \geq H + N, \tag{16}$$

$$1 \geq L + M, \tag{17}$$

and (8) hold for all $A \in [0, \bar{A})$. To satisfy (16) and (17) we assume

$$1 > max \{H + N, L + M\}. \tag{18}$$

Furthermore, by choosing N small enough one can guarantee (8'). To satisfy (15) we assume values of w and M near to 1 and values of $\bar{A}$ and B such that

$$1 > \frac{\bar{A}(p + FA)}{B + PA} \tag{19}$$

for all $A \in (0, \bar{A}]$. Consequently s^c is an equilibrium scenario of our game model.

Although the equilibrium scenario s^c is not often mentioned in the political debate about environmental effects, it may be an empirically important one. It covers all situations where we do not experience illegal pollution since this is no profitable activity due to the efficient control system. Notwithstanding some exceptions like the case of the radioactive material from a run–down hospital in Brazil that had not properly been disposed of, radioactive material is nearly always legally abated where, of course, legal disposal may not always be environmentally adequate. Similarly, most extremely hazardous chemical waste and military weapons are properly disposed of. Most accidents with such substances were not caused by deliberate unlawful action.

One might argue that it is the aim of environmental policy to design a legal system for waste disposal such that the strategy vector s^c is an equilibrium and hopefully the only one. It is obvious from (15) that it is always possible to charge such a high fine $B -$ or to increase $P -$ as to satisfy (15) for any feasible set of values A, $\bar{A}$, F, M, N, and w. Hence in the tradition of "crime and punishment" (Becker, 1968) the obvious policy advice seems to be draconic monetary disincentive (punishment) to deter agents from polluting the environment. However, there are political, legal, and social reasons why societies might want to place upper bounds on the parameters B and P to the effect that the inequality (15) cannot be achieved. The political risk associated with high penalty rates as well as horizontal equity considerations prevent the government from increasing the seemingly costless penalty (Kolm, 1973). Lawyers point to the requirement of keeping means (here: fines) in reasonable proportion to the ends. In particular, with high values of B or P the punishment of low–wealth violators would be unacceptably high. It is for these reasons that incomplete enforcement of environmental standards still is an important feature in many empirical scenarios and cannot be easily overcome by the principle of "crime and punishment".

Even though the "controller's paradise scenario" is characterised by effective enforcement it is not true that the absence of law violations can be attributed to the controller's qualification. Recall that the two types of controller c show pooling behavior. The low expertise of non–experts is sufficient to deter illegal pollution. Therefore, the monitoring agency should pursue a policy of substituting expert controllers by non–experts.

3.4. Intermediate illegal pollution: "constrained polluter's paradise scenario"

Till now only scenarios with either $A = \bar{A}$ or $A = 0$ have been considered. In the following we want to show that intermediate levels $A \in (0, \bar{A})$ of illegal waste disposal can also constitute equilibrium scenarios. To see that, consider strategy vectors of the form

$$s^d := ((0, A^*, A^*, A^*), 0, 0) \quad \text{with } A^* \in (0, \bar{A}). \tag{20}$$

Observe that s^d is exactly like s^a from (4) except that $\bar{A}$ is everywhere replaced by $A^* <$ $\bar{A}$. It implies that both types of controller c would not react to I by a thorough investigation T so that an exploratory accident I cannot provide any information concerning the actually existing type of c.

For s^d to be an equilibrium one must have

$$A^* := \left[\arg \max_{A \in [0, \bar{A}]} g(A) \right] \in (0, \bar{A}), \quad \text{where} \tag{21}$$

$$g'A) := (p + FA)A - [wM + (1-w)N](B + PA)\frac{A}{\bar{A}}. \tag{22}$$

It remains to be demonstrated that the function $g(A)$ assumes its maximal value A^* in the interior of the interval $[0, \bar{A}]$. The first and second order conditions for an interior maximum of function g are

$$g'(A) = p + 2FA^* - \frac{wM + (1-w)N}{\bar{A}} \cdot (B + 2PA^*) = 0, \tag{23}$$

$$\text{and} \quad g''(A) = 2(F - \frac{wM + (1-w)N}{\bar{A}} \cdot P) < 0. \tag{24}$$

These two conditions easily translate into

$$[wM + (1-w)N]P > F\bar{A}, \quad \text{and} \tag{25}$$

$$A^* = \frac{\bar{A}p - [wM + (1-w)N]B}{2\{[wM + (1-w)N]P - F\bar{A}\}}. \tag{26}$$

Obviously, (25) can be satisfied by choosing P large enough. Due to (25) the denominator of the right hand side of (26) is positive. A sufficiently small value of $B \geq 0$

generates therefore $A^* > 0$. The condition $A^* < \bar{A}$ is equivalent to

$$wM + (1-w)N > \frac{\bar{A}(p + 2F\bar{A})}{B + 2P\bar{A}} \tag{27}$$

and can be satisfied by choosing $p > 0$ and $F \geq 0$ small enough. Since P has to be large, the denominator on the right hand side of (27) is not very small. Thus we have shown that intermediate levels of illegal pollution *also constitute an equilibrium scenario*. E-quation (26) lends itself to an easy exercise in comparative statics analysis: The firm will raise its emissions level A^* if, ceteris paribus,

i)   abatement costs increase: $\frac{\partial A^*}{\partial p} > 0, \frac{\partial A^*}{\partial F} > 0$;

ii)   the fine for illegal emissions decrease: $\frac{\partial A^*}{\partial p} < 0, \frac{\partial A^*}{\partial B} < 0$;

iii)   the probability w with which firm f expects to meet an expert controller decreases: $\frac{\partial A^*}{\partial w} < 0$

iv)   the detection probability $W(A, t)$ of illegal pollution decreases: $\frac{\partial A^*}{\partial M}, \frac{\partial A*}{\partial N} < 0$.

All these changes in unlawful pollution conform to one's intuition.

3.5. Equilibrium scenarios and the multiplicity of equilibria

According to the method of equilibrium scenarios one tries to demonstrate that a certain type of behavior is consistent with what we consider the most basic requirement of individually rational decision behavior, namely the equilibrium property, by showing that such a behavior is implied by a generic equilibrium point. What is totally disregarded is whether this equilibrium point is the only one.

In what follows we will first demonstrate the generic multiplicity of equilibria focusing particular attention on so-called *pooling equilibria* and *signaling equilibria*. An equilibrium is said to be a pooling equilibrium, if both types of controller c react in the same way to the exploratory accident I so that the choice of I gives the firm no clue and will therefore be avoided. In contrast, a signaling equilibrium implies, by definition, that the equilibrium solution signals controller c's true type because his two types e and n react differently to the exploratory accident I and that firm f will choose I.

Due to our basic interest in signaling behavior we want to illustrate the generic multiplicity of equilibria by showing that in a generic class of games both types of equilibria, *signaling* ones and *pooling* ones, coexist. More specifically we want to prove that there exists a full–dimensional subset Ω' of Ω such that the two strategy vectors

$$s^s := ((1, 0, \bar{A}, \bar{A}), 1, 0) \quad [= s^\beta \text{ from } (3.7)] \tag{28}$$

and $\quad s^I := ((0, \bar{A}, \bar{A}, \bar{A}), 0, 0) \quad [= s^a \text{ from } (3.4)] \tag{29}$

are equilibria of all games in Ω'. If the signaling equilibrium s^s turns out to be the solution, firm f chooses I. Having observed T, f then knows that it is facing type e whereas it infers that c is of the n–type after having observed $\bar{T}$. As can be readily seen from (29), in case of the pooling equilibrium s^p both types of c react to I by $\bar{T}$ so that firm f does not launch I.

Since $s^s = s^\beta$ and $s^p = s^a$, the equilibrium conditions for s^s are (5), (8), (9), (12), and (13), and for s^p the equilibrium condition is (5).

As mentioned above we now simplify the model by considering only values $A \in \{0, \bar{A}\}$ instead of $A \in [0, 1]$. Note that an alternative route to proceed would have been to state conditions for the function $g_k(A) := (p+FA)A - k(A/\bar{A})(B+PA)$ such that the maximum of $g_k(A)$ on $[0, \bar{A}]$ is either $A = 0$ or $A = \bar{A}$ for all 'relevant' coefficients k to be considered. Here we do not enter into the discussion of such conditions since to apply some of the more advanced game theoretic concepts, e.g. perfectness (Selten, 1975), we have to restrict players to finitely many strategies anyhow. Thus we study a finite extensive game to which some of the more advanced concepts can be applied (Selten 1975, Harsanyi and Selten 1988, and Güth and Kalkofen 1989). If only values $A \in \{0, \bar{A}\}$ are allowed, our equilibrium conditions for s^s and s^p are specified by

$$p\bar{A} + F\bar{A}^2 \geq [wM + (1-w)N](B + P\bar{A}), \tag{5''}$$
$$p\bar{A} + F\bar{A}^2 \geq N(B + P\bar{A}), \tag{8''}$$
$$p\bar{A} + F\bar{A}^2 \leq M(B + P\bar{A}), \tag{9''}$$

in addition to (12) and (13). We want to show that all these conditions can be simultaneously satisfied on a generic subset of the parameter space Ω defined by our game model in Section 2. Since (5") implies (8") conditions (5"), (8") and (9') together can be expressed as

$$M \geq \frac{\bar{A}(p + F\bar{A})}{B + P\bar{A}} \geq wM + (1-w)N. \tag{30}$$

Obviously one can simultaneously satisfy (12) and (30) by choosing $\bar{A}$ such that

$$1 - L > M \geq \frac{\bar{A}(p + F\bar{A})}{B + P\bar{A}} \geq wM + (1-w)N. \tag{31}$$

Moreover, due to $M > N$ and $0 < w < 1$ there exists a non–degenerate interval for the expression $\bar{A}(p + F\bar{A})/(B + P\bar{A})$.

Observe that inequality (13) is equivalent to (9') for $C = 0 = E$. Thus by choosing $C \geq 0$ and $E \geq 0$ sufficiently small we can satisfy (30) and (13) simultaneously if we rely on the more refined condition

$$1 - L > M > \frac{\bar{A}(p + F\bar{A})}{B + P\bar{A}} \geq wM + (1-w)N \tag{31'}$$

rather than on (31). This shows that all requirements for s^S and s^P to be equilibria can be satisfied for a full–dimensional subset Ω' of the parameter space Ω and that therefore *the coexistence of signaling and pooling equilibria is a generic phenomenon.*

This observation leads us to the question which meaning and relevance can be attached to equilibrium points, when in all (or many) games with the equilibrium point s^S the strategy vector s^P is also in equilibrium. From the earlier discussion of these equilibria we know that they characterise markedly different behavior. Obviously, the fact that a certain behavior is implied by one of the equilibria, say s^S, does not mean that this behavior is also the solution behavior. We simply do not know whether a certain model, defined by a non–degenerate sub space of parameters should be characterised as "polluter's paradise" or as scenario of signaling the controller's type.

It is possible to respond to this dilemma in different ways: Either one does not want to distinguish among equilibria. Then all, what one can claim, is that s^s might be the solution. Or one is willing to discriminate between equilibria and to apply more refined notions of individual rationality, e.g. refinement concepts as reviewed by van Damme (1987) or equilibrium selection theories as suggested by Harsanyi and Selten (1988) and by Güth and Kalkofen (1989).

In the remainder of the paper we choose the route to discriminate between equilibria by applying more refined game theoretic solution concepts. For the sake of simplicity and since some of the more refined solution concepts are not yet defined for continuous games, we will restrict the choice of A to $\{0, \bar{A}\}$ instead to $[0, \bar{A}]$ and totally neglect mixed strategy equilibria.

PART II: PERFECT EQUILIBRIA

AND (UNIQUE) SOLUTIONS VIA EQUILIBRIUM SELECTION

4. Uniformly perfect pure strategy equilibria

The weakness of the equilibrium concept, defined by the mutual best reply property (3.1), is that it does not guarantee optimal decisions in information sets off the equilibrium play. For the case at hand the strategy vector s^c as specified in (3.14) can be, for instance, an equilibrium even if conditions (3.16) and (3.17) are not satisfied. The reason is that the relatively high costs of a thorough investigation T do not matter since, due to s^c, firm f chooses I so that no explorative accident occurs. But if (3.16) and (3.17) are not satisfied, the intention to choose T is a non–credible threat since, given the situation I, it is better to use $\bar{T}$ for both types of controller c.

In order to exclude non–optimal choices in unreached information sets, Selten (1975) has introduced the *concept of perfect equilibria* which often is colloquially described as trembling hand perfectness. The basic idea is to derive from the game at hand a so–called *perturbed game* which differs from the former in that each move has to be chosen with a small positive minimum probability (due to a trembling hand). The original game is then viewed as the limit of its perturbed games when all these (artificial) small positive minimum probabilities converge to zero. In a perturbed game all information sets are reached with positive probability so that the choices in all information sets have to be optimal. An equilibrium point of the original game is said to be perfect if it is an equilibrium point in all games of a sequence of perturbed games approaching the original game. A perfect equilibrium point is therefore immune against small perturbations in the sense of small positive minimum probabilities for all moves.

Selten's perfectness idea is a rather weak concept by requiring all minimum choice probabilities for a perturbed game to be positive. Selten wanted to define only a necessary condition for individual rationality, namely an equilibrium concept excluding non–optimal choices in unreached information sets. Some recent *refinement concepts* as those discussed by van Damme (1987) developed more selective equilibrium concepts by imposing more demanding requirements of how immune against perturbations a strategy vector has to be. An extreme requirement of this form is, for instance, to ask that a strategy vector should be immune against all small perturbations. But such extremely stable equilibria do not always exist.

Here we do not want to enter into a discussion of whether one should try to develop more selective equilibrium concepts, which still do not solve many games uniquely, or whether one should design equilibrium selection theories which yield unique solutions but are at least partly based on preliminary ideas. Both approaches are discussed in Harsanyi and Selten (1988) as well as in Güth and Kalkofen (1989). The refinement concept, which will be used in the following, has been suggested by equilibrium selection theory (Harsanyi and Selten, 1988) and seems to be the most attractive refinement since it is not an ad hoc–concept for a special class of games. It rather relies on what we consider a sound philosophical basis of defining individual rationality.

Assume that there are no dominant strategies and that no player has superfluous moves in the sense that there are no two moves which always yield the same result. The idea of the trembling hand is that moves can be chosen by mistake i.e. involuntarily. Making mistakes is not an intentional act so that the probability of making a mistake should be the same for all moves. In an ε – *uniformly perturbed game* of the original game we require therefore the same small positive minimum choice probability ε for all moves in all information sets of personal players excluding chance moves. An *equilibrium* of the original game is called *uniformly perfect* if it is an equilibrium in all games of a sequence of ε–uniformly perturbed games converging to the original game in the sense of $\varepsilon \to 0$. Here it should be clear, of course, that to use a strategy or a strategy vector of the unperturbed game in a perturbed game means to choose it with maximal probability.

The main aim of this section is to determine the set of uniformly perfect pure strategy equilibria if only the two extreme levels $A = 0$ and $A = \bar{A} > 0$ of illegal waste disposal are feasible. Let G denote the game model described in Section 2 with $A \in \{0, \bar{A}\}$ and G^ε its ε–uniformly perturbed games with $\varepsilon > 0$. Clearly, after I firm f's beliefs concerning whether the controller is of type e or n are given by its a priori probabilities w for e and $1{-}w$ for n. The same is also true for the other agents of firm f, if the two types of controller c use identical strategies in G^ε. Let κ_t with $\kappa_t \in (0, 1)$ denote the probability that the necessary moves of firm f and type t of controller c lead to firm f's information after I and T or I and $\bar{T}$, respectively. The assumption that both types of controller c use the same strategy in G^ε implies $\kappa_e = \kappa_n = \kappa$. The probability for reaching firm f's information set is then given by $w\kappa + (1{-}w)\kappa$. Due to $\kappa \in (0, 1)$ this probability is positive. Thus firm f's conditional probability for encountering type e of controller c is given by

$$\frac{w\kappa}{w\kappa + (1{-}w)\kappa} = w,$$

i.e. the a priori probability for meeting type e of controller c. If *the two types of controller c use the same strategy* in G^ε, i.e. in case of pooling behavior, then firm f must choose $\bar{I}$ with maximal probability $1{-}\varepsilon$, and the optimal level A^* of illegal waste disposal is given by

$$A^* = \begin{cases} 0 \ \ \textit{for} \ \dfrac{\bar{A}(p + F\bar{A})}{B + P\bar{A}} \leq wM + (1{-}w)N \\[3mm] \bar{A} \ \ \text{for the reversed inequality} \end{cases} \tag{1}$$

If $A^* = 0$ is chosen with maximal probability, the decision T cannot be optimal if ε is positive but very small. If $A^* = 0$ is the firm's optimal strategy, controller c will therefore use $\bar{T}$ with maximal probability. This proves

Lemma 4.1: *For*

$$\frac{\bar{A}(p + F\bar{A})}{B + P\bar{A}} < wM + (1-w)N \tag{2}$$

the only uniformly perfect pooling equilibrium is

$$s_0^p = ((0, 0, 0, 0), 0, 0).\square \tag{3}$$

If $A^* = \bar{A}$ is firm f's optimal choice, the decision for T is never optimal since it does not pay to invest into a costly signal if firm f does not react to it. From this follows

Lemma 4.2: *For*

$$\frac{\bar{A}(p + F\bar{A})}{B + P\bar{A}} > wM + (1-w)N \tag{4}$$

the only uniformly perfect pooling equilibrium is

$$s_{\bar{A}}^p = ((0, \bar{A}, \bar{A}, \bar{A}), 0, 0).\square \tag{5}$$

Pooling equilibria of the type s^c with the choice of T by both types of controller c are not uniformly perfect since the different decisions for A after T and $\bar{T}$ cannot be justified by different beliefs after T and $\bar{T}$, respectively.

The case where (2) and (4), respectively, hold as an equality is neglected since we do not want to focus attention on degenerate games without special political interest.

If *the two types of controller c use different strategies in* G^{ε}, this always means that type $t = e$ uses T with higher probability than $t = n$. Let π_t denote the probability with which the move T is chosen by type t. Then for given π_e and π_n firm f's probability for observing move T, given its decision for I, is

$$\mu(T) = w\pi_e + (1-w)\pi_n. \tag{6}$$

In an equilibrium of an ε–uniformly perturbed game one has $\pi_e \geq \pi_n \geq \varepsilon > 0$ so that $\mu(T)$ is always positive. We can therefore define firm f's conditional or *posterior probability* for facing type $t = e$ after observing move T by using Bayes–rule as

$$\mu(e \mid T) = \frac{w\pi_e}{w\pi_e + (1-w)\pi_n}. \tag{7}$$

Analogously, the posterior probability $\mu(e \mid \bar{T})$ is given by

$$\mu(e \mid \bar{T}) = \frac{w(1-\pi_e)}{w(1-\pi_e) + (1-w)(1-\pi_n)}. \tag{8}$$

With the help of this notation the optimal decision A^* of firm f can be derived as

$$A^* \Big|_{\delta_T^t \delta_I = 1} = \begin{cases} 0 \text{ for } \mu(e \mid T)M + [1-\mu(e \mid T)]N \geq \dfrac{\bar{A}(p + F\bar{A})}{B + P\bar{A}}, \\[3mm] \bar{A} \text{ for } \mu(e \mid T)M + [1-\mu(e \mid T)]N \leq \dfrac{\bar{A}(p + F\bar{A})}{B + P\bar{A}}, \end{cases} \tag{9}$$

$$A^* \Big|_{\delta_I(1-\delta_T^t)=1} = \begin{cases} 0 \text{ for } \mu(e \mid \bar{T})M+[1-\mu(e \mid \bar{T})]N \geq \dfrac{\bar{A}(p + F\bar{A})}{B + P\bar{A}}, \\[3mm] \bar{A} \text{ for } \mu(e \mid \bar{T})M+[1-\mu(e \mid \bar{T})]N \leq \dfrac{\bar{A}(p + F\bar{A})}{B + P\bar{A}}, \end{cases} \tag{10}$$

$$A^* \Big|_{\delta_I=0} = \begin{cases} 0 \text{ in case of (2)}, \\[2mm] \bar{A} \text{ in case of (4)}, \end{cases} \tag{11}$$

Let us now explore the possibility of signaling behavior in the sense that type e chooses T and type n chooses his move $\bar{T}$ with maximal probability, i.e. $\pi_e = 1-\varepsilon$ and $\pi_n = \varepsilon$. In an ε–uniformly perturbed game with $\varepsilon > 0$ this behavior is optimal if $1-L > M$ and $N > 1-H$. Moreover, one obtains $\mu(e \mid T) = w(1-\varepsilon)/[w(1-\varepsilon) + (1-w)\varepsilon]$ and $\mu(e \mid \bar{T}) = w\varepsilon/[w\varepsilon + (1-w)(1-\varepsilon)]$ so that the posteriori probability $\mu(e \mid T)$ increases when ε decreases and converges to 1 for $\varepsilon \to 0$ whereas $\mu(e \mid \bar{T})$ decreases with ε and converges to 0

for $\varepsilon \to 0$. For ε positive and sufficiently small the following moves are therefore chosen with maximal probability:

$$A^* \Big|_{\delta_I \delta_T^t = 1} = \begin{cases} 0 \ \ for \ M > \dfrac{\bar{A}(p + F\bar{A})}{B + P\bar{A}}, \\[4mm] \bar{A} \ \ for \ M \leq \dfrac{\bar{A}(p + F\bar{A})}{B + P\bar{A}}, \end{cases} \tag{9'}$$

$$A^* \Big|_{\delta_I (1-\delta_T^t) = 1} = \begin{cases} 0 \ \ for \ N \geq \dfrac{\bar{A}(p + F\bar{A})}{B + P\bar{A}}, \\[4mm] \bar{A} \ \ for \ N < \dfrac{\bar{A}(p + F\bar{A})}{B + P\bar{A}}. \end{cases} \tag{10'}$$

Denote by

$$A^* = (A^* \Big|_{\delta_I \delta_T^t = 1}, \ A^* \Big|_{\delta_I (1-\delta_T) = 1}, \ A^* \Big|_{\delta_I = 0}) \tag{12}$$

the vector of firm f's illegal waste disposal levels for its three information sets when only levels $A \in \{0, \bar{A}\}$ are possible. The implications of conditions (9'), (10'), and (11) are graphically illustrated in Figure 4.1 from which it follows that uniformly perfect pure strategy *signaling* equilibria can only exist in the range

$$N \leq \dfrac{\bar{A}(p + F\bar{A})}{B + P\bar{A}} < M. \tag{13}$$

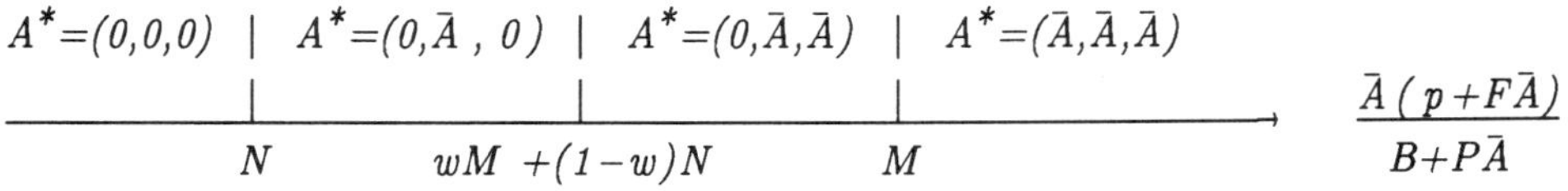

$A^* = (0,0,0) \quad | \quad A^* = (0, \bar{A}, 0) \quad | \quad A^* = (0, \bar{A}, \bar{A}) \quad | \quad A^* = (\bar{A}, \bar{A}, \bar{A})$

$$\xrightarrow{\qquad\qquad\qquad\qquad\qquad\qquad\qquad\qquad\qquad} \dfrac{\bar{A}(p + F\bar{A})}{B + P\bar{A}}$$

$\qquad\qquad N \qquad\qquad wM + (1-w)N \qquad\qquad M$

Figure 4.1: The optimal levels A^* of illegal waste disposal depending on $\dfrac{\bar{A}(p + F\bar{A})}{B + P\bar{A}}$

The decision problem which has not been considered so far is firm f's choice between I and $\bar{I}$. In case of $A^* = (0, \bar{A}, 0)$ the decision I is optimal whenever inequality (3.11) holds. In case of $A^* = (0, \bar{A}, \bar{A})$ the decision is optimal if inequality (3.13) holds. With the help of the inequalities

$$N < \frac{\bar{A}(p + F\bar{A})}{B + P\bar{A}} < wM + (1-w)N, \tag{14}$$

$$wM + (1-w)N < \frac{\bar{A}(p + F\bar{A})}{B + P\bar{A}} < M. \tag{15}$$

we now summarise our results by

Lemma 4.3: *For $1-L > M$ and $N > 1-H$ the only uniformly perfect pure signaling equilibrium is in case of (14):*

- $s^s_{0,1} := ((1, 0, \bar{A}, 0), 1, 0)$, *if (3.11) holds;*

- $s^s_{0,C} := ((0, 0, \bar{A}, 0), 1, 0)$, *if the reversed strict inequality holds;*

and in case of (15):

- $s^s_{\bar{A},1} := (1, 0, \bar{A}, \bar{A}), 1, 0)$, *if (3.13) holds;*

- $s^s_{\bar{A},0} := ((0, 0, \bar{A}, \bar{A}), 1, 0)$, *if the reversed strict inequality holds.* □

All four strategy vectors in Lemma 4.3 prescribe a *type differentiating behavior* in the sense of $\delta^e_T = 0$ and $\delta^n_T = 1$. Strictly speaking, signaling only takes place in case of $s^s_{0,1}$ and $s^s_{\bar{A},1}$ when firm f chooses its move I. But we will also refer to the strategy vectors $s^s_{0,C}$ and $s^s_{\bar{A},0}$ as signaling equilibria; In these strategies the controller would have signaled his type if an exploratory accident would have occurred.

Lemmata 4.1, 4.2, and 4.3 provide a complete overview over all uniformly perfect pure equilibria. Thus, in the range (14) there exist two uniformly perfect pure equilibria, namely s^p_0 and $[s^s_{0,1}$ or $s^s_{0,0}]$, whereas the range (15) contains $s^p_{\bar{A}}$ and $[s^s_{\bar{A},1}$ or $s^s_{\bar{A},0}]$. In all other more degenerate parameter regions there exists exactly one uniformly perfect pure strategy equilibrium point.

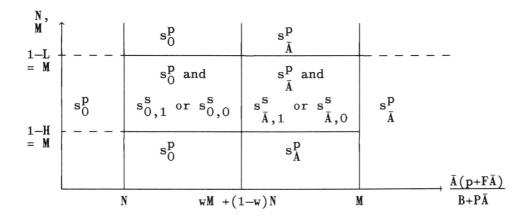

Figure 4.2: All uniformly perfect pure strategy equilibria in the

$[\bar{A}(p+F\bar{A})/(B+P\bar{A}),\ (M,N)]$-plane except for border cases

The possible cases of multiple uniformly perfect pure equilibria are graphically illustrated by Figure 4.2 from which it follows that the coexistence of signaling and pooling equilibria is not resolved by using the more refined concept of uniformly perfect equilibria. Like other refinement concepts the uniformly perfect equilibrium also does not generally yield a unique solution. Consequently strategic uncertainty cannot be completely resolved by relying on this refinement concept.

5. Comparison of signaling and pooling equilibria

As shown in Figure 4.2 we have to distinguish two generic regions with more than one uniformly perfect pure strategy equilibrium, namely the range defined by "$1-L > M > N > 1-H$ and (4.14)" and the range defined by "$1-L > M > N > 1-H$ and (4.15)". Whenever the uniformly perfect pure strategy equilibrium is not unique, we have exactly two such equilibria, namely a signaling and a pooling one. Since the number of uniformly perfect equilibria is generically odd, in all these cases there exists also a uniformly perfect equilibrium in mixed strategies which we chose to ignore. In the terminology of equilibrium selection theory the mixed strategy equilibrium is no initial candidate for the solution of the game (Harsanyi and Selten, 1988; Güth and Kalkofen, 1989).

In the following we will try to *derive a unique solution* for all generic subregions. Whenever there is only one uniformly perfect pure strategy equilibrium, we take this equilibrium to be the solution of the game. In case of more than one such equilibrium we will apply *equilibrium selection theory* in order to decide which of them is the solution of the game.

5.1 Cell and truncation consistency

According to equilibrium selection theory as developed in the pioneering approach of Harsanyi and Selten (1988) one does not solve the game directly but determines its solution g by deriving a unique solution g^ε of its ε–uniformly perturbed games and solves the unperturbed game via the limit

$$g = l\,i\,m\, g^\varepsilon \atop \varepsilon \to 0 \tag{1}$$

of the sequence of equilibria g^ε. Since g^ε is an equilibrium point of the ε–uniformly perturbed game, the limit solution g, if it exists, is obviously a uniformly perfect equilibrium point of the original game. Thus for an equilibrium to become the solution of the unperturbed game it must be uniformly perfect according to equilibrium selection theory.

To determine the unique solution g^ε of an ε–uniformly perturbed game one first has to decompose the game if possible. A game can be *decomposed*, for instance, if it has a proper subgame in the sense of an *informationally closed subtree*. A subtree of the game tree is said to be informationally closed if all information sets containing a decision node of the subtree contain only decision nodes of the subtree. As many games with incomplete information our game model has no proper subgames (see Figure 2.1).

A substructure generalising the notion of the subgame is the *cell game* (Harsanyi and Selten, 1988). Consider the agent normal form of an extensive game which is defined as the normal form game with all agents as players whose strategies are the moves in the respective information sets and whose payoffs are those of the original player (Selten, 1975). Consequently, a player has as many agents as he has information sets. A subset of players in the agent normal form is a *cell* if for all cell players it only depends on the choices of the other cell players whether a certain strategy is a best reply or not. In other words, a cell is a subset of agents which is closed with respect to the best reply correspondence. The cell game has only the cell players as players whereas all other players are assumed to use all their pure strategies with the same probability.

Our basic game as illustrated in Figure 2.1 has no proper cells since in the unperturbed game the agents who make their move after I have all their moves as best replies if $\bar{I}$ is chosen. In the terminology of Harsanyi and Selten (1988, p. 95) the unperturbed game has only a *semi−cell game*. In the ε−uniformly perturbed games with ε > *0* the set of all agents who have to decide after I, is a proper cell. In such a game the move I is chosen with positive probability so that $\bar{I}$ cannot be chosen with certainty. All agents after I have therefore to react optimally to I and to the choices of the other agents after I. Thus all ε−uniformly perturbed games have a proper cell game with all agents after I as players. Also firm f's agent choosing A after $\bar{I}$ is a cell. The residual game has only one player − the agent deciding between I and $\bar{I}$ − who can only react optimally to the two cell game solutions. For details see the decomposition procedure of Harsanyi and Selten (1988) from which we deviate only by using the agent normal form.

Cell consistency requires to solve a cell game as if it were an independent game: The solution of the cell game should not depend on how it is embedded in a larger game context. Given the solution of the cell games the residual game is the game with the non−cell members as players where all cell players are fixed at their strategies according to the cell game solutions. *Truncation consistency* requires to solve the residual game as if it were independent.

When solving an ε−uniformly perturbed game one first looks for the smallest cell games not containing proper subcells, then one looks for the residual games of the second smallest cell games resulting from anticipating the solution of the smallest cell games, etc. This procedure is closely related to the backward induction procedure of dynamic programming. In the case at hand we only have two smallest cell games of our basic model, namely the one with the agents after I as players and the cell game with firm f's agent after $\bar{I}$ as the only player. What is left is only one residual game with just one player, namely firm f's agent choosing between I and $\bar{I}$.

In the following we will distinguish two selection principles, payoff dominance and risk dominance. Cell and truncation consistency requires to apply these principles first to the two cell games and then to the residual game of the ε−uniformly perturbed games. The solution of the original game is then determined by the limit of the combination of the cell game solutions and the residual game solution for the ε—uniformly perturbed games when ε approaches zero.

5.2 Payoff dominance

Let $\hat{s}$ and $\tilde{s}$ be two different strategy vectors and denote by $u_i(\hat{s})$ and $u_i(\tilde{s})$ player i's payoffs implied by $\hat{s}$ and $\tilde{s}$, respectively. The strategy vector $\hat{s}$ is said to *payoff dominate* the strategy vector $\tilde{s}$ if

$$u_i(\hat{s}) > u_i(\tilde{s}) \quad \text{for all players with } \hat{s}_i \neq \tilde{s}_i . \tag{2}$$

Suppose that a game has only two uniformly perfect equilibria in pure strategies, namely $\hat{s}$ and $\tilde{s}$, and let $\hat{s}$ payoff dominate $\tilde{s}$. Equilibrium selection theory then assumes $\hat{s}$ to be selected as the solution (for instance, Harsanyi and Selten, 1988).

The interpretation of payoff dominance as an equilibrium selection concept relies on the hypothetical expectation that all players think that either $\hat{s}$ or $\tilde{s}$ will be the solution. Clearly, players i with $\hat{s}_i = \tilde{s}_i$ will then know what to do, and he or she can therefore be neglected. Players i with $\hat{s}_i \neq \tilde{s}_i$ will be called the *active players* for comparing $\hat{s}_i$ and $\tilde{s}_i$. If (2) holds all remaining players are interested in $\hat{s}$ to become the solution. Payoff dominance assumes that expectations will concentrate on this commonly desired solution (Harsanyi and Selten, 1988, p. 81 and p. 223).

Payoff dominance as a selection principle is not totally convincing since other considerations, e.g. how risky a strategy vector is, might suggest a different result. In a sense payoff dominance is a way to avoid the more appropriate way of formally representing preplay communication which may or may not yield a payoff dominant solution.

For $1-L > M > N > 1-H$ in addition to (4.15) and (3.11) Lemma 4.1 and 4.3 imply that s_0^p and $s_{0,1}^s$ are uniformly perfect equilibria. According to s_0^p and $s_{0,1}^s$ only type e of controller c and firm f after I and $\bar{T}$ use different strategies in the cell game after I, i.e.

are active players. In an ε-uniformly perturbed game with $\varepsilon > 0$ type e receives the payoff

$$\varepsilon(1-\varepsilon) + (1-\varepsilon)^2 + M[\varepsilon^2 + (1-\varepsilon)\varepsilon] - \varepsilon L \qquad (3)$$

given that $t = e$, that firm f has chosen I, and that the choices according to s_0^p are realised with maximal probability. For $s_{0,1}^s$ this payoff is

$$(1-\varepsilon)^2 + \varepsilon^2 + 2\varepsilon(1-\varepsilon)M - (1-\varepsilon)L. \qquad (4)$$

Due to $1 > M$ and $L > 0$ the payoff (3) is greater than payoff (4) for $\varepsilon < 1/2$.

For firm f's agent after I and $\bar{T}$ the payoff expectation implied by s_0^p is

$$[\varepsilon^2 + (1-\varepsilon)\varepsilon]\{(p + F\bar{A})\bar{A} - [wM + (1-w)N](B + P\bar{A})\} - C - \varepsilon E \qquad (5)$$

given that I has been realised. For $s_{0,1}^s$ this payoff is

$$(1-w)\{[\varepsilon^2 + (1-\varepsilon)^2][(p + F\bar{A})\bar{A} - N(B + P\bar{A})] - \varepsilon E\} - C +$$
$$+ w\{2\varepsilon(1-\varepsilon)[(p + F\bar{A})\bar{A} - M(B + P\bar{A})] - (1-\varepsilon)E\}. \qquad (6)$$

For $\varepsilon \to 0$ the payoff (5) converges to $-C$ whereas (6) approaches

$$(1-w)[(p + F\bar{A})\bar{A} - N(B + P\bar{A})] - C - wE. \qquad (6')$$

Due to (4.14) the payoff (6') is smaller than $-C$ if

$$(p + F\bar{A})\bar{A} - N(B + P\bar{A}) < \frac{w}{1-w}E. \qquad (6'')$$

Thus for (6") the equilibrium point s_0^p payoff dominates $s_{0,1}^s$. In case that (6") is not satisfied, one cannot discriminate between s_0^p and $s_{0,1}^s$ by payoff dominance. Since the behavior for the cell game after I does not differ between $s_{0,1}^s$ and $s_{0,0}^s$, the same result is true for the comparison of s_0^p and $s_{0,0}^s$.

For the trivial cell game with firm f's agent after $\bar{I}$ as the only player the trivial solution is $A = 0$ in the range (4.14). The residual game with firm f's agent choosing between I and $\bar{I}$ is not defined if the cell game after I cannot be solved by payoff dominance.

Lemma 5.1: *Suppose that in the range (4.14) two uniformly perfect pure strategy equilibria coexist. Then the pooling equilibrium payoff dominates the signaling one in case of (6") whereas one cannot select one of them as the solution by cell and truncation consistent payoff dominance if (6") is not satisfied.*

For $1-L > M$ and $N > 1-H$ in addition to (4.15) and (3.13) Lemmata 4.2 and 4.3 imply that $s_{\bar{A}}^p$ and $s_{\bar{A},1}^s$ are uniformly perfect equilibria. In the range (4.15) the trivial cell game after $\bar{I}$ has the solution $A = \bar{A}$. When comparing $s_{\bar{A}}^p$ and $s_{\bar{A},1}^s$ the active players of the cell game after I are type e of controller c and firm f's agent after I and T. Given that I has been chosen, type e's conditional payoff expectation is

$$\varepsilon^2 + (1-\varepsilon)\varepsilon + M[\varepsilon(1-\varepsilon) + (1-\varepsilon^2)] - \varepsilon L \tag{7}$$

if the choices according to $s_{\bar{A}}^p$ are made with maximal probability in an ε–uniformly perturbed game with $\varepsilon > 0$. For $s_{\bar{A},1}^s$ the analogous payoff expectation is given by (4). Due to $1-L > M$ type e prefers (4) over (7) if ε is positive and sufficiently small. Therefore, in every ε–uniformly perturbed game with ε positive and sufficiently small type e of controller c prefers the cell game solution of $s_{\bar{A},1}^s$ over the one of $s_{\bar{A}}^p$.

For firm f's agent after I and T the payoff expectation for given I according to $s_{\bar{A}}^p$ is

$$[\varepsilon(1-\varepsilon) + (1-\varepsilon)^2]\{(p + F\bar{A})\bar{A} - [wM + (1-w)N](B + P\bar{A})\} - C - \varepsilon E. \tag{8}$$

The analogous payoff expectation for $s^s_{\underline{A},1}$ is given by (6). For $\varepsilon \to 0$ the payoff (8) converges to

$$(p + F\bar{A})\bar{A} - [wM + (1-w)N](B + F\bar{A}) - C, \tag{8'}$$

whereas (6) converges to (6'). The difference of (8') and (6') is

$$w[(p + F\bar{A})\bar{A} - M(B + P\bar{A})] + wE \tag{9}$$

which is negative in case of

$$M(B + P\bar{A}) - (p + F\bar{A})\bar{A} > E. \tag{8''}$$

For (8'') firm f prefers the cell game equilibrium according to $s^p_{\bar{A},1}$ over the one induced by $s^p_{\bar{A}}$. Otherwise there exists no payoff dominance relationship.

Lemma 5.2: *Suppose that in the range (4.15) two uniformly perfect pure strategy equilibria coexist. Then the signaling equilibrium payoff dominates the pooling one in case of (8") whereas one cannot select one of them as the solution by cell and truncation consistent payoff dominance if (8") is not satisfied.*

According to the Lemmata 5.1 and 5.2 one cannot always rely on payoff dominance to discriminate among the uniformly perfect pure strategy signaling and pooling equilibria. It is interesting to observe that according to (6") payoff dominance of pooling over signaling behavior in the range (4.14) becomes more likely if w increases whereas in the range (4.15) the condition for payoff dominance does not depend at all on w. In parameter region (4.15) signaling is more likely to payoff dominate pooling behavior when costs E to firm f of being inspected become small. Conversely, in parameter region (4.14) pooling payoff dominates signaling behavior if E is sufficiently large. Thus according to the selection criterion of payoff dominance small inspection costs tend to support signaling behavior.

5.3 Risk dominance

Payoff dominance and considerations of strategic risk are mutually inconsistent solution requirements. Equilibrium selection theory (Harsanyi and Selten, 1988, and also Güth and Kalkofen, 1989) relies on both requirement and has avoided their mutual inconsistency by giving priority to payoff dominance. But this is a very premature decision and one that will very likely be reversed in the future. Indeed, earlier versions of the Harsanyi and Selten theory as in Güth (1978) did not rely on payoff dominance at all. Also the recent ad hoc selection concept of Carllson and van Damme (1989) does not use payoff dominance.

In the following we will therefore apply risk dominance as an *alternative* solution requirement even in those regions where the game can also be solved by payoff dominance.

To compare pooling and signaling equilibria one first has to solve the smallest cell games. For the case at hand the only non—trivial game is the cell game after I. The cell game after $\bar{I}$ as well as the residual game are trivial games since they have only one player. In the cell game after I both type n of controller c and one of the firm's agents use the same strategy. Thus the cell game after I has only two active players: type e of controller c and one of the firm's agents. Furthermore, due to $A \in \{0, \bar{A}\}$ both active players have only two pure strategies and both cell game equilibria are strict whenever an ε—uniformly perturbed game with $\varepsilon > 0$ is considered. Here an *equilibrium is said to be strict* if a unilateral deviation by a player yields a lower payoff for the deviator. To solve the game at hand we therefore need a selection concept by which one can solve 2×2—bimatrix games with two strict equilibria. Fortunately, Harsanyi and Selten (1988, Chapter 3.9) have developed a rigorous and easily applicable concept to solve such games. This concept is axiomatically characterised by the following three very convincing requirements: independence of isomorphic transformations (IIT), best reply invariance (BRI), and monotonicity (MO).

Independence of isomorphic transformations requires the solution in isomorphically transformed games to be the same except for differences in strategically unessential details such as the names of players or strategies or positive affine transformations of utilities. Observe that IIT implies symmetry invariance, i.e. this axiom requires the solution of symmetric games to be symmetric.

Since the equilibrium concept implies all players to use mutually best replies, one can argue that it is only the best reply structure what matters for equilibrium analysis – thus contradicting payoff dominance. *Best reply invariance* requires the solution of games with the same best reply structure to be the same.

To explain *monotonicity* consider a pure strategy equilibrium point s of a given game. The game which results from this game by increasing an active player's payoff for s is called the game resulting from strengthening the equilibrium s. If no other pure strategy equilibrium except s is the solution of the original game, payoff monotonicity requires s to be the solution of the game resulting from strengthening s. The stronger incentive for s should then make s the solution.

Harsanyi and Selten (1988, p. 87) show that in the class of 2×2–bimatrix games with two strict equilibria there is only one solution of each such game satisfying the axioms IIT, BRI, and MO. They call this solution the *risk dominant solution*. Expressed in terms of a dominance relation they say that this solution risk dominates the other strict equilibrium.

When determining the solution of the cell game after I we can refer directly to the axioms IIT, BRI, and MO which will allow us to transform the original game into a more appropriate one.

5.4 Solutions in the range (4.14)

In this section it will be generally assumed that condition (4.14) is valid. Recall from Figure 4.2 that if the inequalities $1-L > M > N > 1-H$ do not hold along with (4.14), the pooling equilibrium s_0^p is the solution. But in case of $1-L > M > N > 1-H$ both a pooling and a signaling equilibrium exist. In the following we will therefore presuppose $1-L > M > N > 1-H$ in addition to (4.14).

Since the crucial problem is to solve the cell game after I, we consider the strategic situation after I in an ε–uniformly perturbed game with $\varepsilon > 0$. According to s_0^p and $[s_{0,1}^s$ or $s_{0,0}^s]$ the only active players of this cell game are type e of controller c and firm f's agent after I and $\bar{T}$. Type e's strategies are clearly T and $\bar{T}$ whereas firm f's agent after I and $\bar{T}$ can choose $A = 0$ and $A = \bar{A}$. The 2×2–bimatrix presentation of the cell game is given in Figure 5.1 in which firm *f*'s payoff is the upper left entry and type *e*'s payoff is the lower right entry.

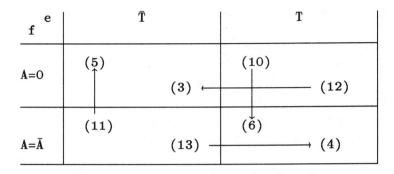

Figure 5.1: The restricted cell game after *I* for the comparison of s_0^p with $[s_{0,1}^s$ or $s_{0,0}^s]$.

The payoff entries in Figure 5.1 are — as far as they have not yet been defined above:

$$(1-w)[(\varepsilon^2+(1-\varepsilon)\varepsilon][(p + F\bar{A})\bar{A} - N(B + P\bar{A})] - \varepsilon E] - C + \tag{10}$$
$$+ w\{[\varepsilon(1-\varepsilon) + \varepsilon^2][(p + F\bar{A})\bar{A} - M(B + P\bar{A})] - (1-\varepsilon)E\},$$

$$[\varepsilon^2 + (1-\varepsilon)^2]\{(p + F\bar{A})\bar{A} - [wM + (1-w)N](B + P\bar{A})\} - C - \varepsilon E, \tag{11}$$

$$(1-\varepsilon)^2 + \varepsilon(1-\varepsilon) + M[\varepsilon(1-\varepsilon) + \varepsilon^2] - (1-\varepsilon)L, \tag{12}$$

$$2\varepsilon(1-\varepsilon) + M[\varepsilon^2 + (1-\varepsilon)^2] - \varepsilon L, \tag{13}$$

where, of course, all payoff expectations are conditional payoffs given the choice of *I*.

In the range (4.18) the expression in curved brackets in (5) and (11) is negative so that (5) is greater than (11). This explains the upward pointing arrow of firm *f*'s agent in the left column of Figure 5.1. Similarly, one can see that (6) is greater than (10) which explains the downward pointing deviation arrow of firm *f*'s agent in the right column.

For $L > 0$ one has, furthermore, $(3) > (12)$ and due to $1 - L > M$ also $(4) > (13)$ if ε is positive and sufficiently small. This explains the direction of the two horizontal deviation arrows and proves that $(A = 0, \bar{T})$ as well as $(A = \bar{A}, T)$ are strict equilibria of the restricted cell game after I. Here "restricted" indicates that only those agents are considered as active players who use different strategies in $s_{0,1}^p$ or $s_{0,0}^s$. Expressed in terms of deviation arrows an equilibrium is strict, if all deviation arrows are pointing to it. Thus the game in Figure 5.1 has two strict equilibria.

The game in Figure 5.2 results from the game in Figure 5.1 by subtracting in each column (row) firm f's (type e's) non–equilibrium payoff. This transformation preserves the best reply structure since the mixed strategy equilibrium and therefore the stability sets of the two games are identical (Harsanyi and Selten, 1988). The *stability set* of a strategy combination is defined as the set of all mixed strategy combinations to which this strategy combination is a best reply. Due to axiom BRI it is therefore possible to solve the game in Figure 5.1 by solving the game in Figure 5.2.

f \ e	$\bar{T}$	T
A=0	$(5)-(11)$ $(3)-(12)$	0 0
A=$\bar{A}$	0	$(6)-(10)$ $(4)-(13)$

Figure 5.2: Best reply preserving transformation of the game in Figure 5.1

In Figure 5.3 the letters X and Y are defined as

$$X = \frac{(5) - (11)}{(6) - (10)} > 0 \quad \text{and} \tag{14}$$

$$Y = \frac{(4) - (13)}{(3) - (12)} > 0. \tag{15}$$

e	$\bar{T}$	T
f		

	$\bar{T}$	T
A=0	X 1	0 0
A=$\bar{A}$	0 0	1 Y

Figure 5.3: Isomorphic transformation of the game in Figure 5.2

With this notation it is clear that the game in Figure 5.3 is derived from that in Figure 5.2 by dividing firm f's payoff by the positive constant $(6) - (10)$ and type e's payoff by the positive constant $(3) - (12)$. These positive affine transformations of utilities are covered by axiom IIT implying that we can solve the game of Figure 5.1 by solving the game of Figure 5.3.

With the help of (14) and (15) it is easy to see that the problem of solving any 2×2–bimatrix game with two strict equilibria can be reduced to solving the class of games described in Figure 5.3.

Now for $X = Y$ the game of Figure 5.3 is completely symmetric. Axiom IIT therefore forbids to select $(A = 0, \bar{T})$ or $(A = \bar{A}, T)$ as the solution. Symmetry invariance implies that the mixed strategy equilibrium is chosen as the solution which is, of course, also uniformly perfect. Thus due to axiom MO the solution is $(A = 0, \bar{T})$ for $X > Y$ and $(A = \bar{A}, T)$ for $X < Y$. Neglecting again the degenerate case $X = Y$ our results are summarised by

Lemma 5.4: *The solution of the restricted cell game after I, as described by Figure 5.1, is*

$- (A = 0, \bar{T})$, *if (14) is greater than (15), and*

$- (A = \bar{A}, T)$, *if (14) is smaller than (15).* □

If $(A = 0, \bar{T})$ is the cell game solution, it does not pay for firm f to invest into an exploratory accident. The solution is the pooling equilibrium s_0^p with no illegal waste disposal. In case of $(A = \bar{A}, T)$ as the cell game solution, the result depends on whether (3.11) or the opposite strict inequality holds: $s_{0,1}^s$ is the solution for (3.11) and $s_{0,0}^s$ for the reversed strict inequality.

Corollary 5.5: *In the range (4.14) the solution of the ε-uniformly perturbed game with $\varepsilon \in (0, 1/2)$ is*

$- s_{0}^p$,   *if (i) $1-L < M$ or $N < 1-H$,*
    or if (ii) $1-L > M > N > 1-H$ and $(14) > (15)$;

$- s_{0,1}^s$,   *if $1-L > M > N > 1-H$, $(14) < (15)$ and (3.11);*

$- s_{0,0}^s$,   *if $1-L > M > N > 1-H$, $(14) < (15)$ and if the reversed strict inequality*
    (3.11) holds. □

In an ε-uniformly perturbed game a solution s means, of course, that the choices according to s are realised with maximal probability. Substitution of (3) to (6) and (10) to (13) into (14) and (15) yields

$$X = - \frac{(1-\varepsilon)\{ (p+F\bar{A})\bar{A} - [wM+(1-w)N](B+P\bar{A}) \}}{(1-w)(1-\varepsilon)[(p+F\bar{A})\bar{A} - N(B+P\bar{A})] + w\varepsilon [(p+F\bar{A})\bar{A} - M(B+P\bar{A})]} \qquad (14')$$

and

$$Y = \frac{(1-2\varepsilon)(1-M) - L}{L}. \qquad (15')$$

Using the notation

$$X^o := \lim_{\varepsilon \to 0} X = - \frac{(p + F\bar{A})\bar{A} - [wM + (1-w)N](B + P\bar{A})}{(1-w)[(p + F\bar{A})\bar{A} - N(B + P\bar{A})]} \quad \text{and} \qquad (14'')$$

$$Y^o := \lim_{\varepsilon \to 0} Y = \frac{1 - M - L}{L} \qquad (15'')$$

the limit solution of the unperturbed game can be described as follows:

Theorem 5.6: *In the range (4.14) the solution of the game with $A \in \{0, \bar{A}\}$ is*

$-s_{0'}^p$ *if (i) $1-L < M$ or $N < 1-H$,*

            or if (ii) $1-L > M > N > 1-H$ and $X^0 > Y^0$;

$-s_{0,1'}^s$ *if $1-L > M > N > 1-H$, $X^0 < Y^0$ and (3.11),*

$-s_{0,0'}^s$ *if $1-L > M > N > 1-H$, $X^0 < Y^0$ and (3.11) reversed.* □

Observe that neither the case $X^0 > Y^0$ nor $Y^0 < X^0$ can be excluded since X^0 and Y^0 are both positive.

With Lemma 5.1 and Theorem 5.6 one would have determined a unique solution for all generic subregions of the multi–dimensional parameter space Ω satisfying (4.14). Either there exists only one uniformly perfect pure strategy equilibrium — the solution is then always a pooling equilibrium — or one can select between the pooling and the signaling equilibrium by risk dominance or by payoff dominance. Actually this would be the result according to the theory of Harsanyi and Selten which defines a dominance relation by payoff dominance or by risk dominance, in case that payoff dominance does not apply. Here we investigate risk dominance also in situations where payoff dominance applies.

5.5. The solution in the range (4.15)

If either $1-L < M$ or $N < 1-H$ in the range (4.15), then the pooling equilibrium $s_{\bar{A}}^p$ is the solution. For $1-L > M$ and $N > 1-H$ the game has also a signaling equilibrium, namely $s_{\bar{A},1}^s$ in case of (3.13) and $s_{\bar{A},0}^s$ in case of the reversed strict inequality. We therefore rely on (4.15), $1-L > M$ and $N > 1-H$ when selecting the solution in what follows.

The restricted cell game after I which we consider for the comparison of $s_{\bar{A}}^p$ with

$[s_{\bar{A},1}^{s}$ or $s_{\bar{A},0}^{s}$] is shown in Figure 5.4. The not yet defined payoff entries in Figure 5.4 are

$$[(1-\varepsilon)^2 + \varepsilon^2]\{(p + F\bar{A})\bar{A} - [wM + (1-w)N](B + P\bar{A})\} - \varepsilon E - C, \tag{16}$$

$$\begin{aligned}(1-w)\{[(1-\varepsilon)^2 + (1-\varepsilon)\varepsilon][(p + F\bar{A})\bar{A} - NB + P\bar{A})] - \varepsilon E\} - C + \\ + w\{[\varepsilon(1-\varepsilon) + (1-\varepsilon)^2][(p + F\bar{A})\bar{A} - M(B + P\bar{A})] - (1-\varepsilon)E] \},\end{aligned} \tag{17}$$

$$\varepsilon^2 + \varepsilon(1-\varepsilon) + M[\varepsilon(1-\varepsilon) + (1-\varepsilon)^2] - (1-\varepsilon)L, \tag{18}$$

$$2\varepsilon(1-\varepsilon) + M(\varepsilon^2 + (1-\varepsilon)^2) - \varepsilon L. \tag{19}$$

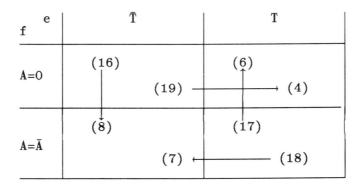

Figure 5.4: The restricted cell game after I for the comparison of $s_{\bar{A}}^{p}$ with $[s_{\bar{A},1}^{s}$ or $s_{\bar{A},0}^{s}]$

For $\varepsilon \in (0, 1/2)$ the payoff (8) is greater than (16) which explains the downward pointing deviation arrow in the left column. Similarly, for the range (4.15) it follows that (6) is greater than (17). Then, in the right column, the deviation arrow has to point upward. For $1-L > M$ and $L > 0$ the horizontal deviation arrows have to be as indicated in Figure 5.4. This proves that the game of Figure 5.4 has two strict equilibria, namely $(A = 0, T)$ and $(A = \bar{A}, T)$.

The next step is to transform the game resulting from Figure 5.4 by a procedure (covered by the axioms BRI and IIT) similar to that used to transform Figure 5.1 into 5.3. For that purpose define

$$U = \frac{(8) - (16)}{(6) - (17)} \quad \text{and} \tag{20}$$

$$V = \frac{(4) - (19)}{(7) - (18)} \tag{21}$$

to obtain the 2×2–bimatrix of Figure 5.5.

	$\bar{T}$	T
$A=0$	0 0	1 V
$A=\bar{A}$	U 1	0 0

Figure 5.5: The transformed restricted cell game after I of Figure 5.4

Now the same arguments as used for proving Lemma 5.4 yield

Lemma 5.7: *The solution of the restricted cell game after I – as described by Figure 5.4 – is*

– $(A = \bar{A}, \bar{T})$, if (20) is greater than (21);

– $(A = C, T)$, if (20) is smaller than (21).   □

In the range (4.15) firm f's agent after $\bar{I}$ uses $A = \bar{A}$ with maximal probability in every ε–uniformly perturbed game. If the pooling behavior $(A = \bar{A}, \bar{T})$ is therefore the solution of the cell game after I, firm f will choose $\bar{I}$, i.e. $s_{\bar{A}}^p$ is the solution of the game. For the signaling solution $(A = 0, T)$ of the cell game after I the solution depends on whether (3.13) holds or not. In case of (3.13) it is $s^s_{\bar{A},1}$ whereas it is $s^s_{\bar{A},0}$ in case of the reversed inequality.

Corollary V.8: *In the range (4.15) the solution of the ε-uniformly perturbed game with $\varepsilon \in (0,\ 1/2)$ is*

$- s^p_A$ *if (i) $1-L < M$ or $N < 1-H$ holds,*

                     or if (ii) $1-L > M > N > 1-H$ and (20) > (21) holds;

$- s^s_{\bar{A},1}$ *if $1-L > M > N > 1-H$, (20) < (21) and (3.13) holds;*

$- s^s_{\bar{A},0}$ *if $1-L > M > N > 1-H$, (20) < (21) and if the reversed strict inequality of*

                   (3.13) holds. □

Since

$$U = \frac{\varepsilon\{\,(p+F\bar{A})\bar{A}-[\,wM+(1-w)N](B+P\bar{A}\,)\}}{(1-w)\varepsilon[(p+F\bar{A})\bar{A}-N(B+P\bar{A}\,)\,]+w(1-\varepsilon)[\,(p+F\bar{A})\bar{A}-M(B+P\bar{A})]} \tag{20'}$$

and

$$V = \frac{(1\,-\,2\varepsilon)(1-M)\,-\,L}{L}, \tag{21'}$$

one has $V > U$ for positive and sufficiently small ε. This proves

Theorem 5.9: *In the range (4.15) the solution of the game with $A \in \{0,\ \bar{A}\}$ is*

$- s^p_{A'}$ *if $1-L < M$ or $N < 1-H$ holds;*

$- s^s_{\bar{A},1}$ *if $1-L > M > N > 1-H$ and (3.13) holds;*

$- s^s_{\bar{A},0}$ *if $1-L > M > N > 1-H$, and (3.13) reversed holds.* □

Observe that Lemma 5.2 and Theorem 5.9 determine identical solutions for the region $1-L > M > N > 1-H$, (8") and (4.15). Thus the signaling solution for this parameter region is very convincing since it is supported both by payoff dominance and by risk dominance. For such games it does not matter whether we rely on payoff dominance or not.

5.6. Discussion of the solution

Except for degenerate cases reflecting the boundaries of parameter regions we have solved all games of the basic game model. We ignore degenerate games since they rely on highly special assumptions for the game parameters and have therefore no practical relevance. A small change of one of the relevant parameters will usually imply that the game falls into one of the generic regions for which the solution has been derived above. Of course, one can also solve the degenerate games uniquely by applying equilibrium selection theory. But this would be a purely game theoretic exercise with hardly any economic relevance.

Let us first look at the ε–uniformly perturbed games with $\varepsilon \in (0, 1/2)$. To illustrate how the solution of such a game depends on the parameters, we use a graphical presentation of results similar to Figure 4.2.

In Figure 5.6 the major dividing line is

$$\frac{\bar{A}(p + F\bar{A})}{P + P\bar{A}} = wM + (1-w)N. \tag{22}$$

With some modifications this dividing line played a major role throughout the paper, e.g. in (3.5'), (3.10'), (3.15), (3.28). The right hand side of (22) is the ratio of what firm f can win and what it can lose from (maximal) illegal waste disposal. This ratio can be interpreted as the firm's "chance to gain" from violating the law as a percentage of fine in case of detection. The right hand side is the a priori probability for being detected as an illegal polluter ($A = \bar{A}$). If the firm's chance to gain is less than the detection probability (i.e. on the left hand side of (22)) firm f will choose $A = 0$ with maximal probability provided that it has to rely on its a priori belief. On the right hand side of (22) the choice of $A = \bar{A}$ is optimal according to the a priori belief. The solution of the game reflects this behavior by the appropriate choice of A after $\bar{I}$ with maximal probability as well as by the pooling solution of the cell game after I.

Other essential dividing lines are $M = 1 - L$ and $N = 1 - H$. For $M > 1 - L$ even type e of controller c prefers not to thoroughly investigate an exploratory accident $(\bar{T})$ since his

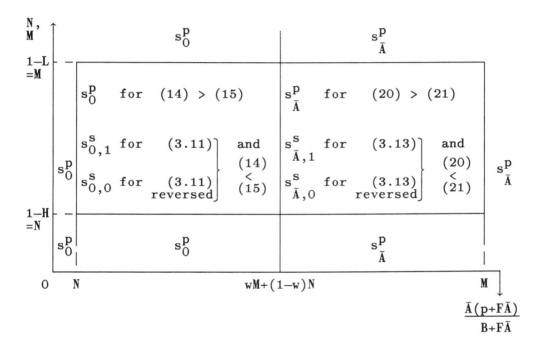

Figure 5.6: Solution of an ε–uniformly perturbed game

with $\varepsilon \in (0, \frac{1}{2})$ in the $\left[\dfrac{\bar{A}(p+F\bar{A})}{B+P\bar{A}},\ (M,N)\right]$ – plane except for border cases.

detection probability M for $A = \bar{A}$ exceeds his payoff $1 - L$ in case of $A = 0$ and a thorough exploration (T). Thus for $M > 1 - L$ only a pooling equilibrium is possible. For $N < 1 - H$ on the other hand even type n of controller c prefers T over $\bar{T}$ since his detection probability N for $A = \bar{A}$ is too low compared to his payoff $1 - H$ for T if T induces the choice of $A = 0$ by firm f. Below $N = 1 - H$ one can therefore have only a pooling solution.

The region where the solution of an ε-uniformly perturbed game is most reactive to the game parameters is the rectangular area determined by

$$1-L > M > N > 1-H \quad \text{and} \tag{23}$$

$$N < \frac{A(p + F\bar{A})}{B + P\bar{A}} < M. \tag{24}$$

The latter range is again subdivided by (22). On the left hand side of (22) it depends on the relation of X and Y whether the solution is a pooling or a signaling equilibrium. Only if the latter is true, condition (3.11) or its reverse determine firm f's initial choice between I and $\bar{I}$. Inequality (3.11) simply says that firm f prefers I over $\bar{I}$ if the solution of the cell game after I is of the signaling type. Similarly, on the right hand side of (22) the variables U and V determine whether the solution is a pooling or signaling equilibrium. Here inequality (3.13) or its reverse matter only in case that the pooling equilibrium is not selected. Like (3.11) the condition (3.13) requires that I is a best reply given that the solution of the cell game after I is the signaling equilibrium.

The limit solution of the unperturbed game, i.e. the solution of our game model with $A \in \{0, \bar{A}\}$, is illustrated in Figure 5.7 in the same way as in Figure 5.6 for its uniformly perturbed games. Compared to the uniformly perturbed games there is a surprising asymmetry between the left and right hand side of the rectangular area, described by (23) and (24). While to the right of (22) a signaling solution prevails whenever such behavior is a uniformly perfect equilibrium, on the left hand side of (22) the solution is of the signaling type only for $X^o < Y^o$. The variable X^o, defined by (14''), can be described as the relation of the a priori expected loss

$$[wM + (1 - w)N](B + P\bar{A}) - (p + F\bar{A})\bar{A} \tag{25}$$

of $A = \bar{A}$ and the expected profit

$$(1 - w)[(p + F\bar{A})\bar{A} - N(B + P\bar{A})] \tag{26}$$

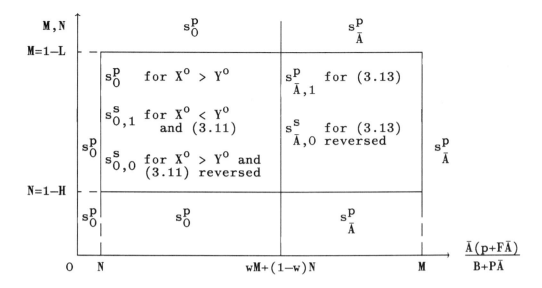

Figure 5.7: Limit solution for the unperturbed game in the $\left[\dfrac{\bar{A}\,(p+F\bar{A})}{B+P\bar{A}},\;(M,N)\right]$ – plane

due to unqualified monitoring by the non–expert type n of controller c. Similarly, Y^0, defined by (15''), relates the difference $(1-L)-M$ to L. Here $(1-L)-M$ is type e's incentive to choose T if firm f reacts to T by $A = 0$ and to $\bar{T}$ by $A = \bar{A}$ whereas L is the incentive to choose $\bar{T}$ if firm f reacts to T and $\bar{T}$ in the same way. This shows that there are intuitive interpretations for the variables X^0 and Y^0 which determine whether the solution on the left hand side of (22) in the rectangular area (23) and (24) is of the signaling or the pooling type.

It is interesting to observe that such different game parameters as p and F, determining the cost advantage of illegal waste disposal as well as the parameters B and P defining the fine in case of detected illegal waste disposal, influence the solution only via the term

$$\frac{\bar{A}(p + F\bar{A})}{B + P\bar{A}} \tag{27}$$

which also captures the impact of the level $\bar{A}$ of illegal waste disposal. One can very well imagine compensating changes of the various parameters constituting (27) which nevertheless leave the value of (27) and thereby the solution unchanged. This indicates that there exist trade off relationships which could be economically and politically very important. So, for example, our solution allows to calculate the necessary increases for the fine parameters B and/or P to offset a higher profitability of illegal waste disposal due to higher values of p and F or due to a larger waste amount $\bar{A}$.

6. Conclusions

A major motivation for our study was to demonstrate the applicability of non–cooperative game theory for analysing illegal pollution, especially the strategic problems involved in enforcing environmental control. That is why we have used quite different methods ranging from equilibrium scenarios to concepts yielding unique solutions. The approach taken here is by no means confined to illegal pollution but easily lends itself to analysing other strategic and institutional problems of environmental management such as strategic interaction between private polluters and pollutees.

In our view, it is very important to take into account that environmental policy has to be determined in situations of uncertainty and private information. For example, important aspects of pollution damages can only be evaluated by the pollutees themselves and are therefore private information. Another information deficit on which our model focuses is that polluters are poorly informed about the effectiveness of environmental control by public authorities. Unlike in conventional principal–agent–relationships (for instance, Hart and Holmström, 1987) neither the firm nor the inspector can be viewed as a subordinate of the other player. Nevertheless the monitoring of private employment contracts can easily be analysed by appropriately reinterpreting the assumptions of our model.

Private information as such does not always lead to signaling. For signaling to occur it is necessary, in addition, to have a sequential decision process which allows a less informed player to elicit the superior information of other players by inferences from their earlier activities. Signaling aspects of environmental problems therefore always require an extensive game form like that in the preceding analysis.

To demonstrate that environmental policy might be improved by institutional ar rangements related to signaling assume that the government considers a new policy instrument with only poor information about the polluter's abatement costs. If these costs are low, the new measure would lead to welfare improvement, whereas high abatement costs, as probably claimed by self—interested polluters, would suggest to refrain from such a measure. In order to elicit cost information, the government might introduce the envisaged measure either on a very small scale or only locally. One can easily imagine market institutions where it does not pay for a polluter to pretend high abatement costs even though they are actually low. Thus the reactions to the exploratory move, closely resembling the move I in Figure 2.1, may allow for updating the government's cost estimates, thus changing its subjective probability for high or low abatement cost and increase its chances for implementing welfare improving environmental management.

References

Avenhaus, Rudolf, 1990, "Überwachung punktförmiger Schadstoffquellen mit Hilfe der Inspektor—Führerschafts—Methode", Universität der Bundeswehr München, manuscript

Avenhaus, Rudolf, Güth, Werner, and Huber, Reiner K., 1991, "Implications of the defense efficiency hypothesis for the choice of military force structures. Part I: Games with and without complete information about the antagonist's intentions" in: Selten, Reinhard (ed.), *Game Equilibrium Models*, Volume IV: *Social and Political Interaction*, Springer—Verlag, Heidelberg et al.

Avenhaus, Rudolf, Okada, Akira, and Zamir, Shmuel, 1991, "Inspector leadership with incomplete information" in: Selten, Reinhard (ed.), *Game Equilibrium Models*, Volume IV: *Social and Political Interaction*, Springer—Verlag, Heidelberg et al.

Becker, Gary S., 1968, "Crime and punishment", *Journal of Political Economy 76*, 169—217

Blümel, Wolfgang, Pethig, Rüdiger, and von dem Hagen, Oskar, 1986, "The theory of public goods: a survey of recent issues", *Journal of Institutional and Theoretical Economics 142*, 241—309

Carllson, H., and van Damme, Eric, 1989, "Global payoff uncertainty and risk dominance", Working Paper, CentER, Tilburg

Gardner, Roy, and Güth, Werner, 1991, "Modelling alliance formation: a noncooperative approach" in: Selten, Reinhard (ed.), *Game Equilibrium Models*, Volume IV: *Social and Political Interaction*, Springer—Verlag, Heidelberg et al.

Güth, Werner, 1990, "Game theory's basic question: Who is the player? Examples, concepts and their behavioral relevance", manuscript

Güth, Werner, 1984, "Egoismus und Altruismus — Eine spieltheoretische und experimentelle Analyse" in: Todt, H. (ed.), *Normengeleitetes Verhalten in den Sozialwissenschaften*, Schriften des Vereins für Socialpolitik N.F. Bd. 141, Duncker & Humblot Berlin, 35–58

Güth, Werner, 1978, *Zur Theorie kollektiver Lohnverhandlungen*, Nomos–Verlag, Baden–Baden

Güth, Werner, and Hellwig, Martin, 1987, "Competition versus monopoly in the supply of public goods", in: Pethig, Rüdiger, and Schlieper, Ulrich (eds.), *Efficiency, Institutions, and Economic Policy*, Springer–Verlag, Heidelberg et al., 183–225

Güth, Werner, and Hellwig, Martin, 1986, "The private supply of a public good", *Zeitschrift für Nationalökonomie*, Supplementum 5, 121–159

Güth, Werner, and Kalkofen, B., 1989, *Unique Solutions for Strategic Games*. Equilibrium Selection Based on Resistance Avoidance, Springer–Verlag, Heidelberg et al.

Hansmeyer, Karl–Heinz, 1989, "Fallstudie: Finanzpolitik im Dienste des Gewässerschutzes", in: Schmidt, Kurt (ed.), *Öffentliche Finanzen und Umweltpolitik II*, Duncker & Humblot, Berlin, 47–76

Harsanyi, H., and Selten, Reinhard, 1988, *A General Theory of Equilibrium Selection in Games*, MIT–Press, Cambridge

Hart, Oliver, and Holmström, T., 1987, "The theory of contracts", in: Bewley, T. (ed.), *Advances in Economic Theory*, Cambridge University Press, Cambridge

Hurwicz, Leonid, 1973, "The design of mechanisms for resource allocation", *American Economic Review*, Papers and Proceedings 63, 1–31

Kolm, S. Chr., 1973, "A note on optimal tax evasion", *Journal of Public Economics 2*, 265–270

Maschler, M., 1966, "A price leadership method for solving the inspector's non–standard–constant–sum game", *Naval Research Logistics Quarterly 13*, 11–13

Myerson, Roger, 1979, "Incentive compatibility and the bargaining problem", *Econometrica 47*, 61–73

Pethig, Rüdiger, 1991, "International environmental policy and enforcement deficits", in: Siebert, Horst (ed.), *Environmental Scarcity — The International Dimension*, J.C.B. Mohr (Paul Siebeck). Tübingen, forthcoming

Rob, Rafael, 1989, "Pollution claim settlement under private information", *Journal of Economic Theory 47*, 307–333

Selten, Reinhard, 1975, "Reexamination of the perfectness concept for equilibrium points in extensive games" *International Journal of Game Theory 4*, 25 n.

van Damme, Eric, 1987, *Stability and Perfection of Nash Equilibria*, Springer–Verlag, Heidelberg et al.

Wilson, Robert, 1987, "Game–theoretic analyses of trading processes",in: Bewley, T. (ed.), *Advances in Economic Theory*, Cambridge Univ. Press, Cambridge, 33 – 70

Comments by Aart de Zeeuw

Werner Güth and Rüdiger Pethig have carefully written a very nice paper with the purpose to show the possibility of using advanced game theory in the analysis of environmental problems with asymmetric information. Most of the paper is concerned with the technicalities of game theory. It draws very heavily on a recent book by Harsanyi and Selten on equilibrium selection theory. Because the analysis is explained step by step, the paper is also useful as an introduction to the exciting new material presented in this book. Judging the paper therefore also means judging the Harsanyi/Selten approach. I agree with Güth and Pethig that the concept of risk dominance is more interesting than the concept of payoff dominance. However, in that case the Harsanyi/Selten approach typically is an axiomatic approach, which is unsatisfactory in the sense that it does not describe how the equilibrium is reached. I see some similarities with bargaining theory. For a long time the axiomatic bargaining solutions derived by Nash and Kalai/Smorodinski were used until the first strategic bargaining model introduced by Rubinstein buried axiomatic bargaining theory in oblivion. In a few years we will see what will happen to equilibrium selection theory.

The paper essentially consists of three parts. In the first part the game is described. A firm is uncertain about the expertise of a monitoring agency. Güth and Pethig argue that controllers can be bad and can prefer to shirk, because the pay is bad in such agencies. This argument can easily loose its strength, when the society starts to care more about the environment and is therefore willing to increase the salaries of controllers. The same remark can be made when Güth and Pethig argue later in the paper that the society does not accept "unreasonably" high fines for illegal pollution. However, even when the controllers are all experts the model remains interesting, because the firm can be uncertain about the level of technology that the controller can employ to detect illegal pollution. An alternative model for this problem is a model where the firm is certain about the qualifications of the controller but where the controller makes random checks, because it is impossible to investigate everything. The firm can try out the controller by means of a small "accident", so that the model is essentially a signaling game. The authors state that their model is a very complex game model. That is true, but from an economic point of view the model is of course still simple. Moreover, in most of the paper the original spectrum of possible illegal waste disposal is simplified to only zero and the maximal level, because the game is otherwise too complex.

In the second part of the paper Güth and Pethig turn to the so—called method of equilibrium scenarios. It is shown that a few specific situations, which the authors see as realistic, are in fact equilibria of the game. In this section three "pooling" equilibria and one "separating" equilibrium for the signaling game are described and interpreted. The main part of the paper, however, is the third part in which the authors apply Harsanyi and Selten's equilibrium selection theory to their model. This theory is based on the refinement concept of uniform perfectness. Güth and Pethig consider this to be the most attractive refinement since, as they write, it is not an ad hoc concept for a special class of games. This is not very fair to the other interesting refinement idea like Cho and Kreps' "intuitive criterion" or Kohlberg and Mertens' "never a weak best response criterion". The game that Güth and Pethig analyse here is strategically equivalent to the following game. In the top decision node the firm decides first to dispose of a small amount of waste or not, and then the same chance move determines in both cases the type of the controller. This game has proper subgames, which can be compared with the proper cells in the analysis of Güth and Pethig. The subgame after the positive decision of the firm to fake an accident is a standard signaling game, which has the same structure as the beer/quiche example in the paper by Cho and Kreps. It could be interesting to compare and discuss the outcomes of this game for the different refinement ideas. Moreover, the model of this paper can then be presented as an extension of the standard signaling game to a situation, in which the less informed player has the choice to play the signaling game or to enter an outside option with only the a priori beliefs. Equilibrium selection theory requires cell and truncation consistency and the use of selection principles. Güth and Pethig convincingly argue that risk dominance is the better selection principle here. For their model risk dominance selects one equilibrium for all parameter values, whereas payoff dominance is not selective for some parameter values. When both principles are selective, the results are the same.

The authors conclude by saying that they have used quite different methods in part two and part three of the paper, because the major motivation was to demonstrate the applicability of non—cooperative game theory for analysing illegal pollution, especially the strategic problems involved in enforcing environmental control. In my view they have achieved this aim. However, they had to be quite restrictive in the economic complexity of the model. This only means that a lot of interesting research remains to be done, starting from the Güth/Pethig paper.

SUBJECT INDEX